Minimal Religion

by   FREDERICK NYMEYER

A book to make Christianity more relevant to

- Business Men
- Professional Men
- Educators
- Scientists

- Nonsectarian
- An interpretation according to the · principle of "strict constructionism" of Scripture
- Mostly cosmological and ethical, leaving creeds and sacraments to denominational interpretation

LIBERTARIAN PRESS   SOUTH HOLLAND, ILLINOIS

First Edition

Library of Congress Catalog Card Number: 63-18098

Copyright © 1964

LIBERTARIAN PRESS

South Holland, Illinois 60473, U.S.A.

Printed in the United States of America by Park Press

Preface

One way to describe the current relationship between religion and nonreligion is that there is disharmony between what religion teaches and what science teaches.

This issue -- conflict -- between religion and science had never been so well formulated and so elaborately worked out until Auguste Comte (1798-1857). Beginning with Comte as the spokesman for "science," religion has faced a new problem.

*   *   *

Another perspective on the current relationship between religion and nonreligion is that their differences concern the ethics of an <u>individualistic</u> self-preservation system versus that of a <u>collectivistic</u> self-preservation system.

This issue -- difference -- between the ethics of an individualistic system and the ethics of a collectivistic program had never been so well formulated and so aggressively worked out until Karl Marx (1818-1883). Beginning with Marx, then, as the spokesman for an alleged higher ethic, religion has faced a new type of battle, on this ethical front.

*   *   *

In other words, the man who formulated the <u>basic issue in cosmology</u> so that religion must most seriously take note of it was Comte. Similarly, the man who first formulated the <u>basic issue in ethics</u> so that the ethics of Moses and Christ need reconsideration was Marx. Both Comte and Marx were nineteenth-century men; the problem is therefore relatively new in the history of human thought.

Major decisions of church councils, the thinking of the scholastics, the views of the founders of religious orders, the deviations from all these by so-called reformers -- these phenomena all antedate Comte and Marx. In a sense, therefore, what preceded Comte and Marx has in part been outdated and outmoded.

Religion needs currently relevant answers to the ideas of Comte and Marx in order to hold its ground or to make gains.

*   *   *

There are two ways to counter Comte and Marx: (1) mere reiteration of the findings of church councils, church fathers, schoolmen, founders of religious orders, reformers, or else slightly varying reformulations of their findings -- in other words, earlier interpretations of the Scriptures are to be repeated; or (2) there can be a return to the basic source itself, that is, to the original statements in Scripture and reformulation in modern terms (that is, post-Comte and post-Marx) of what those original sources teach.

The latter is the method employed in the restatement here presented of the minimum requisites for a realistic present-day Christian religion.

Critiques by Comte and Marx will be found to be invalid, except insofar as those two effectively attack unessential, ambiguous and (in a few cases) erroneous interpretations by the leading religion of the world.

*   *   *

This book does not represent a sectarian view. It is not Greek Orthodox; nor Catholic; nor Protestant. Individuals with strong doctrinal convictions will find that it does not go so far as they consider necessary.

It is hoped that this book will result in greater interest in the cosmology, ethics and theology of the Christian religion.

*   *   *

The author is solely responsible for ideas expressed, but is indebted to those with whose views he has become acquainted, both living or dead. They include Hebrew, early Christian and Roman Catholic writers well into the Middle Ages, including

William of Occam; (2) Reformers; (3) Locke, Burke,
Montesquieu, John Adams, John C. Calhoun; also, but
in an inverse sense, (4) Auguste Comte and Karl
Marx; then (5) classical economists, Adam Smith and
David Ricardo; and (6) Neoclassical economists, in-
cluding Carl Menger, Eugen von Böhm-Bawerk and
Ludwig von Mises.

To the last mentioned there is special indebted-
ness. In comprehensive analyses and critiques and
in positive formulations of his own, he has done
much in defense of the outer ramparts of religion:
it is he who has (1) basically attacked Positivism;
and (2) building on his predecessors but with a
genius all his own, has discredited the whole Marxian system.

South Holland, Illinois

August, 1964

Contents

Contents

III CHRISTIAN ETHICS

Contents   xiii

I

There Are Only Two Basic Religions

Religion Must Be "Two Hundred Years" Behind The Times

A business man or a research man will understand why a good religion must be "two hundred years" behind the times.

As the knowledge of men increases, the special revelation of religion need not change, but its "frame of reference" will change. Men will inter-pret the ancient revelation better than before, and more fittingly according to the changed state of knowledge.

Proposals of change in all fields of life are distressingly frequently wrong. Changes finally adopted will only be a small fraction of many changes proposed. Only a few of the changes can survive testing and experience.

Changes in regard to religion are like a new product. The new product looks wonderful; it is believed to be a great improvement over present products; it is tested a long time; it seems to be all that is expected of it; it is put on the market. But then the trouble begins. The product, as the jargon of business goes, has "bugs" in it, that is, the product in actual use is not satisfactory; some-times, laboriously developed improvements finally make the product market-worthy. Sometimes the pro-duct must be abandoned. In a sense, therefore, new products in business lag far behind ideas.

Similarly, new ideas in religion (or rather, new ideas for a modern interpretation of religion) often have "bugs" in them. It is a mistake for a denom-ination imperiously to accept some new view. There-fore, good denominations are, in the nature of the case, substantially behind the times in their literal official position.

A denomination should be like a good foreign sales manager. He disdains new products until after they have been thoroughly tested in actual use by consum-ers for a considerable time in the domestic market. To have product trouble in a domestic market is bad. To have product trouble in a foreign market, far from good service and rebuilding facilities, can be disastrous.

Therefore, well-managed religions are behind the latest developments. That ought not to discourage experienced intellectuals. Men ought not to condemn a church because it is slow to change, and prudent,

Religion Must Be "Two Hundred Years"
Behind The Times

A business man or a research man will understand
why a good religion must be "two hundred years"
behind the times.

As the knowledge of men increases, the special
revelation of religion need not change; but its
"frame of reference" will change. Men will interpret the ancient revelation better than before, and
more fittingly according to the changed state of
knowledge.

Proposals of change in all fields of life are
distressingly frequently wrong. Changes finally
adopted will only be a small fraction of many changes
proposed. Only a few of the changes can survive
testing and experience.

Changes in regard to religion are like a new
product. The new product looks wonderful; it is
believed to be a great improvement over present
products; it is tested a long time; it seems to be
all that is expected of it; it is put on the market.
But then the trouble begins. The product, as the
jargon of business goes, has "bugs" in it; that is,
the product in actual use is not satisfactory. Sometimes, laboriously developed improvements finally
make the product market-worthy. Sometimes the product must be abandoned. In a sense, therefore, new
products in business lag far behind ideas.

Similarly, new ideas in religion (or rather, new
ideas for a modern interpretation of religion) often
have "bugs" in them. It is a mistake for a denomination impetuously to accept some new view. Therefore, good denominations are, in the nature of the
case, substantially behind the times in their formal,
official position.

A denomination should be like a good foreign sales
manager. He disdains new products until after they
have been thoroughly tested in actual use by consumers for a considerable time in the domestic market.
To have product trouble in a domestic market is bad.
To have product trouble in a foreign market, far
from good service and rebuilding facilities, can
be disastrous.

Therefore, well-managed religions are behind the
latest developments. That ought not to disconcert
experienced intellectuals. Men ought not to condemn
a church because it is slow to change, and prudent.

Dust Is God

Many things pertaining to life and death remain inadequately known to men.

The fact that scientists are still working on explaining the causes of changes (whether motion, energy, mass, life, growth, deterioration, death) is evidence that there is as yet no complete explanation of phenomena. There remains the great realm of the "unknown," some of which may be unknowable.

Some unknowns are "formulated." Some are not even realized. Regarding those that are formulated, correctly or incorrectly, hypothetical explanations are advanced to guide exploratory work.

If the attempted answer is <u>tentatively</u> held, the thought of the researcher is a "temporary faith" or hypothesis which the subject person is prepared to abandon. If the attempted answer is held with a confidence transcending any expected or unexpected evidence, then the explanation is a faith. Not that that confidence might not be changed, but the attitude (the stance) of such a mind is one of a "faith."

Scientists do not appear worried about their own unemployment, about not having something on which to work. They "solve" problems, but raise new ones. The prospects for removing all hypotheses and faith therefore are not good. People will probably agree that there is not a good prospect at the present time that men will eventually know everything, and that hypotheses and faith can be dispensed with. This matter of hypotheses and faith appears to be an imperishable business.

*   *   *

In a broad general way, how should the answer be formulated to the question, <u>What is the origin of the world we know</u>?

The most obvious answer, and to many people the most acceptable answer after long reflection, is that Dust is God. By Dust is meant all the physical elements in the universe.

Such a view holds that there is nothing transcendent above the material. There is no super-God; that idea is a figment. There was no beginning (there could not be); there will be no end.

The changes known as physical laws stem from the physical or energy base known to the common senses

of man (as dust, water, light, air, etc.). Dust
makes its own "laws," if such an expression may be
permitted.

Admirably, by such thought, the universe has been
reduced to a simple, self-contained (unified, monistic) system.

This view is often the view of a physical scientist, and all those whose hope for the solution of
all problems rests with physics, chemistry, etc.
This is also the hope of social scientists when they
explore their subjects according to the same methods
of research as do the physical sciences. (Such, in
fact, is the presently prevailing method in the
social sciences.)

By this approach the scientist can have the
satisfaction of explaining his genius. The universe is a monistic system of closed cause and
effect, and the finest "flowering" of dust is the
activity of the brain of the genius.

What is it that finally "explains" the genius?
It must be something within him. If his wife has
his body cremated immediately after his death, was
that genius the dust which she gets back in an urn?
Will she ponder the urn in sadness; and as she turns
it in her hands, will she wonder how that handful
of dust could have thought so brilliantly? And will
she murmur, "Dust is God, and this was some of the
best of it."? But it is dust that thinks no more;
nor moves, nor senses, nor enjoys. Or did the genius
reside in the moisture and gases driven off in the
crematorium?

Some people in earlier ages have had their god
in their house with them in the symbolic form of an
ikon or an image. A man who believes that Dust is
God might do the same. He could get two ravishingly
beautiful vials or urns, go out to his garden and
get a couple of spoonfuls of dirt, and put it in
the vials and set them on his mantlepiece. To retain "contact with reality," to bring his "religion"
to his consciousness from time to time, to be conscious deliberately what he "believes" -- he should
walk up to his mantlepiece occasionally and pour
the dust back and forth, and he might employ the
formula, "Dust is God; it is the origin of everything; it thinks; it creates; it researches; it is
unfathomable; this which I pour is a part of God;
genius resides in (is) this Dust."

In the world of science this religion gets a

special name, Positivism. The term comes from
Auguste Comte, the Frenchman, but the ideas long
antedate Comte. Positivism is, in fact, an early
and basic religion.

The way for the "common man" to formulate the
idea of Positivism is to repeat the formula --
Dust is God. The average scientist may formulate
the proposition in different terms, and you may not
understand him, but what he will be saying gets
down to that simple "faith."

N O T E

Those who select dust as their god, find some
difficulty worshipping dirt for which they buy
soap to get it out of their clothes. And so they
take dust collectively -- matter in the abstract --
and are pantheists. This is nothing more than an
apotheosis of dust, and is a neat way of beguiling
yourself that the dirt in a shirt cuff is not your
god. Furthermore, Pantheism is a violation of
Occam's Razor, Entia non sunt multiplicandum praeter
necessitatem. Whoever applies Occam's rule shears
the whole idea of Pantheism out of existence.

A Transcendental Being As God

There are not a large number of "theological systems" which explain (or rather, <u>attempt</u> to explain) the universe -- its origin, nature and destiny.

The <u>only</u> distinctive type of explanation of the universe other than Positivism is that there is a Supreme Being, above (transcendent over) dust and its properties.

Associated inseparably with such an idea of the origin and nature of things are the attributes of such a Supreme Being -- that he is a creator; powerful; has knowledge; purpose; plan; is above "mere dust," that is, that he is an intellectual or spiritual (rather than a material or physical) being.

The magnitude of the universe, its existence in time, the concepts of cause and effect, laws of nature, mathematics, justice, protection, mercy are ascribed to a being having those characteristics which are considered characteristically human, but which human beings patently have in a limited or, at any rate, inadequate amount. A transcendent God is <u>infinite</u> in <u>all</u> his characteristics, according to the prevailing definition in the Western World.*

In ancient times the prevailing belief was polytheistic, that there are many gods. Very few really believe that any more, and so the religions of the Greeks and Romans and many other ancient peoples have disappeared.

Ancient Hebrews with singular tenacity clung to the idea of <u>one</u> God, and insofar as a belief in a transcendent God survives, it is associated with monotheism, of either a Jewish, Christian or Mohammedan brand. To these groups, the idea of more than one god is repugnant. Monotheism is the highest form of transcendentalism.

A little reflection will reveal that transcendentalism does not solve the problem of Positivism,

---

* In the <u>Belgic Confession</u> (written by Guido de Brès in 1561) Article I reads: "We all believe with the heart and confess with the mouth that there is one only simple and spiritual Being, which we call God; and that He is eternal, incomprehensible, invisible, immutable, infinite, almighty, perfectly wise, just, good, and the overflowing fountain of all good."

mentioned in Section I, Chapter 1. It is not
obviously clear that the proposition that Dust
is God is reasonable. But to "imagine" a transcendent God is merely to move the problem back
one notch; how in turn explain the origin of God?
By assuming he exists, you have not proved that
he exists. A Positivist will almost surely be
moved to affirm that a "transcendent God" is an
unnecessary assumption. Merely discover, according to his view, all of the laws of matter, and
then you will have all the answers. And so a
transcendental God becomes an unnecessary assumption or belief, for a Positivist.

Shrewdly or naively, those who accept the idea
of the existence of a transcendent God have protected themselves from the necessity of proving
their case. They insist that their god is immaterial, is a spirit, cannot be seen, heard, felt,
touched, tasted. As the Christian religion has
it, its God dwells in the regions of "unapproach-
able light." Even in a future life, according to
Christianity, God as God will never be seen. Christianity's definition given of God is the "safest"
definition that can be formulated. He never needs
to prove his existence to ordinary human senses!
This can be looked at as consistency in thinking,
but it can also be looked at as extremely clever.

There exist, in the world, ideas -- things of
the "spirit," of the intellect, of "symbols," of
the will -- a "world" other than real material
things. We know, however, that when certain material conditions are not met -- a beating heart, the
right temperature, a sound neural system, an un-
damaged human brain, etc. -- that then spiritual
phenomena stop forthwith.

Are then the phenomena named soul or spirit only
certain activities of physical things, namely, body
cells made up of protein, carbohydrates, fats, etc.?
If the spirit of man can exist only when certain
material conditions are present, what assurance is
there that another spirit can exist independent of
appropriate material factors?

The case, therefore, for the existence of a transcendental God is not easily proved, if the person
to be convinced is a confirmed skeptic.

Still, there is "something" that makes the idea
of a transcendent God reasonable. The world may be
looked at as disorderly and evil, but it is very
wonderful, too --`too wonderful for teaspoons of

dirt from your garden (or the "ashes" of your ancestors in an urn) to be adequate as explanation. Consider how wonderfully children are generated, born,
grow, hear, see, smell, move, taste, touch, mature,
and accomplish great things. It is not plausible --
so it seems to believers in a Supreme Being -- that
such marvels of the world could come about by chance
or by activity of mere dust, no matter what the number of chances might be to attain such result by
chance rather than intelligence. It is, they say,
all too wonderful not to have been planned and
ordered; there <u>must</u> then be a Supreme Intelligence.

Now, if in everyday living many desirable results
came about by chance (without effort or logic or
good judgment), then there might be more reason to
have a happy trust that "chance" made this wonderful
world; but that is not what happens in actual fact.
The improvements men obtain and observe come only
in response to intense human effort.

For any man to "make" a machine 1/1000ths as
complex as a baby is an impossibility, in a whole
lifetime. But a brief act of cooperation between
a man and a woman brings a marvelous baby into the
world in less than a year's time. Did Dust "arrange"
that? or a Supreme Being? That the man and the
woman were intermediary agents is not to be questioned, but how did this begetting and being born
"happen" to become so well organized and efficient
and, in a sense, easy.

If the same man, as a famous inventor, set out
to improve an existing product ten percent, he would
have to do much hard work, and remodeling, and im-
proving, and testing.

In short, if men (the "flower" of Dust) can do
so little even in response to so much effort, how
did such a wonderful thing as a baby come about so
easily? Before her first baby, no woman has a prior
experience producing it. How then is the child
usually so well-produced?

But beyond that argument of "design" in nature
there is not much positive evidence that there is
an entity in the universe which should bear the
name of Supreme Intelligence. "Reason," in other
words, makes neither of the alternative hypotheses
acceptable about the origin of things. The two hypotheses are (1) Dust and (2) God. "Proof," obtained
by reason, is inadequate for <u>certainty</u>, and some
might say even for <u>probability</u>. It becomes almost
a matter of preference or temperament whether one
says: Dust is God, or God is God.

Agnosticism

A third position might be taken, but it really does not undertake to answer the question; instead, it rejects the question.

Some people, therefore, answer questions on the origin, nature and destiny of things by saying: We admit we do not know, and we admit we despair of ever knowing; therefore, we neither ask nor endeavor to answer questions regarding the origin, nature and destiny of ourselves and the world in which we find ourselves.

Those who hold such views are called <u>agnostics</u>. They refuse to work on the problem, either because the problem does not interest them (eat, live and be merry for tomorrow we die) or because they consider it unsolvable.

To the question about existence and reality, (1) one positive answer is <u>Dust</u>; (2) another positive answer is <u>God</u>; and (3) one negative answer is that we do not have an answer and that we reject the question.

Let every man's answer be to his taste. The author holds to number 2.

"It All Depends On Whether There Has Been Special Revelation"

A man is fortunate in life, in part, in proportion as he becomes acquainted, in person or through books, with his greatest contemporaries; and through books only, with the great men of the past. It has been the writer's good fortune to know several such men.

In a conversation one day with the greatest of them, the talk was about the mysteries of the origin and destiny of things. This great man is not an easy believer and is a severe critic of much of what passes for religion.

I was repeating in my own language what I had in large part accepted from him, that the answers to the great questions of life cannot be discovered by finite human minds; are unsolvable by human reason; lie lost in the mists of the unknowable; and that consequently we do not "know" and never will fully know.

To my astonishment he looked at me arrestingly, and then in a sense he contradicted me. He said emphatically: "It all depends on whether there has been special revelation."

If the human mind cannot reason its way to a certain conclusion regarding the origin and destiny of things, then there is still the possibility of a correct and definitive answer to those questions, if there has been revelation. The transcendent must make itself known to the finite. The Hebrew religion rests on exactly that foundation for its Old Testament. The Christian religion rests on that foundation for both its Old and New Testaments.

The regular refrain in the Hebrew-Christian Scriptures is, "Thus spake the Lord"; or, "The Word of the Lord came unto me"; or, "The Lord spake by..."

It is worthy of noting that these Scriptures are militantly hostile to falsehood and all other types of evil, and it would be paradoxical that these men would teach righteousness, but simultaneously engage in a fraud about speaking for God or in the name of God. It is possible that they were hypocrites of that crass kind, but that is improbable.

But whether or not there was or was not revelation in fact would probably be more reasonably posed

by saying: (1) these men did receive revelation,
or (2) they were honestly deluded in their belief
that they were recipients of revelation. (It is,
in other words, somewhat implausible that they were
frauds and hypocrites of the crassest sort; they
were merely deluded.)

But the foregoing by no means solves all the
problems. There remain many questions: (1) What
was the character of that revelation? (2) To what
extent was it colored by the character of the human
agent, his foibles, his culture, his ignorance, his
superstition, and by the prevailing climate of
thought in his day? (3) Could this revelation
merely have been above-average intelligence and
judgment? (4) Did these men, when they said, "Then
the Word of the Lord came unto me," merely mean,
"This is sound logic and good sense," and therefore,
"It must be the same as the Word of the Lord, even
though it is only my formulation and my word."
(5) Were these men merely giving their own opinions,
but upgrading them under the guise that these opinions came from the Lord directly?

Analyses of these questions are beyond the scope
of this book. In any event, the Hebrew and the
Christian religions as ultimate stand or fall on
whether or not there was revelation.

In addition to the question of revelation and
the validity of the original inspiration, there remains the question that certain subsequent special-
ists, individually but eventually collectively, have
decided that this work was revelation and that some
other work was not. Who guided these later folk,
individually or acting together in some church
Council? Again, the determination of the Canon,
the determination of which writings are inspired
and revelation (versus which writings are not) is
outside the scope of this book.

But none will be satisfied without giving consideration to what standards might be accepted to
receive or reject specific writings as revelation.
Surely, the mere fact that a man said he was speaking for God does not mean that he should be believed.

Most men would probably require that the following conditions, and maybe others, should be met.

1. The man who alleged revelation was coming
through him must personally have some qualifications
justifying belief in him. His life, for one, must
have been exemplary; or, if not, phases of his life

which were not exemplary must have been held up to
public disapproval and reprobation.

2. The principles, rules and laws declared to
be revelation must commend themselves as generally
being admirable, exalted, severely demanding. The
rules stated as revelation cannot be indefinite,
moderate, nor be mere recommendations. They must
instead be authoritative, explicit, uncompromising,
apodictic, and threatening if not observed.

3. <u>The consequences of living by such recommendations must patently, over the long time -- not the
"short run" -- be salutary to individuals, and to
society in which they live as a whole. In other
words, revelation and foolishness, and revelation
and wickedness, and revelation and bad results are
not reconcilable. Revelation, to have a valid claim
to belief, must be rules by which men, fundamentally
and permanently, can "live." There must be some
common meeting ground where revelation and reason
meet</u>.

The Christian Bible, for example, would probably
not be a reliable book by which to contemplate the
unknown origin and the mysterious future of the universe, if here and now it prescribed bad rules by
which to live; or rules that fail.

Abraham Lincoln, in the year before his death
(according to Charnwood's biography, <u>Abraham Lincoln</u>,
Garden City Publishing Co., Inc., New York, page 440)
wrote to his friend, Speed: "I am profitably engaged in reading the Bible. Take all of this book
upon reason that you can and the balance upon faith
and you will live and die a better man." Although
Lincoln was not a conventional Christian, this was
his favorable opinion of the Bible.

Let us return to the question: Can finite,
human reason give the ultimate answers to the basic
problems of life? The answer is <u>No</u>. Special revelation, and special revelation only -- if there is
revelation -- can give the ultimate answers to
human existence.

Much of the remainder of this book formulates a
modern interpretation of what the Hebrew-Christian
Scriptures teach. Is the Bible really a <u>good</u> book?
Are its basic propositions reasonable or irration-
al? Is its influence "for good"? Is it what
Lincoln said of it?

Three Frames of Reference

If a man addresses himself to the assignment of
"placing" himself in this world, he is faced at
once with the problem: What are the subjects in a
broad way which he must consider; or, in other words,
what are to be his "frames of reference"?

Some folk consider the only frame of reference
to be God. Others do not believe in a god, and so
they reject the approach of the former.

Still others consider the important frame of
reference to be their fellowmen; either individually,
or collectively in some (usually vague) concept of
"society."

If an individual man did not believe in God, and
if he were alone in the world, then the only frame
of reference which he could adopt would be the non-
human world around him, a concept often designated
as things.

In what follows all three concepts, in reverse
order -- (1) a man's relation to things, (2) his
relation to other men, and (3) his relation to a
Supreme Being -- will be considered.

The first, a man's relation to things, is a question of cosmology. The second, a man's relation to
his fellows, is a question of ethics. The third,
a man's relation to a Supreme Being, is a question
of theology.

A comprehensive view of life will require that
a man have ideas on cosmology, ethics and (usually)
theology. The Christian religion has views on all
three subjects: there is a biblical cosmology,
there is (are) biblical ethic(s), and there is a
biblical theology. Interpretations will differ,
but if a man declares he is comprehensively a "Christian," his views will be of a certain general kind
in cosmology, in ethics, and in theology.

The more that Christianity (or any religion)
concerns itself with the here and now, the more it
is exposed to questioning, probing, skepticism,
revision. In other words, cosmology is the most
vulnerable part of Christianity; ethics is next;
theology as such is the safest and least vulnerable,
just because it cannot be verified -- the settlement of the unknowns being blurred in the mists of
uncertainty and the unknowable (except, as has previously been indicated, there is a genuine, special
revelation).

What is the basic <u>cosmology</u> of Christianity?

What is (are) the basic <u>ethic(s)</u> of Christianity?

What is the basic <u>theology</u> of Christianity?

When considering these questions, a man should set
before himself an alternative (that is, <u>his</u> <u>own</u>
alternative), namely: If he does not accept Christian cosmology, ethics and theology -- then what
is indeed <u>his</u> <u>own</u> cosmology, <u>his</u> <u>own</u> ethic, <u>his</u> <u>own</u>
theology?

In this analysis we shall first consider Christian
cosmology.

On Systematically Examining a Religion

Heredity determines most people's religion, namely, who their parents were and what religion (if any) they held; or if parents have not exercised influence on their children in regard to the religion adopted, then the religion of the country -- whether, e.g., England or Turkey or India or Africa -- will have an almost controlling effect. Or else the age in which one was born (for example, whether before or after Christ) will have a bearing on what religion a man has held or holds. In short, most people have a religion determined by their family, country, or the age in which they live.

A few all their life long will continue systematically to examine the propositions of their religion. Sooner or later every premise, every doctrine, dogma, every assumption is thought over objectively, critically and earnestly by them. Their own inclination to examine and appraise their "faith" is often encouraged by their urgent <u>need</u> to do so; they may have heard another view; they may have read a hostile critique; therefore, they find it necessary painstakingly to re-examine their inherited or established beliefs.

It is only such a person -- who has a systematic <u>method</u> of thought -- who is really qualified to be an effective proselyter (missionary) for his own faith. Such a man affirms no more than is necessary, and by such caution keeps his flanks covered. He will also be a man who knows the weaknesses of other faiths, faiths which he has rejected for the very reason that he has become aware of <u>their</u> weaknesses.

<u>A real faith must fully recognize that it is a faith, something unprovable, but that the subject is of a kind for which an answer is needed</u>. Therefore, a genuine faith (strange as it may seem) will welcome critique, listen to doubts, aver no more than is necessary, and will endeavor to show that <u>any</u> alternative is less preferable than its own faith.

Admittedly, the Christian faith inescapably <u>ultimately</u> rests on <u>revelation</u>. But a religion which does not claim revelation cannot give answers based on "reason," just because "reason" cannot explore some things. If there is to be an answer to ultimate questions, then the claim must be to something more than "natural" in the source of the explanations available in this "faith."

But still, reason -- as far as reason <u>can</u> go --
can intelligently confirm the over-all credibility
of the "revelation."

With Augustine a man can say, <u>Credimus ut
intellegamus</u> (We believe in order that we may
know). But there is enough of the reverse in the
situation, namely, <u>Intellegimus ut credamus</u> (We
know in order that we may believe), so that Augustine's statement may be viewed as being a partial
truth rather than the whole truth.

II

Christian

Cosmology

Creation And Evolution

The Christian concept of creation involves a
beginning of things. Things are declared not to
be self-existent. The Christian religion removes
the time of such an event to the illimitable and
undetermined past. Genesis starts off, "in the beginning God made heaven and earth," but the date of
the beginning is not given. (It might be argued
that the quotation contains a paradox.)

The alternative view has been referred to in
Section 1, Chapter 2, "Dust is God." If there were
no creation, then there would be no beginning of
things either. Then things would be eternal.

Let every man make his choice between these two,
according to his reasoning, his judgment, his gambling inclination, his caprice, his temperament,
his education, his taste. But the choice remains
a matter of faith.

*   *   *   *

The creation story is briefly told in Scripture.
It describes the earth as originally being desolate.
Events are checked off by "days," which some take
literally as being twenty-four hours and others as
being periods. According to the narrative, man
(or rather woman) is the last of creation.

Creation can be "imagined" in anthropomorphic
terms. That God had a workshop on and labored
diligently to shape as a bench fashioning Adam or
Eve. Probably, in effect, most people think of
creation in such a sense, except that about their
unconscious assumption is gravely stacked, as just
has been done, they repudiate the idea. Maybe they
think it is genuinely beneath God's dignity to have
an apron on and to be working at a bench. (In a
sense, "creating" a man, with blood in him and
other fluids, must have been a messy business, in
a human sense.)

It might be well to be reluctant about being
doctrinaire on how God created the universe and the
things in it. People once thought of the sun as a
mighty ball of ordinary fire; but in this atomic age
it is known that the "fire" in the sun is no big
bonfire of leaves, wood or coal. Similarly, imagining ordinary methods of creation may be equally
erroneous. Again, every man to his own taste, in
embellishing and enlarging and being more specific
about creation.

Creation And Evolution

The Christian concept of creation involves a beginning of things. Things are declared not to be self-existent. The Christian religion removes the time of such an event to the illimitable and undetermined past. Genesis starts off, "in the beginning God made heaven and earth," but the date of the beginning is not given. (It might be argued that the quotation contains a paradox.)

The alternative view has been referred to in Section I, Chapter 2, "Dust is God." If there were no creation, then there would be no beginning of things either. Then things would be eternal.

Let every man make his choice between these two, according to his reasoning, his judgment, his gambling inclination, his caprice, his temperament, his education, his taste. But the choice remains a matter of faith.

*   *   *

The creation story is briefly told in Scripture. It describes the earth as originally being desolate. Events are checked off by "days," which some take literally as being twenty-four hours and others as being periods. According to the narrative, man (or rather woman) is the last of creation.

Creation can be "imagined" in anthropomorphic terms, that God had a work apron on and labored diligently in a shop at a bench fashioning Adam or Eve. Probably, in effect, most people "think" of creation in such a sense, except that when their unconscious assumption is crassly stated, as just has been done, they repudiate the idea. Maybe they think it is genuinely beneath God's dignity to have an apron on and to be working at a bench. (In a sense, "creating" a man, with blood in him and other fluids, must have been a messy business, in a human sense.)

It might be well to be reluctant about being doctrinaire on how God created the universe and the things in it. People once thought of the sun as a mighty ball of ordinary fire; but in this atomic age it is known that the "fire" in the sun is no big bonfire of leaves, wood or coal. Similarly, imagining ordinary methods of creation may be equally erroneous. Again, every man to his own taste, in embellishing and enlarging and being more specific about creation.

One fact remains indisputable, namely, that the narrative in Genesis is laconic, without many details of great significance: God did it; he took his own time about it; there was a point when he called it quits (after creating Adam and Eve) or, as the narrative puts it, God "rested" from his labors. (In a sense, the idea that a Supreme Being would become weary and need or desire "rest" is another idea subject to anthropomorphic distortion by the human mind.)

Everything considered, the creation narrative is remarkable; it makes several big points: (1) the world did not come by accident, nor by latent capabilities in ordinary dust; instead, God <u>created</u>; (2) lower forms of life came first; and higher, later; and (3) there came a time when creation activity slackened and the world was about what we know it to be today. All that is plausible enough.

There are other realistic features, for example, the origin of language for man -- a phenomenon described as giving names to animals (and other things, too, naturally). Obviously, Moses considered the phenomena of language important enough to make mention of the <u>giving of names</u> as the origin of language.

One kind of grunt by Adam was meant to indicate to Eve that a dangerous animal was near; look out! Another kind of grunt meant that a harmless animal was near. In any event, language in part consists in using names as symbols of real things. Moses recorded the origin of language for humans.

*   *   *

A problem people struggle with is whether there was creation or evolution. Darwin's ideas have shaken the foundations of early Christian cosmology.

A generation ago a professor in the Classical Department at the University of Chicago, Paul Shorey, wrote an article in <u>Atlantic</u> Monthly in which he declared that it was a crime to teach Christianity and evolution on the same campus. (In this article Shorey reveals how he had come to accept Christianity, while attending a church in the southern part of the United States.)

<u>How</u> is it a "crime" to teach evolution and Christianity on the same campus?

If by evolution is meant that Dust is God, that there is no Supreme Intelligence, that purpose is

not a reality in the universe, but that the <u>cause</u>
of everything is in the material (the elements of
the rocks, water, air, etc.), and <u>nothing else</u>; if
indeed <u>that</u> is the proposition advanced as evolution, then Shorey was indubitably right -- to teach
the contrary ideas of a Supreme Creator with intelligence and purpose <u>versus</u> inanimate dust which
"evolved" completely, exclusively and independently
by itself -- all that is to teach such a blatant
contradiction on the same campus as to make it a
"crime" (in a sense, of course)

Evolution can, however, be defined in a much
more limited way, namely, merely as a <u>method</u> or
means used by God for creating. In Scripture, the
record merely says that in response to God's will,
the "earth brought forth after its kind." How?
The record gives no answer.

That a man is not <u>completely</u> different from a
dog everybody knows. A dog has a heart; a man likewise. A dog has ears; a man likewise. A dog can
see; a man likewise. Some people may wish to hold
the idea that therefore there is no relation whatever between a dog and a man in the sense that
hearts, ears and eyes are quite unrelated in the
two species. Others will hold that there is <u>a</u> relationship -- namely, a common creator, and that
obviously various organs in one species often have
parallel organs in other species. On this subject,
too, every man to his taste!

But on the question as posed by Shorey, to wit:
creation by God, by a Supreme Intelligence versus
"creation" via the inanimate dust of the universe
establishing its own almost inscrutable laws of
cause and effect and "evolving" what we know the
world today to be -- on <u>that</u> subject there is no
reconciliation possible. A man is either a
creationist or a positivist. He cannot be both.

<u>NOTE</u> to this chapter (but also appertaining as much or
more to the next): It is disconcerting to men who read
the narrative of creation traditionally to learn that
other Christians accept evolution. If by their use of
the word, evolution, is meant positivism, then they
should not expect to remain in the same communion; positivism and creation are contradictory. But the situation
is different, if evolution is accepted merely as the
<u>method</u> which God employed to bring our world into exist-
ence. It should be remembered that evolution is a term
with several meanings. If it is taken to mean, e.g.,
what John Dewey understood it to be (that is, Positivism),
then no reconciliation is possible. There will always
be war between Christianity and Positivism.

Christianity Versus Positivism

The real issue is defectively stated when the alternative is expressed as creation versus evolution. Such an alternative expresses only a fragment of the full issue, and furthermore that fragment is presented in an ambiguous nomenclature.

The real issue, adequately formulated, is Christianity versus Positivism.

Positivism, as has been noted earlier, is a comprehensive religion, very old and very extensive. It obtained a definitive formulation in the nineteenth century by Auguste Comte, known especially as the man who endeavored to establish sociology as a "science," according to his own specific definition of a science.

Comte observed that physics, chemistry and other "natural" sciences were sciences in the sense that they were developed by observation, comparison, measurement, discovery of uniformity in consequences under identical conditions. In Comte's world the important thing was natural "law," regularity in so-called "cause and effect," and consequently predictability in other but similar situations. For Comte, if there was no control of environment, no uniformity of observation, no measurement, no formulation of laws of cause and effect, then there was no "science" either. Comte moved from cause to effect. For him what was of importance was the factor which initiated something, namely, <u>cause</u>.

As long as Comte was dealing with inanimate things, this definition of science caused no serious problems. The law of gravity for stones is uniform, invariable.

But Comte had another determined ambition or idea -- the concept of science for the "natural sciences" must be extended to, and faithfully applied to, the social sciences, such as politics and economics.

But here a new difficulty presented itself. Living things, at least human beings, appear to have purposes. Further, among human beings these <u>purposes</u> are the motivating factor in determining what causes are to be brought into play in order to accomplish a purpose.

There cannot, in the Comtian world, be any genuine <u>freedom</u> of <u>purpose</u>. If there is any such freedom of purpose, then the chain of cause and effect is broken. A new, unpredictable, disturbing factor (or many factors) is injected in the "scientific world" of cause and effect, as Comte visualized it, and as he was determined to describe it.

Comte's idea for extending his "cause and effect" system beyond the inanimate world to the animate, and especially the purposeful world of human action, was very simple. He categorically denied that any man really has freedom of the will and action.

This was Comte's idea: If you knew everything about X's experience to date from his conception; if you also knew everything about all the things which had influenced X's ancestors from eternity, then under a given set of circumstances it could be exactly predicted what X would do. In other words, X is not capable of being a really free, purposeful human being. In the final analysis X is an automaton. He is part of the "closed system" of cause and effect existing in the universe. Everything is "cause and effect," a monistic system. Man has no real freedom; what he thinks is freedom of purpose only appears to be that. Man is merely a cog in the world of "science."

The extension of purposeless "cause and effect" (in other words, the extension of "science" in the Comtian sense) to all fields of human action is what is known as Positivism.

To make progress in the social sciences (or more correctly said, to make progress in understanding the activity known as human action of any and every kind), the thing to do was to gather statistics, observe, record, measure, and discover "cause and effect." If there are enough observations, measurements, statistics, etc., then the action of human beings can be as predictable as the course of events when you toss a stone off the edge of a roof. The day of science has then finally arrived in the social sciences (the sciences of human action).

Obviously, an idea eventually inseparable from this positivist system is the idea that if X is bad, then he must be bad because of some antecedent cause beyond his control. Find that cause! Then remove that cause. Next substitute a cause which will make X good. Then the problems of the world will be solved. Put in colloquial form, the idea is simply this: People do not make slums; it is slums that make people in slums what they are. The environment, in other words, controls.

Positivism, as a religion first fully formulated by Comte as an attack on Christianity, admits of no compromises.

A reader may say, "let us be reasonable; part of what happens is the effect of the environment, and part is the effect of the individual person's peculiarities; it is unreasonable to deny any influence to the environment, and it is also unreasonable to ascribe it all to the environment; it is some of both."

Such an idea is not Positivism any more. Into such a system, what may be called "free will" has been admitted. Further, into such a system there is a legitimate demand for establishing accountability, or responsibility. For clearly, if a man is merely an automaton in the great and complex and uninfluenceable chain of "cause and effect," then he cannot fairly be held accountable and punished. Then the troubles of the world are not bad men, but bad causes.

It is via Positivism that a great conflict has arisen -- a conflict between "science" (à la Comte) and any system accepting some "freedom" on the part of men in their conduct, and consequently holding them responsible. Science and Christianity clash in head-on conflict, inescapably, when the world is looked at in the manner that a Positivist looks at it.

Christianity allows for both environment and freedom of the will. Positivism allows only for environment. Positivism is a religion consisting of immutable and universal cause and effect. It is an extreme religion. It cannot tolerate any exception to its premise. (Positivism (1) over-applies the methods of the natural sciences; (2) mistakes the nature of the social sciences; and (3) extends the foregoing two in a manner to make them a religion.)

We can now come back to creation and evolution, or more broadly, Christianity versus Positivism. There are finally only two religions left -- (1) a strictly materialistic system as Positivism, or (2) a system allowing for purpose, a purpose by a Creator, and/or a purpose or purposes (which are really free) by human beings.

Christianity allows for purpose -- by God, and by men. Positivism allows for no purpose of any kind whatever. That which is human merely evolved from the sub-human living world; the living world evolved by the grand principle of cause and effect from the inanimate world; the inanimate world has, in turn, no origin, no beginning; it is eternal. Everything that exists is merely the consequence of an earlier purposeless cause -- back, back, back. In short, we are back to the proposition that Dust is God.

There is a mortal fight between Christianity and Positivism. They are not compatible with each other. It is either -- or.

The most popular form in which this fight manifests itself is in the dispute about creation. If the origin of the universe as we know it today is looked upon as evolved according to Positivist ideas, then to teach such evolution on the same campus with Christianity is an absurdity. Either Positivism ought to vacate that campus, or Christianity should.

This does not deny the possibility that some form of evolution, under the direction of a freely purposeful being as God, could.be part of a Christian cosmology in regard to the origin of the world as we presently know it. But then evolution is merely a method; not an autonomous positivist system.

The battle line for Christianity today is not really Christianity versus Mohammedanism, or Christianity versus Confucianism, or Christianity versus Buddhism, or Christianity versus Greek or Roman Mythology. In those terms there is no permanent fight; Christianity, rightly interpreted, has vanquished the Greek and the Roman systems, and advance from present levels of culture will eventually eliminate systems such as Mohammedanism, Confucianism and Buddhism.

But there is that other fight, which means more than Tours, Waterloo or Gettysburg -- the fight between Positivism and Christianity -- the fight between a universal, monistic system of closed cause and effect versus a world in which there can be purposeful intelligence or intelligent purpose.

To be a Positivist is to be anti-Christian at the most fundamental and inescapable point.

Finally -- in the last analysis -- every man is either a Positivist or an anti-Positivist.

The contents of this book are anti-Positivist.

Nature And Status Of The First Man

The nature of man at creation can be idealized, as it often has been and is.

According to Moses, accept his testimony if you will, Adam was a poor and ignorant (but not unintelligent) being. He was a wandering fruit-and-berry picker, trotting from one bush, tree or plant to the next in the hope, probably often vain, of finding something to eat. Eating raw fruits and greens only, he certainly had a nonconstipating diet. As described by Moses, it must have been a long time before Adam had a cooked meal. How could he, unless he knew how to make a fire?

Adam lacked clothes and did not know how to make any. He therefore suffered the full heat of the day, except where there was shade, and the full chill of the night. Scripture makes mention that two can sleep warmer than one, and undoubtedly Eve was needed to contribute to Adam sleeping comfortably.

Maybe as long as Adam lived he never had a shelter (except a tree or a cliff or cave) over his head.

Further, Adam and Eve had no sanitary facilities, no soap, no nail clippers, no razor, no comb. There can be no doubt that, in contrast to present-day descendants, Eve was rancid in spots. What would a modern woman tell her daughter who was planning her wedding without a bath!

Conditions in regard to food, clothing, shelter and sanitation were simply deplorable.

Moses indicates that Adam had considerable intellectual potential capability, but that he was ignorant. It was not that he could not learn; it was a case that he had not yet learned.

Moses indicates that the fact that Adam could survive was due to a favorable circumstance, namely, that God had supplied Adam with something called in this age by the name _capital_, namely, a productive orchard and river-bottom land. Subsequently, Adam lost even that, and subsistence thereafter would be worse.

According to Moses, it took thousands of years before metals were used for tools, in the early bronze age. But, if Moses's record is to be accepted,

Adam was not even a stone-age man who possessed
stone tools. He was instead, originally, a tool-
less and almost helpless human being.

A more favorable picture of the physical condition of Adam is fantasy and not Mosaic realism.

It is equally unrealistic to believe that Adam
had a stock of _theoretical_ knowledge, a knowledge
of mathematics and logic. Why should Adam have
that if he lacked, according to Moses, urgently
needed _practical_ knowledge? We may be sure that
Adam knew no syllogisms, could not originally count,
knew nothing about deductive and inductive reasoning, did not understand the seasons, did not understand the solar system, nor know that the earth
revolves daily and rotates around the sun. The
fact must have been that Adam's mental stock of
knowledge was equally as deplorable as his physical
stock in the form of shelter, clothing and food.

But what Adam did have, according to Moses, was
what no other creature possessed or could possess,
the potential of a capability of acquiring knowledge, prosperity, and cooperative conduct. The
phrase which conveys that idea may sound old-
fashioned or archaic, but is clear enough, namely,
Adam was created in the "image of God" (with a
magnificent potential!) in regard to "knowledge,
righteousness and holiness."

Adam -- pitiable, under deplorable conditions,
with magnificent potentialities -- was a potential
miniature and limited replica of the Creator.

To dispute the foregoing is to read Genesis
idealistically and even foolishly.

Two Sources For The Doctrine
Of The Fall of Man

The Hebrew-Christian Scriptures were written by
many different authors, in radically different circumstances, as much as fifteen centuries apart in
time. These Scriptures can therefore be consistent
and coherent only if read aright and with discre-
tion and common sense. This observation is especially applicable to the Fall of Man. That can be
looked at in the right perspective only by considering that cosmology is the most controversial part
of Christianity, and that the fall of man is in turn
the most controversial part of Christian cosmology.

There are two authors of Scripture who make mention of the fall of man, to wit, Moses and Paul.
Fifteen hundred years separates Paul from Moses.
In that long interval, there is no reference (known
to the writer) to the fall of man. Christ did not
once mention it or refer to it. For fifteen centuries the doctrine was practically a dead letter.

Of the two, Moses and Paul, the latter makes
much more of the fall of man than the former.

Paul was a person whose writings show signifi-
cantly the effect of Greek thought, something not
evident in Moses, the prophets, nor in Christ.
Paul was a "class" or "type" thinker. He appeared
not to be happy about staying with "individuals,"
but wished to make affirmations about categories,
classes, types. This is a characteristic also of
Plato, who was interested in the "grand ideas" as
distinguished from humble, individual facts.

Paul apparently felt there was a serious problem,
to wit, how incorporate believers solidly into the
redemptive work of Christ. To develop his idea on
that important unity he elaborated the idea that
Christ was as representative for "believers" as
Adam was for "all men." That analogous relationship is of critical importance in Paul's thinking.
If Christ was vital for redemption, then (thinking
in categories as Paul did) it was equally important
to view Adam as vital in regard to man's plight and
misery. Hence, the Pauline doctrine of the fall
of all men in Adam.

Moses treats the fall of man importantly, but
does not use the idea as does Paul. Furthermore,
after referring to the consequences of sin as being

pervasive and undesirable, Moses in the remainder
of his Five Books (Genesis through Deuteronomy) does
not again refer to the fall of man.

Apparently the fall of man was not a frequent,
practical bench mark for Moses, whereas it was of
vital theoretical (doctrinal) significance for Paul.

We shall first consider the consequences of the
fall of man in Moses's teaching.

Nature Of The Fall Of Adam

There is a grim and sagacious realism in the way
Scripture looks at the nature of man; here is no
self-deception or superficial optimism or idealism.
Scripture teaches that there is a pervading infirm-
ity or sinfulness even in the best of men. Man is
not good. But if a good God made man good, how
has man become bad? That was (is) a problem.

But before considering the features of the fall
of man, as described by Moses, it will be helpful
to bring the consequences within the range of
reality.

How extensive were the consequences of the fall
of man?

There are varying views on that subject, several
of which will be considered here, because they
touch on a fundamental problem.

The fall of Adam is narrated by Moses in a simple
and understandable manner. Adam was told by God
that he could eat of all the trees in the Garden
of Eden except one, designated as the Tree of the
Knowledge of Good and Evil. Nevertheless, Adam did
eat of that tree.

Moses then records that the consequences were
that Adam became aware of sin (aware of the idea of
having made a mistake, of having done something
ultimately contrary to purpose); that that awareness
became extended to sex matters (which it was not
originally); that he lost his "capital" (the use of
the orchard in the garden -- he was driven out of
it!); that he "died" that day; that Eve thereafter
would have babies in larger number and by painful
birth; and that the earth was "cursed" for Adam's
sake. It is customary to extend these consequences
to Adam's descendants, but Moses does not do that.

At this point the extent of the effect of Adam's
sin will be considered.

In this connection there are four possibilities
which should be kept in mind:

1. Adam's sin had bad consequences for all
    creation, outside of himself as well as
    for himself.

2. Adam's sin had bad consequences on his own
    physical well-being, but not directly on
    nature around him.

3. Adam's sin had bad consequences on his conduct thereafter.

4. Adam's sin was symptomatic of his problem and his failure to solve it, and in that sense his fall was prophetic and provided universal prescience concerning his descendants.

1. Scripture emphasizes that God saw all that he had made and that it was "very good." This expression can be broadly interpreted to mean that everything was so comfortable in the world before the fall that really Adam had no survival problems. This view must patently be unrealistic. A man has needs. Those needs vary. One man needs rain for his particular crop, or thinks he does. Another man needs dry weather for his crop, or thinks he does. Because men's needs differ and because their individual needs are variable from time to time, therefore, the earth could not have been so "very good" that everything was a paradise all of the time for everybody. Such an estimate of the original cosmology of the world is unrealistic.

The original world had "laws of nature" unchanged from what they are now. Some believers may believe that in Adam's original state the sun was never too hot and the wind never too cold, that the rainfall was just perfect! But probably the sun in the Mesopotamian valley was as hot as it is today, and the rainfall there needed to be supplemented by river channels which were really irrigation ditches.

The fall of Adam, therefore, cannot comfortably be believed to have had any effect on "nature." The earth may have become "cursed" in some sense by Adam's (and his descendants') ethical conduct, but its "laws of nature" cannot assuredly be expected to have changed.

2. Adam's sin can, secondly, be considered to have had a bad effect on his own (and his descendants') physical well-being only. The text refers to "the day thou eatest thereof thou shalt surely die." Some believe there was no death in the world until Adam fell. The idea cannot pass muster. Death reigned supreme -- just as supreme in the physical world before Adam fell as after -- cattle had to eat, and "killed" grass and grain. Birds had to survive by consuming bugs and worms. Wolves

kept themselves alive by eating smaller animals.
The cosmology of the world as it is today was the
cosmology of the pre-fall world.

Adam was not created to live forever, but he was
"created to die." Living things were designed by
the Creator to be born, mature, decline, disappear.
That process did not begin with Adam's fall, but
antedated it. There were as many bacteria and
viruses before the fall as after the fall.

Physiological factors did not aggravate Adam's
affairs _after_ he fell. Instead, the physiological
factors were unchanged.

3. A third interpretation of the fall is that
Adam's fall spoiled him _thereafter_ like a disease
he could not shake off. The idea is that he became
bad permanently because he had been bad once.
Scripture does not explicitly teach that idea.
Some may be determined to look at the situation in
that way.

4. The fourth interpretation of the consequences
of Adam's fall is that the defect Adam revealed was
symptomatic of his problem and of his weakness.
This is the simplest and least difficult interpretation of the fall. The logic of this will be considered further in a later chapter.

There remain some problems: Was child-bearing
to be increased (as evidence of misfortune!) and
the pain of delivery aggravated? That idea involves
the idea that the pelvic and muscular structure of
Eve was altered unfavorably by Adam having eaten
particular fruit. Many will doubt that such a
"dislocation" occurred.

The "consequences" of Adam's fall were "moral"
and moral _only_. He rejected, in the test of the
fall, principles which would have made his life
and his wife's life easier if he had observed them.
His productivity would have been higher, his standard of living better, a brood of children would
have been a lesser burden. These are all consequences of Adam's _continued_ conduct, and not of one
representative sin. The fall means a fall from
sound _principles_ _of_ _conduct_, and not a fall (change)
in the _laws_ _of_ _nature_.

The fall adumbrated moral deficiencies and not
the alteration of natural laws. Read Moses simply
and you cannot come to a lesser conclusion than
that. Let others come to broader conclusions regarding the fall, if it is their wish to interpret
the cosmology of the Garden of Eden in that way.

In the foregoing, the maximum and the minimum
has been presented that the cosmology of Moses requires. The minimum is recommended as very acceptable; beyond that, every man to his taste.

Not everything in the narrative of the fall can
be "literally" accepted. Consider the sentence:
"The day thou eatest thereof thou shalt surely die."
This is often interpreted as referring to physical
death. But that is impossible because Adam did not
die physically on the day that he ate from the tree.
(There is the pettifogging quibble that he died in
principle on that day physically; the "seed of
death" was in him.) But the obvious interpretation
appears to be: Adam first experienced on that day
the consequences of unsound policy; in that sense,
he died a "moral" or "spiritual" death. Then the
episode of eating from the tree can have meaning.

What meaning, indeed, did eating from the tree
have?

Meaning of Eating From The Tree Of The Knowledge Of Good And Evil

The scriptural version of the event by which man discovered that he could make a mistake, namely, the fall of Adam, is a unique (and if peculiarly interpreted, a bewildering) narrative.

Adam "sinned," that is, he "missed the mark," or in other words, he "made a mistake." Against which commandment -- the first? second? which? Certainly it should be possible to classify Adam's sin under a specific prohibition in the Decalogue. Otherwise the charge against Adam must be too vague to be convincing.

Some look upon the test applied by God to Adam as having no meaning except a test of obedience to God and respect to him, that is, something having relation to God alone, but no relation to things or to other men. God's prohibition, according to that view, against Adam eating from the tree of the knowledge of good and evil, was arbitrary and had no meaning in itself.

Some look upon the test presented to Adam as pertaining in some way to sex because, after the fall, Adam and Eve are reported to have become sex-conscious. The sex aspects appear, however, to be a _consequence_ rather than a _cause_, or at least posterior in time.

An easy and plausible inference points to another explanation, namely, Adam's sin was against the eighth commandment, _Thou shalt not steal_. A brief explanation will suffice.

Consideration should be given preliminarily to how Adam differed from all other creatures. Animals do not reason in the human sense nor, consequently, do they (or can they) genuinely _cooperate_ with each other. Animals look out for themselves under the guidance of what is covered (usually without adequate definition) by the word, instinct. The law of "tooth and claw," the practice of providing for current needs only, the absence of property rights, etc., all set off beasts from humans.

The question for Adam was: would he operate instinctively and opportunistically as animals do, or would he operate rationally and with foresight as a being with human reason (created, as Scripture says, in the "image of God") should operate?

In the ethical section of this book the meaning
of <u>cooperation</u> among men will be defined in some
detail. At this point the statement will have to
suffice that the question before Adam was whether
he was able or willing to <u>cooperate</u>, in the manner
that <u>cooperation</u> is essential for human society,
and for man to rise above the level of beasts.

<u>Cooperation</u> (as will be explained later) cannot
be accomplished except there be property rights.
If individual men <u>cannot</u> have property rights, then
the advantages of <u>cooperation</u> among men vanishes.
Associated with the destruction of cooperation is
the calamitous result of humans not being able to
elevate themselves above beasts, or to develop a
welfare for themselves beyond the lamentable bestial
level.

The Mosaic narrative in Genesis about Adam's fall
is, therefore, perspicuously enlightening. It
declares God made it easy for Adam to learn the
"idea," by restricting for himself only <u>one</u> tree,
the tree symbolically and illuminatingly designated
as the Tree of the Knowledge of Good and Evil. The
idea can be paraphrased easily -- the Tree of the
Knowledge of the Proper Property Rights of Others.
God, in effect, said: if you will not allow me to
restrict for myself just one tree, you will not
naturally allow it for other (later) humans either;
then, as a consequence, you will have torpedoed the
idea of cooperation among human beings. You will
have sinned, or as the original has it appropriately,
you will have <u>missed</u> <u>the</u> <u>mark</u>, you will have fallen
short of the goal of which you are capable.

How, in any form, could the idea involved in the
fall of Adam be more simply and cogently told?

The narrative of the fall is therefore no meaningless figment of the imagination; it is, at least,
profound education and admonition.

The Garden of Eden may properly be looked upon
in the Genesis narrative as an especially favorable
place for man to survive. The place was fruitful
enough to make clear the idea of <u>capital</u> (something
that increases production; in this case, many food-
bearing trees and shrubs). Involved in the narrative is the idea that God had a <u>prior</u> claim, but
he limited his claim (in order to "get his idea
across") to only one tree. As a penalty for not
respecting that one tree, Adam was driven out of
the Garden, symbolizing that failing to respect

proper property rights of others results in the
loss of capital to everybody. <u>Capital</u> will then
not be <u>formed</u>. When <u>capital</u> is not <u>formed</u>, existence returns to an animal level.

The Garden of Eden had meaning then, and has
meaning today, in the sense that where there is no
respect for property rights the <u>garden</u> disappears.
In fact, all <u>cooperation</u> in the special human sense
(to be explained later under the explanation of a
<u>contract</u> <u>society</u>) is a fundamental requirement for
human advancement beyond the beasts.

More On The Minimum Of The Fall of Adam

The Christian religion is probably weakened by interpreting the fall of Adam as a combination of (1) a capricious command by God, and (2) an unaccountable perverseness of Adam.

It has been shown in the previous chapter that God required that Adam leave one tree in the Garden of Eden untouched, as private property of God (and therefore symbolic of the significance of private property generally for human prosperity, as will be shown in more detail later). The command regarding the tree of the knowledge of good and evil was therefore not capricious, nor even provocative.

How must Adam's alleged perverseness be interpreted? As peculiarly heinous? as malignant? as singularly depraved? Was it inevitable that he would succumb to temptation (which, if true, would make God accountable for Adam's fall!)? Answers to these questions will vary, as they will to many others that might be asked. What is the minimum which must be read into the event in the light of comments in the Old and New Testaments?

The realism of the record in Genesis has been detailed in earlier chapters; Adam was poor, naked, tool-less, ignorant; but nevertheless capable of language, marvelous rationality, and wonderful cooperation with fellow men; that is, he had the potentiality of "knowledge, righteousness and holiness." But it has turned out that he nor any of his descendants would attain to the practice of knowledge, righteousness and holiness except by intense effort.

Now granting that Adam did not accomplish what was asked by God of him at the first test -- not to eat of the tree -- was he however to be exonerated, and was the requirement of self-discipline (not manifested in this event) to be abandoned? Everything in Scripture disputes this defeatist view. The ideal must be retained. Adam must be rated as having failed. The penalty of failure may not be escaped. Adam missed his mark; he fell short of requirements; he, in scriptural language, sinned.

Now, how can maximum blame be put on him, or contrarily, what is the minimum for which he can be blamed? Let each reader ask the question in whichever form he or she wishes, in order to place

the most or the least blame on our progenitor. We
shall, in this book, here deal in minimums.

Let us not begin by blandly declaring Adam to
have been malignant. Let us look at his potentiality for good and with Scripture say sincerely that
he was created so that he possessed (at least potentially) "knowledge, righteousness and holiness."

Further, there is nothing in the narrative that
would indicate aggressive, deliberately motivated
rebellion by Adam against God. He did not set out
perversely to do what God had forbidden, specifically
in order to affront God.

Quite the contrary, his motivation was to do
something for himself, because he saw that the fruit
of the tree was good to eat. It must be in this
aspect of the problem that the solution should be
sought.

What now was the "nature" of Adam, and is the
"nature" of man?

1. First, Adam had _needs_, as men still have.

2. Secondly, _things_ can satisfy those needs.

3. Thirdly, men can prefer satisfying their own
    needs ahead of the satisfaction of the needs
    of others (in this case God, as there were
    no other men).

4. Fourthly, they can satisfy their needs, not
    only ahead of others, but at the expense of
    others.

Propositions 1 and 2 are fundamental but not
disputable. The difference between propositions 3
and 4 are significant; there are in Scripture no
objections to proposition 3; it is proposition 4
only that constitutes "missing the mark," that is,
"falling," that is "sinning."

For clarification of an idea the following is
quoted from the book written by the American political theorist, John C. Calhoun, near the very end
of his life, with the title, A Disquisition on
Government. Calhoun gave a singularly accurate and
moderate description of the nature of man -- of Adam
and Adam's descendants.

...while man is created for the social state
and is accordingly so formed as to feel what

affects others as well as what affects himself,
he is, at the same time, so constituted as to
feel more intensely what affects him directly
than what affects him indirectly through others,
or, to express it differently, he is so constituted that his direct or individual affections
are stronger than his sympathetic or social
feelings. I intentionally avoid the expression
"selfish feelings" as applicable to the former,
because, as commonly used, it implies an unusual excess of the individual over the social
feelings in the person to whom it is applied
and, consequently, something depraved and vicious.
My object is to exclude such inference and to
restrict the inquiry exclusively to facts in
their bearings on the subject under consideration,
viewed as mere phenomena appertaining to our
nature -- constituted as it is; and which are as
unquestionable as is that of gravitation or any
other phenomenon of the material world.

In asserting that our individual are stronger
than our social feelings, it is not intended to
deny that there are instances, growing out of
peculiar relations -- as that of a mother and
her infant -- or resulting from the force of
education and habit over peculiar constitutions,
in which the latter have overpowered the former;
but these instances are few and always regarded
as something extraordinary. The deep impression
they make, whenever they occur, is the strongest
proof that they are regarded as exceptions to
some general and well-understood law of our
nature, just as some of the minor powers of the
material world are apparently to gravitation.

I might go farther and assert this to be a
phenomenon not of our nature only, but of all
animated existence throughout its entire range,
so far as our knowledge extends. It would,
indeed, seem to be essentially connected with
the great law of self-preservation which per-
vades all that feels, from man down to the
lowest and most insignificant reptile or insect.
In none is it stronger than in man. His social
feelings may, indeed, in a state of safety and
abundance, combined with high intellectual and
moral culture, acquire great expansion and
force, but not so great as to overpower this
all-pervading and essential law of animated
existence.

But that constitution of our nature which
makes us feel more intensely what affects us

directly than what affects us indirectly through
others necessarily leads to conflict between
individuals. Each, in consequence, has a greater
regard for his own safety or happiness than for
the safety or happiness of others, and, where
these come in opposition, is ready to sacrifice
the interests of others to his own. And hence
the tendency to a universal state of conflict
between individual and individual, accompanied
by the connected passions of suspicion, jealousy,
anger, and revenge -- followed by insolence,
fraud, and cruelty -- and, if not prevented by
some controlling power, ending in a state of
universal discord and confusion destructive of
the social state and the ends for which it is
ordained.   (P. 4f.)

Men were created, according to Calhoun, to prefer
their own interests over those of others. It may
be added that it is fortunate that men were created
that way; their individual intelligences are inadequate to be responsible for others (which in effect
would mean all others). It is the limitations of
the human mind which make altruism an impracticable
program. For each man there is only one rule that
he is competent (considering his intellectual limitations) to follow, namely, to evaluate his own
needs and seek to supply them first; he knows his
own needs with a degree of thoroughness that he
cannot know the needs of others. (There will be
more on this later.)

Wherein then did Adam fail -- fall -- sin?

That he wished to take care of his needs was
all right, even admirable.

That he wished to take care of his needs ahead
of birds, for example, who might have eaten the
fruit, or ahead of some theoretical other person
was also no failure, no falling, and no sinning.

But that he proposed to take care of his need
at the expense of another (in this case God),
that is, that he proposed to take care of his
need by theft, that was where the "sin" entered in.
It was when Adam permitted himself to satisfy his
properly preferred needs by a nonpermissible
method -- a method destructive of human cooperation
and prosperity (namely, by theft) -- it was then
that he failed, fell, sinned.

The pursuit of self-regarding interests is not

sin; they ought most of the time to be pursued
ahead of the interests of others; it is, instead,
the pursuit of self-regarding interests _in certain
improper_ manners (coercion, fraud, and theft)
which constitutes sin today, and which must have
been involved in the fall of Adam.

At least, it is impossible to read less than
that into the fall of Adam unless one is prepared
to "correct" rather than interpret the record.

On Paul's Emphasis On The Representative Character Of The Fall Of Adam

In the New Testament the Apostle Paul, in his Epistle to the Romans (especially in Chapter 5), repeatedly emphasizes the "representative" character of Adam's fall for all men.

Old Testament Hebrew thought was individualistic, and so are the gospels in the New Testament. But Paul had apparently been influenced by Platonic thought, which considered the general concept, man, more significant than individual man. To make participation in salvation through Christ plausible, Paul undertook to affirm that participation in a universal condemnation prior to salvation afflicted all men through the initial sin of Adam.

A "rationally minded" man may be disposed to boggle at that idea; and there is again the need to explain what at least this idea, that "all men have fallen in Adam," can mean in an acceptable sense.

As a minimum it can mean that, if we each had the same choice Adam had under identical circumstances, we each and all would have made the same decision, and suffered the same "fall." In that sense, Adam represented us.

Some Christian theoreticians teach that God had "predestined" Adam's fall; if this means that God gave Adam no real choice then, considering that Adam was created that way, it must be accepted that Adam's fall was indeed predestined. Maybe it was rather too much to expect that an ignorant (but not stupid) and desperately poor, wandering fruit-nut-and-berry picker, trotting from bush to bush and tree to tree, would make a far-reaching, perspicuous decision in favor of "principles of cooperation" for a complex society which he had not yet experienced. In that sense, the "predestination" to fall can be given meaning.

Adam, according to the narrative, made his choice as a mature person, albeit an ignorant one. His descendants make their first choices as infants, children and adolescents. What handicaps Adam had from ignorance and lack of social knowledge are paralleled among his descendants by their ignorance associated with their immaturity. Again, the representativeness of Adam's fall in respect to his descendants, as insisted upon by Paul, is understandable and has meaning.

Finally, what person has ever approached such a
level of self-discipline that it can be said of
him or her that it was so perfect that Adam's lack
of self-discipline was unrepresentative, and that
that person did not fall in Adam?

Behind the narrative of the fall, and behind the
extended interpretation of the fall by Paul in the
New Testament, there is a basic and indisputable
idea, namely: in the pursuit by even the very best
people of their appropriate self-regarding interests
there is an apparently inescapable tendency to engage more or less in inappropriate means to attain
self-regarding ends -- means destructive to a well-
ordered, prosperous and cooperative society,
namely, the sinful means of coercion, fraud, theft,
and the related psychological states of ill-will,
anger, envy, revenge, etc.

Adam is indeed our psychological progenitor as
well as our physical progenitor.

N O T E

The Apostle Paul, being interested in the "unity"
of the human race, wrote especially in Romans 5
about Adam being the representative in the fall and
Christ in the recovery from the fall. The Apostle
taught great truths by his analysis. The interpretation of Romans 5:12, selected as minimal in this
book, is summarized on pages 294-5, but could well
be placed even later, after the reader has read not
only pages 278-9, but also 372-7.

Fall Of Adam And The Resultant Reduction
In Well-Being

Separate penalties are itemized for Adam and Eve
in the narrative of the fall in Genesis.

In regard to Eve the text reads as follows:

> Unto the woman (Eve) he (God) said, I will
> greatly multiply thy pain and thy conception;
> in pain thou shalt bring forth children; and
> thy desire shall be to thy husband; and he
> shall rule over thee. (Genesis 3:16)

This is a formidable list of penalties to Eve:

1. More pain when giving childbirth;
2. More children, or more miscarriages, or both;
3. More appetite for sexual intercourse;
4. More submission to domination by husband.

One interpretation of the foregoing may be that
the pelvic, organic and muscular structure of Eve
was changed by Adam's fall; also, she became more
fertile; also, she became more sexy; and she lost
strength so that she could not resist so effectively
as previously the wishes or abuses of Adam. Further,
it may be inferred that (these changes having taken
place in Eve) they were transmitted to her daughters
in their succeeding generations.

There may be difficulties, however, from reading
all such ideas into the text quoted.

Overwhelmingly, the prevailing idea in Scripture
is that children are a blessing. Here a greater
number of children is _impliedly_ mentioned as a
curse! Or else, the conclusion must be that the
number of miscarriages was to increase.

That women have a great appetite for sexual intercourse can be observed by anyone and everyone.
Maybe after Adam fell the appetite increased. This
female appetite, however, does not appear to be
stronger than in the animal female world, nor stronger
than may be "natural."

That wives are dominated by husbands is declared
in Scripture at a later point to be a very good and
desirable thing, and wives are _instructed_ to submit
to the rule of their husbands. How can this then
be in a list of penalties for women, if submission
is a good thing and elsewhere commanded?

In this connection the practical viewpoint of
David Hume may be considered. Reasoning <u>rational-
istically</u>, Hume concluded that there was nothing
surprising about men ruling over their wives. Hume
observed that men have the <u>physical strength</u>, because of size and weight, to lord it over their
wives. Hume concluded that men are not the heads
of families because the bachelor or widower, Saul
of Tarsus, said men <u>should</u> be the head, but that
men are the head because they <u>can</u> if necessary
"beat up" their wives and make them submit. On the
basis of Hume's thesis, Paul was simply agreeing
with obvious facts, rather than stating a law which
did not but ought to exist.

From the screams women emit during childbirth
the inference is obvious that the temporary pain
is excruciating. However, maternity wards in
hospitals are relatively cheerful, certainly the
most cheerful <u>in hospitals</u>. As no children were
born before the fall, not even Eve could have testified how much the change in the situation amounted
to because of the fall.

In any event, the character of the penalties
listed for Eve is such that a crass explanation may
look foolish. For those who doubt that Eve's body
was altered by the fall (that she became more
fertile, or more sexy, or that she lost strength
more than Adam did so that he could coerce her more
than previously) a more general explanation may
suffice, namely, Adam's fall (being symptomatic of
his unpreparedness to <u>cooperate</u> peacefully and
mutually helpfully in an organized human society)
entailed that the sciences generally would be much
slower to develop, that the science of medicine
specifically would be delayed, and that pain-reducing
drugs would come later than otherwise; that children
(because of poverty resulting from lack of peaceful
economic cooperation among men) would be a greater
burden than otherwise; and that in the violent,
fraudulent and thieving society which would come
into existence each woman would more urgently than
otherwise seek the protection of a stronger man who
would undertake to shelter her, even though that
meant taking some abuse; further, that women would
aim to pay off their respective protectors by being
more sexy mates. As a minimum, on such a basis the
list of "penalties" makes good sense.

*   *   *

In regard to Adam, the penalties of the fall
are outlined as follows:

And unto Adam he said, Because thou hast
harkened unto the voice of thy wife, and hast
eaten of the tree, of which I commanded thee,
saying, Thou shalt not eat of it: cursed is
the ground for thy sake: in toil shalt thou
eat of it all the days of thy life; thorns also
and thistles shall it bring forth to thee; and
thou shalt eat of the herb of the field; in the
sweat of thy face shalt thou eat bread, till
thou return unto the ground; for out of it wast
thou taken: for dust thou art, and unto dust
thou shalt return. (Genesis 3:17-19)

This, too, is a formidable list:

1. The earth is cursed;
2. Thorns and thistles appear to be created
   belatedly;
3. Human beings were to remain vegetarians;
4. Labor would be burdensome;
5. Each man will revert to dust, because that
   is all that he is.

Some may regard the curse of the earth to be
figuratively directed at it, whereas possibly the
curse really applies to Adam's erroneous method of
operating which would bring less-desirable results
than appropriate conduct would bring. They may
also doubt whether thorns and thistles had not
existed at all previously. They may further wonder
whether men would permanently remain vegetarians
(the fact is that they have not). They may also
suspect that Adam had found the labor of trotting
from bush to bush and tree to tree burdensome
before the fall (which was the practical reason that
he ate from the forbidden tree), and consequently
that the unpleasantness of sustained labor was not
something really new to him. And finally, seeing
how God must have created the world, providing for
a high birth rate in the human and the sub-human
species, some people may infer that death had always
played a significant role in the plans of the
Creator, and therefore that death could not have
been a mere afterthought, and consequently only at
this late time fitted into God's scheme of things.

Those who may wish to keep their interpretation
of Genesis 3:16-19 possibly wisely simple, may interpret the foregoing penalties of the fall rationalis-
tically as a series of logical consequences, just
plain cause and effect: (1) that because men will
not cooperate (as the commandment not to eat of the

tree of the knowledge of good and evil required),
therefore the enormous benefits of cooperation among
men, so great in magnitude as to be almost unbelievable (as will be demonstrated later), will be lost
and men will inescapably therefore be much the
poorer; (2) that also because of noncooperation the
hindrances to prosperity, such as weeds in a primitive field, will be a greater burden; (3) that all
phases of life will be less prosperous and will
require more work -- more sweat, too; and (4) that
death was scheduled for man anyway as the nature of
the universe reveals, but that because of sin it
may come earlier, and more painfully, and be feared
almost in a panic because men when dying have such
a bad conscience. (If their conscience were fully
at ease, human beings would approach death maybe
with regret but not with terror.)

*   *   *

The nature of the penalty for Adam's (at least
symptomatic) sin, namely, the pervasive and primitive nature of the inescapable consequences, cannot
appropriately be pursued further at this point, but
it will be considered in some detail in the ethical
section of this book. Then the consequences of
Adam's fall, as described by Moses in terms which
were meaningful for early generations, will be discovered to be equally meaningful in a modern, complex, industrial, commercial and world-wide society.

The descendants of Adam and Eve cannot possibly
(this much is not only to be accepted but is very
obvious) be so well off as they would be if they
did not, systematically, fail to <u>cooperate</u> with
each other under the terms specified in the Decalogue (of which theft was one phase, and of which
the tree of knowledge of good and evil was made a
symbol).

N O T E

The following is quoted from Edwin Cannan's
<u>A</u> <u>Review</u> <u>of</u> <u>Economic</u> <u>Theory</u>, page 1:

The story of Adam and Eve...suggests the
advantage of capital invested in the <u>improvement</u>
of land when it pictures Adam as having an easy
and pleasant job so long as he was required only
to "dress and keep" the "garden" of Eden, and a
very hard one when he was thrown out of it and

driven to contend with a "cursed" ground all
covered with "thorns" and "thistles" or their
Eastern equivalents. (Emphasis supplied.)

Whoever knows farm life knows that unimproved
land is not so productive as improved land. By
the word <u>unimproved</u> is meant land with no orchard
or crops already on it; no drainage ditches; soil
preparation by several years of plowing, discing,
harrowing, planting, weed extermination, etc. A
man can buy a "run-down" farm and then spend much
labor and money "building it up." Such improvements
can, using Cannan's phrase, be viewed as "capital
invested in the improvement of the land."

The Garden of Eden may be understood as having
been put, by favorable natural conditions, in a
cultivated state, by the Creator; it may further
be assumed to have had an orchard, unusually good
compared to what was available elsewhere. On those
assumptions, Adam was a caretaker and not a developer
of "capital"; he was a maintenance man instructed to
"dress and keep" the orchard in condition.

Then Cannan assumes further that wherever the
Creator had not in a sense invested capital in the
form of an orchard, or in some other way, the land
was considered to be in uncultivated condition --
that is, "cursed," and covered with the usual crop
of "thorns and thistles."

On this theory, the world did not become "cursed"
because of Adam's sin, but merely lacked "capital"
(in the form of land improvements), outside of the
Garden of Eden.

It is an interesting question <u>how</u> Adam and Eve
were driven out of this favorable "garden" into the
"cursed" world outside, reading the story as Cannan
does. Maybe Adam and Eve were driven out by flood
water. Maybe after long and heavy storms with much
lightning and thunder our first ancestors moved to
higher ground, land not so good as Eden's river
bottom land, and hilly and stony land covered with
thorns and thistles. And the play of the lightning
behind them on their path out of the flooding low-
lands may have flashed from horizon to horizon in
so awesome a manner that they never endeavored to
return; for them the way was barred by an angel with
a flaming sword.

Auguste Comte As Founder of Positivism

Speaking in terms of human personalities, the
two great founders of religions are Moses (1280?-
1400 B.C.) and Auguste Comte (1798-1857); compared
to these, all others are secondary. The former
founded transcendentalism; the latter founded
materialism.

The religions of these two men are separated by
about three thousand years. According to Comte's
ideas, the differences between their two religions
are understandable phenomena; it was impossible for
his "religion" to be formulated except long after
the kind of religion which Moses founded.

In this connection, the "religion of Comte" to
which reference is made is not the foolish formal
religion which he developed in his later years, a
religion headed by a goddess. Reference is here
made to _assumptions_ underlying Comte's ideas on
science generally and individual sciences particularly. Those _assumptions_ constitute the "faith,"
the neglected premises, almost always unapprehended
and in fact unprovable, which constitute the religion of Positivism, or science _as_ _Comte_ _interpreted_
_it_.

It should be noted that Comte refused to restrict
his Positivism to the operation of cause and effect
to the inanimate and sub-human world. He considered
his great (even immeasurable) contribution to human
thought to be _his_ _extension_ _of_ _the_ _methods_ _of_ _the_
physical _sciences_ _to_ _the_ _social_ _sciences_ (better
and more broadly described as the sciences of
human action). The actions of men, Comte held, were
as controlled and should be as predictable, in response to remote or recent stimuli, as the reactions
of chemicals in a test tube.

Comte undertook to be the founder of an alleged
new and comprehensive social science which he called
sociology. The _methods_ of research for this "science"
were to be patterned on the methods of research in
the physical sciences. _Causes_ were assumed to reign
supreme; _purposes_ in the real sense were assumed
not to exist; when philosophers talked of _final_
cause (by which term they meant _purpose_), they were
talking of something, according to Comte's premises,
that did not really have reality, something imaginary.

As mentioned earlier, Comte's view required that
the universe be viewed as a closed system of cause
and effect, a system which had no breaks in it, but

which was self-contained -- with no origin; no
interference; self-developing; based on a principle
of evolution which should be discoverable, and comprehensive for all existing beings.

Christianity, in short, has unprovable premises
involving <u>origins</u> and <u>purposes</u>. Positivism, in
short, allows for no origins and has unprovable
premises involving <u>causes</u>.

*   *   *

Comte made a shrewd approach to presenting his
views by selecting an effective "sales" approach.
He "sold" his own wares by "running down" his competitor's merchandise; he attacked the premises
(admittedly unprovable) of historic religion, and
he probably had Christianity mostly in mind. An
effective way to attack an opponent is to show his
premises to be unsound; having accomplished that,
most onlookers have thereby been sufficiently
brainwashed to accept credulously and gullibly what
the clever critic proposes instead of what he has
previously attacked.

It must be admitted that Comte's attack on religion possesses great suasion.

Comte's method consisted in his making an interpretation of the <u>history</u> <u>of</u> <u>thought</u>. He affirmed
that the progress of thought from the primitive to
the modern scientific was from (1) religion, to
(2) metaphysics, to (3) positivism (scientific control, observation and measurement of cause and
effect). He makes a plausible case for his theory.

1. He shows how originally ignorant men
<u>imagined</u> a world of spirits, nonmaterial beings,
which they imagined explained those things which
as primitive men they did not already understand.
In grossest form this is <u>animism</u>, that is, there is
a "spirit" in everything, which "explains" its
really not-understood characteristics and operations
(in the series of causes and effects in this world).

From animism it is but a short step to polytheism -- Jupiters, Venuses, Mercuries, etc.; and
then there is a final rather larger jump to monotheism -- <u>one</u> God.

But, according to Comte, there are no "spirits";
nor is there a plurality of gods; nor is there <u>one</u>
God. These are all facile, imaginary and incorrect
explanations of events for which people in an ineffective manner seek an explanation.

2. Then there was secondly, according to Comte, "progress" from religion to metaphysics.

Metaphysics means something parallel to the physical, or rather something parallel but both different and higher. The physical itself was held to be inadequate as an explanation, and so a parallel meta-physical world was developed by philosophers, but their meta-physical explanations were mere imaginary creations and in reality often mere words.

To lean on metaphysics, says Comte, is to lean on a broken reed that will pierce the hand, just as religion is a broken reed on which none should rely.

3. Then there is the grand third phase, science, which when properly appreciated and universally applied, becomes Positivism -- that is enlightenment, reality, nothing imaginary, in the form of chemistry, physics, biology, anatomy, psychology, sociology, etc. At this stage, religion (degrees of animism) has been abandoned, and likewise metaphysics. The method has been changed; it is no longer imaginary thought, nor reflective thought, but the controlled laboratory methods of the sciences. As the sciences pertain only to the material, the explanation too cannot introduce anything except material antecedent events, as causes. Positivism is pure materialism.

Getting rid of religion and metaphysics was a process which Comte described as hygiene cérébrale, mental hygiene.

This is what the Encyclopedia Britannica says (in part) of Comte's system:

> The Positive Philosophy opens with the statement of a certain law of which Comte was the discoverer, and which has always been treated both by disciples and dissidents as the key to his system. This is the Law of the Three States. It is as follows: Each of our leading conceptions, each branch of knowledge, passes successively through three different phases. There are three different ways in which the human mind explains phenomena, each way following the other in order. These three stages are the theological, the metaphysical and the positive.
>
> Knowledge, ...is in the theological state, when it supposes the phenomena under consideration to be due to immediate volition, either in

the object or in some supernatural being.

In the metaphysical state, for volition is
substituted abstract force residing in the
object, yet existing independently of the object; the phenomena are viewed as if apart from
the bodies manifesting them, and the properties
of each substance have attributed to them an
existence distinct from the substance.

In the positive state inherent volition or
external volition and inherent force or abstraction personified have both disappeared from
men's minds, and the explanation of a phenomenon
means a reference of it, by way of succession or
resemblance, to some other phenomenon -- means
the establishment of a relation between the
given fact and some more general fact.

In the theological and metaphysical state men
seek a cause or an essence; in the positive
they are content with a law.

To borrow an illustration from an able English
disciple of Comte: "Take the phenomenon of the
sleep produced by opium, (a) the Arabs are content to attribute it to the 'will of God' (religion); (b) Molière's medical student accounts
for it (metaphysically) by a soporific principle
contained in the opium (these are mere words);
(c) the modern physiologist knows that he cannot
account for it at all. He can simply observe,
analyze and experiment upon the phenomena attending the action of the drug and classify it with
other agents analogous in character."
                              -- Dr. Bridges

The distinction made in the foregoing that Positivism seeks no cause but only describes what happens
and calls that a law and not a cause should blind no
one to the fact that in effect Positivism admits the
existence of the material world only, and of cause
and effect here designated by the word law, which
is supposed to be limited to mere description of
events, but which involves the assumption of what
is usually understood by cause and effect.

Several problems associated with Positivism
should not be overlooked.

1. There cannot have been a beginning; what
exists must be eternal in its origins and in its
destinies.

2. The marvels of the universe have emerged

without guidance, without purpose, aimlessly, out
of primeval rock or mud or elements; it has all
just happened, even man.

3. Men are not "free"; instead they are bound
helplessly in a mighty system of law -- of cause
and effect. This idea involves, in the final analysis, that men are irresponsible, that is, they cannot reasonably be held accountable. They are
puppets.

4. Therefore, the science of sociology should
consist in <u>changing the environment for the better</u>,
because men are dominated by their environment;
their environment explains their conduct.

Briefly, in contradiction Christianity (1) affirms
a beginning, a Creation by God; (2) affirms a purpose in God's program; and (3) holds that men are
also purposeful and therefore responsible.

N O T E

To what extent a natural scientist rejects a
system other than Positivism, consider the remarks
of Albert Einstein in his Introduction to Carola
Baumgardt's <u>Johannes Kepler</u>, <u>Life</u> and <u>Letters</u>
(Philosophical Library, New York, 1951). (Kepler
has been appraised by Immanuel Kant as "the most
acute thinker ever born.") Einstein writes (p. 12f.):

Kepler was a pious Protestant, who made no
secret of the fact that he did not approve all
decisions of the Church; he was, for this reason,
looked on as a sort of moderate heretic, and
treated accordingly. This leads me to the
internal difficulties already touched on that
Kepler had to conquer. . . .

He had to free himself from an animistic,
teleologically oriented manner of thinking in
scientific research.

The required method of thinking according to Einstein, namely, <u>abandoning</u> a "teleologically oriented
manner of thinking" indicates that Einstein thought
as a Positivist, and considered the banishment of
<u>purpose</u>, out of research work in the natural sci-
ences, as a requisite for Kepler's progress.

Christianity Is Not A Variant Of Animism

Christianity assumes immaterial entities such as: a Creator; souls; it also assumes a "beginning"; a "purposeful creation."

It should be admitted that other religions have some absurdities regarding which Comte made some valid criticisms.

Further, it should unhesitatingly be conceded that much of metaphysics ("essences," and the like) has been logomachy -- just words, pure blarney. (Consider, for example, various aspects of what in the Middle Ages was known as Realism, by which was meant the opposite of what the name implies to the modern person, uninitiated in Medieval terminology.)

Let us, however, look at what the Scriptures of the Old and New Testaments teach about cause and effect, or natural law.

(Before doing that, there is a general observation about the diversity of statements in Scripture which should be recognized. Scripture in specific locations makes statements which appear to need qualification, which therefore appear to be inadequate. But how can Scripture properly be expected in its many pages and with its variety of events always to "qualify" everything it says at each occasion? Scripture must therefore be read broadly and as an integrated whole. There is such a thing as too much literalism; the interpretation of Scripture can degenerate into absurdities.)

It is granted, Scripture specifically provides for a "variable" element in the control of the affairs of men. God watches over and controls all things. That introduces a "personal" element in the affairs of men which partially negates determinate natural law.

The ideal in regard to natural law, on the one hand, and the interposition by direct action of God, on the other, would appear necessarily to be a combination of the two. Religion becomes meaningless if everything is entirely and exclusively natural law. On the other hand, the world becomes chaos if nothing is natural law and everything is variable under the "caprice" of God. Common sense would therefore expect a combination of natural law and interposition by God.

The point Comte made was that religion did not

have any place for natural law, did not provide for
regularity in cause and effect, and therefore lacked
being law in the Comtian sense.

To make clear that the Hebrew-Christian religion
has avoided absurdities in this regard, we shall
summarize the teaching of the book of Job in the
Old Testament, and the teachings of Christ (in regard to the uniformity of natural law) in the New
Testament.

*   *   *

The story of Job is famous; his prosperity, his
piety, his massive misfortunes, the unvarnished
critique of his friends that his misfortunes proved
he had been a great but successfully hypocritical
sinner, his rejection of those charges, and his
final vindication by God.

The theme of the book of Job is that God does
not alter his physical laws just because a man (Job)
or any man has been good; such a man (or men) is
(are) as subject to physical laws as evil men are.
This is a view of the uniformity of physical law
to which Comte could take no exception.

Here is the structure of the book of Job. There
is a prose prologue telling of Job's prosperity and
rectitude. First, according to the dramatic theme,
Satan is permitted to devastate the possessions of
Job; later Satan is permitted to break the health
of Job, but not to take his life.

Then the extended body of the book contains, in
verse, (1) the lamentations of Job and (2) the re-
criminations of his three special friends, Eliphaz,
Bildad and Zophar. They did not believe in invariable natural law, but in the exact opposite --
variation of natural law in order to reward the
good and punish the evil. Natural law was made dependent on the morality of men; natural law was
neither invariable nor universal.

Job pertinaciously defends himself and rejects
their charges. However, he has no satisfactory
explanation for his vicissitudes. He limits himself
to rejecting the accusations of his three friends,
but he does not analyze a relationship between evil
moral conduct and natural law penalties, and good
moral conduct and natural law rewards, if any such
exists. He attacks the facts of his friends rather
than their reasoning. He affirms: I have not been
a bad man. He does not critically analyze their
theory regarding physical penalties necessarily
being the consequence of morally being a bad man.

—— Another friend, much junior in standing, Elihu,
presents his ideas.

Finally, though, the author of Job ascribes the
appropriate answer to God. In a way, it appears to
be a curious and irrelevant answer; it lists the
great things God has made and controls in the physical world. The argument is lifted bodily, as it
were, by God, out of the moral field and put over
into the physical field of creation -- great creatures, storms and what have you. And then God declares: Those are the laws of the physical world
and who shall critize me for them!

In other words, the explanation of Job's specific
physical ailments must be found not in some moral
defect of Job, but in the character of the physical
universe created by God, and in the natural laws
that he has established.

In the altogether different field of human action,
Scripture teaches that immorality brings its own
specific penalties, and virtue brings its own specific rewards. But that is another "world," or
another phase of life than the physical laws -- the
laws of viruses, infections, contagions, diseases,
malnutritions, poisonings, allergies, mechanics,
electricity, etc.

However, Scripture teaches that the physical
world is sometimes utilized by God to combat something in the moral world, but these are conspicuously indicated to be exceptions.

The scriptural picture then is (1) that there is
a "closed" physical system; (2) that there is a
"closed" moral system; and (3) that there is some
crossing over, in special cases, between the two.

It is, in a sense, defective to say that the
problem discussed in the book of Job is the "suffering of Job" or of the righteous generally. It is
better to say that it is the problem of the relationship of physical laws to moral laws. To that the
general answer is that there is no relationship
except in exceptional cases. The attempt of Job's
friends to establish such a relationship is sharply
condemned.

The presentation of the epic list of great items
in creation, catalogued by God, are a poetic method
of calling attention to the significance of natural
law -- a field autonomous except when used for a
very special purpose.

*   *   *

In the New Testament, the same view is taken of natural law, and its <u>universality</u> and its <u>invariability</u>.

In this case the spokesman is Christ. The context is the Sermon on the Mount.

By misinterpretation, the prevailing doctrine of that time was that violation of the moral law by A against B, permitted B to consider that the moral law had, in effect, been annulled by A's violation, so that B could <u>retaliate</u> -- avenge himself; an "eye for an eye, and a tooth for a tooth."

That idea Christ rejected unqualifiedly. To indicate the <u>universality</u> of the requirement to consider the <u>moral law never to be annulled by the action of any man</u> whoever he might be, Christ specifically refers to the invariability of natural law. The text is simple and self-explanatory; in Matthew 5:44-46 we read:

> ...but I say unto you, Love your enemies, and pray for them that persecute you; that ye may be sons of your Father who is in heaven: for <u>he maketh his sun to rise on the evil and the good, and sendeth rain on the just and the unjust</u>.

The universality of natural law, undifferentiated over the morally good and the morally evil, is taught in the words underscored. Christ taught that <u>the requirement to "love your enemies" was properly as invariable and universal as the physical laws of sunshine and rain</u>.

(It should be observed that Christ was not referring by the term <u>love</u> to a sentimental affection for enemies. Love is always defined in the New Testament as being identical with the commandments in the Decalogue. In other words, "love" in Scripture refers to a <u>profound social policy of human action</u>, and not to an <u>emotion</u>. There will be more on this in Section III.)

Comtian aspersions on religions are not, it should therefore be obvious, properly applicable to the Hebrew-Christian religion. They are applicable to cases of gross animism, and to polytheism such as that of the Greeks and the Romans.

*   *   *

Two problems remain which are associated with the problem of universal natural law, the problems of _miracles_ and the problem of real _answers to prayers_. These are obviously both cosmological problems. They will be treated in the next following chapters.

*   *   *

Comte practically made a "god" out of natural law, out of a rigidly operating system, inflexibly controlling everything. In a sense, some branches of Christianity have on this subject almost outdone Comte: there is an extensive belief among Christians in predestination, which is defined as a predetermined and unalterable system of control by God. There is as much "fatalism" in such branches of Christianity as there is in Comtian Positivism; indeed, there is more.

Prayer As A Phase Of Cosmology

Requests, in the form of prayer, are primarily
in physical matters questions of cosmology.

Prayer aims to change the course of events --
in the world of the natural sciences, subjective
psychology, personal welfare, society.

Thanksgiving in the form of prayer is primarily
a question of theology, the relation of a person
to God. Prayer in this sense is worship.

Prayers can further be looked upon as a question
of ethics, a method to improve a person's own conduct, and the conduct of others.

But an important aspect of prayer is cosmological.

Prayer is repeatedly and energetically urged upon
those who profess the Christian religion. What significance can prayer have to someone who is objectively looking at that religion?

It is common to pray for life and for health.
If a man is really sick, he may call in a preacher
to pray over him -- for his recovery. People often
take to prayer as a last recourse.

Eventually, however, all such prayer fails. Even
though a man recovers once in answer to prayer --
or a hundred times -- eventually he dies. In that
sense, that is, objectively, prayer fails.

Nobody knows either whether the earlier recover-
ies were natural events, that is, that the recovery
would have occurred without the prayer as well as
with it or by it. Answer to prayer is, therefore,
substantially a subjective phenomenon rather than
an objective one.

If a man believes in "natural law" (for example,
that if you are infected by smallpox germs, assuming you have never been vaccinated, you will become
very sick and maybe die), then for him to pray for
your recovery really involves his belief in prayer
being able to influence the infection and reducing
or even eliminating it. The prayer is intended to
frustrate natural law.

Now if "natural law" is the means by which the
world is orderly, and so that cause and effect can
be known, and plans can therefore be made, and the
future to a degree forecast -- then to pray to
frustrate "natural law" is in a sense a prayer for

chaos. Do we really wish that there be so much
variation in cause and effect that there is really
no certainty of anything in the world anymore?

In fact, most prayers <u>must</u> fail. Let us imagine
that every time we had some difficulty or danger we
could objectively take care of it by mumbling a
prayer to God. If that would "work," then it would
only require a day or two before all human effort
would cease; prayers would be substituted for action; all work and incentive would end. The abuse
of prayer would become perfect. Therefore, prayer
<u>cannot</u> involve frequent favorable response, in the
form of an objective change in events.

The fact is that prayer is not objectively and
directly answered often enough to cause chaos in
the world. Maybe this is fortunate.

Appropriate Subjects of Petitionary
Prayers

To a reasoning Positivist (a person who believes
the universe is a purposeless, closed system of
immutable cause and effect, with no "interference"
by Creator or creature; a monolithic and remorse-
less universe) any and all prayer must appear ridiculous. Why should anyone have expectation by
petitions to change unchangeable, inescapable, ir-
resistible events! Comtian Positivism and prayer
are perfectly irreconcilable.

The situation is different in several respects
for Christians who must believe in an anti-positivist world system.

*   *   *

1. The most appropriate subject of petitionary
prayers is the <u>improvement</u> of <u>self</u>.

A young man in his middle twenties came under
the employ of a nonreligious businessman with abilities approximating genius. The employee soon learned that the explanation of the spectacular achievements of his superior was that the latter always
"blamed himself" for <u>any</u> failure in any part of the
business. If something had gone wrong through a
faithless or incompetent employee, the employer
blamed himself -- he should have more correctly appraised the man whom he had trusted. If another
employee had made an error because he had not understood instructions, then the instructions had not
been clear or emphatic enough. If an associate had
the wrong ideas, that was not really the associate's
fault; instead it was the employer's own fault --
he had not yet used the right arguments in the right
way, nor provided all the facts. In short, it was
always <u>his</u> <u>own</u> <u>fault</u>.

Casually one day, he incidentally was dismissing
a man from consideration for some work, with the
remark: "He is no good; it is <u>never</u> his fault; it
is always somebody else who is to be blamed, never
himself; he thinks the world is out of joint when
it is he himself who is out of joint; we really cannot use him for that job."

If that "approach" of a great businessman has
significance -- and surely it has -- then petitionary prayer is a manifestation of wisdom, if that
prayer concerns itself, as it should, first of all
with admission of failure and need of self-
improvement.

There is no prospect of self-improvement for a
man if he thinks he has done nothing amiss nor neglected anything. The old saying is, "You cannot
get religion unless you get on the mourner's bench,"
(mourner here meaning not weeping for somebody's
death, but regretting, "mourning" for, your fail-
ings and deficiencies). Why "get religion" if you
have failed in nothing in your thoughts, words and
conduct?

Just as the requisite first step in "getting
religion" is "conviction of sin," or in ordinary
language, awareness of grave shortcomings, so in
prayer for self-improvement the requisite first
step is a lively consciousness that you have not
been so good as you should have been. The "psychology" of wise prayer is, therefore, genuinely sound.

If someone with pride affirms that he can develop
the right psychology for the first requisite step
for self-improvement (namely, awareness of imper-
fection that ought to be removed) without the for-
mality of prayer, he will do well to heed the remark
of William James, the psychologist, that if you
would be cheerful then activities which are cheerful in character will help you to be cheerful, just
as noncheerful acts will injure your prospect of
being cheerful. Similarly, formulating your deficiencies specifically, in words, in prayer, will
clarify awareness of them and will heighten the
desire for improvement.

In the Christian religion much emphasis has historically been placed on "prayer in the inner chamber," that is, solitarily, by oneself. Probably
the purpose of recommending that kind of exercise
is based on the perception that full confession will
hardly be formulated in words with a wife present
(she might be greatly shocked) or members of the
family, or the public (your reputation might soon
be ruined). Inner chamber prayers are not the
kind to advertise anywhere, if they are to be the
most valuable prayers, namely, prayers which begin
by recognizing deficiencies, shortcomings, sins,
dishonors, contemptible weakness, pusillanimity,
treachery, envy, theft, violence, lies, and what
have you.

The great merit of accomplishing improvement in
general -- for others as well as for self -- by
reforming the self first hardly needs to be argued.
It ought always to be easier to accomplish general
improvement by beginning with the self first. Why
should others respond favorably to your attempts

to reform them, when there is no conspicuous evidence that you have begun by reforming yourself! Only an obviously perfect person can dispense with self-improvement before he (she) begins to work on others. There are no such perfect persons!

*   *   *

2. After beginning with deficiencies of the self and confessing them sincerely, and appealing for the grace of forgiveness, petitionary self-improvement prayers should concern means and not ends. The "gimme, gimme" prayers are probably generally of little value; similarly, prayers which are apparently designed to put God to work, by asking him to "bless this" and "bless that," "vouchsafe me this" and "guard me against that," are maybe correctly described as an impertinence and maybe are not wisely uttered. It is different if the prayers are again "self-directed," wherein the petitioner asks the Almighty to give the petitioner the soundness of judgment, the will, the humility, the conscientiousness, the perseverance, to get something done. If a person is to go under dangerous surgery, it is one thing to pray abstractly "bless this operation," as distinguished from praying, "may I take the necessary steps to choose the right surgeon, and the right hospital, and may I be a conscientious follower of instructions given me, and may I cooperate with the surgeon promptly, and completely; may I not depress myself by unnecessary fears; nor whimper and make those nervous who are endeavoring to help me."

Prayer cannot be magic words, or an incantation. "Bless me, bless me" is not the formula, in all probability, of getting from the Almighty what you wish to have, when you merely ask, without effort on your part.

Christian prayer has always been Janus-faced (like January facing two ways, backward and forward), or to change the expression, it has always been ambivalent. Devout Christians have prayed, but also adopted carefully all the necessary means. The nature of the incident escapes the writer at the moment, but there is the story of the man in battle, or going into battle, who was fervently praying and urging others to do so, but his prayers were interspersed with practical admonitions "to keep the powder dry."

Prayers to mean much must pertain to means, and be accompanied by suitable action to accomplish the means. The prayer action is not an integrated

whole unless the psychology of prayer is accompanied by the suitability of practical action.

*   *   *

3.   Another suitable subject of petitionary
prayers consists in prayers <u>for</u> <u>others</u>, or that
others might do something.

What is the prospect of result?

There is considerable prospect if (1) and (2)
have first been patiently performed, and further
if the other person now <u>hears</u> the prayer which pertains to him.

A patently sincere, humble petition to God for
relief from wrongs by another, when heard by the
perpetrator, may soften his heart, change his purpose and his conduct.

Furthermore, the <u>public</u>, whose <u>public</u> <u>opinion</u>
is the ultimate police power in society, when it
hears such a petition may become fully aware for
the first time of some iniquity that ought to be
stopped, and then public opinion goes into action
to stop it.   Such prayers, for relief by God, can
turn out to be implemented by the perpetrators of
evils themselves, or by public opinion, or by the
state.

Such prayers are a simpler, and often an easier
way of getting things done than filing a lawsuit,
or taking the law into one's own hands.

Christians who think must eventually come to a
difficult and grave question; does God <u>always</u> work
<u>through</u> <u>means</u>; if not, how limited or how much does
he operate <u>directly</u> without using means.   A whole
"view of life" or "system of thought" will be determined by the answer to <u>that</u> question.   Not only
does the answer affect the subjects just discussed,
but also those that follow.

4.   Finally, prayer can be looked upon as a means
of <u>influencing</u> God's control of current effects.

Maybe, so the thought may be, God has not
planned -- predestined? -- certain events as A hopes
for and wishes.   Therefore, A petitions God to
change his mind, his plan, and the course of events.

The non-Christian will have two problems in this
situation: (1) if there is predestination as some
Christians believe, then events cannot be changed
by prayer, and prayer is ineffective; and (2) if
God is "operating the universe" by natural laws (in

the direction of Comtian Positivism), then the laws
-- cause and effect -- will grind out their inevitable consequences inexorably. On these bases,
prayers to change events by direct action of God
are futile because God's predestination is fixed
and his natural laws are immutable. As an example
of the latter, a fall from a great height resulting
in a broken back and severed spinal chord means
death, according to natural laws; why then pray a-
bout that if natural laws are indeed immutable, and
if God works through them in governing the universe
rather than through any direct action.

Patently, this "positivistic" problem is a serious one. What follows is one interpretation -- it
may be in error -- of the Christian cosmology involved.

(a) There is, indeed, a world of systemic
natural law. If there are exceptions, then they
cannot be multitudinous; if there are such exceptions, then they are ex definitione miracles. And
miracles by implied definition are infrequent.

(b) There is also a world of freedom -- that
is, freedom from invariable cause and effect, the
world of man's "freedom of his will." This is
independent of inexorable cause and effect, of immutable natural law. It can probably be categorically affirmed that if man has no "freedom of the
will" -- no independence of Comtian or "scientific"
cause and effect -- then man has no soul either;
or if he has one, then that soul is of no significance. The idea of a "soul" is irreconcilable with
Comtian Positivism. Now in this "world of freedom"
(as explained earlier in this chapter) prayer, and
the faithful exercise of prayer, are of vital,
requisite significance.

(c) But the Christian Scripture teaches one
thing more, namely, that there is some cross-over
between natural law and the independent field of
human freedom from that law. These cross-overs are
miracles. They have happened in the past, with long
intervals of nonoccurrence. In these cases, the
independent world is not made subordinate to the
world of natural law, but the reverse is the case;
the orderly sequence of natural law is changed in
the service of the independent government of God
and the welfare of an individual for some special
purpose. The cases may be relatively very, very
few in number, but that they exist is an essential
part of the Christian religion. If they have not

existed in the past, and if they do not exist still
in answer to prayer, then from a cosmological viewpoint a man might just as well be a positivist as
a Christian.

Petitionary prayers, petitions to God to inter-
vene with natural law, remain in order, but a
"sophisticated" view of the necessity of <u>order</u> in
the world will give the petitioner an awareness that
answers to such prayers have historically been
limited and will probably continue to be limited
in the present and future.

*   *   *

This discussion of subjects for prayers is not
complete, but that cannot be expected in a book of
this character.

Miracles

Miracles, in the Christian religion, are varied and are subject to various interpretations.

Some _physical_ phenomena may have had a psychological origin, and the correction of the physical difficulties by a change in psychology may be considered by some not to have been a genuine miracle -- an intervention into natural law. This is possible, and in some cases may be probable.

The walls of Jericho, according to Scripture, fell down when the Israelites shouted on the seventh day after they had marched silently around the city for six, and had finished on that day the seventh march around the city. The reliability of the story may be questioned by a skeptical Christian; it may be doubted that it is _history_. But Jericho has been excavated, and it is now known that the city had existed for two thousand years or more before the Israelites appeared before it; had been destroyed several times and rebuilt; that the wall in the time of Joshua was built on the foundations of an old wall but improperly on the edge so that the footings of the new wall were not genuinely sturdy; that there is evidence which indicates the walls collapsed from an earthquake, an event rather frequent in that area. On the basis of that evidence, was there a miracle in the wall collapsing? in the earthquake? in an alleged effect from the shout of the Israelites? in the _timing_ of the shout and the earthquake? Obviously, interpretations _can_ differ. A skeptic may declare that the defect in the structure of the wall, the earthquake and the shout all constituted a chance concatenation of circumstances and that no miracle occurred. It is _possible_ that the event was such a mere concatenation.

Later in the conquest of Canaan by the Israelites under the leadership of Joshua, Joshua prayed in a crucial battle (probably with a few thousand men at the most, on each side) that sun and moon would stand still, and the implication is that the event took place. In the narrative mention is made of a terrible hailstorm, undoubtedly accompanied by extraordinary darkness which may have hindered pursuit by the Israelites. Some may argue that the day was not lengthened but that the darkness from the storm cleared up. The "proof" presented is quoted in Joshua 10:12-14 in the form of poetry from

a book called Jashar. This book was probably a
book of minstrel poems. Minstrel poems have usually
had characteristics which indicate poetic license.
The clearance of the storm may be looked upon, under
poetic license, as a lengthening of the day, as a
sun and moon standing still. Interpretations may
again differ -- from outright skepticism, to emphasis on the hailstorm, to the earth temporarily ceas-
ing its spinning, a most truly extraordinary event.

There must, however, if the source of the Christian religion is to be considered reliable, be a
limit to skepticism in regard to miracles. Deny
them all; reason them all away; declare that instead
natural law has never been altered by miracles, by
intervention by God; into what position has such
skepticism reasoned itself? Simply into the position that the world has been "positivistic" all the
time -- a closed system which God nor man can
change, or at least has not changed.

Christianity is the antithesis of Positivism. It
is not the antithesis in the sense that Positivism
means unalterable law and that Christianity is perfect animism assuming no natural law at all but that
everything is capricious. The facts are quite different. Miracles in the Christian religion are not
common events, but are indicated to be uncommon,
most exceptional kind of events. Christianity,
therefore, does not assume a world that is a complete
antithesis of cause and effect in natural law, but
only that there are infrequent and exceptional oc-
currences which are independent of natural law.

The problem is a matter of principle. If there
never were miracles, if they were all hallucinations
or forgeries, if then natural law has never been
interrupted, then a man is back to Positivism;
which (as has been indicated previously) means,
Dust is God. To dispute all miracles is to adopt
a position that if there is a God, he may properly
be ignored, because he is letting his system unwind
itself with never any attention to it, nor any
change. Perfect skepticism on miracles merely makes
a Positivist of a man.

Deism, which looks upon the Universe as a clock
which has been wound up and is running down, therefore, cannot be Christianity. Christianity involves
acceptance of theism, that is, that God is the
active natural and moral governor of the universe.
He tinkers some with his clock.

Blaise Pascal, distinguished French mathematician and physicist, considered the phenomena of miracles to be a necessary support of the scriptural narratives. The idea is that if there were no miracles, then the narrative may be untrue; the miracles therefore validate the reliability of the narrative. Pascal appears to be right, but it also appears preferable to restate his proposition: if there were no miracles -- none whatever ever -- then there can be no religion for Dust is indeed God; without purpose and by chance and not by design everything has just "come about"; mathematics is all accident, chance; natural law is itself a fiction; there is no law, but just uniformity determined by nothing but what originally was only inanimate dust. Dust developed life, intelligence, but no "freedom," no ability by men really to influence events; men, too, are mere automatons of "forces" in Dust. Dust is God! (Now, if you wish a miracle, such belief is indeed a miracle, in the judgment of most Christians!)

Faith in Positivism requires a greater faith than the Hebrew-Christian faith requires.

Cosmology And The Rest Of Religion

Religion may be looked upon as a fortress that has outer bastions; then a second moat; and finally an inner citadel, the ultimate rampart of defense.

One way to represent this is by concentric rings; the outermost bastion is in the field of cosmology; then, more important, is the second line of defense, ethics; and finally there is the inner citadel, theology.

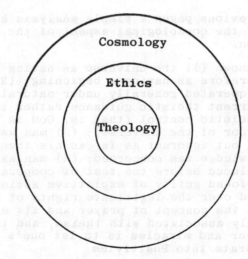

Cosmology

Ethics

Theology

Another way to represent the situation is to divide the circle into three segments of 120° each. In this representation the whole of religion -- combined cosmology, ethics and theology -- can be weakened almost fatally by the failure of any one of the three fronts.

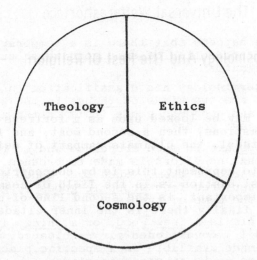

In the previous pages a simple analysis has been made of the cosmological aspect of the Christian religion.

We have shown (1) the universe as having a Creator, and therefore as having a beginning; (2) this universe as operated generally under natural law, but under current theistic guidance rather than mechanical deistic control (that is, God is the active governor of the universe); (3) man as created intelligent, but ignorant as far as his then current stock of knowledge was concerned; (4) man as inadequate when placed before the test of cooperative action, and found guilty of exploitive action (driving roughshod over the legitimate rights of others); and (5) that the concept of prayer and its efficacy is inseparably associated with theism, and that to abandon prayer and miracles is to let one's opinions deteriorate into Positivism.

The only real alternative to Christianity is Positivism, which is a religion that can briefly be described as holding (rather astonishingly) that Dust is God. Such a religion appears to require more faith than does Christianity.

It is conceded that there are no answers to the ultimate riddles of life except by special revelation. Mundane proof positive has never been claimed by Christianity. In fact, no such evidence is possible.

The Universal Welfareshortage

It often happens that there is a temporary and limited overproduction of some good which can satisfy a human want.

In the terminology and classification in economics there are two kinds of things in the world, free goods and economic goods (this latter group for short, just goods).

Free goods are in such abundance and so readily available that no effort is made to produce, conserve or distribute them. Such free goods are often distinguished from economic goods by giving the former the name of things.

Outside air is a free good, or a thing, in economics. B u t   conditioned air -- cleaned, cooled or heated, made available in a specific place at a specific time -- is an economic good.

Things can shift from free goods to economic goods, and from economic goods to free goods; it depends on circumstances. Water is an economic good in a canteen in the desert, but is a free good next to a copious mountain stream. But the mountain stream might dry up at times, and then it might be necessary to store water there, and then it has become an economic good. Whether something becomes an economic good depends on the ratio of the quantity of the thing to the need of potential users.

If someone owns a good (for which there is a demand relative to the supply so that effort must be put forth to produce, conserve and distribute that good), and thinks that he has a valuable asset, only to discover that for some reason or other his good has changed into a mere thing, he may lament his "loss," and whimper for help or compensation.

Or, the ratio of supply and demand may not change enough to convert an economic good entirely to a free good, but only enough to lower the price so that the supplier does not recover his costs; he "loses money" on those goods. Again he may regret the change, whimper and complain, and facilely demand, inappropriately, that society do something for him.

From circumstances as the foregoing men sometimes jump to invalid conclusions, which on reflection they would reject. Sometimes they deduce that there

is _general_ overproduction -- too much of everything.
However, there has never been anything like that,
nor can it ever occur. There is the possibility,
probability (certainty, in fact) that there will be
intermittent overproduction of _specific_ items --
because of the lack of perfect foresight. But such
overproduction is always accompanied by _underpro-
duction_ of something else.

Instead of there ever being _general_ overproduction, the real situation consists in there always
being a _universal welfareshortage_. Observation sub-
stantiates this; in the world today more people are
alleged to go to bed hungry than surfeited.

The _fact_ of a universal welfareshortage is supported by sound logic, too. The world is _finite_;
the demands of men (and especially of women) are
infinite. That combination means that total _demand_
is _always_ pressing against total _supply_; it is inescapable.

Moses in Genesis 3:19 proclaimed an inevitable,
inescapable and usually distressing fact -- that
there generally would be a _universal welfareshortage_.
It is a fact of life -- in Adam's day, in Moses's
day, in our day, in every day.

This _welfareshortage_ -- this imbalance between,
on the one hand, men's needs and, on the other,
goods to supply those needs -- constitutes the great
practical problem in this life. The welfare _short-
age_ is the most important benchmark in this life.
In some way or other, everything has to be interpreted in relationship to that welfareshortage.

So that none may think that the emphasis here on
universal welfareshortage is evidence of unawareness of serious economic problems, it may be added
that the phenomena of economic instability and
especially economic depressions do not negate the
principle of a universal welfareshortage. In depressions, _needs_ _seem_ to disappear. Business
activity is paralyzed. Few of the many who bought
clothes yesterday seem to need them today; those
who were eager to buy houses last week have abandoned the idea; the would-be investor who planned
to buy stocks last month now tries to sell what he
has long had in his portfolio. Suddenly everywhere
there seems to be an oversupply, and demand has
evaporated.

The _cause_ of booms and depressions will be considered later. That _cause_ does not rest in the

basic ratio between demand and supply. That <u>cause</u>
is something different, and is not a cosmological
phenomenon, but an ethical one (namely, theft).
In this situation, it is ethics that are askew,
not cosmology. Therefore, this poignant phenomena --
depressions -- will be considered under ethics, in
the next section in this book.

Where And How Cosmology And Ethics
Dovetail Together

Ethics is not an autonomous science, but a derivative one; or if not derivative, it is no more than an associated science. The underlying or antecedent science is cosmology as the term is here used, to wit, the nature of man, the world around him, and man's relationship to that world.

It might, therefore, appear to be proper to go further at this time into the relationship of men to things. An additional reason for that would be the fact that the relationship of men to things is not simple.

If the Hebrew-Christian Scriptures have a defect, in the form of an omission, then that defect may be considered to be the important lack of analysis of the complex and varied relationships of men to things. Moses did not seem to realize the problem; he went ahead and assumed, although he made correct assumptions; but he did not analyze the principles involved; maybe he was unaware of their crucial importance; at any rate, there is no evidence that he was able to or did "formulate them.

Problems of ethics (relationships of men to men) stem from antecedent problems of cosmology (relationship of men to things). Remove problems in the latter field, and there are few left in the former.

(If there is an exception to the foregoing statement, it will be in the field of sex. But if a mate (man or woman) be considered a "thing" for the moment, and if the possession or nonpossession of the mate be appreciated to be the problem between the sexes, then even sexual ethical problems are not separable from cosmology.)

The complexities of the relationships of men to things were not only unformulated in ages gone by; they are generally unrecognized and unformulated even in this age. The overshadowing economic and political problems of the twentieth century would be "approached" differently, and more effectively, if the characteristics of the relationships of men to things were properly understood before the

endeavor was made to solve the relationships of men
to men, by specific economic and political policies.

In regard to the position of the Hebrew-Christian
religion in this situation, it can probably best be
described by saying that it came to the right
answer by revelation without giving evidence that
it was humanly capable at the time of <u>analyzing</u> the
problem. A skeptic might say that it "blundered"
into the right answer, but was unable to explain
<u>how</u> that right answer was found.

This raises the question: if the relationship
of men to things is genuinely antecedent to the
relationship of men to men, is it not only appropriate but even necessary to analyze this "mysterious" and "unappreciated" complexity associated with
the relationship of men to things in this cosmological section, <u>before</u> taking up ethics in the next
section?

The apparent answer is probably <u>yes</u>, but for
reasons of exposition the remainder of consideration
of cosmological problems in this book will be inter-
mingled with the ethical questions themselves.

Cosmology and ethics dovetail too much to justify
separating the explanation of the relationship of
men to things in a watertight way from the explanation of the relationship of men to men. Therefore,
the remainder of discussion regarding cosmological
problems is in the next section.

III

Christian

Ethics

Definition Of The Christian Religion

There are various ways to define what is meant
by the Christian religion.

One definition might consist of three parts:

1. Acknowledgment of a Creator, that is,
   acceptance of him as the particular explanation of the origin of all things.

2. A specific set of ethics -- rules for
   conduct in this life.

3. An anodyne of hope, a promise of a future,
   to wit, a future life, associated with
   either reward or penalty.

In other words, Christianity is a doctrine on
origin and destiny, with this life for and sandwiched in between, and for which the rules of conduct are given a fantastic importance and are also
declared to be apodictic.

Disobedience of these rules is inseparably associated with gravest punishment, except the grace of
the Creator intervenes.

Emphasis on conduct -- on ethics -- begins on
the earliest pages of the Hebrew-Christian Scriptures, and revives and revolves around that theme.

When reading Scripture, its extraordinary preoccupation with "conduct" should ever be kept in
mind. It is also well to remember that when reading this section.

Definition Of The Christian Religion

There are various ways to define what is meant by the Christian religion.

One definition might consist of three parts:

1. Acknowledgment of a Creator, that is, acceptance of him as the particular explanation of the origin of all things.

2. A specific set of ethics -- rules for conduct in this life.

3. An anodyne of hope, a promise of a destiny, to wit, a future life; associated with either reward or penalty.

In other words, Christianity is a doctrine on origin and destiny, with this life for man sandwiched in between, and for which the rules of conduct are given a fantastic importance and are also declared to be apodictic.

Disobedience of those rules is inseparably associated with gravest punishment, except the grace of the Creator intervenes.

Emphasis on conduct -- on ethics -- begins on the earliest pages of the Hebrew-Christian Scriptures, and revolves and revolves around that theme.

When reading Scripture, its extraordinary preoccupation with "conduct" should ever be kept in mind. It is also well to remember that when reading this section.

Preliminary Remarks On Christian Ethics

Christian ethics are at least 3,500 years old, but agreement on them is not yet complete. They have ever been in dispute because of differing interpretations and applications.

Moses presented the <u>Decalogue</u> (of which ethics constituted the second half) about 1,400 B.C. In 30 A.D. Christ, by giving his own version of ethics in the Sermon on the Mount, disputed some of the then-prevailing interpretations of Moses's ethics. His refrain was: "Ye have heard that it was said, ... but I say unto you, ..." It is certain that at that time there were real and important issues at stake.

Today Moses's ethics are subject to still different interpretations, some of the new interpretations having been influenced by another system of thought, the Marxian Communist.

It may be expected that the interpretation of Hebrew-Christian ethics will remain in some flux.

*   *   *

It is customary to consider <u>love</u> as the keynote to Hebrew-Christian ethics. This raises an interesting question: Does <u>love</u> define and explain the Decalogue, or does the Decalogue explain love?

The prevailing twentieth-century view is probably the sentimental one, that love really defines and explains and maybe adds something to the Decalogue. In many churches, as a means for further enlightenment of members, <u>after</u> the Decalogue has been read in the liturgy of the service, the minister in "explanation" or "elucidation" of that Decalogue, with a happy smile on his face, summarizes it as being, "to love God above all and the neighbor as the self"; in other words, the mere word <u>love</u> is presumably used to explain the Decalogue. But very probably the idea lacks merit.

In the first century of the Christian era it was the reverse: the Decalogue defined and explained the word <u>love</u>.

The sober and rational view is the one just

expressed, that Christian ethics is founded on the
rules of the Decalogue, and not on the sound and
letters of a mere word, l-o-v-e, regardless how
much value a love-sick swain or a fevered maiden
puts on the word itself; or for that matter, a sentimental teacher of ethics.

*   *   *

If love, which so often and so strongly <u>implies</u>
affection, is the essence of Christian ethics, or
if sentimental love is its hope -- then Christian
ethics is probably on the wrong track. More rationalism than that kind motivation is needed.

If in their ethics the ancient Hebrews gradually
shifted through the centuries from the specific
rules of the Decalogue to the variably defined term
<u>love</u>, then their intellectual quality was probably
gradually deteriorating.

*   *   *

The expression, Thou shalt love thy neighbor as
thyself, is as old as the time of Moses; he wrote
in Leviticus 19:18b: "Thou shalt love thy neighbor
as thyself."

Christ and his contemporaries defined <u>love</u> by the
Decalogue, and not the Decalogue by love. See
Mark 10:17-19.

The Apostle Paul wrote in Romans 13:8-10:

Owe no man anything, save to love one another; for he that loveth his neighbor has
fulfilled the law. For this, Thou shalt
not commit adultery, Thou shalt not kill,
Thou shalt not steal, Thou shalt not covet;
and if there is any other commandment, it
is summed up in this word, namely, Thou
shalt love thy neighbor as thyself. Love
worketh no ill to his neighbor: love therefore is the fulfillment of the law.

The Apostle John wrote in his First Epistle
General 5:2, 3:

Hereby we know that we love the children
of God, when we love God and do his commandments.

Love, As A Term Summarizing Hebrew-Christian Ethics, Must Be Defined

If <u>love</u> is significant in Christian ethics, then the term urgently needs careful definition.

Love is, even in the Hebrew-Christian Scriptures, a flexible, ambiguous, <u>equivocal</u> term.

Love is used in Scripture to designate shameful, brutal rape; it is also used to designate alms-giving, charity, sacrificial sharing. The mere word <u>love</u> is therefore inadequate to designate by itself alone what is meant by Hebrew-Christian ethics. Standing alone the word is too flexible to be useful.

This book deals with minimals and not with maximals. In conformity with that principle, the definition here given may be looked upon as a minimal one. Strict constructionism of Scripture will be the rule that will be followed.

But this minimal definition will carry enough demands that its force will be massive.

Ethics is not a science of emotions, but a science of appropriate action relative to fellow men. Ethics is properly based on intellect, rather than on feeling. Using the nomenclature of the science of electricity, in the science of ethics the intellect must supply the real amperage, and emotion no more than the requisite voltage. It should not be otherwise, with feeling supplying the content of the meaning of love and the intellect merely contributing some supplementary features. The definition here developed will therefore be rationalistic and analytical as well as minimal.

Voluntary equal sharing -- treating another as well as a man treats himself -- can be considered the acme of ethical love, according to Hebrew-Christian principles. Another name for kindly, affectionate and voluntary sharing is <u>charity</u>. In a sense then, charity is the maximal definition of Hebrew-Christian ethical love.

Charity, it must be conceded, is the loveliest flower of Christian ethics, but it is the ornament and not the framework. It should not be over-valued, at least not in an analytical study.

Charity is not mentioned in the foundation docu-

ment of Hebrew-Christian ethics, the Mosaic Decalogue (Ten Commandments); charity is a modest supplement to the Decalogue.

As a basic principle for ethics, charity has a
defect. Christ said, "It is more blessed to give
than to receive." In other words, receiving charity
has some unattractive features. Christ's statement
might be paraphrased in this manner: "Charity often
involves unhappy and unedifying sentiments on the
part of recipients, and charity may be a curse to
them, even though the giver of the gifts may be
moved by a noble emotion and reasonable judgment;
therefore, charity is not an unmixed but an adulterated good."

The foundation stones of Hebrew-Christian ethics
are of coarser material than charity, namely, the
so-called Second Table of the Law: do not coerce
(sixth commandment); nor commit adultery (seventh);
nor steal (eighth); nor lie (ninth); nor covet
(tenth); nor fail to honor parents (fifth).

Three of these are of especial interest for this
economic age, namely, the prohibition of coercion,
of theft and of fraud. A crucial question is: what
is the positive "opposite" to the prohibition of
coercion, theft and fraud; what is the counter, the
antonym, to these three ideas taken collectively?

It is believed that the correct answer to that
question is the idea of cooperation.

Although cooperation may initially be prejudged
as something of a lowlier order than charity, in
what follows the idea will be advanced that cooperation is the real foundation stone of Hebrew-Christian
ethics, or if not that, then it is the minimal that
anyone can accept and still affirm that he holds to
Hebrew-Christian ethics.

                    *   *   *

The illuminating analytical principle on which
Hebrew-Christian ethics is founded is explained in
Ricardo's LAW OF ASSOCIATION (COOPERATION). To
understand Hebrew-Christian ethics requires a thorough grasp of what Ricardo presented. But there
are assumptions underlying Ricardo's irrefutable
mathematics, and those assumptions are the operation
of the sixth, eighth and ninth commandments. The
indulgence of the reader is petitioned in regard to
what follows, because the most admirable features

of Hebrew-Christian ethics cannot come to light
except by some analysis and mathematics.

N O T E

The following questions assume something,
namely, that "indiscriminate almsgiving" will give
rise to "universal poverty and degradation." That
assumption appears to be correct; almsgiving is,
therefore, not an invariable good but a good that
depends on circumstances. The merit of alms depends on the wisdom of the giver, or the person
whom he utilizes to make the distribution of his
alms. Only wisely discriminated alms are meritorious.

The two questions below are taken from A Review
of Economic Theory by Edwin Cannan, p. 3f. (P. S.
King and Son, Limited, London, 1929):

> Can we really make up our mind
> whether we ought as Christians
> to give money to a beggar with-
> out raising the question whether
> he will buy whisky for himself
> or food for his alleged starving
> children?

> Can we recommend indiscriminate
> almsgiving in spite of the
> universal poverty and degradation
> to which it is certain to give
> rise?

Ricardo's Law Of Cooperation

An admittedly rather novel position is here taken,
that Hebrew-Christian ethics can best be explained
by first ignoring any revelation of its authoritar-
ian conclusions and by postponing attention to its
exhortations, and instead beginning with a factual,
or rather a mathematical, analysis of its not-
always-obvious (and usually only vaguely sensed)
framework in which it operates.

There is in a sense an "internal mechanism"
within ethics which, if first and fully understood,
will affect the evaluation and interpretation of
ethical rules.

In what follows there is submitted for consideration an illustration, in simplest form, of a law in
economics -- not too well understood and not often
mentioned in the science of economics -- known as
Ricardo's LAW OF COOPERATION or ASSOCIATION. This
law is not ethics, but this law will not operate
satisfactorily unless the appropriate ethics permit
the law to operate. The problem then is one of
associating (1) economic mathematics with (2) Hebrew-Christian ethical principles.

*   *   *

It is possible to describe Ricardo's Law of Cooperation in words, but that will entail being
complex and even unconvincing. Instead, therefore,
of talking about cooperation abstractly, a computation which is a simple demonstration will be submitted.

The mathematics will distress no one who can
divide and add. No algebraic symbols will be used;
no formulae; no complexities.

We shall take the case of two farmers, with farms
equal in size and quality, growing the same crops,
and with equal harvests, consisting of 80 bushels
of nuts and 600 bushels of potatoes. Further, it
is assumed that the men have the same equipment for
harvesting: ladders, baskets, spading forks, and
storage facilities.

Shall these men associate together or cooperate
in harvesting their crops, or shall they harvest
separately in isolation from each other? From the
words employed in the name of Ricardo's Law of
Cooperation there is an implication that there is
a benefit from association or cooperation. After

all, the principal practical purpose of association is an advantage to be gained from cooperation.
But how and under what terms can these men cooperate to mutual profit, if at all?

*   *   *

Now, by tailoring the circumstances in a biased
manner a case could undoubtedly be made that these
two farmers could best harvest their crops to
<u>mutual</u> profit, and also in a socially agreeable
manner, by working side by side.

Ricardo, however, did not bias the data for his
computation in that direction, but in the contrary
direction -- against his thesis.

He deliberately assumed data which, rather
patently, would yield a result against attempted
association; and therefore against cooperation.

Ricardo assumed that one of the farmers was more
capable as a harvester <u>in every respect</u> than the
other farmer. Let us call the farmers, Fastman and
Slowman. Let us assume that Fastman can pick 5
bushels of nuts a day, but Slowman only 2 bushels;
and that Fastman can dig 30 bushels of potatoes a
day, but Slowman only 20 bushels. This is shown
in Table 1.

Table 1

Harvesting Capability Per Day Of Two Farmers
(In Bushels)

Product	FASTMAN	SLOWMAN
N u t s	5	2
Potatoes	30	20

It <u>appears</u> obvious that Fastman will do best by
picking his own nuts and digging his own potatoes,
and not bothering with Slowman. If then each man
harvests his own crop, how many days labor will it
take? For Fastman the figure is 36 days; and for
Slowman, 70 days.

For Fastman the detailed computation is shown
in Table 2, columns (1), (2) and (3); for Slowman
the detailed computation is shown in Table 2,
columns (1), (4) and (5).

Table 2

Days Required By Two Farmers To Harvest Two Crops

		F A S T M A N		S L O W M A N	
Product	Crop (Bushels) (1)	Bushels Per Day (2)	Tot. Days Required (1) + (2) (3)	Bushels Per Day (4)	Tot. Days Required (1) + (4) (5)
N u t s	80	5	16	2	40
Potatoes	600	30	20	20	30
T O T A L :	Each		36		70
	Combined			106	

Together the two men, working separately, can harvest their crops in 106 days: Fastman requiring 36 days for his crops, and Slowman requiring 70 days for his. Slowman will have to work nearly twice as long as Fastman.

     *   *   *

Let us suppose that Slowman is a fearful man and that he is terrified and becomes dizzy when on a ladder, and that he goes over to his neighbor, Fastman, and tells him of that predicament and pleads with Fastman to pick part or all of his (Slowman's) nuts, and that in return he (Slowman) will dig all of Fastman's potatoes. Fastman thinks long and hard; he knows how slow his neighbor is both at picking nuts and at digging potatoes. He knows that he cannot cooperate with Slowman except at a loss to himself, because Slowman does nothing so fast as Fastman himself does it. Slowman pleads desperately, and Fastman wracks his brain to find a way out so that he does not need to help Slowman. Finally, however, Fastman makes a concession; pity controls his decision; he decides to engage in some charity to Slowman; Fastman knows his wife will object and ridicule him; but he finally says, "Okay, Slowman, I'll do it for once, but not for another time."

Under this arrangement Fastman will have to pick 160 bushels of nuts, and Slowman will have to dig 1,200 bushels of potatoes. This is now association or cooperation, with Fastman doing some of Slowman's work and Slowman doing some of Fastman's. Slowman realizes that Fastman is doing him a favor; Fastman thinks that he is sacrificing himself for Slowman; neither has "worked out the problem on paper" nor realizes "how he will come out." Two simple divisions will, however, give the answer; see Table 3.

Table 3

Result Of FASTMAN Picking All Nuts and
SLOWMAN Digging All Potatoes

Product	Quantity to be Harvested	Harvesting Rate	Days Required
N u t s	160 bushels	5 bushels per day by FASTMAN	32
Potatoes	1,200 bushels	20 bushels per day by SLOWMAN	60
		T o t a l	92

We can now compare the gain or loss from cooperation; presumably Slowman will have gained and Fastman will have lost. See Table 4.

Table 4

Effect Of "Cooperation" By FASTMAN and SLOWMAN,
With FASTMAN Harvesting All Nuts and
SLOWMAN Digging All Potatoes

		Days - In Isolation	Days - In Cooperation	Saving For Each Man
FASTMAN:	N u t s	16	Nuts only, 32	
	Potatoes	20	-	
		36	32	4 days
SLOWMAN:	N u t s	40	-	
	Potatoes	30	Potatoes, 60	
		70	60	10 days
	Grand Total	106	92	14

In still more abbreviated and simplified form the final data are presented in Table 5.

Table 5

Savings In Days and Percentages From Cooperation

	Days - In Isolation	Days - In Cooperation	Net Saving In Days	In Percent
FASTMAN	36	32	4	11.1%
SLOWMAN	70	60	10	14.3
Together	106	92	14	13.2%

Many readers will think a trick has been played
on them, or that there is a subtle error in the
calculation. But let every one check the figures,
and re-examine the reasoning. They can come to
only one conclusion, to wit: there is a "mysterious" advantage in cooperation. That "mystery" will
be explained later to readers to whom it is not
already obvious.

        *   *   *

Let us return to ethics for a moment.

The Hebrew-Christian religion talks and talks
of love, as the essence of its ethics.

And what, then, does love mean? Does it refer
to the kindly motivation that Fastman had of doing
a good turn at his own expense to Slowman, his less
capable neighbor?

Note that it turned out, in our illustration,
that Fastman made a gain of 11.1% and Slowman a
slightly greater gain of 14.3%.

The illustration here presented raises an important ethical question: Is Hebrew-Christian love in
essence a charitable motivation, or is it something
entirely different, a mysteriously profitable
cooperation as just analyzed?

The answer is that Hebrew-Christian ethics is
something of both -- cooperation and charity -- but
it is overwhelmingly more cooperation than charity.

Then where does the "ethics" come in? The ethics
enter the phenomena of cooperation at an antecedent
point: the benefits from cooperation are obtained
only when certain rules of conduct are followed,
namely, the sixth, eighth and ninth commandments.

All those familiar with the Hebrew-Christian
Decalogue will remember the insistent reiteration
that love means only what the Ten Commandments
specify. Therefore, that love -- the hard-headed
"love" of the commandments (and not some insipid
sentimentality) -- underlies the Hebrew-Christian
ethic.

The arrogance of the Hebrew-Christian ethic is
almost insufferable. It promises this world (and
paradise to boot!) to those who will really live
according to that ethic. Is it boasting when it
promises so much? Not at all; the good results are
inescapable.

The human body would be a pulpy mass without a
skeleton to give form and vigor. Similarly, underlying <u>love</u> in Hebrew-Christian ethics there is a
firm skeleton consisting (wholly independent of
pulpy sentimentality) of the principles of Ricardo's
Law of Cooperation and those hard commandments
against coercion, theft and fraud.

The Great Principle Of Division Of Labor

In the case of Fastman and Slowman, cited in the previous chapter, these two men "associated themselves"; "cooperated"; or, in other words, they engaged in "division of labor."

Division of labor is the most important technical fact in social life and in economics. Civilized society is verily founded on the principle of the division of labor.

The idea of division of labor, and the practice of division of labor, is mentioned early in human history. Cain and Abel were the two oldest sons of the original human pair, Adam and Eve. There was already division of labor between these two, for Cain is described as a farmer, a tiller of the soil; and Abel as a sheep rancher. Cain undoubtedly exchanged his grain and vegetables for Abel's wool and mutton, and vice versa. In other words, about the earliest economic fact of life that the earliest humans discovered was advantage from the division of labor.

Advantages from the division of labor were discovered early elsewhere, too, as among the early Greeks. Socrates, principal spokesman in Plato's Republic, makes a big point of division of labor.

One of the convincing passages in Adam Smith's Wealth of Nations concerns itself about the advantages of division of labor; Smith tells in simple and dramatic style the advantages from division of labor in making ordinary pins; in Book I, Chapter 1, he writes:

> The greatest improvement in the productive powers of labour, and the greater part of the skill, dexterity, and judgment with which it is anywhere directed, or applied, seem to have been the effects of the division of labour.
>
> The effects of the division of labour, in the general business of society, will be more easily understood, by considering in what manner it operates in some particular manufactures. It is commonly supposed to be carried furthest in some very trifling ones; not perhaps that it really is carried further in them than in others of more importance: but in those trifling manufactures which are destined to supply the small wants of but a small number of people, the whole number of workmen must necessarily be small; and those employed in every different branch of the work can often be collected into the same workhouse, and placed at once under the view of the spectator. In those great manufactures, on the contrary, which are destined to supply the great wants of the great body of the people, every different branch of the work employs so great a number of workmen, that it is impossible to collect them all into the same workhouse. We can seldom see more, at one time, than

those employed in one single branch. Though in such manufac-
tures, therefore, the work may really be divided into a much
greater number of parts, than in those of a more trifling
nature, the division is not near so obvious, and has accordingly been much less observed.

To take an example, therefore, from a very trifling manufacture; but one in which the division of labour has been very
often taken notice of, the trade of the pinmaker; a workman
not educated to this business (which the division of labour
has rendered a distinct trade), nor acquainted with the use
of the machinery employed in it (to the invention of which
the same division of labour has probably given occasion), could
scarce, perhaps, with his utmost industry, make one pin in a
day, and certainly could not make twenty. But in the way in
which this business is now carried on, not only the whole work
is a peculiar trade, but it is divided into a number of branches, of which the greater part are likewise peculiar trades.
One man draws out the wire, another straights it, a third cuts
it, a fourth points it, a fifth grinds it at the top for receiving the head; to make the head requires two or three distinct operations; to put it on, is a peculiar business, to
whiten the pins is another; it is even a trade by itself to
put them into the paper; and the important business of making
a pin is, in this manner, divided into about eighteen distinct operations, which, in some manufactories, are all performed by distinct hands, though in others the same man will
sometimes perform two or three of them. I have seen a small
manufactory of this kind where ten men only were employed,
and where some of them consequently performed two or three
distinct operations. But though they were very poor, and
therefore but indifferently accommodated with the necessary
machinery, they could, when they exerted themselves, make among
them about twelve pounds of pins in a day. There are in a
pound upwards of four thousand pins of a middling size. Those
ten persons, therefore, could make among them upwards of forty-
eight thousand pins in a day. Each person, therefore, making
a tenth part of forty-eight thousand pins, might be considered
as making four thousand eight hundred pins in a day. But if
they had all wrought separately and independently, and without
any of them having been educated to this peculiar business,
they certainly could not each of them have made twenty, perhaps not one pin in a day; that is, certainly, not the two
hundred and fortieth, perhaps not the four thousand eight
hundredth part of what they are at present capable of perform-
ing, in consequence of a proper division and combination of
their different operations.

In every other art and manufacture, the effects of the
division of labour are similar to what they are in this very
trifling one; though, in many of them, the labour can neither
be so much subdivided, nor reduced to so great a simplicity
of operation. The division of labour, however, so far as it
can be introduced, occasions, in every art, a proportionable
increase of the productive powers of labour.

Advantages from division of labor rest upon various bases: (1) differences in native abilities;
(2) differences in acquired skills; (3) differences
in quality, location and availability of natural
resources; (4) differences in the amount of capital
available; (5) differences in the intensity of division of labor; (6) differences in the smoothness of
the mechanism for exchanging the products of division of labor; (7) etc.

In our illustration in the preceding chapter, we assumed all factors to be the same except the native abilities of Fastman and Slowman. This assumption of inequality of native abilities was deliberate, but certainly not contrary-to-fact. Everywhere we see that people differ in native abilities -- one is good at a certain activity; another is good at another activity. The one extraordinary assumption which was made is that Fastman was better in everything than Slowman. For simplicity, we used the harvesting of only two crops, nuts and potatoes, but the principle involved is identical whether there be two activities or a thousand. If we had used an illustration where Fastman was better in one activity and Slowman in another, then the advantages of division of labor and cooperation would have been considered obvious, and no "mystery" would have seemed to have appeared. Too ready recognition of the benefits of division of labor have the result that there is a failing to understand the real reason why there are such advantages.

There is another reason why exploring the full consequences of division of labor is desirable. There is the sensitive psychological problem of the inferiority complex of less-talented individuals. There is the still more sensitive problem of the inferiority complex of less-talented nations, the so-called under-developed.

Several mistaken ideas unfortunately arise from an incomplete understanding of noticeable differences in talents: (1) there is, first, the erroneous idea of altruists that charity (in effect, almsgiving) is the solution to the problem of the less-gifted or under-developed; (2) a poisonous and bitter discontent on the part of the less-talented with the allotment of talents they have received; (3) especially an unawareness on the part of the less-gifted that they contribute as much to social welfare as the more-gifted, which (if they realized that fully) would enhance their self-respect and legitimate pride in economic and social situations; and further (4) a failure to understand that, under the control of Christian ethics, there will be amazing equity in the distribution of the mutual benefits from division of labor.

A sound system of ethics will be able to show that it can and does meet these problems successfully.

But first a very interesting question remains: do the benefits of division of labor ever fail; if so, when and why?

Failure Of The Principle Of Division Of Labor

By uncovering when benefits of division of labor do not occur, a fundamental requirement for the achievement of those benefits will be brought into proper prominence.

This exposition will be accomplished by an apparently unimportant change in the data used in Section III, Chapter 4 describing the joint harvesting by Fastman and Slowman. We shall now assume that Fastman is _exactly_ as much faster than Slowman on potato harvesting, as he (Fastman) on nut harvesting.

The original figures were that Fastman could harvest 5 bushels of nuts per day to Slowman's 2 bushels, and 30 bushels of potatoes per day to Slowman's 20. Slowman was only 40% as good at picking nuts and 66-2/3% as good at digging potatoes.

We shall now change the figures so that the ratio on harvesting nuts (which is 5 to 2) will be equalled by the ratio for harvesting potatoes; then Fastman must be able to dig 50 bushels a day (instead of 30 bushels as previously assumed) compared to Slowman's 20.

Working alone, in isolation of each other, these two men will harvest their crops as follows (compare Table 2, page 89, for different earlier data):

Table 6

Days Required For FASTMAN To Harvest His Two Crops (under revised assumption)

Product	Quantity to be Harvested	Rate Per Day	Days Required
N u t s	80 bushels	5 bushels	16
Potatoes	600 bushels	50 bushels	12
		T o t a l	28

For Slowman the computation is shown in Table 7 (unchanged as in Table 2 on page 89; the figures are repeated here).

Table 7

Days Required For SLOWMAN To Harvest His Two Crops

Product	Quantity to be Harvested	Rate Per Day	Days Required
N u t s	80 bushels	2 bushels	40
Potatoes	600 bushels	20 bushels	30
		T o t a l	70

Together, the two men, working separately, will harvest their crop in 98 days -- Fastman requiring 28 days and Slowman, 70 days.

Now, suppose they "cooperate," and engage in division of labor with Fastman doing all the nut picking and Slowman doing all the potato digging. The problem is: will there be a total saving in time, that is, will there be a mutual gain which can be distributed (divided) between them?

The answer now is that there is no longer any gain from division of labor, but rather than working the problem in a manner as if we did not know the answer in advance, the analysis will be easier to understand when we work the problem as if we did know.

For ease of computation, we shall assume that Fastman experiences neither gain nor loss in time required. Then Slowman's gain or loss, in total time required, if there is any change, will show up in the residual time required by him.

In Table 6 it is apparent that under the new assumption Fastman will have to work 28 days in isolation, harvesting his two crops alone. As before, he works at picking nuts, at the rate of 5 bushels a day. If he works 28 days at 5 bushels a day, he will harvest 140 bushels. That is, however, 20 bushels less than the total quantity to be harvested. Therefore, Slowman will have to harvest the remaining 20 bushels, and in addition dig all of the potatoes. Gain or loss from division of labor will then all show up in Slowman's required time. The calculation in Table 8 reveals what now develops.

Table 8

Computation Of SLOWMAN's Required Time To Complete
All Of Harvesting Left Undone By FASTMAN, After The Latter
Had Worked As Long As His Required Time In Isolation

Product	Quantity to be Harvested	SLOWMAN's Rate Per Day	Days Required
N u t s	20 bushels	2 bushels	10
Potatoes	1,200 bushels	20 bushels	60
		T o t a l	70

Table 9 summarizes the results:

Table 9

Results Of "Cooperation" By FASTMAN And SLOWMAN
Under The Very Special Assumption That They Are Equal
In Their Inequalities In Harvesting Capability
(Compare this with Table 4 on page 90)

	Days - In Isolation	Days - In Cooperation	Saving For Each Man
FASTMAN: N u t s	16	28	
Potatoes	12	-	
	28	28	0 days
SLOWMAN: N u t s	40	10	
Potatoes	30	60	
	70	70	0 days
Grand Total	98	98	0 days

Gone is the saving from division of labor! As
astonishingly as the gain showed up in the previous
calculation in Chapter 4, equally astonishingly it
has now disappeared. Apparently, society can easily
fall apart, because gains from division of labor
can disappear easily.

Such, however, is not the case. The assumption
underlying the present illustration is an unreal
one. The condition here assumed is never fully met.
That assumption is that (1) not merely two men were
unequal, but that (2) they were equally unequal.

Their first inequality was that both men were
unequal: Fastman can pick 5 bushels of nuts to
Slowman's 2 bushels; and dig 30 bushels of potatoes
to Slowman's 20. Then the ratios were changed so

that Slowman was equally inferior to Fastman on
both nut picking and potato digging. (Fastman could
now pick nuts in the ratio of 5 to 2; and could dig
potatoes in the ratio of 50 to 20. Obviously 5:2
and 50:20 are identical ratios.)

Here is the fundamental rule: advantages accrue
universally from division of labor only when there
is unequal inequality. If a man is equally inferior
to another in every activity -- as in this illustration he is 60% inferior on both picking nuts and
digging potatoes -- then there is no benefit to
either of them from division of labor, from "association" or from attempted "cooperation."

Society, therefore, depends -- stands or falls --
on universal inequality. Men would have no more
cohesion than grains of sand, were it not for the
benefits of division of labor, according to Ricardo's Law of Cooperation, which in turn requires the
most pervasive and universal inequality in productivity on the part of every man.

In a sense, society rests on just that corner-
stone which unfortunately some moralists suspect
and even dislike -- namely, on inequality.

Egalitarianism -- activity to make men equal
rather than freely to permit their being unequal --
must be, in the logic of the world in which we find
ourselves, a nonsensical ideal.

The Creator made men unequal. The wiser men are,
the more they will endeavor to make men even more
differentiated in productive capabilities. If the
Creator had made the mistake of making men equal,
men should have assiduously endeavored to improve
the situation by making themselves unequal in the
most varied manner. For anyone to endeavor to neutralize the inequality of creation by making men
equal -- to have an egalitarian program -- is literally to undermine society or, in another figure,
literally to burn as with fire the greatest bond
that holds society together.

Certainly egalitarianism cannot be an intelligent
goal for Christian ethics; and it is not. Further,
for anyone who can read what is plainly written in
Scripture, there will be no thought of seeking
egalitarianism under a Christian set of ethics.

Ethics And Ricardo's Law --
A Contract Society

On the basis of the preceding chapters, a prime
function of ethics or morality should be to facilitate rather than to hinder <u>cooperation</u>, because
Ricardian cooperation does more than anything else
to promote general prosperity. The crucial question is: what policies will hinder cooperation;
or, vice versa, what policies will promote cooperation?

                    *   *   *

Before stating those rules, it will be well to
recapitulate the framework, based on creation
(inequality, mathematics, logic), within which the
rules must operate, or which (if it is desired to
state the case differently) must control the cooperation in order that cooperation be not frustrated
(because it is certainly true that Ricardo's Law
of Cooperation <u>can</u> be frustrated).   It is the frustration of Ricardo's Law which constitutes a major
part -- the largest -- of what the Hebrew-Christian
ethic calls ethical <u>sin</u>.

First, then, a recapitulation of the framework:

1. Universal inequality, by birth, inheritance,
creation -- use what term you wish.

2. <u>Further</u> inequality, by location, natural
resources, and all adventitious circumstances.

3. <u>Additional</u> inequality, by deliberate training, specialization.

These factors permit one man to become much better
than another in one occupation; and another man to
be much better in another occupation.   Then patently,
no great mathematical knowledge being necessary,
specialization, cooperation and exchange become
enormously beneficial for everybody.   To obtain high
productivity each man does what he can do most pro-
ductively, especially if he can do it better than
others.   Clearly, if some man (or a group of men)
is genuinely best at something, productivity will
be increased if they produce that something not
only for themselves, but in mass quantity for other
men.

4. <u>Fortunately</u>, men are not created equal; and

even more fortunately they strive to become more
unequal, by increasing their specialized production,
thereby enhancing the possibility of profiting by
the mathematics -- the principle -- underlying
Ricardo's Law of Cooperation.

5. _Equal_ men, or _equally_ unequal men (as defined
in the preceding chapter) _cannot_ profitably cooperate. Such men might as well live in isolation as
in society. The more equality, the less potential
cooperation; equality and cooperation are antagon-
istic principles, as fire and water.

6. Creation, conditions, lack of good education,
depravity, accidents, sicknesses make some people
generally inferior, i.e., inferior in every respect,
in a specific time and place. (They may have great
unused capabilities, or they may not; the fact of
their being inferior in activity A, and activity B,
and activity C -- in everything -- does not make
them nonuseful members of society. They can, despite their _general_ inferiority, make a net contribution to the welfare of all men, even to the individual who is the most brilliant, and most productive member of that society. The _lowest_ man _in_
society _contributes_ to the _welfare_ of that society,
if he associates himself with his fellows (rather
than withdraws from them), that is, if he special-
izes and exchanges services -- _cooperates_, in that
sense.

This fact of contributing to society is a matter
of great importance, because it provides an indis-
pensable element to _everybody's_ self-respect,
namely, an awareness (despite maximum inferiority)
of nevertheless being able to contribute _genuinely_
to the welfare of all others.

The real benefactors of society are _those who_
stay in it. Ricardo's Law should be expounded from
every pulpit as a joyful message, to relieve everyone -- except the most talented person in the
audience -- of any inferiority complex in regard to
his contribution to society. It should also humble
the most-talented person and all well-talented
people, in the sense of making them aware that their
prosperity is in part due to the less talented, and
even to the least talented person in the audience.

                    *   *   *

Now, here is the question: Can Ricardo's Law
fail for any other reason than a failure to have
unequal inequality (a requirement already shown to

be critically essential)? It can fail, namely, by
(1) coercion, (2) theft, and (3) fraud. And it is
here that ethics comes in; in fact, becomes determinative.

In Chapter 3 of this section, the total labor
required to harvest Fastman's and Slowman's crops
with each working in isolation was 106 days, but
with them working in cooperation only 92 days, a
saving of 14 days, or 13.2%.

By specific assumptions which were made, this
saving was distributed rather equally between Fastman and Slowman, namely, Fastman saved 4 days and
Slowman saved 10 days, or 11.1% and 14.3% respectively. In other words, both men gained.

Innumerable differences can be assumed, and then
computed to determine how much of the gain Fastman
is to receive, and how much Slowman. Assumptions
might have been made on how the assignments were
to be made so that all the benefit of 14 days had
gone to Fastman only, or to Slowman only. Readers
can make their own mathematical assumptions to
experiment with this crucial problem -- on what
principle will the benefits of cooperation be distributed to the participants?

When all the benefits of cooperation go to one
man only rather than some to both; and even more,
when all the benefits and more besides go to one
of the men only (which means that the other man is
actually hurt by the "cooperation"), then the
voluntary motivation for cooperation disappears for
the man who makes no gains and/or actually has a
loss.

Therefore, in the case of the 14 days saved in
our illustration, the motivation to cooperate will
begin to fail when the distribution is such that
whichever man gets the smaller part of the gain, he
nevertheless does not get, say, at least one day;
then one man gets 13 days gain and the other one
day. That looks rather unfair, but against the
alternative of not cooperating at all, a rational
man will still cooperate and save at least one day
of his own time.

In a later chapter (Chapter 32) attention will
be given to the factors which will control the
division, or distribution, between participants.
That is a computation by itself.

At this point, the significant idea is: unless
both partners gain from the way the savings of

Ricardo's Law are <u>distributed</u> they will <u>not</u> cooperate <u>voluntarily</u>. They will, instead, cooperate
only under <u>coercion</u>.

As will be developed later, the greatest of the
ethical commandments is: Thou shalt not kill (the
sixth commandment in the Decalogue). But no one
will affirm that the commandment goes no further
than prohibiting murder. Everyone will agree that
the commandment logically prohibits violence, say,
wounding without actually killing. Further, everyone will agree that it is logical to go further and
affirm that the sixth commandment prohibits <u>coercion</u>.
Then, another way to express the sixth commandment
is to say, <u>Thou</u> <u>shalt</u> <u>not</u> <u>coerce</u>.

It is <u>coercion</u> (to be more carefully defined
later) which most comprehensively designates what
is forbidden in the sixth commandment.

In other words, Fastman may not coerce Slowman
to cooperate, if he (Fastman) claims the total saving of 14 days; and ditto, Slowman; and worse still,
if either claims more than 14 days benefit for
himself!

All of this rational reasoning rests on the basic
proposition that a man is entitled to engage in
self-preservation, which (as the extension in the
reasoning in the preceding paragraph -- from killing
to coercion) is equally applicable here, to wit:
the extension from self-preservation to the pursuit
of legitimate self-regarding interests of any kind.
In principle, self-preservation and pursuit of the
self-regarding interests are manifestations of one
fundamental principle.

There are two alternative (basically different)
principles on which society can be organized, (1)
on the principle of coercion, or (2) the principle
of <u>contract</u> (voluntary cooperation).

The Hebrew-Christian religion, by the sixth commandment of the Decalogue, establishes a <u>contract</u>
<u>society</u>, where people <u>agree</u> to a division of the
proceeds, because they get a <u>benefit</u> from that division of the proceeds, or (to change the words)
the distribution of the proceeds.

A <u>contract</u> society is a <u>just</u> society. A <u>coer-</u>
<u>cive</u> society is an <u>unjust</u> society; it will not be
necessary to be coercive, if there is <u>mutual</u>
benefit -- at least <u>some</u> benefit to both (or all)
participants. The mutuality does not need to be
<u>equal</u> for a society to be a just society, but there
<u>must</u> be mutuality.

The benefits of Ricardo's Law of Cooperation
become perverted, if its benefits are not distributed by contract, that is, without coercion, as
required by the sixth commandment of the Decalogue.

The benefits of Ricardo's Law will effervesce,
too -- just bubble away -- if there is fraud or
theft, on the part of either party under cooperation beyond the limits of mutuality. The purpose
of fraud and of theft are to take away from one
party what would otherwise accrue to the other party.
Under such circumstances men become reluctant to
cooperate with another man who defrauds and steals.
These are the sins forbidden by the eighth and
ninth commandments in the Decalogue: Thou shalt
not steal, and Thou shalt not bear false witness
against thy neighbor.

Coercion, deception and theft lessen and in extreme cases destroy the willingness of men to cooperate. Contract, honesty and property rights
are the fundamentals on which cooperation rests.

Ricardo's Law is not ethics. Ricardo's Law
merely provides an opportunity for maximum productivity. The ethics come in at the point that the
proceeds must be distributed to participants. Most
fundamental of all, the proceeds must be distributed by contract, that is, by honoring the sixth
commandment.

N O T E

Here I may perhaps mention that only because men are in fact unequal can we treat
them equally. If all men were completely equal
in their gifts and inclinations, we should
have to treat them differently in order to
achieve any sort of social organization. Fortunately, they are not equal; and it is only
owing to this that the differentiation of
functions need not be determined by the arbitrary decision of some organizing will but
that, after creating formal equality of the
rules applying in the same manner to all, we
can leave each individual to find his own level.

There is all the difference in the world
between treating people equally and attempting
to make them equal. While the first is the
condition of a free society, the second means,
as De Tocqueville described it, "a new form
of servitude."

                    -- Hayek, Individualism and
                       Economic Order, page 15f.

Anarchy, Tyranny And Freedom

Anarchy is a system for organizing society, under which each does what he pleases. Anarchy assumes that men are good, or will be good. Anarchy removes law as a helpful factor in society and social relations; it despises organized law. Anarchy is unlimited freedom. Because its premise, the goodness of man, is unrealistic, its conclusion is also wrong; society requires more for its existence than the principle of unlimited -- and therefore excessive -- freedom.

Tyranny is the other extreme; too much law, whether general legislation or personal autocracy; and not enough residual freedom. Of the two forms in which tyranny manifests itself, too much legislation or arbitrary personal rule, the latter is the worse.

Generally, mankind has abominated both anarchy and tyranny. What mankind has wanted, and rather steadily strives for, is a limited freedom to which the rather careless term, freedom, is unqualifiedly given, but this should confuse no one, because the great principle of real freedom is a combination of freedom and law, of freedom to do some things and restraint on doing other things. Freedom is an ideal -- to find the golden mean between anarchy and tyranny.

Of the three -- anarchy, tyranny and freedom -- anarchy is the worst; it means chaos. A man owes much to his natural father; he owes more to his corporate father, the state. If a man loves his natural father because of benefits received, he should love his corporate father even more for the greater benefits received from it.

Gross tyranny can be an unbearable burden, but it is worse to remove tyranny and introduce anarchy. Those who rebel against tyrants should have a program of well-balanced law and freedom. Rebels who cannot govern better than those against whom they rebel are not justified in rebelling.

Ethics and the social system merge at every joint. Good ethics, too, is a combination of freedom and law; it is not a system of all law and no freedom (a moral tyranny), nor is it a system of all freedom and no law (license).

Hebrew-Christian ethics, with admirable balance,

draws the best line between unlimited freedom (anarchy) and too much government (tyranny).

Because anarchy is not survivable and therefore really only a theoretical system (whereas tyranny is survivable), the approach here made to ethics will not be from the side of anarchy but tyranny.

What is forbidden, what is law, in Hebrew-Christian ethics? Then what freedom is thereafter left; what is that residue which makes me "free" (but not anarchical)? These are questions to be answered in the following chapters.

One thought more on anarchy before it is practically dropped from consideration. It is not a viable -- survivable -- system for two reasons: (1) men are generally not good enough to be permitted to be anarchists; and (2) ambitious evil men do not fail to attempt to fill the vacuum created by "no law," and they usually succeed; they seize power. The customary course then is from anarchy to tyranny; and from tyranny to freedom (the residual freedom which is the right combination of freedom and law).

Spurious Reasons For Justifying Tyranny
Of One Man Over Another; Or Of The
Majority Over The Minority

There are four reasons -- generally spurious --
for justifying tyranny, namely: (1) that one man's
judgment is better than that of another; (2) that
the government's judgment is better than that of
individuals; (3) that one man's interest is to be
preferred over another's, and (4) that the presumed
or alleged welfare of the majority is to be preferred over that of the minority and of individuals
generally.

The first two are alleged <u>intellectual</u> supports
to tyranny; the second two are alleged <u>moral</u> supports.

On first thought the moral supports appear the
stronger, especially the last mentioned, welfare of
the majority should take precedence over that of the
minority, or in crass language, the majority may
exploit the minority.

Nevertheless, it remains false that one man may
tyrannize over another for his own benefit at the
expense of the other; and equally so that a majority
may pass laws for its benefit at the expense of the
minority.

The logical foundation of liberty lies deeper,
to wit, it is more intellectual than moral. The
reason why laws should be limited to certain subjects is that men do not have the omniscience --
neither <u>one</u> man nor a <u>bureaucracy</u> -- to regulate
and decide the <u>manifold details</u> of life. Most of
life <u>must</u> be left <u>free</u>, because other men cannot
make decisions so well as the individuals who
themselves are directly involved.

The ultimate case for freedom is that A knows
better what makes life worth living for A, than do
B, C, D and all his other neighbors.

The case for freedom (as here defined) rests on
the fact that men have finite -- <u>very</u> finite and
limited -- minds, and cannot in detail wisely rule
over the multitudinous decisions which an individual
man should make.

The primary intellectual foundation for true
liberty rests upon several not-well-known facts.

It is conceded that the case for liberty is
energetically agitated, but not by reasoning from

cause to effect, but by reasoning back from bad
effects. The absence of liberty is found to be
annoying and unprofitable, and therefore men clamor
for liberty.

But it is profitable to reason from cause to
effect. Men should have liberty because:

1.   The relation of men to things is exceed-
ingly complex. These relations are governed
by a law known as the law of _marginal_ _utility_
(of which more later);

2.   The relation of men to men is largely
controlled by the complex relation of men to
things; in _that_ sense, is dependent on cosmology
(creation and the nature of things), as was
mentioned in the previous section; and

3.   Mortal men, with finite minds cannot wisely
determine the _infinite_ variety involved in
numbers 1 and 2, and should not attempt it;
and

4.   God, who is considered infinite, himself
did not attempt to regulate the _details_ of
men's lives and activities.

The basic source of Hebrew-Christian ethics,
the Second Table in the Decalogue, leaves most of
life _free_. However, it does not give a reason for
leaving the largest part of life free. It simply
speaks didactically, authoritatively, briefly. However, the unspoken, ungiven reason for the unsuit-
ability of a system of all-law and no-freedom is
the limitation and restricted finiteness of men's
minds.

Liberty in the proper sense _must_ exist because
of human _intellectual_ limitations.

How Much Of Life Does The Hebrew-
Christian Decalogue Leave Free?

The Hebrew-Christian ethic leaves everything
free between men, except (1) no coercion, (2) no
theft, (3) no fraud, (4) no adultery, (5) no envy;
and (6), it requires respect to parents.

The rest of life is left both unprohibited or
uncommanded. Do what you will; live your own life
your own way; eat, drink and be merry, if you will;
or work, slave and save; be pleasant or be a cur-
mudgeon; have your own goals; do not let your parents dominate your <u>adult</u> life; pick your own wife
(or husband), and leave your parents. None of
these things is forbidden, and not being forbidden,
it is permitted; not being commanded, it need not
be done.

Freedom was too great an area to be defined in
the Decalogue. It was better to specify the few
things forbidden (the first five in the foregoing
list). The <u>negative</u> feature of these ethical rules
constitutes one of its admirable features. Good
laws <u>generally</u> are negative.

How large an area of life is cut off by these
commandments?

The answer depends on the individual person;
practically nothing is cut off from the life of
the person who sets his aims and adopts his means
so as not to violate these commandments; in the
case of another person whose aim is to get along
in the world <u>at the expense of others</u> (that is, a
person whose preferred method is to violate these
ethical rules) these laws may appear to him to restrict his life and reduce his idea of happiness
intolerably.

The situation can be illustrated graphically;
the diagram (on the following page) at the left
shows how much of a man's life is <u>free</u> who aims to
live without violating the Decalogue; the diagram
at the right shows how a man's life is hemmed in
by law, if his prime method of operating is to
violate that law.

The Area Of Life
Circumscribed By
Law For <u>A</u> Who Aims
To Operate With Minimum
Injury To His Neighbor

The Area Of Life
Circumscribed By
Law For <u>B</u> Who Aims To
Help Himself By Maximum
Injury To His Neighbor

Remainder of
life free
for <u>A</u>

Law

Left free for <u>B</u>

Forbidden

by

Law

In a sense, the diagrams say no more than that
a man whose <u>method</u> of helping himself is by injuring his neighbor will find the law burdensome, and
may land in jail. But the man whose method is to
operate by <u>voluntary contracts</u> with his neighbor
(without using forbidden methods) will prosper,
will be popular, will be "free."

That is, the "good" man will be free unless overpowered by an evil man, or by an evil government.

The "burden (or benefit) of the law" is then
partly a matter of the method of operation of a man
himself, and partly a matter in what regard and how
much society restrains the evil doer. If society,
through the state, does not restrain the evildoer,
the "good" life may still be burdensome, because
other individuals frustrate the good effects of the
good methods of good men.

Under anarchy a man <u>cannot</u> be free, unless all
men are good. It is commonplace that all men are
not good.

But the <u>law</u> which the Hebrew-Christian religion
prescribes is limited to prohibiting injury to
others (except the positive requirement to honor
parents). It is a minimum of law.

The application of its ethical rule is not made
to depend, in the Hebrew-Christian system, on some
form of government.

Undoubtedly, in some respects a government accountable to a majority is safer than another
system. But the Hebrew-Christian system does not
submit to any changes because there is a majority;
the rule applies to <u>any</u> organization of society --
a monarchy, an aristocracy, a republic, or a
democracy.

A monarchy which applies the Hebrew-Christian
rules meticulously is a good government; a republic
which does not apply the Hebrew-Christian rules is
a bad government.

The Hebrew-Christian rules are apodictic and
supersede any contrary rule elected to be followed
by someone, or by many, who are powerful enough to
follow their own inclination at the cost of injuring others.

Nothing makes a man so extensively free as to
follow the Hebrew-Christian rules in a society
where those rules are enforced.

In the foregoing there has been a free switch
back and forth between ethics and the laws of a
state. The two should be identical. Laws should
not be more rigorous than ethical rules, and ethical rules should not demand more than what a state
may properly legislate. The free shifting back
and forth is not a proper ground for reproach. The
two must in fact be in proper harmony if a society
is to be a "good society."

Is Christian Love No Warmer Than That!

It will be helpful to revert for a moment to the question: Does love define and elucidate the law; or does the law define and elucidate love? Next, there is the succeeding question: Does the law end with the prohibitions against injuring the neighbor, and the requirement of honoring parents?

The first question has been answered earlier: The law defines love; not love the law.

Taken in the large, there are three supplementary ideas to what has already been defined as ethical love between men. The whole list, of four, consists of the following:

1. You must avoid injuring the neighbor; those injuries are specified in and pro- hibited by the law.

2. The law is <u>never</u> abrogated. If A strikes B, B is not authorized to strike back <u>in</u> <u>vengeance</u>. The law is <u>never</u> vengeful; only utilitarian. See later comment on this.

3. Those stricken by the vicissitudes of life, or overwhelmed by their own folly, need assistance, that is, <u>charity</u>, in as limited amounts as is feasible and utili- tarian.

4. Every man owes it to other men to help them get their thinking straight, propagating wisdom and information and sound advice as enjoined on all men toward those they can reach. This can be expressed as "spreading the gospel" in a narrow sense, or as trying to educate others in <u>every</u> way possible, including the gospel specifically.

1. It will after some thought be obvious that the list consists really of only three concepts. The second is merely a variation, a specific case, of the first. Some have considered it valid to "avenge" wrong. Some Hebrews and some Christians have affirmed that Mosaic laws tolerate vengeance. This is a misconception, but a so-common one that it is desirable to list number 2 specially, that is, <u>nothing</u> abrogates the commandments against injuring others; the prohibitions <u>always</u> remain in force.

Utilitarianism is a factor in punishing for injuries, but that will be discussed later.

2. _Charity_ must be looked at as a supplement to the law. It is not mentioned in the law. It is not the quintessence of ethical love, but a beautiful flower on the plant. For various reasons people need help from time to time. How much help? Nobody knows _exactly_; therefore, charity _cannot_ be a part of the law; charity is a matter of degree and judgment; the law is a command and not a question of degree or variation. Nevertheless, the Hebrew-Christian religion has been sound in its not separating charity from the law and from love. It is against sound policy to fail to help the stricken, or the fallen, or the forlorn. The help A gives today to B, may be reciprocated to him the next year by B's help to A. The welfare of all is greatly promoted by trying to get the unfortunate and beaten back on the road to productivity, or at least to help them survive. The best-organized charities of the world are those of the Hebrew-Christian religions. Mankind ought to appreciate those religions for that reason only, if for no other. In this analysis, it being one of strict constructionism and _minimal_ religion, _charity_ is _not_ equated with love. It _is_ a part of love; but only a _minor_ part; but it is the most beautiful part. The traditional percentage for charity has been 10%. Ordinarily, that (it seems to the writer) is a proper figure; only in emergencies would he go above it; in ultimate disasters the figure might go to 100%. As previously mentioned, the very nature of charity is its nonmeasurability for particular cases and circumstances. Let a man's conscience and wisdom be his guide beyond the 10%. In conclusion on _charity_: charity does add to the "warmth" of Hebrew-Christian ethics.

3. The third and last element of what has historically come to be accepted as a part of the requirements of Christian ethics is "spreading the gospel." This is, finally, by far the greatest, most onerous, demand in Christian ethics. Here a man _is_ responsible for his neighbor in the sense of being prepared to and energetically endeavoring to help him. It is criminal for A to see B plunging himself into destruction, and A not warning B nor admonishing him. If A does not warn B or fails to dissuade him, B is injured, and that indirectly will injure A also, like a recoil on a gun when it is fired. The more a man ponders the Christian

religion, the more he discovers that the one practically unlimited claim which his neighbors have
on him is their claim to receive voluntarily from
him everything which will set all of their thinking
straight, including their thinking on the life to
come. This is the greatest "warmth" of the Christian religion, and the only warmth that does not
have a phase to it which creates problems.

In short then, the ethics of the Christian religion requires -- (1) do not injure others,
(2) limited and wise charity, and (3) doing everything in one's power to get other people's thinking
straight. The "warmth" of Christian ethics comes
wonderfully from number 2, but still more benefi-
cially from number 3.

The Sensible Meaning To The Injunction, Thou Shalt Love Thy Neighbor As Thyself

The "summary" of ethical law in Hebrew-Christian ethics is, Thou shalt love thy neighbor as thyself.

There are several possible ways to interpret this statement in the abstract: (1) love your neighbor equally well with yourself in all matters; (2) in some matters; (3) or, if number 2 is para- phrased, love your neighbor really less than your- self; or (4) love your neighbor more than yourself, or have what is known in Greek language as agape (ag-a-pe) for him, as distinguished from eros; agape is equivalent to treating another perfectly, self-effacingly for yourself, regardless of the other person's merits.

In regard to number 4, famous present-day Chris- tian ethical teachers affirm that the ethics of the Christian religion are inferior unless it is endued with the spirit of agape (sacrifice and service) and purified of eros, the kind of love which has a self-regarding taint.

It will be noted that, in the foregoing, number 2 and number 3 are essentially the same. In a practical way there are then, in the ethical air in which Christian ethics lives, three definite interpretations of, Thou shalt love thy neighbor as thyself: (1) love him exactly equally; (2) love him less than entirely equally; and (3) love him more than exactly equally.

No luminous thought will be possible on this problem unless the analysis again turns on defini- tion of the word love, that equivocal term, with confusing and contradictory meaning.

Attention has already been directed to the multiple meanings of the word love in Scripture, and that for ethics, love (as a term) must be specifically defined. In accordance with the re- quirements of the title of this book -- to avoid extensionism -- the general direction of this phase of the discovery of the definition of the ethical meaning of the word love will be restricted and minimal. In fact, if that is not done, the defini- tion of ethical love can become grotesque. There- fore, in this analysis, to love your neighbor as thyself will again be given a minimal meaning, as it appears to be intended in Scripture.

Among the foregoing definitions the only one
that can possibly be practical is the definition
which really calls for loving your neighbor <u>less</u>
than yourself.

But that appears to violate the commandment. It
is, therefore, desirable to restate "less than thyself" into the form of "as thyself <u>but</u> <u>only</u> <u>in</u>
<u>certain</u> <u>specific</u> <u>respects</u>." (This latter is the
statement numbered 2 in the second paragraph of
this chapter.)

This "restriction" (see underscoring above) may
arouse wonderment and reluctance to accept it, but
it can here be dismissed on authoritative grounds
(and also rational, but that will be later).

Should a man "love" his neighbor equally with
himself in <u>all</u> matters, and should he and his neighbor share <u>everything</u>? If so, let them share the
best they have, their wives; and wives, their husbands!

The Decalogue, however, strictly forbids sharing
wives or husbands. Therefore, on the basis of the
Decalogue itself a person is not supposed to share
his (her) best asset, his (her) mate. It is therefore absurd to affirm that a neighbor must be
"loved" equally in <u>all</u> matters. He must be loved
equally only in <u>some</u> matters.

It was outlined in preceding chapters that
ethical <u>love</u> in Scripture was not an emotion but a
profound policy -- (1) no injuries of a certain
sort, (2) forbearance, (3) almsgiving, and (4) attempted good advice. There is <u>some</u> sharing involved
in this definition, namely, limited almsgiving; and,
there is extensive sharing of thoughts (advice) to
help the other man; (but it should be noted that
not all advice is good, and that the proposed re-
cipient must be left free the choice of rejecting
it; advice certainly cannot be <u>forced</u> on the re-
cipient and still be considered Christian ethics).

In other words, to love the neighbor <u>as</u> <u>thyself</u>
means that you love him <u>in</u> <u>some</u> <u>respects</u> as you
<u>love</u> <u>yourself</u>, not in all respects.

But the term, <u>as</u> <u>thyself</u>, has not been fully
defined yet. In what precedes, attention was directed on how to love the neighbor -- not hurt him,
have patience with him, engage in almsgiving in his
need, and give him good advice -- that is, the
definition is directed toward "love" for him in

those specific senses. But what happens to the
definition when attention is directed to the <u>self</u>,
as is required by the phraseology, <u>as</u> <u>thyself</u>?

What does a rational man prize most highly, almost as life itself? The answer to that is: free-
dom to <u>live</u> <u>his</u> <u>own</u> <u>life</u>; do what he himself wishes
to do. Surely, toward his fellows he has the four-
fold obligation repeatedly mentioned in the foregoing, but <u>all</u> <u>else</u> was declared in Chapter 10 of
this section to be <u>free</u> for him. His life was
described as being <u>his</u> <u>own</u>. To love yourself is
to love your own legitimate <u>freedom</u>, to claim it,
to defend it, to exercise it.

The purpose of the four restrictions previously
mentioned is to grant greater freedom to all. Freedom is in fact the great <u>intermediary</u> purpose of
the ethical part of the Decalogue; the <u>ultimate</u>
purpose is <u>happiness</u>. The right kind of freedom
maximizes every man's prospects of attaining happiness. How can a man be happy if he cannot have
maximum legitimate freedom!

What then does <u>as</u> <u>thyself</u> mean in the famous
(but almost meaningless when undefined) cliché,
Love thy neighbor <u>as</u> <u>thyself</u>? It means: loving
your freedom outside of what is forbidden or specifically required.

And how is a neighbor loved <u>as</u> <u>thyself</u>? By
allowing him his <u>corresponding</u> freedom.

When a man puts more restrictions on his neighbor than Christian ethics calls for, then that man
does <u>not</u> love his neighbor <u>as</u> <u>himself</u>.

(The difficult problems raised by the <u>agape</u>-
cult will be discussed later.)

The World's Most Revolutionary Ethical Proposition

The most revolutionary ethical proposition in the world is that you must live _for_ your neighbor; or that you must in _all_ things love him as you love yourself. These propositions have <u>never</u> been the ethical propositions advanced by the Hebrew or the Christian religions, <u>soberly interpreted</u>.

The following commonsense anecdote appeared recently as a humorous item in a national daily:

> "The reason we are on earth is to help others," the Sunday school teacher informed her class of small boys and girls.

> A thoughtful youngster raised his hand and asked, "What are the others here for?"

>   - <u>Wall Street Journal</u>
>   March 1, 1963

The basic Hebrew-Christian ethic has been that a man lives <u>for</u> <u>himself</u>, but <u>not</u> <u>at</u> <u>the</u> <u>expense</u> <u>of</u> <u>injuring</u> <u>his</u> <u>neighbor</u>, nor rejecting all charity, <u>nor</u> <u>being</u> <u>indifferent</u> <u>to</u> <u>educating</u> <u>the</u> <u>neighbor</u> <u>in</u> <u>regard</u> <u>to</u> <u>the</u> <u>latter's</u> <u>true</u> <u>welfare</u>.

The trouble in the world is not that people primarily live for themselves, but that they live for themselves in a manner which has been given by Albert J. Nock the name, Epstean's Law.

In a conversation with a friend named Epstean, Nock defended, as appropriate, pursuit of the self-regarding interests. Epstean is reported to have responded, quick as a flash, that if the principal motivation of life is to look out for yourself -- self-preservation -- then right on the heels of <u>that</u> motivation is a <u>second</u> motivation, to wit, to look out for yourself <u>at</u> <u>the</u> <u>expense</u> <u>of</u> -- by damaging -- the neighbor.

It is Epstean's Law that should be the target of critique of conduct. It is not self-preservation that is sin, but self-preservation in the <u>wrong</u> way, self-preservation the Epstean-Law way, that <u>is</u>, self-preservation by violating the ethical commandments in the Decalogue as has been explained.

Scripture does not dispute Epstean's Law. It
agrees with Epstean's Law, or rather, Epstean's
quick rejoinder in the conversation mentioned agrees
with the Biblical teaching of the perverse nature
of man.

Now "looking out for yourself" has a very bad
name. Seeking your own happiness is called "selfishness" which rings very badly in the ears of most
people; or is called "hedonism" -- a low, rather
despicable, appetite for pleasure.

Those connotations are unfortunate because they
always confuse (1) self-interest with (2) improper
pursuit of self-interest. Unless that paralogism
can be avoided, any conclusion regarding ethics
will be completely confused.

How can the infusion of undesirable connotations
be kept from confusing the subject?

To that the answer is: abandon the word selfishness, and the word hedonism, and even eudaemonism.
Shift instead at least to the term, self-regarding
interests, because that sounds better.

But even that term is finally inadequate; there
is a different and more ideal formulation; remove
the word self entirely from the terminology because
here we are talking about objectives and not means;
nor should we, in this situation drag in second
parties; we are here talking aims only; what then
do we get: a man should have the liberty to pursue
what he prefers more to what he prefers less. This
is the best formulation of the real purpose of
sound objectives. (Of course, injuring a neighbor
is specifically forbidden as not a proper means --
and of course, aim -- as previously reiterated.)

Those who would deny men the extensive --
immense -- liberty left outside the restrictions of
the Decalogue deny that a man has the right to pursue what he prefers more to what he prefers less.

If there is any proposition which needs reiteration, it is the statement that the Christian religion demands inestimably less of men than do socialism and communism. Under Christian ethics men may
pursue what they prefer more to what they prefer
less. Under socialism and communism men are not
considered entitled to pursue what they prefer more
to what they prefer less; they must instead "live
for others." What a monstrous claim! And surely
a spurious ethic!

The ethics of socialism and communism are over-
zealous, are sanctimonious, are revolutionarily
more demanding than historic Hebrew and Christian
ethics. If you seek a fantastically unreasonable
personal ethic, become a socialist or a communist.
If you seek a reasonable -- and superior -- personal
ethic, adopt the ethics of the Christian religion.

Christian ethics are (relatively) easy; socialist-communist ethics are intolerably heavy and
invariably fail. If you choose the latter, you
undertake to be Atlas, carrying the world.

But in that attempt you will violate <u>all</u> sound
ethical rules. Socialist-communist ethics are
supremely burdensome.

What Did The Sermon-On-The-Mount Change In Hebrew Ethics?

An analysis of Christian ethics is facilitated by distinguishing between <u>aims</u> and <u>means</u>. Further, a man can have good aims or bad aims; and good means or bad means.

Living <u>for</u> the neighbor is essentially a bad aim; living for yourself is essentially a good aim. The explanation of this will come later.

In regard to means, they are bad when they entail coercion, fraud, theft; however, <u>appropriate collective</u> coercion (through the legal apparatus of the state) against those evil means is not only permitted, but necessary. Everything else should be <u>free</u>.

But at once Christian ethics appears to be in trouble. The second-most-famous formulation of Christian ethics is in the Sermon on the Mount by Christ; (the <u>most</u> famous is the Decalogue).

This oration or discourse has in it the illogical statement, <u>Resist not evil</u>. This appears to be the negation of any ethical system; it advocates -- <u>seems</u> to advocate -- ethical and social chaos. Putting it plainly, it advises, as an example, women not to resist rape! Of course, there must be something wrong with <u>that</u> interpretation. We shall in this chapter concern ourselves with some of the astounding statements of Christ in the Sermon on the Mount. On examination, they are not so astounding.

*   *   *

In the first place, this sermon can not have been completely reported. All we have (almost certainly) are small extracts or short abbreviations.

Secondly, the Sermon on the Mount does not stand on its own foundation. It is expressly affirmed to stand on the Decalogue. It is declared that <u>nothing</u> is really added to the Decalogue beyond what was always in it.

By its own statements, the Sermon on the Mount is a derivative, secondary document; nevertheless, it is of decisive importance.

The Sermon on the Mount rejects then-prevalent,

improper _interpretations_ of the Decalogue. The
refrain is, "Thou hast heard (some particular _inter-
pretation_), but I say unto you (the differing _inter-
pretation_)."

*   *   *

Let us begin with the three, famous and absurd,
words: "Resist not evil." When read _in_ context,
what do they mean?

The expression is elliptical; something is
omitted; what is omitted is patently assumed to be
understood, or understandable, from the context.
The full statement obviously is: Resist not evil
by a VENGEFULLY MOTIVATED equivalent, or worse,
evil or evils.

On first thought it might be assumed that the
foregoing formulation can be abbreviated to, Resist
not evil _with_ evil. This seems to go far enough,
but does not. A murderer is punished for murder
by execution, which is certainly an evil to him.
The key words therefore are _vengefully_ motivated.

Moses apparently did not fully understand the
Decalogue, which is possibly circumstantial evidence
that the Decalogue was _inspired_. If Moses had con-
cocted the Decalogue entirely himself and _fully_
understood it, he would probably not have ambigu-
ously legislated elsewhere "an eye for an eye and
a tooth for a tooth."

When Moses put in his parochial Israelitish law
"an eye for an eye and a tooth for a tooth," he
opened his legislation to the interpretation (essentially erroneous) that there is such a thing as
vengeance, or "primitive justice," which is permissible.

As has been explained in Chapter 10 of this
section, such response to injury in effect _annuls_
the sixth commandment. If the minute that A wrongs
B, B may retaliate and wrong A; then A will react
by re-wronging B, etc.; the whole system collapses
in an endless chain of _vengeance_. To permit vengeance is to scuttle the Decalogue. Christ attacked
that scuttling, and denied the validity of a _venge-
ful_ taking of an eye for an eye. That was what
Christ legislated on _that_ subject, but by doing
that he "saved" the Decalogue.

*   *   *

Then there are the peculiar statements in the
Sermon on the Mount: if a man strikes you on one
cheek, turn him the other; and, if a man compels
you unrightfully to go one mile, go two miles with
him.

The laws of the United States are <u>essentially</u>
similar but nobody considers them peculiar.

If an armed robber has seized your valuables and
is climbing out of your window in flight, and it is
clear that he is fleeing, you are <u>not</u> authorized to
shoot at him or kill or maim him.

If a man seduces the wife of another, the wronged
man may <u>not</u> claim license to kill the seducer. If
that is his <u>only</u> defense, the law of the United
States can send the wronged man to the gallows!
About the only adequate defense, according to American law, in such a case, is "temporary insanity."
Interesting, is it not, that forbidding retaliation
is the rule which has also been developed <u>by experi-
ence</u> for secular law! One wrong does not authorize
and validate <u>another</u>; never. (Christ merely, in
the Sermon on the Mount, anticipated American common law.

What does United States common law endeavor to
avoid? Legal, moral and ethical chaos. To accom-
plish that the <u>spontaneous</u> <u>reactions</u> <u>to</u> <u>injury</u> <u>are</u>
<u>required</u> <u>to</u> <u>be</u> <u>inhibited</u>. That is what United
States law does.

Christ's legislation on "turning the other
cheek" and "going the second mile" are "very strong"
statements designed to prevent, in the heat of anger,
a man taking the law into his own hands. That principle is unqualifiedly rejected. The response to
injustice must not be an infuriated answer. That
is not the way to build a good society.

There is also a profound wisdom in this advice.

A strikes B on his cheek. Almost certainly
there was a dispute. People do not ordinarily come
to blows except often under mutual provocation.
Maybe B was really the aggressor and had goaded A
to strike him. None of these relevant facts are
given in the Sermon on the Mount.

What then do these commandments establish? This:
men should not take the "law" into their own hands;
actions should not be based on situations where
powerful emotions are currently involved; the less

excitable a man is in times of stress, the wiser
he conducts himself.

To "fight it out" is like the old trial by con-
test. The strongest man, the most skillful fighter,
wins. Is that the way society should be organized?
Christ, by implication, rejected that rule, saying
in effect, might does not make right.

But there is a subtlety to the advice that
should be noted. What is the consequence of Christ's
advice to turn the other cheek and go the second
mile? The consequence is that public opinion will
be behind the man wronged, or showing the greatest
forbearance. Public opinion finally controls everything. If A continues to wrong B, it is only a
short time before C, D, E, F and all the rest say:
"This must stop." And that will be the end of A
striking B's cheek, and forcing him to go another
mile. Christ, in his rules, put in strong and almost exaggerated terms, advises reliance on ultimate
public opinion, the world's greatest policeman.

These rules of "turning the other cheek" and
"going the second mile" are not doctrines on genuine nonresistance to evil, but the soberest and
most effective and ultimately the most successful
means to resist evil.

                *   *   *

There is also the expression in the Sermon on
the Mount, Blessed are the meek, for they shall
inherit the earth. Nothing is added to explain
this statement, which permits considerable latitude
in interpretation.

Does "meek" in this instance mean someone who
permits others to beat him into pulp and abuse him?
Probably not. Instead it can mean, and makes good
sense, to paraphrase the statement this way, Blessed
are those who do not employ coercion, for they shall
inherit the earth.

Every businessman knows that the best way to make
money -- big and permanently -- is to give the
public what it wants, that is, not try to coerce
the public. And then what? The businessman who
serves the public best -- who is meekest in that
sense -- makes the most money, and "inherits the
earth."

                *   *   *

Christ's advice on lending money and not asking
for it back cannot possibly refer to a business

loan, which the borrower asks for so that he can
make more money than the interest charge and also
pay back the loan. Instead, the context implies
a consumer loan to a destitute person, and it
advises treating the loan as almsgiving, if the
borrower cannot repay. (The question of "interest,"
erroneously thought literally to be forbidden in
Scripture, will be treated later.)

There are also discussed in the Sermon on the
Mount questions of sexual morality -- divorce and
remarriage, lust and incontinence. On these the
rules of Moses are not relaxed, but tightened. The
root psychological cause, concupiscence, is condemned as well as immoral acts themselves, which
ruin people's lives and disorganize society.

*   *   *

What, then, do the teachings in the Sermon on
the Mount add up to?

A forbearing, patient society; a nonviolent
society; a contract society; an orderly society;
a society in which law is fortified by developed
public opinion, a compassionate society in which
widows and orphans get loans that they do not repay
unless they can; a society safe for women so that
they cannot be turned out by a husband when he
tires of his wife. In short, an ideal society.

The Sermon on the Mount was needed in order to
interpret rightly the ethical laws of the Decalogue. But to make that interpretation one must
be more than a woodenish literalist. Christ was
not.

The means to accomplish ends, as stated in the
Sermon on the Mount, are good means.

In remaining chapters there will be other references to ideas in the Sermon on the Mount.

Misunderstanding The Apostle Paul On Love

One of the New Testament authors who writes extensively on <u>love</u> is the Apostle Paul.

It is especially what Paul writes in Chapter 13 of his First Epistle to the Corinthians which is often quoted and accepted as a great presentation of the doctrine of love. Such it may have been for Corinth, but there is nothing new or radical in it, even though Paul had the temperament of a zealot -- first as a Pharisee, then as a persecutor of Christians, and then as a Christian missionary. He was not naturally <u>temperate</u>.

Chapter 13 in First Corinthians must be read <u>in context</u>.

The context pertains to the egregious faults of the missionary church in Corinth, founded by Paul.

That church would be described in the modern world as unseemly and disorderly. A church today conducted on the basis of the one in Corinth would probably be reported to the police as a nuisance.

When they had communion in Corinth, some would attend quite drunk. Give your imagination a little play on that sad subject. When drunk, some men become quarrelsome; others maudlin; others talk vulgarly and indecently; etc.

In other parts of their religious services they shouted not-understood mouthings -- and not one at a time -- and they called that "speaking in tongues." Paul indicates that this was a means to release subjective emotional tension, of little value except to the (maybe hysterical) person himself or herself.

Others roared (over the din being created by the "speaking in tongues") what are called "prophecies." (See I Corinthians 14.)

The women especially were hysterical. Paul categorically forbade them to speak at all. That, he said, <u>must</u> stop.

In regard to the seeming nonsense, known as "speaking in tongues," Paul endeavored to restrain that uttered by the men in three ways: (1) only <u>one</u> might speak at one time, rather than having bedlam; (2) the maximum number who might speak should be not more than three; and (3) the meaningless sounds, which would be uttered, had to be explained as having a rational meaning, and if that were not possible then that person should not speak in tongues.

In this age, a well-organized denomination would order discontinued improprieties of the kind at Corinth.

The same might have been expected of Paul. One would have thought that he would have given a peremptory order to that effect. (However, it should not be overlooked that Paul confesses or boasts that he himself spoke more in tongues than anyone else!) But, contrary to his nature, and as a pioneering missionary, he restrains himself to urging no more than _moderating_ the excesses at Corinth. He does not endeavor to eradicate them abruptly, but gradually.

The restraint which he puts on the Corinthians apparently was the limit to which they could (would) submit and not disintegrate as a congregation.

Some salesmanship or "soft-soaping" was necessary. And so, in the midst of Paul's itemizing of the Corinthian excesses in Chapters 10, 11 and 12 and especially later in Chapter 14, Paul sandwiches in an appeal for _tolerance_ on the part of the Corinthian members. It is that appeal (which is set off by itself, in Chapter 13) which is so often quoted detached -- and therefore _meaningless_ -- from the context.

The chapter sounds rhetorical. It begins with the sonorous sentence, "If I speak with the tongues of men and of angels, but have not _charity_, I am become as sounding brass or a clanging cymbal." The rest of the chapter is in the same vein. "Tongues" here refers to no angel's psalm, but to not-understood, or even un-understandable, sounds.

An intelligent reader immediately notes that there is a problem whether the crucial word should be _charity_ or _love_. The King James version uses _charity_, as quoted in the foregoing. Later versions substitute _love_. Of these two translations, charity is preferable, but neither word appears to be a correct translation.

Although fitting the context better than love, charity should not here be taken to mean almsgiving; instead, it means _forbearance_ or _tolerance_. Paul is arguing to the individual members in this way: overlook the foibles of others; do not disintegrate

the church; be patient; wait gently until this
excitement quiets down. That is what, and only
what, <u>charity</u> or <u>love</u> can mean in <u>this</u> context.

But analyze Chapter 13 for yourself and you
will discover that Paul ties in what he here
writes, with his adverse comments on the Corinthian
disorder; note his references in this chapter to
<u>tongues</u> and <u>prophecies</u> which he denigrates in Chap-
ter 14. From verses 1 through 7 he pleads for
toleration which is called <u>caritas</u> in the Greek,
and translated as <u>charity</u> or <u>love</u> in the English.
But it means nothing more than the equivalent of
the patience of a mother with an immature and
imaginative -- and very trying -- child.

Then in verses 8, 9 and 10 he declares that the
immaturity (and "foolishness" (?)) of tongues and
prophecies will end in due time.

Next, in verses 11 and 12, he admits that the
Corinthians are conducting themselves as children,
but that eventually they will "put away" these
childish antics.

The last verse, 13, brings in two other virtues,
<u>faith</u> and <u>hope</u>, both very fine, but which according
to Paul in the Corinthian situation, are subordinate to the then-and-there need of brotherly <u>toler-
ance</u> -- "love," if you wish inaccurately to call
it that.

Readers should begin with Chapter 10 and continue at least through Chapter 14. The famous, but
notoriously misinterpreted, Chapter 13 reads as
follows (American Standard Version):

1. If I speak with the tongues of men and of
   angels, but have not love, I am become
   sounding brass or a clanging cymbal.

2. And if I have the gift of prophecy, and
   know all mysteries and all knowledge; and
   if I have all faith, so as to remove moun-
   tains, but have not love, I am nothing.

3. And if I bestow all my goods to feed the
   poor, and if I give my body to be burned,
   but have not love, it profiteth me nothing.

4. Love suffereth long, and is kind; love
   envieth not; love vaunteth not itself, is
   not puffed up,

5. doth not behave itself unseemly, seeketh
   not its own, is not provoked, taketh not
   account of evil;

6. rejoiceth not in unrighteousness, but
   rejoiceth with truth;

7. beareth all things, believeth all things,
   hopeth all things, endureth all things.

(Comment: In the foregoing Paul affirms that the
dubious "speaking in tongues" and the "prophecies"
are not very important, but that the desperate need
in Corinth was to overlook these excesses. Paul
admits that a tremendous amount of toleration --
translated as charity or love -- was needed in
order to do that; he urged, "endure" it. Have that
"charity" toward each other.)

8. Love never faileth: but whether there be
   prophecies, they shall be done away; whether
   there be tongues, they shall cease; whether
   there be knowledge, it shall be done away.

9. For we know in part, and we prophesy in part;

10. but when that which is perfect is come,
    that which is in part shall be done away.

(Comment: In the foregoing, Paul further disparages
"tongues" and "prophecies.")

11. When I was a child, I spake as a child, I
    felt as a child, I thought as a child: now
    that I am become a man, I have put away
    childish things.

12. For now we see in a mirror, darkly, but then
    face to face: now I know in part, but then
    shall I know fully even as also I was fully
    known.

(Comment: In the foregoing, Paul declares that it
is time to end the immature, childish conduct in
Corinth; the "kid stuff," that is, "speaking in
tongues," and "prophesying.")

13. But now abideth faith, hope, love, these
    three; and the greatest of these is love.

(Comment: In the foregoing, Paul implies that
"love" means forbearance or tolerance.)

It should be noted that there is nothing <u>general</u>
in the definition of <u>charity</u> or <u>love</u> in I Corinthians 13; quite to the contrary, the meaning of
<u>charity</u> or <u>love</u> is here limited to urging on the
members of the congregation that they be gentle
and patient about specific excesses.

Paul's I Corinthians 13 is of limited value for
the <u>logic</u> of Christian ethics. It is a polite
chapter, soothing and gently rebuking.

Why this special comment here on this beloved
chapter in Corinthians? (1) So that the confusion
be removed, which would inevitably result from not
defining the word <u>love</u> in this chapter as it should
be defined, namely, in a very limited way; and (2)
so that the word here be not idealized in response
to Paul's sonorous rhetoric, on the assumption
that everything in Corinth was "sweetness and light,"
(which it certainly was not).

I Corinthians 13 is a synthetic chapter -- a
combination of Pauline ethics, manners and salesmanship, especially the last.

N O T E
    Context and <u>logic</u> will determine meanings, re-
gardless what a dictionary may show are several (but
not necessarily all) of the meanings of a <u>general</u>
term, as the word <u>love</u>. Context and reason indicate
that the real meaning of the word <u>love</u> in the First
Epistle to the Corinthians, can best be designated
by the English word, <u>toleration</u>.

Then we read, using the King James version:
    "Though I speak with the tongues of men
    and of angels, and have not toleration,
    I am become as sounding brass, or a
    tinkling cymbal."

If in the rest of the chapter a reader substitutes
<u>toleration</u> for <u>love</u>, then the chapter makes good
sense -- especially in the light of what is written
in the fourteenth chapter.

Or a reader may even read the verse:

    "Though I speak with the not-understood
    sounds of men and of angels, and have
    not toleration, I am become as sounding
    brass, or a tinkling cymbal."

Nothing New In What Apostle John Writes On Love

Another New Testament writer who places outstanding emphasis on <u>love</u> is the Apostle John.

In his gospel, John modestly keeps from referring to himself by name; instead, he uses the phrase, "the disciple whom Jesus loved." Possibly he was boasting.

John was, it appears reasonable to believe, an emotional person -- warm-hearted, impulsive, and explosive (the last probably against his will, but a rather regular phenomenon in a temperament of his kind).

The crucial question is: what did John, when he was in a rational rather than emotional mood, mean by love? Did he define the word love by rules for conduct, or did he define rules for conduct by the word love?

The answer is definitive: for John the commandments explained love; and not the word, love, the commandments. In his old age he wrote in his Second Epistle General, verses 5 and 6a:

> And now I beseech thee,..., not as though I
> wrote to thee a new commandment, but that
> which we had from the beginning, that we love
> one another. <u>And this is love, that we should
> walk after his</u> (God's) <u>commandments</u>.
> (Emphasis supplied.)

However emotional John may have been, he was in the last analysis rational and logical, namely, love meant to him walking <u>according to God's commandments</u>.

Nor is there a problem from what John wrote, quoting Christ, in his Gospel, Chapter 13, verse 34:

> A <u>new</u> commandment I give unto you, that ye
> love one another; even as I have loved you,
> that ye also love one another. By this shall
> all men know that ye are my disciples, if ye
> have love one to another. (Emphasis supplied.)

"A <u>new</u> commandment" by Christ? Does that mean sacrificing his life for others as eventually occurred? That cannot be the meaning because the past tense is used here; the reference is to Christ's past life. But presumably, because the word <u>new</u> is used, there must be something new in the commandment.

What was "new" was only the <u>interpretation</u> of the commandment, not a new commandment <u>per se</u>. The new interpretation has been explained in Chapter 14 in this section. That new interpretation was that the <u>old</u> commandment controlled conduct <u>toward enemies</u> as well as toward friends, controlled conduct of A after he had been injured by B, as well as before he had been injured by B.

In his general epistles John reiterates the <u>old</u> commandments more than the "new." In his First Epistle General, Chapter 2, verses 3 to 7 he writes:

And hereby we know that we know him (God, Christ) if we keep his commandments. He that saith, I know him, and keepeth not his commandments, is a liar, and the truth is not in him; but <u>whoso</u> <u>keepeth</u> <u>his</u> <u>word</u>, <u>in</u> <u>him</u> <u>verily</u> <u>hath</u> <u>the</u> <u>love</u> <u>of</u> <u>God</u> <u>been</u> <u>perfected</u>. Hereby we know that we are in him: he that saith he abideth in him ought himself also to walk even as he walked. <u>Beloved</u>, <u>no</u> <u>new</u> <u>command-</u> <u>ment</u> <u>write</u> <u>I</u> <u>unto</u> <u>you</u>, <u>but</u> <u>an</u> <u>old</u> <u>commandment</u> <u>which</u> <u>ye</u> <u>had</u> <u>from</u> <u>the</u> <u>beginning</u>: <u>the</u> <u>old</u> <u>commandment</u> <u>is</u> <u>the</u> <u>word</u> <u>which</u> <u>ye</u> <u>heard</u>.

Then John himself makes the same play on <u>old</u> and <u>new</u>, which he had quoted in his gospel from Christ; he continues: "Again, a new commandment write I unto you, which is true in him and in you,..." But that <u>new</u> commandment is nothing more than the <u>old</u> commandment <u>applied</u> <u>now</u> <u>to</u> <u>all</u>, to <u>enemy</u> as well as to <u>friend</u>.

What John writes is a repetition of the basic idea of the Sermon on the Mount. Hate toward <u>anyone</u> and <u>everyone</u> is forbidden. The conduct re- quired by the Decalogue is <u>universally</u> required, rather than only toward certain people, your friends. It is therein that the newness lies. The commandment itself is old and unchanged; the pre- viously erroneously permitted exceptions are ruled out; it is the ruling out of the exceptions that was new.

In short, John steadily follows the basic idea in the Sermon on the Mount. When he refers to love, he is talking about the Decalogue and not about a <u>sentiment</u>; he soberly turns to cooperative conduct rather than to an altogether different thing, an emotion, also covered by the word love.

Potentially Conflicting Goals Of Ethics --
Liberty Versus Justice

Principles of ethics can be considered goods in
themselves. But they are primarily means to ends.

When the question is asked, "What are the ends
of ethics?" a two-fold answer may be given: "Liberty
and justice."

Heretofore in this section, liberty has by implication been assumed to be the chief end of Hebrew-
Christian ethics. Those ethics -- the Decalogue --
arrange for magnificent liberty (except you may not
injure your neighbor, you should in certain circumstances help him with alms, and you must always
endeavor to educate him rightly -- tell him the
whole "gospel"). This gets down to (1) liberty;
(2) no injuring; (3) limited alms; and (4) an in-
destructible obligation to persuade (but not to
coerce).

But justice? Has adequate attention yet been
given to that?

Indeed, justice has been provided for by the
Decalogue against clear-cut cases of violence,
theft and coercion -- the kind of evil deeds that
the law can control -- through statutes, judges and
police. But some will declare: What a caricature
of true justice that is! Who, or what, they may
say, will truly protect the weak against the strong;
and the foolish against the wise?

Do you not realize, they may ask, that every
time a wise man deals with a foolish man, that the
wise man will almost surely come off better than
the foolish man? Did he do something illegal? No,
nothing illegal if you ask whether the wise man
lied or otherwise deceived the foolish man; but
that misses the point here; it is not the open
violation of the commandments that must be proved;
that may be hard to do; but the injustice is sure
to be there, because, as the commandments have been
defined (in what precedes) as every man properly
looking out for himself, the wise man (because he
is wise) can look out for himself better (and he
surely will), than the foolish man can look out for
himself (he being by nature less wise). The differences and inequalities in men make injustice
certain, so the argument goes, unless something
more is done to protect the foolish and weak than
merely enforcing the Decalogue.

According to this viewpoint, which is widely
taken, the ethics of the Decalogue yields justice
for the weak and foolish only against blatant injury by coercion, theft and fraud, but does not
provide justice in the multitudinous exchanges of
life in buying and selling, employing and hiring --
which constitute the largest part of life.

It is as if a prosecuting attorney working for
the weak and foolish, in order to insure them justice, argues this way:

An iceberg is 14% above water; it may look like
a colossal mass; but 86% -- six times as much --
is under water. The 14% is visible; it is visible
like sins against the Decalogue are visible. The
captain of a ship should be far more afraid of the
86% of the iceberg under water, than the 14% above;
there is where his ship's real danger is. Similarly,
so the weak and the foolish must be more afraid of
the greater danger to them from the ability and
strength of the wise and strong than from the latter's direct violation of the commandments. It is
the not-on-the-surface advantages of the wise and
strong which enable men to pervert justice without
being caught and punished!

Justice, this is the argument, cannot be assured
to the weak and the foolish, if they have no more
protection than the enforcement of the Decalogue,
as that has been defined.

What then should be done? One answer is that
everything should be regulated by detailed laws;
just prices must be set; just wages must be paid;
nobody should own the means of production, that is,
the tools men use to produce, because ownership
grants power which is sure to be unjust. Officers
of the state must protect the very weak from the
very strong; and the moderately weak from the
moderately strong. Justice, in short, is attainable only through the operation of a benevolent and
paternalistic bureaucratic state.

What is more, it should be fully realized that
it is unwarranted optimism to believe that liberty
and justice are both attainable at the same time;
they are opposites, as fire and water. If liberty
is to prevail, there can be no real justice; if
justice is to prevail, there can be no real liberty;
these are contradictory ends! And the real end of
society is justice, not liberty! And an all-
powerful state is needed to attain justice!

There is nothing, however, in the Hebrew-
Christian Scriptures which sustains that argument.
If it is correct, then Hebrew-Christian ethics are
defective. Further, the presumed strong argument,
that the Hebrew-Christian revelation as a whole was
belief-worthy because its ethics were so superb,
falls to the ground.

Unless the argument (that justice will not prevail in the ordinary transactions of life except
when there is more control than the Decalogue) can
be answered, a grave limitation of Christian ethics
will have to be admitted.

Problems mount. Earlier it was shown that God
was supremely wise in making men unequally unequal,
in order to permit Ricardo's Law of Cooperation to
operate, thereby enormously increasing production
of goods which men need. Those inequalities were
looked upon as fortunate, and as being the binding
glue that holds men together voluntarily in society.
But now those inequalities have seemingly become a
grievous liability rather than a great asset. Inequality, by this approach to justice, has become
a mistake of Creation; the Almighty did not, so it
now seems, know what he was doing! He has frustrated his own work and purposes.

It is well to face this difficult problem frankly.
It divides men into two irreconcilable classes --
(1) those who argue for liberty, and (2) those who
argue for justice. They may even sit in the same
pew in the church and call themselves brothers, but
they are mentally far apart. They find it hard to
understand each other. They do not communicate
well. Outside of church they avoid each other.
Talking together gets them nowhere; it seems to put
them farther apart.

The church calls them "brethren" and they themselves use the term, but the term is a fiction,
and the idea that they spiritually are brethren is
hardly realistic. Basically, they are unsympathetic.
Their priest or pastor takes sides. On the most
practical problems of life they will vote contrarily,
and fight each other pertinaciously. And what is
more, they do not really like each other, because
they do not know how to come to an understanding.

As Minimal Religion is a book proselyting for --
seeking converts for -- the Christian religion, it
should not ignore this difficulty about justice,
which is generally so frustrating. It is freely
admitted that there is a problem here, and an

important one. It is admitted that the problem
should be stated and emphasized. Further, that it
should be thoroughly analyzed. And, an answer <u>must</u>
be found, or Christian ethics may have had its best
days. (It is probably a mistake to attempt to
solve the problem by a pious appeal to "love," whatever that may mean in this instance; probably such
an approach is merely obfuscation.)

Today, the <u>trend of opinion</u> is that because it
is believed that justice is in jeopardy when men
are protected <u>only</u> by the Decalogue, therefore something more than the Decalogue is needed and must be
provided -- through a welfare state, which sacri-
fices (and allegedly properly so) freedom for
justice.

Problem of Defining Justice

<u>Justice</u> is merely a word of seven letters, or a
gust of air and a sound coming out of a man's
mouth, both of which will be meaningless unless
defined.

The word, justice, does not appear in the Decalogue, which is some ground for believing that it
is not a primary idea in ethics, but maybe a verbal
abstraction, which violates the (not-always-
understood) dictum of William of Ockham (Occam),
<u>Entia</u> <u>non</u> <u>sunt</u> <u>multiplicanda</u> <u>praeter</u> <u>necessitatem</u> --
that is, terms should not be multiplied beyond
necessity. If ideas and terms already exist which
define actions which themselves determine justice,
then there is no urgent need for the term, justice;
it is then somewhat redundant and it may be a mis-
use of a word and a confusion of thought. To add
a word as a new term implies that it has a meaning
not adequately covered by existing terms. Under
such a rule, justice is a half-suspect term.

Plato wrote a book about <u>justice</u>, entitled <u>The</u>
<u>Republic</u>, in which he finally reached the simple
conclusion that justice consists in every man getting his proper due and place in life. That is an
idea which has associated with it the idea of
<u>proper</u> <u>rewards</u> -- good or bad. This conclusion
sounds all right and even profound, despite the
theoretical and impractical ideas which constitute
the main part of <u>The</u> <u>Republic</u>.

Nevertheless the conclusion itself which has
just been quoted is of limited value. It is a
"question-begging" proposition that a man should
be given his proper place in life -- in order to
attain justice for himself. <u>What</u> is truly a <u>proper</u>
reward for a man's services and goods, and <u>who</u> is
to decide what is a man's <u>proper</u> place? Plato
did not undertake to answer those questions, but
it is they which are crucial.

*   *   *

Suppose we concern ourselves with justice for a
man named A. Suppose the people he deals with
daily are B, C, D, E, F and G. Suppose further
that the rest of the community consists of H, I, J,
etc., on to Z.

Altogether A to Z constitute society. A to G
constitute folk connected with each other in

employer-employee relationships; and buyers and
sellers among each other; they exchange services
and goods; and, let us assume when doing that,
that they are not averse to achieving justice among
themselves. Then, further, let us also assume that
the remainder of this society, the people from H to
Z, are also interested in the noble goal of justice.

The Hebrew-Christian Scriptures talk some about
justice, as in the famous (and ambiguous) text in
Micah 6:8: "He hath showed thee, O man, what is
good; and what doth Jehovah require of thee, but to
do justly, and to love kindness, and to walk humbly
with thy God?" (Emphasis supplied.) We are told
to "do justly"; but what is it?

Justice -- whatever it is -- can be "determined"
in a specific case by people in any of one (or more)
of three categories. These three are:

1. A can define justice for himself. He may
    say, "This is my due. This is my proper
    reward; my daily income should be so and
    so."

2. The people A deals with, B through G, can
    undertake to say what is justice for A.
    They can say to him, "This is what we will
    voluntarily pay for your services and for
    your goods; that is all that they are worth
    to us." This might be much less than A
    declares is the minimum if justice is to
    be shown to him.

3. Then, also, H to Z may enter the situation
    as third and not-directly-interested parties,
    and they may assert that they have a peculiar
    capability enabling them to ascertain
    justice between A on the one hand, and B to
    G on the other.

It is necessary to indicate what role people in
these three categories can play in a practical
situation. They all can play some role, although
their importance in determining justice varies greatly.

(It may be well to state, anticipatorily, where
justice can be determined, according to the Hebrew-
Christian Scriptures; it is solely determined by
category 2, B to G.)

Let us begin, however, with category 3. If H
to Z, the public, are to decide what justice is,

they are (by definition) third parties; their dis-
pensing of justice will supersede A's ideas of
justice, or B's to G's ideas of justice. They, as
third parties, take from one and give to others;
or take from others and give to one. The justice
which they dispense touches others but not themselves. It is not painful for them to give to B
to G at the expense of A; or vice versa; as the
colloquial expression goes, it is no skin off their
(H to Z's) noses. Therefore, this third class is
suspect, in principle; it is likely to be impractical, sanctimonious, arbitrary, maybe foolish, and
worst of all, potentially wicked.

                *   *   *

When we look at A himself as a determinator of
justice for himself, we are estopped at once. If
A can determine justice for himself, what is to
keep him from being unreasonable? Will he not have
a bias in his own favor? Will he not, when he
wishes to sell, ask too much for his services or
goods; or, if he wishes to buy, will he not expect
to buy services and goods from others too cheaply?

The common-sense answer is that occasionally
there may be an A, so wise and so fair that he can
really be about right on what is "justice" for himself when he buys or when he sells. But this will
be so infrequently the case that it should be removed from consideration; a man must not be his own
judge, because he is not generally qualified for
that. (It should be remembered that our A represents a class -- all men individually, when they
deal with their fellows.) If the average man can
claim for himself what he considers justice, it may
confidently be expected that society will fall
apart, because such claims will generally be too
high.

Two situations can then develop. In one, the
people represented by B to G will simply neither
buy nor sell to A; exchange between them will stop.
Then A gets "justice" but without exchange; he
will be cast back on his own resources; he will be
withdrawing from society. The alternative is that
A will be granted the power to "claim" -- insist
on -- his demands, which means that B to G must
submit to A's coercion.

This is a system by which every man determines
the final claim for himself, but it will not work.
It results in exchange paralysis; or else in
coercion of everybody by everybody -- obviously a
chaotic and evil system.

                *   *   *

We come now to the group designated B to G, that part of the public with whom A deals as employer or employee, as buyer or seller. Let us assume that A is a carpenter and B to G are householders who need repairs for their dwellings and occasionally a new house. Let us assume A says that he must have so many dollars an hour to receive a "just wage." Let us further assume that B to G say that they are willing to pay only one-half that many dollars an hour. What will happen? Either the householders (the buyers in this case) will repair and build for themselves; or they will forgo both repairs and building; or they will hire somebody else willing to do the work for less than A will do it.

*   *   *

It is apparent that <u>justice</u> is determined by <u>who</u> is in a position to make the decisive decision. Society is faced with three alternatives:

1. Mutual <u>agreement</u>.

2. <u>Coercion</u> by one or the other party.

3. <u>Nonaction</u>.

Number 1 will be followed when both parties prefer it to nonaction. Number 3 will be followed when a mutual agreement cannot be reached. Number 2 will be followed when <u>coercion</u> is considered a sound principle for organizing society. But number 2 violates the sixth commandment of Hebrew-Christian ethics, which reads, "Thou shalt not kill," but which patently covers, Thou shalt not wound, and also, Thou shalt not coerce.

*   *   *

But, someone may say, "society" (H to Z) has an interest in justice -- that each man gets his <u>proper</u> share -- and here is an opportunity for "conciliation" or "arbitration," and here is where the "third parties" should step in. However, if such interference has <u>compulsory</u> power, it too is a violation of the sixth commandment.

The situation is different if "arbitration" is genuinely voluntary. Then the parties to the voluntary arbitration in effect say, I would rather make a deal somewhere within the range on which we are still at odds with each other, rather than wait longer for a settlement.

Often, this is "face-saving." Both parties would probably be willing to settle on the other

party's terms, but they will appear more courageous
and doughty if they themselves do not make the
concession, but if it is imposed by an "arbitrator."

The difference between compulsory arbitration
and voluntary arbitration is, obviously, fundamental. They involve contrary principles of morality.

It should now be evident that justice is basically an aspect of noncoercion; justice is a result,
not a cause. The cause of injustice is a violation
of the sixth commandment. The existence of justice
depends upon observance of the sixth commandment.

*   *   *

Insofar as injustice might be the result of
falsehood or theft, the same conclusion can be
reached -- justice is not a means to an end, it is
basically an end in itself. The means to attain
that end, justice, is by avoiding coercion, by
avoiding theft, by avoiding fraud. In other words,
obedience to these commandments promotes the good
life, of which justice is part. Justice is not
mentioned in the Decalogue, because the Decalogue
deals with causes rather than with results (although
certain other results are mentioned).

When the prophet Micah admonished Israelites to
"do justly" (as the translation has it), he might
as well have said, "Do not coerce, rob or defraud."
That is all the meaning that a "minimal religion"
approach can read into the word, justice.

Hard Bargaining Or "Jewing Down" Another
Man's Price

In an issue in April, 1962 of the Deutsche
Zeitung (published in Cologne) Hans Hellwig, editor,
wrote in an editorial:

> Diplomatie setzt, wie alle Verhandlungs-
> kunst, bis zum Resultaat volle Geheim-
> haltung voraus.

In an English translation, this would read about
as follows:

> Diplomacy, as in the case of all negotia-
> tions, presupposes complete secrecy in
> regard to how far each party will go,
> until the very end when the deal is made.
> (Emphasis supplied.)

Suppose a man has a son who has outgrown a small
bicycle, which can no longer be used in the family
and ought to be sold. Suppose that a few houses
down the street there is another family which has
a boy who wants the bicycle. Suppose further that
both fathers have all the purchasing power problems
(welfare shortages) of young men with families.
How should they make a deal?

Suppose that the father who is selling will "let
the bicycle go" for $13, if he must go that low in
price. Suppose, too, that the father who is buying
will pay $17, if that is what it takes to obtain
the bicycle.

But what in practice will they do? The seller
will begin, say, with a $20 asking price. Is that
honest? Christian? Is it good ethics?

The buyer, contrarily, will offer (maybe half
disdainfully) $10 for that "pretty well worn-out"
bicycle. But he is really willing to pay $17. Is
this man "brotherly"? Does he practice Christian
ethics when he begins by bidding $10?

Why all this apparent flim-flam of asking $20
and bidding only $10? Such action, it may be
argued, is not honorable, nor meek, nor gentle,
as the requirement is taught, say, in the Sermon
on the Mount.

However, such an appraisal of the situation
appears incorrect.

The writer, when a boy, was conditioned against
hard bargaining. "Jewing down" another man's price
was looked at with some disapproval, and "beneath
the family." With growing sophistication, however,
the writer has changed his mind. Each of these
fathers is quite right -- to begin as seller with
a high asking price, and to begin as buyer with a
low offering price. It is not "wrong" to do that,
but it is "right" and <u>wise</u>.

What will happen in this situation? As the buyer
and seller argue and wait each other out, of one
thing we may be sure, unless one or the other gives
up too soon; they will make a deal, because the buyer
will go up to $17 and the seller will go down to $13.
In that sense they are very "capable" of buying and
selling.

Maybe the price will be at the average point
between $17 and $13, or $15; (or for that matter the
average, too, between the original quotations, $20
asked and $10 bid).

However, that does not by any means necessarily
follow. All that can be known from the facts (that
the seller will go as low as $13, and the buyer as
high as $17) is that the price will be agreed upon
between $13 and $17.

Exactly what the price within that range will
turn out to be depends on the sales and trading
skill, and on the respective firmness, of the men.
If the seller is a much better bargainer, the price
may be $17. If the buyer is a much better bargainer,
the price may be $13. There is, therefore, a range
of $4 within which the price will fall.

As long as the seller does not <u>coerce</u> the buyer
to pay more than $17, and as long as the buyer does
not <u>coerce</u> the seller to take less than $13, there
has been no violation of good ethics; why? Because
the seller prefers the money down to $13 (but pre-
fers the bicycle to $12.99 and less); and because
the buyer prefers the bicycle up to $17 (but pre-
fers $17.01 and more to the bicycle). <u>Coercion</u> of
the buyer or the seller -- that is, when they are
compelled by the other party to give up what they
prefer more for something they prefer less -- is a
violation of the Commandments. Under our present
assumptions there is no coercion.

The question is: are these two men entitled

morally to be secret about how far they will go in
a trade, or may they "conceal" that at the beginning and reveal it only when they are prepared to
do so? If the idea of "justice" may be used care-
lessly for the moment, what is a "just price"?

All that may be known from the data already at
hand is that any price between $13 and $17 is a
"just price."

Will both of the men ever know what the full
range of prices (which is up to $4) is? The answer
is, No. If the final price is $13, the seller
could hardly know that he could have obtained $17.
If, on the other hand, the final price is $17, the
buyer will almost certainly not know that he could
have bought the bicycle for $13.

The gaunt fact remains, whatever price is nego-
tiated between $13 and $17, that that is a price on
which <u>both</u> buyer and seller were agreed. Society
nor ethics should concern itself any more with the
"justice" of the price in such a situation.

But was it not unconscionable for the seller to
ask $20? Why? It is one thing to ask it; he could
always come down, and he did under our assumption.
And was the man, as seller, not entitled to endeavor to discover how much he <u>could</u> get? And would
he not, if that were his purpose, be obliged to
start with a high asking price?

And the same holds true for the buyer. Was he
not entitled to endeavor to discover how cheaply
he <u>could</u> buy the bicycle? Was it wrong for him to
begin with an opening bid of $10? For all he knew,
the seller might have been willing to sell for $10,
or $11.

Why should a buyer undertake to buy as dearly as
he can, and why should a seller undertake to sell
as cheaply as he can, in a case of <u>isolated exchange</u>
as this one, that is, when there is <u>one</u> buyer and
<u>one</u> seller? Neither was <u>coercing</u> the other. As
soon as the seller lowered his price to $17, the
buyer knew he <u>could</u> have a deal; the moment the
buyer raised his price to $13, the seller knew he
<u>could</u> have a deal. Neither man was wronged by
asking much or offering little at the beginning.
They were undertaking a risk of their own however,
namely, of not making a deal, because if either
buyer or seller had lost interest while the negotiations were above $17 in the asking price and
under $13 in the offering price, then there would

have been no exchange. The "problem" between the
$20 and the $17 prices was a risk problem of the
seller, which he created for himself. The "problem"
between the $10 and the $13 prices was a risk problem of the buyer, which he, in turn, created for
himself.

*   *   *

Suppose for the moment, that this transaction
was not likely to turn out to be a case of
<u>isolated exchange</u> (<u>one</u> buyer and <u>one</u> seller), but
a case of genuine <u>two-sided competition</u>, by which
is meant that there would be several bicycles for
sale, say four; and several buyers, say five. What
then?

Maybe <u>one</u> of those five buyers might have been
willing to pay $20. In such a case, the seller at
$20 <u>could</u> (maybe) have got his asking price.

Maybe <u>one</u> of the four sellers might have been
willing to sell for $10. In such a case, the buyer
who offered $10 <u>could</u> (maybe) have acquired a
bicycle at that price.

In these two cases just assumed, the buyer and
seller whom we have discussed would not have been
"outside the ball field" in their original asking
and bidding prices.

However, in <u>two-sided competition</u> important new
factors enter the situation, which will be treated
in the next chapter, because of their significance
for ethics.

What Happens Under Genuine Two-Sided Competition Among Buyers And Sellers

The subject still being considered is whether the Hebrew-Christian Decalogue by itself alone is adequate protection to insure justice for the weaker and less-competent members of society, or whether they must have more protection of some sort whatever it may be.

Is more than the Decalogue necessary to establish justice? The answer being developed in these chapters is (1) that anything less-than-the-Decalogue permits injustice; (2) that anything more-than-the-Decalogue entails injustice; and (3) that the Decalogue solitarily alone provides not only justice but also a maximum of liberty; any attempted addition or subtraction from the Decalogue involves individual and general loss of justice and liberty.

The thesis of this chapter is that when people are left free to buy and sell <u>according to their own subjective evaluations</u>, that is, to compete with each other in their own way, they then establish a market framework which itself is the best protection possible for the less strong and the less wise individuals.

*   *   *

In order to make clear how <u>competition</u> protects both buyers and sellers, in the most effective way that they can be protected, an illustration will be given involving seven potential sellers of boys' secondhand bicycles and seven potential buyers. For purposes of illustration, it is assumed that all the bicycles are equal quality, appearance, size, color, etc.

It is further assumed that the sellers will all have the principle in mind of asking at first more than they are willing to sell for; further, that the buyers will all begin with offering less than they are willing to pay. In the "play" between bid prices and asking prices, some kind of a price, or prices, will emerge.

The seven sellers are assumed each to have in mind what their ultimate minimum asking price is; listing these sellers according to the lowness of their price, we shall use the following figures: $14, $15, $15, $16, $17, $18 and $20. Obviously,

the seller who is "most capable" of selling is the
man who is willing to go as low as $14; the second
most capable sellers are the two whose minimum
selling price is $15; etc. The "least capable"
seller is the man who will finally hold at $20 as
his firm minimum price.

In the computation to be made, the buyers are
assumed to be willing to pay $20, $19, $16, $16,
$14, $12 and $10. These buyers too in each instance
will begin by bidding less than they are really
willing to pay. It is not necessary for every one
of them to speak up. Each man can learn considerable regarding who is a real competitor in buying
by listening to what the others offer and what
sellers ask. For example, the buyer who is willing
to pay only $10 will soon realize that his oppor-
tunities for buying are reduced by higher bids by
any of the other buyers.

In Table 10 the data are arranged in such a
manner that it will be readily obvious how many
bicycles can be sold out of the seven, and at what
price they will go. In this table the sellers are
ranked according to their "capability to sell."
The lower the seller in the table, the less his
capability to make a deal. Therefore, sellers are
ranked from low prices asked to high prices asked.

Buyers are ranked according to the same principle,
namely, capability to deal, and of course the higher
the price that a man is willing to pay, the more
capable he is of making a deal. Therefore, in the
buyers' column the man willing to pay $20 comes
first, and the man willing to pay $10 comes last.

Table 10

Determination Of Price For Bicycles Under
Genuinely Two-Sided Competition

Capability to Deal	Sellers Prices	Buyers Prices	Can they make a deal?
Best	$14	$20	Yes, in $14-20 range
Good	15	19	Yes, in $15-19 range
Medium	15	16	Yes, in $15-16 range
Medium	16	16	Yes, at $16
Medium	17	14	No
Bad	18	12	No
Worst	20	10	No

It is obvious that whenever the buyer's price
is more than, or equal to, the seller's price, a
deal can be made. The seller willing to sell for
$14 and the buyer willing to pay $20 can make a
deal somewhere between $14 and $20. Similarly, the
seller willing to sell for $15 and the buyer will-
ing to pay $19 can make a deal in the range between
$15 and $19, and so on through the fourth pair.

The fifth, sixth and seventh pairs cannot make
a deal because the sellers all want more than the
buyers will pay; the fifth seller wants $17 and the
fifth buyer will only pay $14.

Clearly, four of the seven bicycles will be
sold. The remaining three buyers and sellers are
"incapable" of buying or selling.

One question is: Will the four bicycles which
are sold all go for the same price or at different
prices within the whole range between $16 and $20?
The answer depends on how buyers and sellers are
matched. Such matching can be attempted in several
ways. To illustrate the problem, one example will
be given.

Table 11 shows the same data as Table 10, but
reverses the sequence in the sellers' column.

Table 11

Determination Of Price For Bicycles Under Two-Sided Competition By Matching Buyers And Sellers In An Order Different From Capability To Deal

Sellers Prices	Buyers Prices	Price In Such A Market
$20	$20	$20
18	19	Between $18 and $19
17	16	No deal
16	16	$16
15	14	No deal
15	12	No deal
14	10	No deal

This is a chaotic situation with necessarily three
different prices, $20, between $18 and $19, and $16.
In this kind of a market the buyers and sellers do
not "protect" each other; there is not enough
"bidding" and "asking," nor enough deliberation on
the part of participants. This is not, in fact,
the way free and orderly markets operate.

Who <u>ought</u> to make a deal? Those most capable
ought to do so. Therefore, the sequence in
Table 10 is the proper sequence for matching sellers
and buyers, because there the principle for matching was <u>capability</u>. The result in this kind of a
situation permits the determination of one single
price for all the bicycles to be sold, namely, $16.
This is, in fact, <u>the</u> principle which is followed,
or at least tends to be followed in <u>free</u> markets.

As the buyers' bids climb finally to $16, and
as the sellers' offers finally drop to $16, the
buyers and sellers, when they are alert, will discover that there are four bicycles which can be
matched at $16. In this situation, the four most
competent sellers will realize that there are four
bicycles for each of which somebody is willing to
pay $16, and four of the buyers will realize that
$16 is all that is necessary in order to get those
four bicycles. (If they do not realize this at the
first "go around," they will before trading stops.)

It is evident that two-sided competition, that
is, competition among sellers and competition among
buyers, narrowed the price among those most capable
of buying or selling from a maximum range of $14
to $20 down to $16.

Once a market is set at $16, most would-be (but
unsuccessful) buyers will know that they cannot get
that kind of a bicycle for much less than $16, and
most stand-by sellers will realize that they cannot
get much more than $16, unless there is a radical
change in the market. A market today is almost
always different from the market the day before,
but except when there are drastic changes in circumstances, or unless the market is an irregular one,
price changes from day to day will be related to
the price the previous day.

The important point to observe of what happens
under two-sided competition is that all sellers
are helped by the competition among buyers; and
vice versa, that all buyers are helped by the competition among sellers. In fact, as far as inform-
ing each other is concerned, each is helped by <u>all</u>
the others in the market. In a sense, the "market"
is a school to educate people on prices.

It is, therefore, an error to believe that the
weak and the foolish are unprotected unless the
government or some other authority sets a price
and fictionally calls it a "just price." In fact,
no government <u>can</u> set a just price; a just price

has no meaning except it be determined by free
competition on both the buying and selling side.

It would have been helpful, but would require
too much space, to show what would have happened
under "one-sided competition" on the part of buyers,
and "one-sided competition" on the part of sellers.
That would have indicated the powerful effect of
competition. (For details of competition of this
kind, see First Principles In Morality And Economics,
pp. 313-365, Libertarian Press, South Holland,
Illinois, Volume VI, 1960.)

*   *   *

What may happen on the morrow in regard to
bicycles? The fifth pair consisted of a seller who
wanted $17, and a buyer who balked at going above
$14. But the seller may be weakened in his reso-
lution; maybe after sleeping over it, he decides to
come down one dollar, to $16; after all, his son may
have outgrown the bicycle. And the father who bid
only $14 may feel uncomfortable when he sees dis-
appointment written large on the face of his hopeful son; he may quickly resolve to come up one
dollar in his bid, to $15. Now there is a seller
at $16 and a buyer at $15. The spread is no longer
so great.

Such a situation illustrates how the activity
of the market educates buyers and sellers. In a
sense they all help each other. It is, really, no
longer a case of every wise man and every foolish
man (whether buyer or seller) standing isolated,
solitary and unhelped in his dealings with his fellows. It is not a case of every relatively weak
and foolish man being unprotected against the
machinations of the strong and wise. There will be
foolish men and wise men on both sides of nearly
every market. They counterbalance each other.

The situation is radically different if there
is violence or fraud permitted in this market.
Then the weak and the foolish will be at a grave
disadvantage compared to the strong and the crafty.
But the sixth and the ninth commandments protect
the weak and foolish by forbidding coercion and
deception.

The weak and the foolish are then protected in
a well-organized society by (1) enforcement of the
sixth and ninth commandments, by the strong arm of
the law, and (2) by the free exercise of liberty,
in the form of competition, by everybody who bids

and asks what he pleases, thereby revealing the
facts on "supply and demand" and educating all
would-be participants. It is this second protection of the weak and less-alert, which is not always
fully appreciated; it is, in fact, fully as powerful and in practice more beneficial than item 1.

Understood in the foregoing sense, men are generally protected by (1) law AND (2) freedom. Many
think, inadequately, that they are protected by
law only. It follows, then, that it is those who
are against market freedom who gravely expose the
weak and foolish.

                    *   *   *

The problem of pricing becomes much more compli-
cated when there is little uniformity in the product. It was assumed that these seven bicycles
were all the same quality, etc. In the Oriental
world in the time that Scripture was written there
was little mass production; every rug woven was
different from every other rug. Such lack of uniformity created opportunities for sellers to be
exorbitant in their asking prices, and buyers to be
cut-throat buyers.

In the United States in the twentieth century
nearly everything is mass-produced and consequently,
for practical purposes, identical. The tires on
one automobile are equal to the tires of the same
size on another; branded merchandise is available
in practically every product line and the brand
indicates the quality of the goods and uniformity
of the price.

Suppliers (sellers) have had so much experience
in regard to the cost of producing their products
that they know what price they must get in order
to avoid losing money. Buyers read the newspapers
and see who is selling various items of known merchandise cheapest. In other words, buying and
selling in the United States is less complex than
it was in primitive Hebrew-Christian society.

Unsatisfactory market conditions prevail to a
considerable extent even today in the Near East and
Orient. If a Westerner walks into a bazaar in the
Near East to buy a rug, he will be known to have
been foolish if he pays the full asking price. One
consequence of retaining that type of market is that
considerable time is "wasted" haggling over the price.
Markets to buy and sell are better organized in the
Western countries (for the protection of the weak
and inexperienced) than in the Eastern countries.

Subjective Value And Its Effect On
Avoiding Price Extremes

In the preceding chapter an illustration was given of "price determination in a free market."

By "free market" is meant (1) no coercion or fraud, that is, no violation of the ethics of Christianity; and (2) complete freedom beyond that, for each participant in the market to buy or sell, or do nothing, at whatever value he puts on bicycles.

In Table 10 on page 147 it was clear that there was considerable variation in valuations. One seller wanted $20; another wanted only $14. One buyer was willing to pay $20, but another was willing to pay only $10. Clearly, the subjective evaluations of all participants differed for some reason or other.

In economics, subjective evaluations must be considered as "ultimate data." Unless individual, variable subjective evaluations are accepted as of prime importance for determining exchanges, society becomes either tyrannical or anarchical.

Similarly, in ethics variable subjective evaluations must equally be tolerated, or else freedom will disappear and "society" will not be a contract society (involving mutual agreement), but will be instead a coercive society.

By giving untrammeled subjective evaluations maximum opportunity to control action, men individually have an opportunity to obtain maximum satisfactions for themselves as human beings. They will be happiest that way. By constantly comparing and ranking their subjective evaluations and deciding what they want most, and considering what they must pay to get it, free exchange maximizes psychological satisfactions. That is one reason why a free society is a rich society. It is rich psychologically, as well as rich in goods. Contrasted to that, a coercive society is always poorer psychologically; and it is also poorer in goods.

Modern neoclassical economics has a different foundation from all other and all earlier economics; its foundation is the autonomy of subjective evaluations, from which is derived the term subjective value. Such subjective value is ethical, according to Hebrew-Christian ethics, because it is uncoerced.

Any other economic system cannot be reconciled with Hebrew-Christian ethics.

What do the figures in Table 10 on page 147 show about the subjective value of bicycles in the evaluations of fourteen people, owners or would-be owners of bicycles?

In the first place, "demand and supply" were <u>balanced</u> by the transactions that took place. What happened?

Three would-be sellers valued bicycles more than the money they could get for them. They preferred to keep the bicycles they had unless they could get more than $16 for them; these buyers manifested a <u>demand</u> <u>to</u> <u>hold</u> <u>bicycles</u>.

Three would-be buyers, on the other hand, preferred to keep their money rather than buy a bicycle because they did not wish to pay what it would take to buy. These unsuccessful buyers and sellers did not act, in order to keep themselves happier according to their own individual <u>subjective evaluations</u>. They were not injured. There was no injustice. They legitimately pursued their own happiness, according to their own subjective evaluations.

In the four other cases it was different. Four men had bicycles, but they preferred the money they could get for them. Likewise, there were four men who had money but preferred bicycles to money. These four pairs traded. Nobody coerced them either to buy or sell. They acted according to their subjective evaluations.

Altogether there were seven people who preferred bicycles to money, and those seven held or obtained the bicycles. Altogether, too, there were seven people who preferred the money they had or could get from the sale of bicycles, and these seven held or obtained the money. There was no injustice here.

(Much of modern neoclassical economics pertains to an analysis of subjective evaluations, but that is beyond the scope of this book.)

Everybody was benefited, then, either by action or by nonaction; assuming (as is proper) that these respective subjective evaluations should be sovereign.

*   *   *

But there is a group who gained especially, namely five people of the eight who traded, but who would have been willing to trade at different prices than $16. These five are numbered in the following, and the premiums (discounts) which they obtained are shown.

1. Willing buyer at $20 who obtained discount for himself of $4 down to $16.

2. Willing buyer at $19 who obtained discount for himself of $3 down to $16.
   Willing buyer at $16 who obtained no discount for himself.
   Willing buyer at $16 who obtained no discount for himself.

3. Willing seller at $14 who obtained premium for himself of $2 up to $16.

4. Willing seller at $15 who obtained premium for himself of $1 up to $16.

5. Willing seller at $15 who obtained premium for himself of $1 up to $16.
   Willing seller at $16 who obtained no premium for himself.

The three shown in the foregoing list as not getting a "premium" or a "discount" for themselves obtained satisfaction from dealing, but not so great as the other five. All gained, but five gained more psychologically than the others.

Now, might _that_ be an injustice -- that some obtained greater psychological benefits than others? Anyone can have his own opinion on that, but to think of this as injustice is to expect what is too idealistic. (It will take too long to go into details in regard to this problem, and it is here dismissed; see Rothbard, Man, Economy, and State, Volume I, pages 222-225, D. Van Nostrand Company, Inc., 1962.) The basic fact is that all these eight people preferred to do what they did to the alternative. They obtained "justice" in that sense. Any man who sets out to seek to require equal psychological satisfactions from every transaction for everybody sets out on an impossibly idealistic program. It _cannot_ be done.

The $16 price finally arrived at was determined by the _marginal_ _pair_, the weakest buyer still able to buy and the weakest seller still able to sell.

The marginal pair in this case is the buyer at $16
and the seller at $16. That means that the price,
determined in this way, always avoids extremes. It
is always less than the highest price, and more than
the lowest price. It maximizes happiness because
it leaves bicycles at the lowest possible price in
the hands of those for whom they are worth at least
that much.

                *   *   *

   But, someone may say, these bicycles when new
all cost $60. They are not half-worn-out yet.
Therefore, the prices should have been at least $30.

   This injects a new -- and nonacceptable --
principle into the situation, namely, cost (something "in the past history" of the bicycles).

   Prices cannot properly be set by history. The
past is past. It is only today's subjective evaluations that count, or estimates of tomorrow's subjective evaluations. The present and the future
properly control prices; not the past.

   If the past is considered to have a claim, then
the approach is that the bicycle owner as producer
is sovereign, to use a term from Chapter 22.
If one and the same person is to be sovereign as
producer, he cannot be sovereign as consumer. As
shown in Chapter 22,   men must choose between
being sovereign one way or the other. Nobody, by
requiring that choice of men, is taking sovereignty
away from their persons. All that is said is that
no man can be sovereign both as producer and consumer.

   When the price for these bicycles settles at $16
(rather than at a theoretical historical cost
figure of, say, $31), then all these fourteen men
remain sovereign, as consumers, but not as producers
(in which function they should never, according to
Christian ethics be sovereign anyway).

   Men must not live for the past. They must not
evaluate on the basis of past costs. They must
live only for the present and the future. Justice
is not served by using costs -- incurred in the
past -- in determining a "just price."

   It is not only a question of the past being the
past and, therefore, irrelevant. It is also possible
that the "cost" was excessively high, or especially
low. In neither case will that determine the

current demand for these bicycles. Ultimately, demand only determines prices in a free economy. (Analysis how cost seems to enter into price determination is outside the scope of this book. See "The Ultimate Standard (Determinant) of Value" in Shorter Classics of Böhm-Bawerk, Libertarian Press, South Holland, Illinois, 1962.) If costs cannot be recovered by sale, buyers should not be coerced; those who made the error of miscalculating demand must suffer the penalty of their own miscalculations. It is lamentable that there are losses, but those who brought them on themselves should suffer them. It would be "injustice" to make B suffer for the errors of A.

It is agreed that a great deal of the complaint about "unjust prices" stems from the disappointments of producers who are unable to recover costs (and thereby suffer losses), or who only break even. If these bunglers or unfortunates are subsidized to lighten their load, they will not learn agonizingly enough that they made an error. It is damaging to society not to let cause and effect operate. Rather than to frustrate cause and effect, they should be permitted free operation. If relief must be given, it should come under the label of alms.

*   *   *

At the risk of boring repetition, it is nevertheless desirable to call attention again to the principal justification for freedom to all men on all matters (except not freedom to do specified evils), namely, other men cannot decide for others -- because they lack the intellectual capability properly to do so -- at what price any man should offer (1) to hold, (2) to sell, or (3) to buy a bicycle. Indeed, who can determine a "just price"? And is a "just price" the same for all?

Let us imagine why one man asks a minimum of $20 for a bicycle, and another only $14.

Suppose the former will not sell for less than $20, because that is what he needs to buy fishing tackle for his son. This father would rather have his son retain the bicycle than that he (the father) gets $19.50, which is inadequate to buy the fishing tackle. The father, let us say, merely represents the preferences of the son; first, fishing tackle; second, bicycle; third, $20. If the $20 is not forthcoming from the sale of the bicycle by which

the fishing tackle can be bought, then the boy
prefers the bicycle. How can some man or some
committee take into account the "motivations" of
this boy? They would not know that he existed or
what his "valuations" were.

Or consider the father and his son who will sell
for as little as $14. Let us assume that this boy
has "shot up like a weed," and cannot ride his
bicycle any more with comfort; as he peddles, his
knees have to be flexed to the angle of a grass-
hopper's. Suppose, too, he urgently needs a larger
bicycle in order to ride to school. A quick sale
at $14 is a genuine convenience to this boy, and
to his mother who must otherwise deliver him to
school and pick him up to bring him home. How
would any man or any committee be qualified to set
a price, supposedly a "just price," at which this
bicycle could permissibly be sold?

In short, all those who undertake to set "just
prices," by their general judgment on what is "just"
and "unjust," are suffering from hallucinations
that they do know -- or even can know -- what the
price "should" be. They overrate their own intelligence. They, in effect, aim to play at being wiser
than God.

There is nothing in Scripture which indicates
that God has ever undertaken to "set prices." That
is something to be thankful for, and prayers may be
desirable to keep any mortal man from undertaking
to be a "price setter," and particularly if he has
the mistaken belief that he can set that unknown,
mythical and hallucinary "just price."

Some People See Only The Visible, But Are Blind To The Invisible (Or, Is Every Man To Be Sovereign As Consumer Or As Producer?)

Beatrice and Sidney Webb were two of the important founders of the Fabian Society (Socialist) in England in the nineteenth century, which developed into what is now known as the Labour Party in England.

Beatrice was the daughter of a big business man, and as a little girl she would occasionally accompany her father to the office of the company.

She noticed that everybody bowed and scraped and deferred to her father. Upon reflection, she concluded, and apparently retained the opinion throughout her whole life, that there was something wrong about that. Here was a man, her own father, who had too much power, to whom other people deferred; a father who "controlled" the lives of the others in the company. Beatrice apparently decided, further, that such a system was wrong -- one which gave her father so much "power"; and further, she concluded that the economic organization of society should be changed to remove such concentration of authority (even though that authority was in a particular case concentrated in somebody of whom she was fond). At home her father was nice to live with, but there people did not bow and scrape to him; and maybe she even heard her mother "talk back" occasionally or frequently!

However, Beatrice was really confused about this. Her father was not an arbitrarily autocratic tycoon in business, as she childishly appraised him to be.

He was only a link in a chain of command, and he was not the original or most important link, by any means.

Beatrice's father had a "boss" to whom he conducted himself like a respectful servant, just as his employees in turn showed respect to him. But this "boss" of her father was not visible to Beatrice, because he, or rather, they were not present in her father's office. If they had been, then she would probably have marvelled how the roles were reversed, and how respectful her father was to those people.

The bosses of Beatrice's father, who in a way

held his fortune in their hands, were the <u>customers</u>
<u>of the company</u>, the consumers or users of the
goods produced or supplied by the company of which
her father was the head, the administrator.

The function of her father was to endeavor to
supply to customers goods of better quality, or at
a lower price, or accompanied by better service
than any other supplier could or would.

In a <u>free</u> market society customers are unrestric-
ted to buy where they can buy cheapest and best.
That kept Beatrice's father "on his toes," doing
his best to serve.

Any strong, authoritative action, which the
father took toward the others in the company was
surely designed single-mindedly to keeping the real
bosses of the business satisfied and firmly "attached"
to the business of which he and they were all members.

Beatrice lacked penetrating insight into reality,
when she was a little girl, and she did not grow
up to see the less obvious, or the seemingly invisible. She was merely one of many people in the
world who are inadequate as economists, that is,
they see only what is visible <u>on the surface</u>.

                  *   *   *

As there are only two ultimate systems of religion, namely, (1) that God is God, or (2) that
Dust is God, so there are only two ultimate economic systems: (1) a system in which the consumers
are sovereign, or (2) a system in which the producers, subdivided into groups, are sovereign.
This latter system, because it is basically fragmented, tends toward friction, poverty, confusion,
and eventually tyranny.

When Beatrice criticized her father, she was in
effect criticizing the one economic system that
is ethically defensible, because it makes <u>everybody</u>
a "servant" to <u>all others</u> (the public), namely, a
consumer-oriented society.

It will be well to avoid exploring the production
and distribution systems in a gigantic and complex
economy and instead to use a simple illustration
which anyone will readily understand. What is true
in a small society is as true in a large one.

Let us assume five families in an isolated
community. Let us also assume that there is division of labor among them: A is to produce food and

drink; B is to produce wearing apparel; C is to produce shelter and heating; D is to produce all equipment and hardware; and E is to provide entertainment and all miscellanea.

These men (and the mature members of their families) are each _dual_ personalities; they are producers on the one hand, and consumers on the other. Tacitly or explicitly, they must decide how they will organize, whether (1) with themselves sovereign _as consumers_, or (2) with themselves sovereign _as producers_. It is not disputed that sovereignty should rest in them, but they cannot be sovereign in two ways at one time, both as consumers and as producers. If they are sovereign here and now as consumers, they cannot here and now be sovereign as producers; it is one or the other.

If they decide to be sovereign as producers, they immediately reduce their unity. To be sovereign as producers means that each will himself decide (1) _what_ to produce (kind, quality, color, size, etc.) and (2) what price to demand. Then all of them, the individual producer as well as the other four, will be obliged to accept what the producer decided to make and pay his price.

If, on the other hand, these five men agree that they are to be sovereign as consumers, then the farmer will take a poll what the other four (and he himself) want in foodstuffs; the apparel man will make inquiry of the others (and of his own family, too) what they want in wearing apparel; the contractor will build, repair and provide heating materials, not as he himself wishes to do, but as the others (as well as his family) wish, and he will act accordingly; and so on. In this society it is the same people who are sovereign but now they are sovereign _as consumers_.

Wherever people _as consumers_, rather than as producers, are recognized as being sovereign, society is properly considered to be free, and such a society is described alternatively as a _capitalist_ or _free market_ society.

Wherever people _as producers_, rather than as consumers, are recognized as being sovereign, (1) society is regulated in order to favor producer groups who are operating as pressure groups, such as those who demand and get special tariff protection; or (2) other groups get special protection, as employees in certain crafts, to which admission is limited, as in certain labor unions; or (3) groups

are favored by special laws so that their coercion
against others is effective, as in the case of
unions generally; or (4) a whole industry is looked
upon as a unit, as in Italy in Mussolini's days,
and under which system an employer-employee combination, by industries, engages in "civil war" against
all other industries; or (5) everything is regulated
in regard to investments, ownership of land and
capital, as under socialism-communism. All these
categories are, more or less, based on an unstated,
hidden principle -- to wit, we are to be sovereign
<u>as</u> <u>producers</u>, not as consumers.

The position of Christian ethics in regard to
this issue is <u>that</u> <u>it</u> <u>is</u> as <u>consumers</u> <u>that</u> <u>men</u> <u>must</u>
<u>be</u> <u>sovereign</u>. The reason for this is that Christian
ethics is opposed to compulsion or coercion.

A producer-oriented society <u>coerces</u> the consumer
to take what is produced.

A consumer-oriented society requires that the
producers produce what consumers want, but if they
do not like what is produced they are not obliged
to take it. If it is alleged that a consumer-
oriented society is also coercion, the answer is
in the negative. The consumer does not compel the
producer to produce what he wants; he merely will
not buy what he does not want; he will instead buy
something else that he does prefer.

A consumer-oriented society is, therefore, a free
society; a producer-oriented society is a regulated
society; and in part or seriously, always a tyrannical society.

Christian ethics is on the side of freedom, in
this situation, as was outlined in this section,
Chapter 10.

Beatrice Webb's father was a cog in the machinery
of a consumer-as-sovereign society, but she did not
have the perspicacity to see that. Her father was
boss of a business, <u>because</u> he served his bosses --
consumers -- effectively. If he had failed at that,
the business of which he was a manager would have
gone bankrupt. He would probably have been removed, or would have resigned, before that happened.

*   *   *

A world-famous business recently employed a new
manager for its main works -- a hard-driving, young
man, of the kind the management thought was needed
to improve operations.

Shortly after he took over, he and his key associates were in a meeting. One of the men was called

out to answer a telephone call. Upon his return,
the new boss asked about the nature of the call.

The associate dismissed the matter as rather
trivial; some customer was complaining and worry-
ing about a late delivery; the employee said the
matter could wait, and the meeting could go on.

But the new manager thought differently. He
said something to the effect: "Go and trace the
shipment this minute; do you not know who our
bosses are -- our customers! Find out when that
merchandise can and will be shipped, and inform
the customer at once." A considerable to-do was
created by the new works manager about this customer complaint.

And how did the bosses in the general office
(situated as Beatrice Webb's father) react when
they heard of the incident? They grinned with
pleasure. Their hope was increased that the business was headed for better days just because the
new plant manager was customer-oriented rather
than producer-oriented.

Here was a practical case: The consumer was
treated as boss and sovereign. He was to be
served -- not coerced.

This is in the spirit of Christian ethics --
service to others. (Of course, this has no relation to almsgiving. Passages in Scripture urging
service upon Christians are often erroneously
interpreted to mean almsgiving; instead, depending
on the context, those texts frequently mean service
as just defined.)

         *   *   *

The people of the United States should be
reluctant to think that they can have a mixed
society, one with the same person, at a given time,
sovereign both as consumer and producer. It is
impossible.

Further Considerations About Doing Evil
To Others

In his First Epistle to Thessalonians (Chapter V, verse 15) the Apostle Paul, writing in an incisively imperative tone, commands: "See that none render unto anyone evil for evil; but always follow after that which is good, one toward another; and toward all."

This brief statement by the Apostle Paul instructs that members of the church in the city in northeast Greece still known as Thessaloniki do not render evil for evil, either to fellow church members, or to anybody.

It will be recognized at once that this is one of the fundamental changes which Christ made in the Sermon on the Mount, in his interpretation of the Decalogue. The prevailing contrary <u>interpretation among the scribes in the first century of the present era</u> was that evil might properly be rendered for evil, as indicated by the Mosaic expression: "an eye for an eye, and a tooth for a tooth."

One question that arises is: What all may be included in the expression "rendering evil," regardless whether such rendering of evil is in response to a prior evil, or without such incitement?

*   *   *

Suppose that one man has been buying merchandise from another, or that the former has been employing the latter; further suppose that the former stops buying merchandise, or that he dismisses the latter. In either case the second man has been "injured" by the nonbuying or by the nonemploying.

Or suppose that one man has been associating with another and then for some reason or other, wisely or unwisely, or kindly or unkindly, the former no longer wishes to be associated with the latter. Assume that the association was for the latter pleasant and profitable. Does the former, according to Scripture, now "render evil" to the latter by disassociation?

Or suppose that a man who is a <u>nouveau riche</u> buys a residence in a block occupied by members of "distinguished old families," and that one of the reasons for his doing that is to provide himself

the real or supposed advantages from having such
an address and associating with such people.
Suppose further, however, that they are unsympathetic to his intentions and that they ignore him
and his family. In such a case, does Scripture
say or imply that evil has been rendered to the
newcomer by the old Brahmins who neglect and ignore,
or even reject him when he invites them or solicits
invitations from them?

If in these cases evil has been rendered, which
of the commandments in the Decalogue has been
violated, the commandments against coercion, fraud,
theft, or what?

Reflection will indicate at once that it will
require considerable "extension" of the meaning of
the commandments in the Decalogue to justify declaring that evil has been rendered in the cases cited.

According to the "strict constructionism" employed
in this book, the second and third clauses in the
text quoted, from the Apostle Paul in the foregoing
(to wit, "always follow after that which is good
one toward another; and toward all") does not restrain each man's freedom to buy or _not to buy_; to
employ or _not to employ_; to associate or _not to
associate_.

Really, the difficulty is that the problem
suffers from considerable danger from the proposition under discussion being changed subtly from
one of prohibiting _doing evil_ to being required
compulsorily to do "good." In ethics there is a
basic difference between those two propositions.

Nevertheless in the cases cited, actions may be
subject to condemnation if the buyer ceased buying
with the specific purpose to injure the seller;
and if the employer ceased employing in order to
injure the employee; and if the neighbors reject a
newcomer in order to injure him or hurt his feelings.

If this motivation is indeed involved in the
actions of a buyer, employer and neighbors, then
probably the injunction of Paul "always to follow
after that which is good one toward another" is
inadequately honored.

However, if that was not the motivation of the
buyer, employer and neighbors, then the situation
should be viewed differently. All men are entitled
to be motivated by their legitimate self-interest.
Maybe the buyer no longer wished to buy because he

did not need the product, or preferred to give the business to somebody else whom he liked better. Maybe the employer estimated that he was not getting "value for value received," or he wished to give the employment to a nephew; or maybe the neighbors thought the newcomer in the neighborhood was unpleasant company and his children a bad influence on their own children. In these cases, the motivation was not to injure the other person, but to protect one's self. Under "strict constructionism," it is estimated that no evil was rendered under such circumstances.

If the problem is raised which asks who is to have the final voice in regard to interpreting motivations, then the only safe answer is that each person must be the ultimate judge for himself. It would be easy enough for a seller to say that the buyer had stopped buying because of malice; or for the employee to say that the employer had ceased employing because of hatred; or for the newcomer to declare that he was rejected because of envy of his new-found prosperity; but ethics (and society in practice) will find it unsafe to rely upon the assertions of claimants in such cases.

Neither can society rely upon some third party which sets itself up as judge in regard to the "facts" about the motivations of those who have discontinued buying, ceased employing, or those who will not associate.

The legal apparatus of society can hardly ever be employed safely to coerce a buyer, an employer, or a neighbor, even though there may be suspicion that the motivations are to injure others rather than protect the self. The Christian religion can go a little further and condemn morally "in principle" what is done to injure others rather than to protect the self, but it too lacks sure knowledge of subjective motivations and, consequently, it cannot make it a part of its "discipline" to compel a man to continue to buy, or to continue to employ, or to associate.

*   *   *

Of the three cases cited, the one on which society has never been so explicit, as on the other two, is the case involving social association. If one is inclined to condemn the unneighborliness of the Brahmins who would not accept the newcomer, and if they are to be reproved or disciplined for that, then the laws of the land, in order to be

consistent, would also have to be altered to require a man to continue to buy, and to continue to
employ on the demands of the other party. This is
patently a subversion of the historic scheme of
things in the Western world under Christian ethics
and Christian principles.

John Stuart Mill put the proposition rather well,
on the basis of his utilitarian principles, when
he wrote in his essay, On Liberty, that a man may
not be compelled to do good, but that he may be prohibited from doing evil (and that only). Mill was
no "believer" in the Christian religion, but he was
here clearly voicing Christian ethics.

(It is interesting to note what system of morals
two of the greatest skeptics that the Western world
has produced, David Hume and John Stuart Mill, have
taught in regard to principles in morality, the
former in his An Enquiry Concerning The Principles
Of Morals and the latter in his essay, On Liberty.
In broad outlines both of these men hold to the
same set of rules for morality as the Hebrew-
Christian religion; their deviations are minor;
they should both be looked upon as "conformists"
to Hebrew-Christian ethics.)

It is interesting to note that Mill, when he
argued unqualifiedly for everybody being entitled
to have his own liberty regarding with whom to associate (and even in cases where the unwillingness to
associate involved contempt), declared that the
right not-to-associate was unchallengeable, but
that a man was not entitled to supplement such
nonassociation by showing his contempt in order to
injure the other. (The subject of contempt will
be considered in the next chapter.)

*   *   *

The liberty to refuse to act and the liberty to
reject for personal subjective reasons, particularly
self-regarding reasons, whether rightly or wrongly
evaluated, cannot be restricted by any alleged claims
of morality without, in fact, subverting society.

Public opinion is the most powerful police force
in the world. True, police and courts of law restrain people every day and in many ways, but much
more broadly every day we all strive for the favorable opinion of our neighbors so that they will
buy from us, employ us and associate with us. If
we do not have to earn the esteem of people, on
their own terms, the most powerful disciplinary
force in society has been removed.

Individual men, therefore, must be permitted the
liberty to retain the options to buy or not to buy,
to employ or not to employ, to associate or not
associate, in order to manifest their approval or
disapproval of the particular acts of their neighbors. This is, first, legitimate self-defense;
it is, second, salutary disciplinary action toward
others; it is, third, not deliberate bad manners
nor grossly offensive to feelings; and it is,
fourth, salutary for society because it induces
everyone to exert himself to please others more so
that they will resume their wish to buy, to employ
and to associate.

Hebrew-Christian ethics therefore wisely does
not require the doing of a positive good to another
beyond one's own inclination. What it teaches
instead is that we may not be motivated by the desire to injure another, nor may we do it by overt
acts of coercion, theft and fraud.

$$* \qquad * \qquad *$$

There can be no question that the last rejoinder
of those who wish to go farther will be that refusal to buy, refusal to employ, and refusal to
associate are all forms of coercion against the
wishes of others. The threat not to buy, not to
employ and not to associate puts pressure on those
against whom such "discrimination" is exercised;
and "pressure" is coercion! The ethics of the
Christian religion, however, have never required
such an "extension" of the definition of the word
coercion.

Any inclination to declare that noncompliance
with the wishes of others is really an indirect
form of coercion (as by not buying, not employing,
not associating) must finally be rejected on grounds
of a priori logic based on Scripture.

It is in dialectics an unconscious (or sometimes
conscious) practice to extend the meanings of terms
inappropriately, and then to argue against that
extension. To consider "nonaction" (nonpurchase,
nonemployment and nonassociation) a violation of
the rule against coercion would be a case in point.

This can probably be made clearer by a brief
further analysis.

For the purposes of that analysis, let us consider two kinds of alleged coercion: (1) aggressive
or offensive coercion; and (2) self-defensive
coercion, characterized by motivations of self-

protection, self-interest, and manifested by in-
action or discontinuance of action, such as in the
cases considered earlier in this chapter.

Some may say that both kinds of coercion,
(1) aggressive coercion (as violence, theft, fraud)
and (2) self-defensive coercion (as nonpurchase,
nonemployment and nonassociation) must be considered to be violations of the ethics of the Christian
religion.

Merely examining one of these terms will reveal
a grave difficulty, the term self-defensive coercion.
The ideas "self-defense" and "coercion" are mutually
exclusive. They are in principle the same as saying
that there is a "white black" or a "black white,"
as if such a color were possible. It really does
not need lengthy proof that "self-defensive" action
and "coercive" action are "opposite" terms and can
never cover one and the same idea. In fact, they
are more than opposites; they are contradictory,
and to endeavor to unite them is to violate one of
the three famous axioms of logic, the second (known
as the Law of Contradiction, that is, Nothing can
both be and not be) which, applied to our problem,
means that if something is self-defense it cannot
be coercion, and if something is coercion it cannot
be self-defense.

Just for the argument, let it be granted that A
may not (according to his own opinion on what is
self-defensive for himself) act on that opinion by
not-buying, not-employing or not-associating. Then
what implicitly does that entail? It entails that
B is indeed permitted to be aggressively and offen-
sively coercive toward A!

In other words, by extending the definition of
coercion to forbid defensive actions by A, the door
in effect has been opened to permit aggressive
coercion by B. Patently, the aim to develop a
super-ideal (or super-sanctimonious) ethic has
over-reached itself, and a breach of gravest proportions has been opened on the really significant
front.

                *   *   *

There are others who wish to extend the term
coercion in yet a different manner, and equally il-
legitimately. The argument runs about as follows:
A does not coerce B (by violence, theft and fraud),
nor does A coerce B by pursuing his (A's) own
interests legitimately, but A employs "circumstances"
to his own benefit at B's expense and coerces B in
that improper manner.

Suppose that suddenly there is a shortage of
wheat. Suppose, too, that A has storage bins full
of wheat, but B has none; either by chance or foresight A is "long" on wheat, and again by chance or
lack of foresight B is "short" on wheat. Now let
us assume further that A (apparently) doubles the
price of wheat to B and, because B must eat, B is
obliged to pay, and is in effect "robbed" by A.
In short, A is employing "circumstances" to coerce
B.

If there is, in fact, a shortage, then the smaller
stock left must be husbanded and made to stretch as
far as needed. The way to do that is to raise the
price. But seldom does A, in the case assumed, raise
the price. Potential buyers C, D, E and all the
rest bid up the price. If there is "coercion" in
this situation, the coercion is among the competitive buyers -- B, C, D, E, etc. (In this connection
see the analysis in First Principles In Morality
and Economics, Volume VI, 1960, pages 315-317; or
Böhm-Bawerk, CAPITAL AND INTEREST, Volume II,
Positive Theory of Capital, pages 218-219; or the
extract, Value and Price, pages 218-219.)

Many seemingly complex problems arise in cases
of radical changes in supply and demand, but the
untrammeled price mechanism will always (or almost
always) be the best way for everybody to adjust to
the circumstances.

One thing is obvious from the Hebrew-Christian
Scriptures: moral problems about coercion are not
associated, in those Scriptures, with "coercion by
circumstances." Coercion, in Hebrew-Christian
ethics, applies not to events, but to the overt acts
of men: murder, violence, threats of violence,
psychological intimidation, etc. Those Scriptures
are realistic enough to assume that there is always
the pressure (coercion) of circumstances; everywhere
in those Scriptures there is the assumption of a
ubiquitous and ever-present "universal welfareshortage" which was described in Chapter 16 in
Section II of this book.

*   *   *

Coercion in Hebrew-Christian ethics never refers
to the pressure of circumstances, nor to defensive
actions, but to offensive actions only. Defensive
actions are not condemned in Hebrew-Christian ethics.
Where actions fall in the generally large category
of defensive actions, but are supplementarily motivated by the malicious will to injure someone else

rather than to defend the self, then a moral condemnation is in order, but practical ethics cannot
arrogate to itself safely the judging of the motives
behind the actions of people.

Vengeance, malice, efforts to injure others are
all "Dead Sea fruits," but they are basically
entirely different from defensive nonactions. (The
term, nonactions, is not a fortunate one, but readers
will understand what is meant from the context.)

*   *   *

In some vague ways the Christian religion does
seem to require in some situations that especially
good treatment is due to fellow-believers, even if
not extended to nonbelievers. There are expressions,
for example, about being especially good to those
of the same "household of faith." These expressions,
however, are not conclusive. It should be noted,
for example, in the text given at the beginning of
this chapter that Paul makes no distinction between
believers and unbelievers, but says "always follow
after that which is good one toward another; and
toward all." In a sense, there seems to be a distinction, but it is certainly hard to determine
what it is.

Limited Attention In Christian Ethics Against Manifesting Contempt Of Others

Non-Christian ethics legislates strongly against showing <u>contempt</u> of others. Christian ethics has very little to say on that subject.

Non-Christian ethics concerns itself extensively with "human dignity" and often calls for the suppression of adverse opinions of others (which more or less involves the risk of such ethics fostering hypocrisy). Contrarily, although Christian ethics sets a high value on human beings, it does not set a high estimate on man's innate goodness, or wisdom, or worthiness of respect. Hence, there appears to be room left for the exercise of contempt.

In the secular world, manners and ethics merge. Scripture almost entirely neglects manners.

<u>There is a generic difference in a system of ethics which has its attention largely fixated on discouraging and condemning sin, versus another system of ethics which has its attention fixated on evaluating all men kindly and equally; or at most only reluctantly showing unfavorable appraisal, and explaining shortcomings as the result of unfavorable environment, inadequate education, discrimination, prejudice, and the lack of gentle ethics.</u>

How then harmonize harsh Christian ethics and polite manners? How reconcile Christianity's condemnation of man's sin and his propensity to do evil on the one hand, with a seemingly very worthy policy of not breaking down a man's morale by letting him know how poorly he is regarded by others, on the other hand?

Whenever an employer prefers A to B, and B to C, and C to D, etc., there is an unfavorable comparison for the one not favored. If in preceding chapters the propriety of evaluating everything strictly on the basis of what they are subjectively worth to others is justified -- which in fact is so common-sense that the subject should not be debatable -- how can social, political and economic life be prevented from being unideal, harshly comparative, and psychologically wounding?

If Jones and Smith both produce shoes, but Smith's shoes are better than Jones's shoes, and if buyers

of shoes refuse to buy from Jones, his feelings may
be hurt, his morale may be lessened, and he may
suffer a spiritual trauma. The public, in short, by
pursuing its own interest has openly showed "contempt"
of Jones's shoes, and therefore shown "contempt" of
him as a shoemaker. If a man's labor and product
may be treated with contempt (by rejecting them for
the labor and product of others), may contempt be
shown generally on other matters, as in association,
membership in various organizations, etc.?

All our actions in life are based on "rankings";
we prefer this to that; every action we take involves
a "judgment," which puts one thing ahead of another.
Christianity latches on to that idea, and acknowl-
edges the right to make comparative judgments. Whoever is low in ranking is despised compared to those
high in ranking. Christianity may, therefore, by
loose reasoning, be considered as contributing to
"classes," as measuring men harshly, as not "loving"
men equally.

Such also, as will be readily agreed to, is the
indictment of socialism-communism against Christianity. According to socialism-communism, matters
in life must be equalized between men; life must be
made egalitarian; equality must not exist in the
same "set of rules" for everybody, because that will
end in inequality because of inequalities in abilities and environment and opportunity. An ideal
society -- a really "loving" society -- will suppress
differences in evaluations of things and men; men
will "love" one another equally regardless of differences in merit between the objects loved; men
will have agape (ag'-a-pe), that is, nondiscriminating love.

Some Christian theologians and ethical teachers
affirm that God has agape (nondiscriminating love)
toward all men, and that Christian ethics requires
that men have such agape toward one another, too.

However, as a descriptive publication, Minimal
Religion will not make acceptance of the Christian
religion unpalatable by affirming that to accept
Christianity it is necessary to subscribe to such
an enormous requirement. Instead, it will continue,
on this subject too, its standard practice of stating the minimum that Christianity requires rather
than a supposed maximum. We shall approach this
subject from the viewpoint of "strict constructionism."

However, the problem will not be ignored that

Scripture hardly has a word of condemnation for contempt.

The fact is that Scripture approaches the problem of contempt from a <u>radically</u> different <u>starting</u> <u>point</u>.

But first it will be interesting to note what various moralists have written against <u>contempt</u> or against the <u>manifestation</u> <u>of</u> <u>contempt</u>.

Machiavelli, Locke, Hume and Mill On Contempt

Machiavelli has written some of the wisest words
ever expressed against contempt. He wrote in his
The Discourses, Second Book, Chapter XXVI, under
the title, "Contempt and Insults Engender Hatred
Against Those Who Indulge In Them, Without Being
Of Any Advantage To Them" (emphasis supplied):

> I hold it to be a proof of great prudence
> for men to abstain from threats and insulting
> words toward any one, for neither the one nor
> the other in any way diminishes the strength
> of the enemy; but the one makes him more
> cautious, and the other increases his hatred
> of you, and makes him more persevering in his
> efforts to injure you... It is the duty,
> therefore, of every good general...or chief
> of a republic, to use all proper means to
> prevent...insults and reproaches from being
> indulged in by citizens or soldiers, either
> amongst themselves or against the enemy;
> ...Tiberius Gracchus, who in the war with
> Hannibal had been called to the command of
> a certain number of slaves, who had been
> armed because of the scarcity of free men,
> ordered amongst the first things that the
> penalty of death should be inflicted upon
> whoever reproached any of them with their
> former servitude; so dangerous did the Romans
> esteem it to treat men with contempt, or to
> reproach them with any previous disgrace,
> because nothing is more irritating and cal-
> culated to excite greater indignation than
> such reproaches, whether founded upon truth
> or not; "for harsh sarcasms, even if they have
> but the least truth in them, leave their bit-
> terness rankling in the memory."

Any man wise enough to have attempted to conform
to Machiavelli's advice, namely, never to show contempt, will know how difficult it is to achieve;
only the very, very wisest approximate Machiavelli's
advice.

John Locke is reported to have been strongly
disposed toward good manners, and the avoidance of
the showing of contempt. A biographer wrote of him
(Life and Character of John Locke, in an Introduction

by Mr. Le Clerc to Locke's <u>Essay Concerning Human Understanding</u>, page 49, Open Court Publishing Company, Chicago, 1949):

> If there was anything he (Locke) could not bear, it was ill manners, which were indeed very ungrateful to him, when he perceived they did not arise from want of conversation, and knowledge of the world, but from pride, ill-nature, brutality, and other vices of that nature. Otherwise he was very far from despising any persons, though their persons were never so mean. He looked on civility to be not only something very agreeable and proper to win upon men, but also a duty of Christianity, and which ought to be more pressed, <u>and</u> <u>urged</u> <u>upon</u> <u>men</u>, than it commonly is...

Hume expressed his views on contempt, when he wrote his famous definition of good manners in his, <u>An Enquiry Concerning The Principles Of Morals</u>, Section VIII. Hume summarized the rules of good manners as follows (emphasis supplied):

1. Engage in mutual deference;
2. <u>Disguise</u> <u>contempt</u> <u>of</u> <u>others</u>;
3. Conceal authority (or power);
4. Give attention to each in turn; and
5. In conversation have:
   a. an easy flow;
   b. without vehemence;
   c. without interruption;
   d. without eagerness of victory;
   e. without airs of superiority.

Mill commented on the same subject in his essay, <u>On Liberty</u>, Chapter IV (emphasis supplied):

> We have a right, also, in various ways, to act upon our unfavorable opinion of any one, not to the oppression of his individuality, but in the exercise of ours. We are not bound, for example, to seek his society; we have a right to avoid it (<u>though</u> <u>not</u> <u>to</u> <u>parade</u> <u>the</u> <u>avoidance</u>), for we have the right to choose the society most acceptable to us. We have a right, and it may be our duty, to caution others against him, if we think his example or conversation likely to have a pernicious effect on those with whom he associates. We may give others a preference over him in optional good

offices, except those which tend to his improvement. In these various modes a person
may suffer very severe penalties at the hands
of others, for faults which directly concern
only himself; but he suffers these penalties
only in so far as they are natural, and, as
it were, the spontaneous consequences of the
faults themselves, not because they are purposely inflicted on him for the sake of
punishment.

The foregoing are all great statements, wise
and lucid.

The outstanding observation to be made, however,
is that neither Machiavelli, Hume nor Mill recommends abolishing contempt <u>per se</u>, but they oppose
<u>manifesting</u> contempt. The latter, of course, is
quite something else from the former.

There will always be some taint of hypocrisy to
having contempt but of suppressing the expression
of it. (The Christian religion approaches the
problem from a less-challengeable position as will
be explained later.)

What is there to be learned from these secular
thinkers?

First, they are not foolish enough to deny that
there are differences between men, nor do they
recommend that those differences be pretended not
to exist.

Secondly, you may protect yourself against what
you prefer less compared to what you prefer more.

Thirdly, you may betray your opinions by your
actions and words; but

Fourthly, you may not "parade" your contempt or
disfavor unnecessarily, that is, beyond your own
need of self-protection or your warning others
whom you hold will benefit from your warning.

Observation and reflection will make clear that
there are many ways in which there is unnecessary
ostentation in showing contempt. All such actions,
according to Machiavelli, Locke, Hume and Mill are
blunders.

For an intellectual to realize how difficult it

is not to show contempt, he need only reflect how
seldom, in a sharp argument, he limits his final
presentation only to endeavoring to convince, as
distinguished from seeking even more to humiliate
his opponent. An argument almost always degener-
ates into an occasion to show contempt; that is why
men in conversation together so quickly engage in
what Hume discouraged, namely, the showing of "eagerness for victory" and the displaying of "airs of
superiority." And Hobbes's cynical remark, in his
Elementa philosophica de Cive, should not be for-
gotten, that all mental pleasure consists in being
able to compare oneself with others to one's own
advantage!

If the foregoing represents a rational approach,
what is the approach of Christian ethics, which
has hardly a word to say against contempt?

Condemnation Of Pride In Christian Ethics

From what starting point can Christian ethics condemn contempt without involving itself with (1) the taint of hypocrisy, or (2) the "shallowness" of good manners only?

Scripture condemns pride; it condemns the person who is showing contempt. By condemning pride Scripture avoids abstractness, and ties the sin and the sinner together. The advantage from concentrating attack on pride lies in the fact that the man who thinks well of himself when he compares himself to others, and therefore has contempt for them, loses his grounds for pride when he compares himself with what he ought to be, rather than with others. The scriptural position is that when a man compares himself with what he ought to be, he cannot come to a favorable conclusion; he must come to the humbling conclusion that he is very deficient.

Psychologists warn parents against voicing comparisons about their children, thereby discouraging those who come off badly in the comparisons; such procedure may discourage the less-meritorious child. Psychologists recommend that each child be compared to his own past; hopefully gains have been made by the child, or can be made or regained. In short, one child is not built up at the expense of breaking the other down.

Similarly in ethics, contempt based on comparing one man unfavorably to another should be avoided. Nor should a man, according to Christian ethics, even compare himself favorably with his own past; instead, a man should compare himself with what he ought to be, according to the Decalogue. There will then be no swollen pride.

One of the most remarkable men whom the writer has known fully realized that he was a harder worker, more thorough, more deliberative, more fair-minded than almost any other living man. In those respects he was, or could have been, as proud as Lucifer. But he never made such comparisons. It was obvious that he was always comparing himself against an ideal standard rather than with other men. The consequence was that this most-able man was conspicuously humble. He was not, however, engaging in any spurious or mock humility by pretending others

were better than he when they were not. No good
system of ethics can be founded on unreality --
violation of facts.

There is a basic difference in Greek ethics from
Hebrew ethics. The Greeks affirmed that the most
pervasive and disorganizing motivation in society
is <u>sex</u>. That is the theme of their tragedies,
comedies and dissertations. The Hebrew God, however,
declared that the most pervasive and disorganizing
motivation in society is <u>pride</u>. In this matter,
the Hebrews appear to have been more perspicuous
than the Greeks. Pride is the mainspring of our
evil actions; but sex comes trudging on behind
equally unfailingly.

*   *   *

Whereas secular thinkers concentrate on removing
<u>manifestations</u> of contempt, Scripture concentrates
on removing the foundation for contempt, an excessive self-estimation. Having challenged the foundation for contempt, it does not need to devote
much attention to manners.

But there is nothing in Scripture which converts
its attacks on pride into the unrealistic proposition that nothing may be discriminated against, merely
because that itself would be a manifestation of
pride.

The fact is that Christian ethics are unrelent-
ingly discriminatory. It does not recommend association with fools, scoundrels, triflers, the idle,
the fickle, the unsteady, the improvident. The
list of those disparaged by Christian ethics is
long and the critique is uncompromising. Christianity recommends <u>against</u> association with such folk,
and in favor of seeking association with the wise,
the good, the earnest, the industrious, the stead-
fast, the provident. The church has historically
been an exclusive club and you get into it (if it
is a church true to the Scriptures) only by comply-
ing with its requirements.

To the question, "Does this mean that the wise
may properly leave fools to their folly, and the
wicked to their wickedness, and that the world will
be divided into groups which do not concern themselves about others?", the answer is, "<u>No</u>." As
previously explained, the most extensive requirement of Christian ethics is to "spread the gospel"
which was defined as in-season and out-of-season
endeavoring, by persuasion and example (not by

force), to set people's thinking straight on all
matters pertaining to human existence in this life
and a life to come. Christian ethics requires
association to help and admonish people; it does
not require association to manifest equality; or
to concede that there is equal merit; or to flatter
the vanity of those who may claim what they have
not earned; or to equalize benefits of unequal
efforts; or to make fuzzy the sharp boundaries
between right and wrong, wisdom and folly.

Christian ethics and Christian love do not require that "cause and effect" (relentless reward
for the good and relentless penalty for evil) be
annulled.

The way to destroy a family (the relationship
between parents and children, and between each of
the children) is simple: merely fail to discriminate on the basis of merit; fail to reward the
admirable child; fail to penalize the unadmirable
child (of course, in both cases taking relevant
differences into account); prattle of "one, nice,
big family" and have the word "love" disguise unreality, bad habits, injustices, injuries -- and
the "one nice big family" will eventually become
hateful to its members.

And no more than nondiscrimination will work in
a family, will it work in a church, or a society,
or a city, or a nation, or in the world. But pride
and arrogance? On those, Christian ethics is invariably condemnatory.

Permissible Discrimination Against The Hopelessly Incorrectable

Discrimination against undesirable but correctable deficiencies may appear not only logical and useful, but even essential in a good society. The case may appear to be different, however, when discrimination is directed against that which cannot be changed, or improved, or made to be more pleasant.

Is it, for example, valid to discriminate against ugliness, a particular sex, old age, color of skin, nationality, dullness, deformity, handicaps? The person discriminated against is (at least, relatively) helpless to "correct" his (her) defect. Why then "victimize" him (her)?

Nothing in Scripture, however, requires that a person should like everything as it occurs in nature equally, and the answer to the question that has been asked undoubtedly is: discriminate according to your inclination.

If the Almighty had desired to require nondiscrimination in what he created, then he could have solved that easily by making everything in nature absolutely uniform; for example, all women exactly alike and indistinguishable; would that not have been a mess! Fortunately, he did not.

There are degrees of ugliness, or stupidity, and of everything else. Every degree of difference justifies a difference in the reaction. Perfect ugliness will inspire more revulsion than a mild degree. If one were authorized to condemn anyone for objecting to ugliness, then who would be qualified to determine at what point "ugliness" begins?

And tastes differ, too. What one person may consider charming, another may despise. One man may prefer a brunette; another, a blonde. One man wishes a large wife; another a diminutive one. Good ethics avoids legislation on matters of taste -- that is, on all matters of liking or not-liking.

As natural objects (men, women, things) vary one from another, correctably or incorrectably, and as people's tastes differ also, so there is only one answer to the question whether all persons and things are open to discrimination, according to

each person's pleasure or caprice, and that is that
there should be the right of untrammeled discrimination regarding every person, thing or subject.
This will naturally include the right to be wrong
and foolish and nonsensical in discriminations, as
well as to be correct and wise.

Christian ethics, as was outlined in Chapter 10
of this section, legislates _for_ liberty; everything
is free (except there is no freedom to do certain
specified evils).

A society based on Christian ethics cannot appropriately legislate against discrimination in choices
of all kinds. A Christian society, for example,
should not legislate against dancing, or card play-
ing, or theater going; sumptuary laws go beyond
what Christian ethics may legislate. Christian
ethics may, however, vigorously employ persuasion
against such activities, but not legislation.

To be realistic in regard to what Christian
ethics permits, the basic propositions which follow
should be noted:

1. We are required to _love_ our neighbors; (but
love in Christian ethics does not refer to a senti-
ment or emotion, but to "fundamental policies for
conduct," as outlined already in this section in
Chapters 8 to 18).

2. We are not required to _like_ anything or
anybody. We are free to like or not-to-like. (The
reason for that is that _to like_ cannot be defined
for purposes of legislation; because it involves
degrees of liking, ethics become dangerous in proportion as it concerns itself with problems that
involve "degrees"; it can operate only with matters
which partake of the nature of absolutes. (Consider the disaster which afflicts everyone who
ventures in the morass of casuistry.)

3. The blunder of those who "extend" the
field of Christian ethics to questions of liking
(which involves _degrees_ of liking) is that they
finally find themselves in the impossible position
of declaring that there _must be universal equality
of liking_, that is, you must _like_ (usually they say,
love) everybody _equally_. This is an unwarranted
extension of Christian ethics, and an absurdity.

4. Christian ethics, therefore, does not really
legislate against discrimination, but for discrimi-

nation or, in other words, Christian ethics legislates _for_ liberty and _against_ tyranny, especially
the tyranny of being required to like what you do
not like, or the hypocrisy of pretending you like
what you really dislike. Christian ethics does
not thrive under either compulsion or hypocrisy --
of such sorts.

Suppose two saplings grow to big trees, but the
one is ugly and the other is beautiful. What a
fool a man would be to say that he liked (or "loved")
the ugly tree as much as the beautiful tree. Suppose, too, that the ugly tree is ugly because, when
the sapling was small, a cow stepped on it. That
was no fault of the sapling or the now ugly and
mature tree; it was just "one of those things." A
sentimental moralist, however, might think that it
would be sensible to like (love) the ugly tree as
much as the beautiful tree.

Similarly, there is no merit in saying that a
natural fool should be appreciated as much as a
natural wise man, or that the company of the fool
should be sought as much as the company of a wise
man; or that (_other_ _things_ _being_ _equal_) a handsome
woman is not to be preferred to a homely one; or a
healthy relative to an ailing one. Why -- if one
at one's own pleasure may prefer certain kinds of
weather, or certain kinds of scenery -- may one
also not prefer colors, shapes, and other characteristics in people over which they themselves have
no more control than the weather or a landscape has
of itself? Some Christians may sincerely strive
for certain lofty (?) ideals, but Christian ethics
is really sober and realistic; it is not delineated
in Scripture as some sort of humbug or unreality.

*   *   *

At the same time that it is affirmed that Christian ethics does not entail any hypocrisy or silli-
ness about nondiscrimination, it must immediately
be admitted that it has a powerful and systematic
bias in favor of the "underdog" -- the weak, the
foolish, the wicked, the handicapped, the ugly, the
unfortunate. Further, Scripture is not given to
praising the strong, the wise, the good, the beautiful, except in an invariably restricted sense.
Surely, strength, wisdom, goodness and loveliness
are good, but such characteristics should never be
the basis for pride; nor a cover for some iniquity;
nor a basis for taking advantages over those weaker,
or less wise; and the strong, wise, good and fortunate are never relieved of the obligation of charity

(see Chapter 11 in this section); nor are they ever relieved either from persevering, patient and well-intentioned endeavors to help all others elevate themselves.

There is no division (separation) authorized in Scripture between the wise and the foolish -- that the wise should not endeavor to make the foolish wise; but beyond that, the wise man need not go out of his way to associate with the foolish.

There is no division (separation) authorized in Scripture between the strong and the weak -- that the strong should not endeavor to make the weak strong; but beyond such efforts the strong may associate with whom they please.

There is no division (separation) authorized in Scripture between good folk and evil folk -- that the good should not endeavor to persuade the evil to become good; but beyond association for that purpose the good need not lower themselves to un-desirable association with those who prefer evil.

There is no division (separation) authorized in Scripture between the beautiful and the ugly -- that the beautiful should not endeavor to alleviate what is ugly; but neither is the beautiful enjoined to get itself obliterated by association with ugli-ness.

Christian ethics, in short, are not against discrimination, that is, the free exercise of choices; it is in favor of that. But it is (1) against pride, always; (2) against resulting con-tempt and arrogance; (3) against not only contempt and arrogance per se, but also against the manifes-tation of lack of appreciation, and good will and gentleness, except when lack of appreciation is appropriate in order to motivate efforts on the part of others to improve and elevate themselves.

*   *   *

Not infrequently there are notes of dissatisfac-tion (or shall we say, envy) in Scripture, of the poor against the rich -- as the statements of Mary, the mother of Jesus, in her Magnificat, and of the Apostle James in his Epistle General. One wonders whether these expressions are unalloyedly appro-priate; but why should not the poor and the weak voice their psychological unhappiness. At any rate, such expressions occur in Scripture.

The psychology of the poor and the weak can
easily be illustrated. A hundred years ago a
European left his native land for the United States.
In the church he had attended abroad, the rich had
reserved (rented) pews -- the best. In the United
States, the immigrant "landed" in a frontier community with no "rich," and the best seats in church
were available to anybody. A half-century later
this man, having become prosperous and honored, was
asked why he did not revisit his native European
town. This is the reason he gave: I do not wish
to return to a community so stratified and congealed
in classes as my native land; and then the illustration he gave, in order to make his point, was: "If
I went to church back there, I would have to sit
in one of the poorer, nonrented pews!" (The "have-
nots" are always sensitive; indeed, all people are
sensitive to distinctions, which is wonderful because they are then provided with strong incentives.)

The psychology involved in this case is typical --
indeed, it is universal. And why, then, should
Scripture be unrealistic, and have no notes in it
which sound "envious," and carping, and even whining.

Nor is it to be gainsaid that every man, having
risen from the lowly to the high, from the poor to
the rich, from the weak to the strong, does not bend
every effort to hold himself, his family, and his
descendants for generations after him, in the high,
rich and powerful position which he has attained.
He builds houses, factories; he establishes trusts
and other devices, as permanent as the laws allow,
to continue what he has attained!

Not unreasonably, therefore, is Scripture practically systematically biased in favor of the
"underdog" -- the publicans, sinners, prostitutes,
poor, weak, widowed, orphaned, old, sick, the
"down-and-outers," and the "lost."

                *   *   *

The idea of "egalitarianism" is generally foreign
to Christian ethics; it does not strive to make men
equal by holding back the energetic, or equalizing
rewards, or redistributing property; or making
declarations against multitudinous discriminations;
nor does it blame environment for the deficiencies
of individuals. Christian ethics is instead
individualistic -- every man on his own; rewards
for achievement are to be variable according to

individual achievements and chance characteristics;
penalties according to lack of achievements or
chance characteristics are to be equally individualistic.

Acts of generosity by the strong to the weak,
and the wise to the foolish, and the good to the
bad are not described as due the latter, and therefore appropriately made compulsory, but are designated as being exactly what they are, almsgiving,
in one form or another; but profitable to the giver
and to society generally, as well as to the recipi-
ent.

In non-Christian ethics "society" often becomes
a great and sacred concept, a mystical something.
Christian ethics has no mystique of that sort, but
remains individualistic and rationalistic.

Every religion must run the risk of becoming
pious, or maybe better said, sanctimonious. The
Christian religion, with its many spokesmen, does
not always keep itself free from that trait; however, in principle it is a singularly nonpious and
nonsanctimonious phenomenon.

                *   *   *

Interpretations of Scripture of a non-strict-
constructionist character against discrimination
are often based on either of two syllogisms:
(1) one syllogism is based on creation; and (2)
the other on a future life. Neither of these
syllogisms is logical or scriptural.

1. To argue that people may not discriminate
in regard to each other because God made them all,
or that they all "come from one blood" is to engage
in a paralogism; the reasoning involves a non
sequitur. A dutiful husband favors (discriminates
for) his own wife, against other women. But God
made all women. Are all women then to have the
same privileges as a particular wife? Nobody employs
that argument, equally based on creation, for such
a conclusion; similarly all other arguments against
other discriminations, based on creation, fail
equally. One is reminded of other non sequiturs
such as: "Debt is no problem, because we owe it to
ourselves." It sounds plausible, but is absurd.

2. Then others argue that we may not discriminate because in the hereafter we shall be integrated
with each other. This argument is based, although

it is not obvious, on the premise that the life
hereafter will be similar to this life; however,
that is a premise explicit rejected in Scripture.
We know practically nothing about the hereafter.
In the argument between Christ and the Sadducees,
described in Matthew 22:23-33, the _assumption_ of
the Sadducees's argument was that life in the hereafter would be similar to this one. This is the
story of the seven brothers who had had one woman
to wife, and regarding whom the Sadducees asked:
"In the resurrection, therefore, whose wife shall
she be?" Christ, in his answer, attacked the unstated assumption; namely, translating the conditions of this life into the next. His basic (and
astute) proposition, simple enough, was this: you
cannot reason _from_ this life to the next. The
corollary, of course, is that you cannot reason
from the next life back to this one. (See Chapter 7
in Section IV.)

Therefore, arguments against discrimination
based either on _Creation_ or on a _Future Life_ are
illogical and unscriptural.

*   *   *

There is also the argument against the unchallengeable principle of discrimination which is based
on the "church" and the "mystical union" of its
members.

On a strict-constructionist basis there is not
much to be said for such reasoning.

It depends on what is meant by the "church."
There are some grand theories about it. But for
the idea of "church" and "church membership" to have
any bearing on questions of discrimination, it is
necessary to affirm that the church goes beyond
conformity in certain beliefs and conduct. In all
probability, it cannot. The church is _not_ a social
institution; nor political; nor economic. If it
is proper to separate _church_ and _state_, what reason
can be given for not separating _church_ and _social
life_? Obviously none. The fact is that _church_ is
a limited concept, and reasoning from _church_ to
segregation or nonsegregation, or from _church_ to
discrimination or nondiscrimination, are both
non sequiturs. (The church is not exclusive on the
basis of pride, but on the basis of its requirements.)

*   *   *

There are certain problems of discrimination, especially segregation or desegregation in schools, which have been aggravated by laws and court decisions.

Of acute interest to parents is the character of the schools which their children attend. The quality of a school depends on (1) the faculty, (2) the facilities, and (3) the quality and character of the mass of the students. Parents naturally wish all three characteristics to be favorable.

Any good law regulating schools will legislate for maximum freedom of the establishment and administration of schools. Education is primarily the function of parents, and only secondarily of State and Church. The parents should, preferably, found and own schools. Then they can control faculty, facilities and attendance themselves -- that is, have maximum freedom to elevate their children by a good education. The words of Erasmus are apropos: "More people are ennobled by education than by birth."

Historically, the difference between the white and negro races is considerable, and governments have often legislated for segregated facilities, although the requirement has usually been that faculty and facilities should be equal. In other cases, legislation has coerced integration of white and colored in schools.

The "thrust" of either of these two kinds of legislation is contrary to Christian ethics. If there is segregation, there is no choice, although there are two kinds of schools. If there is integration, there is no choice, and there is only one kind of school. Both types of legislation are tyrannous, and will continue to be unless at least three kinds of schools are provided: (1) all negro, (2) all white, and (3) negro and white. Only then will the school system be tolerable. Parents can then choose what they want.

In other words, the school system should be altered in the direction of real freedom to get what one wants, rather than in the direction of restriction of what one wants. The dispute now is which particular coercion should prevail, whereas that dispute should be liquidated by the elimination of the unjustified limitation of choices.

The validity to claim greater freedom in education

than now prevails -- by <u>granting</u> choices rather
than <u>restricting</u> choices -- can rest on either of
two grounds: (1) preference in regard to alterable
factors; or (2) preference in regard to unalterable
factors. Either or both grounds should be respected, as explained earlier in this chapter; that means
that a negro can legitimately prefer to send his
child to an all-negro school which white children
may not attend, either (1) because he thinks the
character of white children to be inferior and harmful to his child; or (2) because he does not wish
his child to associate with children who have a
white skin, which he does not happen to prefer.

It is eventually unworkable -- and unethical --
to coerce one person onto another. Coercion promotes friction; not peace. It is foolish to legislate the emotion of "liking."

But the rule still holds, that it is always un-
wise to <u>parade</u> preferences whether in regard to
alterable or unalterable characteristics; it is
unmannerly, it is essentially contrary to purpose,
as Machiavelli analyzed the problem. To <u>parade</u>
preferences is certain to be a manifestation of
pride; but to have and act on preferences is not
<u>per se</u> to be guilty of pride.

*   *   *

The foregoing can be summarized as follows:

1. Everybody is master or mistress of his own
life, and can choose and discriminate to please
his or her own subjective choices. (The reason
is: everything is different and unique, and not
to be free in discrimination is unrealistic.)

2. Christian ethics legislates for maximum
liberty -- decide and do what you please -- except
no violation of the Decalogue. Except for this
narrow restriction, all the rest of life is glor-
iously free. (It is a perversion of Christian
ethics to interpret it as <u>generally</u> a restriction
of liberty.)

3. Discrimination is necessary for social discipline -- in order to have corrected easily that
which ought to be corrected.

4. But discrimination is equally justified in
regard to what is incorrectable. It is just too

bad, but why make A unhappy about B's ugliness when
it is bad that B is already unhappy about it himself. (Again, the right to discriminate is based
on the variety in nature.)

5. Discrimination associated with pride and
arrogance is condemned in Scripture as one of the
worst sins; this is undoubtedly because pride and
arrogance are hindrances for help by those who can
contribute toward helping those who need help. The
"thrust" of scriptural thinking is that pride is
the root sin of mankind, and handicaps genuine
helpfulness.

6. Contempt, which has its origin in pride, is
in principle equally condemned in Scripture, although
it does not receive the "going over" that pride gets.

7. Nor does Scripture specifically condemn the
manifestation of contempt, more than the contempt
itself, but indubitably the manifestation of contempt is equally condemned with pride. (Good manners
and good public relations entail suppression of
manifestations of contempt.)

8. Christian ethics, therefore, must be considered opposed to discriminations betraying contempt,
as distinguished from (a) those discriminations
which are appropriately disciplinary; or (b) those
discriminations which manifest merely subjective
preference. In short, you may discriminate for
appropriate disciplinary purposes, and to please
yourself, but not purposely to injure someone else
directly, or to incite third parties to injure others,
or simply to parade your contempt.

All in all, Christian ethics on these subjects
is realistic and constructive, rather than idealistic and sentimental.

The Love Of Money As The Root Of All Evil

Some people misquote Scripture and say: "Money is the root of all evil." Scripture does not say that.

Others quote more correctly: "The love of money is the root of all kinds of evils." (I Timothy 6:10a) But what does the "love of money" mean?

In any event, few people want money for itself. The money they want is only indirectly loved; they love "things," that is, goods and services which will give them pleasure. Money is the means to acquiring the goods they crave. (It is only the relatively few misers in the world, who love money itself directly; it probably makes them feel secure.)

The text then can mean: a prime and excessive interest in material things only can so deflect a person from an appropriate perspective of life that material goods may properly be described as the root of all evil. This is a phase of the problem which has been phrased in this book as "the problem of the relationship of men to things."

It has been affirmed earlier that there are three primary relationships affecting men in their lives: (1) their relationship to things (cosmology); (2) their relationship to each other (ethics); and (3) their relationship to the Creator of everything (theology). It was also affirmed that the relation of men to men (ethics) cannot properly be understood unless the prior relationship of men to things (cosmology) is thoroughly understood. In a sense, this is saying the same thing as saying that "the love of money is the root of all kinds of evils." If the "love of money" creates the problem of evil, and if the "love of money" really means "love for the things money will enable a man to buy," then the "love of the good things of life" is the root of all kinds of evils.

But just as money itself is not what people really want (they want instead what money can buy), so, finally, a man does not really want houses, lands, jewels, factories, food, clothing, etc., for their own sake, but because they are the "bearers" of services, to wit, they provide the service of shelter and privacy; provide the service of space

on which to live; the <u>services</u> of ornamentation; of
better production; of nutriment, of warmth, etc.

If someone then interprets the text to mean that
it is wrong to wish shelter and privacy (a house);
space on which to live (land); adornment and ornamentation (jewels); lower-cost means of production
(factories); nutriment to maintain health, animal
heat, vitality and strength to work (food); or
warmth (clothing), then too much has been read into
the text.

But what then, as a minimal interpretation, may
be read into the text?

Existence, health, comfort and pleasure are
everywhere (and properly) eagerly sought after by
human beings. Such motivations take a high place
in life, in time and in ranking. These are aspects
of self-preservation. Here is no sin in itself.
But when acting on these motivations, if the desire
to attain fulfillment may become so intense that
it results in injuring the neighbor (coercion,
theft, fraud, adultery), <u>then</u> there is evil and
sin. Further, when the pursuit of material things
overwhelms and excludes other desirable motivations,
the result is bad and the cause is condemned.

It took thousands of years before men addressed
themselves systematically to the problem of the
relationship of men to things, that relationship
which underlies the urgent desire for the services
which goods can yield. In the last quarter of the
nineteenth century Carl Menger, Eugen von Böhm-Bawerk,
(and later in the twentieth century) Ludwig von Mises
(and others belonging to the Neoclassical school of
economic thought) began fundamentally to analyze
the <u>relationship</u> of men to things. They are the
originators of what is known in economics as the
idea of <u>subjective value</u>.

It is beyond the scope of this book to explore
this field, but the concept of <u>subjective value</u> (on
which concept Neoclassical economics is founded)
cannot have reality or significance unless coercion,
theft and fraud are condemned and maximally restricted. <u>Subjective value</u> cannot be effective subjective
value in the Neoclassical sense, if a person's activity of making subjective valuations is performed
under coercion and deception.

Classical economics, which flourished in the
century preceding the Neoclassical, never rightly

studied the problem of the relationship of men to things. In that regard the classicists (Adam Smith, David Ricardo and lesser lights as John Stuart Mill) built on an inadequate foundation; they built on sand, although parts of the house they built were most admirable. The socialist flood came, and its winds blew, and swept some of the house away.

Scripture strongly condemns (1) exclusive attention to the material things of life, and (2) acquiring material goods improperly. But it does not condemn material things as such, nor negate the common-sense need for the "services" which goods supply to keep people alive and comfortable.

*   *   *

Summarizing:

1. Money itself is not sin, either as money or things money will buy.

2. Love of money generally is not sin either, but the root, the neutral origin, of potential sins of another kind. Otherwise the text should read, "The love of money is evil," but instead it reads that the love of money is (merely) the root of evil. (Scripture does say in diverse places that some kinds of love of money is evil.)

3. By using the word root, the text affirms that persons have needs. Our needs are the ultimate origin (not the specific cause) of persons sinning. It is (a) not sin to have needs; nor (b) to desire to satisfy needs; but only to satisfy needs in the wrong way.

It is confusing when distinctions are not made between (1) human needs (roots), (2) desire to have means to satisfy needs (love of money), and (3) the wrong way to satisfy the needs (sin). The text quoted at the beginning refers to all needs, which are called "roots," and to wrong motivations and methods stemming from those roots.

By similar careless reasoning it is possible to conclude that it is sin to have a mate. A man has a "need" for a mate; that is the "root" for his hunting for one. Presto, so the reasoning might go: "Love for a mate is sin"! That proposition is nonsensical.

One might also say: the need of the body for food is sin; therefore, the love of food (hunger) is sin. Hunger can be the "root" of sin; not sin itself.

The Erroneous Slogan That Charity Should Take Precedence Over Cooperation And Production

On the bulletin board of a church in the Bavarian Alps the following slogan was recently displayed:

> "Nie soll das Geld König sein,
> sondern die Barmherzigkeit."

This can be translated as follows:

> "Never shall money be king,
> but charity instead."

The language is figurative, but the meaning is obvious -- that charity is better than business (money-making).

Money is used to facilitate exchange. Exchange in turn rests on cooperation, that is, that each party to the exchange of goods or services acts voluntarily and considers himself benefited by the exchange. This is cooperation according to the terms of the Decalogue (as analyzed and dissected by Ricardian mathematics, for which see Chapter 4 of this Section III). In short, in the foregoing quotation, charity is elevated above that cooperation according to the Decalogue, which is known as business.

That proposition is erroneous in itself, nor does it agree with the basic ethical teaching of Scripture as formulated in the Decalogue. The correct proposition is the reverse: Whatever contributes to cooperation (that is, increased production, exchange, business) takes precedence over charity.

To rank charity below production is not to affirm that charity is itself inconsequential. It is one of the greatest principles in life, and requires energetic recommendation.

Because charity is so often neglected, reiterated emphasis on it in Scripture is indubitably in order. But to rank charity higher than cooperation (higher than production, exchange, that is, business à la Ricardo's Law of Cooperation) is like valuing a man's little toe higher than his brains; thereby charity is over-valued.

*   *   *

Not even socialists, nor socialist-influenced
unions, make any more the mistake emblazoned on the
bulletin board of that church in Bavaria. It is
not difficult to supply evidence on this.

To be sure, socialism and such unionism as is
basically hostile to capitalism, talk continually
about more for the employee and less for the employer. This proposition is really a variation of the
theme of Barmherzigkeit, or charity, because (although sound moral principles require that an employee be paid for his full production) the claim
that employees must be paid so that there is nothing
left for the employer is -- paradoxically -- wrong.
This will be explained in the next chapter. Socialism demands -- genuinely claims -- a redivision of
the proceeds of production and, astonishingly, more
than the laborer produces.

Further, some versions of Christianity in principle declare that an unlimited voluntary redivision,
via charity, ought to take place, and that that is
really a moral imperative.

But, and this but is very significant, socialistic labor unions and socialist governments (and
also capitalist governments induced by "competition"
to go along with them) now are emphasizing the need
for "economic growth."

The emphasis is no longer exclusively on "redistribution" of the existing income, that is, on a
different slicing of the pie, but instead on a
"larger production," that is, on growth. This is
very significant.

And what is meant by "growth" in this case? Obviously, nothing more than that there should be
"more capital investment"; so that in turn there
is more "capital" behind each working man; so that,
in turn again, his production will increase. This
all means there is a new demand for more cooperation
and production; and more cooperation means more
"Geld" in the terminology of the church bulletin
board; in so many words: Money after all should
be king!

There will, of course, be differences of opinion
on how to "save" the "increased capital" in order
to obtain the "growth" wanted, but the fact that
stands out stark and clear is that production is
coming to be appraised even by the "redistributors"
as being more important than redistribution; or in

other words, <u>Nie</u> <u>soll</u> <u>die</u> <u>Barmherzigkeit</u> <u>König</u> <u>sein</u>,
<u>sondern</u> <u>das</u> <u>Geld</u>,   that is, Never shall redivision
or redistribution of income be the key objective,
but rather increased production. This is the reverse of what the bulletin board declared.

It required the Industrial Revolution in the
eighteenth century, and the continued expansion
of production in the Western world in the nineteenth
and twentieth centuries to rediscover the importance
of the Decalogue in order to obtain prosperity.
Certainly, at that time pioneering thinkers as Adam
Smith led the way. Then businessmen followed; now
labor-union leaders and socialists. The church will
follow them all eventually, and acknowledge that
in the interests of prosperity the commandments are
far more important than almsgiving.

Socialists, and those folk who have been influenced by the ideology of socialism, have, although belatedly in this respect, come back to the
basic idea of the Decalogue. It will be regrettable
if some of the churches are the last stragglers to
return to basically scriptural ideas.

*   *   *

An essential part of the capitalist system is
that it provides an incentive for as much "growth"
in the economy as people wish (are willing to save
for and invest in), and for which they have the
technological capability. Capitalism, when in
operation according to its own principles, does not --
and some folk may consider this unfortunate -- contribute to <u>unwanted</u> growth. However, any forced and
unwanted growth, or growth based on misleading information, will eventually prove unstable and imper-
manent. As it will not "work," there is little to
be said for it. (See Chapters 33 to 38.)

*   *   *

Really, it is not desirable to contrast production
and charity, <u>Geld</u> and <u>Barmherzigkeit</u>. It should
never be -- one versus the other. The idea of con-
trasting them is wrong.

Furthermore, on the question of ranking, first
rank must be given to increased production (and the
prerequisite of increased production, viz., the
rules of the Decalogue), and then a high and appre-
ciative rating -- but lower than increased production -- should be given to charity.

*   *   *

What might there be in it, for the mass of the citizens of the United States, to "redistribute" the existing income of the United States? The answer is: eventually, less than nothing, that is, a _net_ loss.

The income on owned assets (interest on money, rent on land, profits in business) has in the United States been traditionally about 11% of the total income.

Let us arbitrarily assume that presently 2% of the population are the capitalists who receive that 11%.

If National Income is $673 billion a year, if 11% goes as a return on capital, the amount in round figures is $73 billion for capital owners, and $600 billion for noncapital owners. The $73 billion now going to capital owners is to be re-distributed over the whole population (100%).

If there are 200 million people in the United States, and if 2% constitute the capital owners, then there are 4 million capital owners, and 196 million noncapital owners.

Presently, the distribution would be:

	In Millions		
	Dollars	People	Average
Earned National Income	$600,000	200	$ 3,000
Return on Capital	73,000	4	18,250
The redistributed amount would be	$673,000	200	$ 3,365

Roughly, the first two lines in the foregoing give the pattern of what exists now. The next line shows the consequence, if the Return on Capital of $73 billion is redistributed. It amounts (in this very rough calculation) to $365 a year, or $30 a month. Roughly in percentage, it is a difference of 11% (as, of course, on the basis of the assumptions it had to be).

It is this $30 a month not received by the noncapital-owning population which has put the per capita income in the United States for everybody to five to twenty times the per capita income in those parts of the world where capital is not pri-vately owned (and, therefore, there is there in-adequate inducement to accumulate capital because it is either not-rewarding or not-safe).

The average high income in the United States can
initially be redistributed by an increase of $30 a
month. But to do that will eventually result in a
reduction in total productivity to lower than $3,000
a year. The extra $365 a year is an important part
of the "foundation" for the $3,000 of earned income.
In a figure of speech, the $365 is the goose that
lays the golden eggs. (True, a government rather
than its private citizens can accumulate capital,
but this will always involve tyranny, a violation
of the sixth commandment. Further, as Mises has
shown, no calculation can exist where there are no
free markets and therefore socialism is not intrinsically viable. See Mises's Socialism, Yale University Press, 1951.)

The Laborer Is Entitled To All That He Produces; His Employer Should Subtract Nothing From That

Since the middle of the nineteenth century any survey of ethics would be out-of-date which did not consider this problem: whether under capitalism the employees are, or are not, systematically exploited by their employers.

In the nineteenth century a German socialist, Rodbertus, affirmed that income derived from ownership of capital was at the expense of employees. Karl Marx coming after Rodbertus parroted the same allegation, namely, unearned income can come to those who get it only by filching it from others.

Definition of Originary Interest

The unearned income to which reference is here made is of three specific kinds: (1) interest on money, (2) rent on land, and (3) profit in business.

It is important to realize that the term interest is in economics used in two different senses: in a narrow sense and in a broad sense. In a narrow sense it means a return on loaned money only; in a broad sense it means that, and in addition, rent on land and profit in business. To distinguish these two meanings of the word, interest, the broad meaning is here usually designated as originary interest, but the context will also make clear which meaning is intended.

The socialist affirmation is that originary interest (interest on loans, rent on land and profit in business) is immoral; that it takes from borrower, tenant or employee, in order to give that amount to the owner of the capital, to wit, to the owner of money, to the landlord, or to the owner of a business.

The socialist argument goes this way: capitalism involves private ownership of the means of production. That permits the capitalists to exploit the employees. The exploitation consists in paying employees less than they produce. Exploitation is morally wrong. Therefore, capitalism -- in this sense, meaning the private ownership of the means of production -- involves moral turpitude.

This type of reasoning beguiles the covetous and deceives abstract reasoners. However, regardless how convincing the argument may sound, it is fallacious, and a lamentable paralogism. There is no truth in it.

Hebrew-Christian Scriptures
Do Not Prohibit Originary Interest

Presently, and also in the past, some phases of Hebrew-Christian ethics have seemed to agree with the socialist argument, but this is not the fact.

Consider, for example, the alleged Mosaic prohibition against interest on money only (interest in the narrow sense), which is repeated in various locations in Scripture: Exodus 22:25, Leviticus 25:35-37; Deuteronomy 23:19,20; Psalm 15:5a. This prohibition was restricted (1) to Hebrews; (2) was not applicable when interest was collected from non-Hebrews; and (3) between Hebrews was only against loans to other Hebrews who were desperate.

This argument is against interest in the narrow sense, as a return on a money loan only; and was intended only for the protection of necessitous Hebrews, not business or money-making Hebrews.

But nowhere in Scripture is there an attack on rent on land, or on profits in business. A clear thinker will realize that if it is valid to attack interest on money loans because such interest is "unearned," then it is also necessary to attack rents on land and profits in business because they are equally unearned.

But Scripture nowhere affirms that rent on land is immoral; nor that profit in business is forbidden. Therefore, the narrow prohibition in Scripture to interest (1) on money only, (2) among Hebrews only, and (3) in necessitous cases only (rather than comprehensively to originary interest), makes clear that Moses had a limited and restricted purpose in mind; and definitely that he did not express a general objection of a nature similar to the nature of the broad socialist objection to originary interest.

One of the characteristics of the Catholic church is its historic faithfulness and steadfastness to interpret Scripture literally, or as literally as reasonable interpretation permits. The mother church of Western Christendom, therefore, fought

pertinaciously for centuries to take literally --
and in an extended sense -- the Mosaic objection
to interest <u>on</u> <u>money</u>. It proved a losing fight, as
it had to be. The error lay in the "extension," a
practice not followed in this book.

The eighth commandment reads: Thou shalt not
steal. If originary interest is exploitation, it
is therefore also theft. Then all interest, all
rents and all profits are immoral. Then the origin
of this immorality must be immoral also, namely,
private ownership.

But how can private ownership be immoral if in
Scripture ownership is assumed to be moral, so that
it is immoral to steal? If ownership were immoral,
then theft would not be immoral. An inconsistency
(as is assumed in the acceptance of contradictory
ideas) that originary interest is immoral but ownership of capital is moral -- is too great an inconsistency to be tolerable in any belief-worthy system
of ethics, whether Christian or otherwise.

Christ in statements attributed to him always
assumed (and he was also explicit in specific cases
in an affirmative way) that ownership of capital
was a legitimate part of the moral order of things.
If a "moralist" as austere as Christ accepted
originary interest, then the case in a Christian
ethical system against originary interest must be
viewed as hopeless -- as, in truth, it is.

The shrewdest Christian reasoners have generally
come to the conclusion that Christian ethics do
not require rejection of originary interest but,
on the contrary, must accept and insist upon it.

Originary interest, in short, does have the
approval of Christian ethics; but such an assertion
is based on the mere affirmations in Scripture,
rather than on illuminating reasoning.

The much-needed enlightening analytical work has
been done by secular economists, with mental furniture of the foremost order. The analytical answer
is as recent as one hundred years, proof enough in
itself that the answer was elusive. (Neither the
Classical economists nor the Socialists found the
answer.) The basic analysis was done by Eugen von
Böhm-Bawerk in his <u>Capital and Interest</u>. For
further developments, see Ludwig von Mises's
<u>Human Action</u>. For an easier-to-read nontechnical

account, see <u>First Principles In Morality And
Economics</u>, Libertarian Press, Volume VI, 1960,
pp. 227-253.

Nevertheless, why merely rely on what Scripture
teaches on the basis of its apodictic authority and
why fail to understand rationally, when a logical,
analytical answer is available? On this crucial
subject it is practically a requisite to fortify
revelation by reasoning.

Socialists Have Been Excellent Critics Of Inadequate Capitalist Justification Of Originary Interest; But Poor Constructive Reasoners

Businessmen, both borrowers and lenders, accept
originary interest and are emphatic in their demands for it, but they have made little or no contribution to its real analysis, and explanation,
and (consequently) to its defense. They declare
that it is both natural and necessary, but those
two adjectives are only sounds unless further explanation is forthcoming.

In fact, even today almost universally, businessmen assume the wrong reason for justifying originary
interest. They affirm that interest is a reward
for productivity, or abstinence, etc. Böhm-Bawerk
in his first volume of CAPITAL AND INTEREST (with
the specific title, <u>History and Critique Of Interest
Theories</u>) shatters one by one the prevailing arguments of businessmen, defending originary interest.
The critique is devastating.

For the <u>theoretical</u> analysis and defense of
originary interest, businessmen and economists both
might have continued to be sterile indefinitely had
it not been for valid socialist criticism of the
illogical defenses advanced for originary interest.
The socialists have been good critics of defective
capitalist explanations of originary interest.

However, what the socialists were able to achieve
by their critiques, they were unable to match by a
positive correct theory of their own; they came up
with their own Exploitation Theory, which is as much
a delusion as any explanation by capitalists or
their spokesmen.

The Employee Is Entitled To All That
He Produces, Which Seems To Leave
The Employer Nothing; Paradoxes

The problem would be interesting solely because
of its dramatic history and its long-unsolved
plight, but becomes even more interesting when the
problems and paradoxes which are involved are set
out starkly and uncompromisingly. Here are the
important problems:

1. The employee is entitled to everything --
all -- that he produces. If he does not get all
that he produces, then he is indeed, as the socialists affirm, exploited; that is, robbed; that is,
treated unethically; that is, treated in violation
of the eighth commandment, Thou shalt not steal;
that is, not treated as required by Biblical ethics.

2. Nevertheless, the worker does not seem to
get all that he seems to produce. People sense
that there must also be a "return on capital," that
is, in the three forms of originary interest:
(a) interest, in the narrow sense, on loans; (b)
rent on land; and (c) profits in business. How,
indeed, can the employee get all that he produces,
if there is anybody who gets a so-called unearned
income?

3. Then (as if the contradiction of items 1 and
2 were not enough) there is a third mystery to add,
namely, that the origin of originary interest does
not really rest on an ethical basis, but on a non-
ethical one; it rests on a "natural" base, namely,
the mortality of man; that is, (a) that he will die;
(b) that he knows that he will die; and (c) that
that makes him act in such a manner that originary
interest is inescapable, and as long-lasting as the
present dispensation will last. Not until the "last
trump shall sound," and not until the "dead are
raised," will originary interest cease to exist.

Summarizing, it comes to this: (1) the employee
is entitled to ALL that he produces, which pretty
well seems to eliminate any legitimate originary
interest (but in fact does not); (2) originary
interest nevertheless will be paid everywhere and
somehow, but it comes neither (a) from employee, nor
(b) supplier, nor (c) consumer; and (3) the validity
of originary interest rests (a) in creation rather
than ethics, (b) in natural law rather than in moral
law, and (c) will continue openly or disguisedly in
one form or another as long as mortal men continue

to be in existence. Everybody laboring for the
elimination of originary interest is laboring in
vain; just as did poor Sisyphus, condemned in Hades
to roll a big stone to the top of a mountain, but
whose stone kept rolling down just before he had
it at the top.

Definitions Of Various Terms

For clarity, some definitions are necessary.

1. <u>Employee</u>. This cannot mean merely the physical laborer, but must also include the mental laborer; the manager as well as the sweeper; the account-
ant as well as the machine hand; the salesman as
well as the research man. All these people, and
many besides, contribute to business; if they could
be dispensed with, and if a real gain could be obtained from their elimination, then they would have
been dismissed peremptorily long ago. (So-called
nondirect labor (overhead) exists in socialist-
communist countries, too.)

2. <u>Exploitation</u>. In <u>specific</u> cases there is
undoubtedly exploitation. Some employer will,
ignorantly or knowingly, be paying some employee
too little. Sometimes this will, when done knowingly, be literal exploitation. One argument for
unions is that they reduce the opportunity for such
"exploitation." Grievance cases are (in theory at
least) intended to eliminate exploitation. If
there are good arguments for unions, this is one of
the best. A legitimate conclusion from the existence of super-powerful unions is that there must
now be only relatively few cases of <u>specific</u> exploitation. But the important thing to note is that
the argument is not about ever-newly-occurring and
ever-being-resolved <u>individual</u> exploitation cases.
The argument is far more basic and fundamental,
namely, about the fact that the whole capitalist
system on the average <u>regularly</u> yields originary
interest. The unions have not "touched" this problem; they cannot solve it; and they will not be
able to do so.

Of course, there are specific cases where employers pay too much, just as there also are cases
where they pay too little. This "play" around the
"average" is again beside the real point, for that
"average" <u>perennially</u> has originary interest in it.
The argument here concerns a hard, uncompromising
and unalterable problem.

3. <u>Interest</u>, <u>Rent</u> and <u>Profit</u>. These terms are
ambiguous and need definition.

     a. _Interest_ at a given time and place, as
in the United States today (1964), may vary from
1% to 8%. This is a wide spread. But what interest
are we talking about when we talk of originary interest? We are referring to a _theoretical_ (unquoted)
figure, probably somewhere between 3% and 5%, without including any risk factor that is large enough
to be measurable and which is therefore included in
the total rate; and without very-limited-use-values
(which reduce the utility of the loan, as in the
case of so-called "Fed" money, available for so
short a time -- one day -- that it will carry maybe
only 1% interest or less).

    The originary interest rate is not _exactly_ know-
able. It is the average rate at which men "discount
the future." But the composite (total) rate of
interest today for a corporate loan will include
charges for:

    (1)   originary interest (the discount of the
          future);

    (2)   an "insurance premium," against potential
          non-repayment;

    (3)   a "charge" to allow for loss of purchas-
          ing power because of inflationism; or,
          in different circumstances, a "credit"
          for deflationism;

    (4)   errors in judgment by negotiators on
          interest rates in all the foregoing, and
          in other temporary and variable relevant
          factors; and

    (5)   expenses associated with making and
          collecting the loan.

But all that is being considered here is the originary interest rate only.

     b. _Rent on Land_. Rents on land vary "all
over the map" from a nominal figure for desert
grazing land, to fantastic figures for urban lots
in commercial or industrial centers. Which are we
here considering? For simplicity sake, assume
a good Midwestern farm, whose fertility and improvements are steadily maintained (neither increased
nor decreased) and which yields on the average a
net of $4,000 annually to the owner as landlord.
This is economic rent or "originary interest."
Such a farm would probably sell for $80,000, that

is, to yield 5% _net_ annually. (Of course, sometimes there are net losses on rented farms. If
long continued, such farms are abandoned.)

    c. <u>Profits (or Losses) In Business</u>. Every-
body knows that these vary from truly extraordinarily
high figures to bankrupting losses. The writer was
in a meeting recently where a single division of
the business was computed to show a profit rate of
71% annually, but indubitably the figure was wrong;
the business as a whole was merely average! In
another case, the writer knows of losses upon
losses, year after year, in a case which turned out
to be a disastrous investment. But the profits
here talked about are not the <u>extraordinary</u> profits
(because of luck, surpassing skill, spectacular
foresight, monopoly, exploitation, bad accounting,
windfalls, patents, dishonesty); nor, on the other
hand, is consideration here being given to low returns or even losses (because of bad luck, stupidity,
excessive competition, disasters, dishonesty of
others). What is considered here as originary
interest is a net return not far from 3% to 5% --
again that hard core around which actual profits
fluctuate from year to year, and from company to
company. The prices of stocks of the large compa-
nies listed on the New York Stock Exchange currently
sell to yield earnings at a rate of approximately
5%. The common expression is that the price/earn-
ings ratio is "times 20," that is, stocks (in, for
example, the Dow-Jones Industrial Average) sell to
yield 5% (100 ÷ 20 as the "multiplier" = 5%). On
this basis, a stock earning $4 sells for $80.

Examples How Men "Discount The Future"

    We are now ready to turn to the solution of the
mystery of originary interest. What explains it?

    Illustrations will make it easier to grasp the
principle that is the solution.

    1. Suppose your neighbor who is very rich has
a delightful fondness for you, and he visits you
and says: "I have decided to give you $100,000;
when would you like to get it?; anytime is agree-
able to me between now and ten years from now."
What will you answer, and why?

    These are some thoughts that will go through
your mind: (a) I might be dead in ten years; then

that $100,000 will not do me an iota of good;
(b) my neighbor might have reverses, or change his
mind; now is better than later; (c) I can get an
income of about 5% a year for ten years if I get
the money now; at compound interest, the $100,000
now will accumulate to $163,000 _then_; or, vice
versa, $100,000 _then_ is at 5% compound interest
worth only $62,000 _now_.

And so you speak up boldly and say, "If that is
your wish, sir, and if you give me the option, then
I shall gladly thank you for the $100,000 _now_."
You would be a fool not to answer that way.

But what have you done?

You have evaluated the $100,000 in the present
as worth more to you than in the future. As the
expression goes, you have discounted the future!
(_Strictly_, it is only item (a) in the foregoing
that explains originary interest. To go into details will be to go beyond the scope of this book.)

All originary interest is of _that_ nature.

2.   Or take another example of "discounting the
future." Consider a soldier going into battle
next week. He is on leave. He has $300 -- all
his savings -- in his pocket. What may he do? He
may reason this way: Maybe I shall be dead this
day next week. What good will the money do me
then? I have never had possession of a woman. For
me, it may be now or never. Whatever this money
will buy me in sexual satisfaction is going to be
spent on that. And so he may make the round of the
houses of prostitution that he can find. He has
discounted the future benefit that $300 will have
for him, because he does not have confidence that
he will have a future.

Would he do that if he thought life was certain?
Or that he would next year be able to marry the
girl in his home town whom he had always admired
and respected? Would he so rashly let his $300 go,
even for an _appropriate_ satisfaction, if he confidently thought that he would live? Might he not
say to himself: "This is the first of the money I
need to buy a car which I wish to have when I get
home; I shall not spend it."

The more certain we are of life and of the
events in the future, the higher we tend to value
something available in the future. The less certain
we are of life, the less we value something in the
future. Each man's originary interest rate changes
with his own changing circumstances. The average

in the United States apparently establishes a rate
between 3% and 5% annually.

3. If you are "poor as a church mouse" but if
you wish to play the role of a rich and generous
man, tell your friends that you will give each of
them $1,000,000 -- if they will come to collect
one hundred years from now. You look soberly at
them and say: "I shall have the money for you
then." But they look at you and grin. They think
you are joking. They know that neither you nor
they will be alive then; you all will be mouldering
in a grave, or be dust in the urns of a crematorium.

Your big talk of $1,000,000 for each of them is
blarney; it means nothing. You make the promise
because it will never be fulfilled. In other words,
the farther away a "good" is for you in future time,
the less you value it. Even a billion dollars means
nothing to you two hundred years from now. In this
life, all earthly "values" for individuals tend to
become zero when they are beyond the expected life
span (except that assets can be passed on by inheritance).

Natural Rather Than Ethical
Origin Of Originary Interest

Clearly, in the case of originary interest we
are not dealing with something that is ethical in
origin, but that which rests in our "mortality."
If time -- the difference between now and the
future -- meant nothing to us, there would be no
originary interest. The phenomenon of originary
interest rests on our mortality rather than on
morality. (This of course does not mean that men
cannot cluster various sins around originary interest. They do that, but those sins are irrelevant
appendages to the explanation of originary interest
itself.)

Anything that exists by "creation" and the "conditions of life" (as has just been explained how
mortal men "discount the future") is ineradicable.
It will always exist. Whoever tries to remove it
will surely fail, and end with frustration.

How A Reader Can Convince Himself
That Originary Interest Is Ineradicable

As a man ponders his way through the truly difficult problem of originary interest, he may say to

himself: I grant that "discounting the future" is
a plausible explanation of originary interest, but
how then can the employee obtain the full proceeds
of his labor; will he not receive as much less than
his full production as is subtracted for originary
interest? The answer is <u>No</u>.

The most interesting way to analyze the problem,
and to provide the correct answer for the foregoing
question, is to investigate whether under genuine
socialism -- no private ownership of the means of
production -- the phenomena of originary interest
will occur. To help the reader understand such an
analysis, the conclusion of such an investigation
will be here anticipated; the answer is as follows:
in a socialist society the phenomena of originary
interest will, in order to attain justice, certainly
occur openly or disguisedly. In other words,
originary interest <u>cannot</u> be abandoned justly even
in a pure socialist society, where there is no
private ownership of the means of production.

A conclusive analysis, in order to show that,
has been ideally worked out by Böhm-Bawerk in the
first volume of his three-volume work, CAPITAL AND
INTEREST, namely, <u>History and Critique of Interest</u>
<u>Theories</u>. The pertinent information appears on
pages 263-271 under subheading "B".

Böhm-Bawerk assumes (1) that five socialists
wish to build a steam engine; (2) that none of them
is a capitalist who can or will "put up the money";
(3) that this is to be a joint venture of all five
of them; (4) that these five men will pay no originary interest to any outsider who would thereby be
their exploiter; (5) that the whole value of the
engine will accrue to the five; (6) that it will
take "time" to build the engine, namely, five years;
(7) that the men will contribute equal amounts of
work; (8) that the men will work in sequence; and
(9) that the engine will sell for $5,500 when it is
ready to be delivered to a buyer.

Immediately it should be clear -- seemingly --
that each man should get, in order to insure justice,
one-fifth of the proceeds of the sale, that is, one-
fifth of $5,500 or $1,100.

But there is a critical question: <u>when</u> is each
man, who will participate, to do his work? And
which man (or men) will have his own way regarding
whether he works the first year, or the fifth year,
or any other year?

Some thought on that question will result in
readers finally answering the question in this
manner: "I myself would prefer to work the fifth
year, because then I must wait only to the end of
my work-year for my $1,100; I least prefer working
the first year, because then I must wait five years
for my $1,100."

The foregoing is standard; all five men, then,
will naturally wish to work the last year; none,
the first year. Böhm-Bawerk shows that <u>real</u>
justice -- not the mere word, justice -- will require (under an originary interest rate assumption
of 5%) payments to these five men as follows:

First worker, who waits	five years for pay:	$1,200
Second " " "	four " " " :	1,150
Third " " "	three " " " :	1,100
Fourth " " "	two " " " :	1,050
Fifth " " "	one " " " :	1,000
	Total	$5,500

Readers should now have less difficulty understanding Böhm-Bawerk's analysis, which follows
directly; the Rodbertus referred to in the text is
the well-known German socialist, previously mentioned,. whom Böhm-Bawerk is refuting.

**Böhm-Bawerk's Explanation Which
Shows That Justice Requires Originary
Interest In A Socialist Society**

B] Rodbertus's next thesis is that by the laws of nature and according to the "idea of pure justice" the entire product, having been produced by the worker alone, must belong to the worker, or in lieu of it,
its full value without deduction. I am fully in accord with this thesis,
too, since under the terms of the limiting presupposition which I stipu-
lated before, there can be no question of its correctness and its fairness.
But I do think that Rodbertus and all the other socialists have a false
conception of the realization of this truly just principle. Misled by that
misconception they desire the creation of a condition which is not in
accordance with the principle, but directly opposed to it. I consider it
remarkable that the numerous attempts that have been made hitherto
to refute the exploitation theory have touched on this decisive point only
superficially at best, but never presented it in its true light. I shall therefore
take the liberty of requesting my readers to devote some measure of
attention to the following development of the point. This difficult subject certainly requires it.

The error that I censure I shall first name and then elucidate. The
completely just proposition that the worker is to receive the entire value
of his product can reasonably be interpreted to mean either that he is
to receive the full *present* value of his product *now* or that he is to get

the entire *future* value in the *future*. But Rodbertus and the socialists interpret it to mean that the worker is to receive the entire *future* value of his product *now*. At the same time they act as if that were entirely self-evident and the only possible interpretation of that proposition.

Let us illustrate the matter by a concrete example. Let us imagine that the production of a good, for instance a steam engine, costs five years' labor, and that the completed machine commands a price of $5,500. Let us further ignore for the moment that in actual practice the labor is distributed among many workers, and imagine that a single workman produces the machine by five years' continuous labor. Now let us ask what wage is due him in the sense of the proposition that the worker is to receive his whole product, or the full value of his product. There cannot be a moment's doubt that the answer is the whole steam engine or $5,500. But *when*? On that score, too, there can be no slightest doubt. Obviously at the expiration of five years. For by the laws of nature he cannot receive the steam engine before it is in existence, cannot gain possession of a good valued at $5,500 and created by himself, before he has created it. In that case he will have received his compensation according to the formula, "the whole future product, or its whole future value at a future time."

But it often happens that the worker cannot or will not wait until his product has been fully completed. Our worker wishes, for instance, after the expiration of one year to receive a corresponding partial compensation. The question arises, as to how that is to be measured in accordance with the aforementioned principle. I think this, too, can be settled without a moment's hesitation. The worker will get justice if he gets all that he has labored to produce up to this point. If, for instance, he has up to this time produced a pile of unfinished ore, or of iron, or of steel material, then he will be justly treated if he receives the pile of ore, of iron, or of steel, or receives the full exchange value which this pile of material has, and of course has *now*. I do not think any socialist could find fault with that decision.

How large will that value be, in relation to the price of the finished machine? Here is the point at which a superficial thinker can easily go wrong. The worker has up to this time performed a fifth of the technical work which the production of the entire machine demands. Accordingly, a superficial consideration of the problem might tempt us to answer, the present product will possess an exchange value of one-fifth of that of the whole product, that is to say, $1,100. The worker is to receive a year's wage of $1,100.

That is wrong. One thousand one hundred dollars is one-fifth of the price of a completed, present steam engine. But what the worker has produced up to this time is not one-fifth of a machine that is already finished, but only one-fifth of a machine which will not be finished for another four years. And those are two different things. Not different by a sophistical splitting of verbal hairs, but actually different as to the thing itself. The former fifth has a value different from that of the latter fifth, just as surely as a complete present machine has a different value in terms of present valuation from that of a machine that will not be available for another four years. And it will be so, just as surely as it is true in general that present goods have a value different from that of future goods.

That present goods have a higher value, in the esteem of that present in which the economic events take place, than future goods of the same kind and quality, belongs to the most widely known and most important economic facts. The causes to which this fact owes its origin, the multifarious variations in which it is manifested, and the equally multifarious consequences to which it leads in economic life, will be the subject of detailed investigation in the second volume of this work. That investigation will be neither so easy nor so simple as the simplicity of the basic idea might lead us to expect. But even before I have completed that investigation, I think it justifiable to rely on the fact, as a fact, that present goods do have a higher value than identical future goods. The crudest empirical tests of everyday life establish it beyond any question of a doubt. If you ask 1,000 persons to choose between a gift of $1,000 today and $1,000 50 years from today all 1,000 of them will prefer to have it today. Or ask another 1,000 persons who are in need of a car, and who would be willing to pay $2,000 for a good one, how much they would give today for an equally good car to be delivered in 10 or 15 years. All of them would offer a far smaller sum, if indeed they offered anything at all, thus demonstrating that people, when acting economically, universally regard present goods as more valuable than identical future goods.

Accordingly our worker at the end of a year's work on the steam engine that will be finished in another four years has not yet earned the entire value of one-fifth of a completed engine. He has earned some smaller amount. Smaller by how much? I cannot at this point explain that without a lot of awkward anticipation. Let the remark suffice here that the amount of that difference bears an ascertained relationship to the rate of interest prevailing in the locality as well as to the remoteness of the time at which the whole product is scheduled to be completed. If I assume a prevailing interest rate of 5% then the product of the first year's labor will, at the end of the first year, be worth about $1,000. And so, if the principle is valid that the worker is entitled to the full produce of his labor, or to the entire value thereof, then the wage for the first year of labor will amount to $1,000.

If anyone has the impression, in spite of the line of reasoning laid down above, that this is too little, I offer the following for consideration. No one will question the statement that the worker is not being underpaid if at the end of five years he receives the whole steam engine or its whole price of $5,500. Let us for the sake of comparison also compute the price of the anticipated payment of wages in terms of its price at the end of the fifth year. Since the $1,000 that he receives at the end of the first year can be deposited for another four years at interest he can thus earn interest at 5% for four years. That is to say, he can receive an additional $200 (ignoring the compounding of interest) for the possibility of using his money that way is open to the worker when he has received his wage. Obviously then, $1,000 paid at the end of the first year is the equivalent of $1,200 paid at the end of the fifth year. So if the worker gets $1,000 at the end of a year for one-fifth of the technical work, he is clearly being compensated by a standard which is not less favorable than if he had received $5,500 at the expiration of five years.

But how do Rodbertus and the socialists envision the principle that the worker is entitled to receive the entire value of his product? They demand that the entire value which the product is going to have when completed shall be used for payment of wages, but not at the conclusion of the whole process of production, but made available in installments during the course of the work. Let us weigh carefully what that means. That means, in the case of our steam engine, that the entire $5,500 which the engine will be worth at the end of five years, is received by the worker at the end of 2½ years, which is the result attained by averaging the installments received over five years. I must confess I find it absolutely impossible to justify this demand by that premise. How can it be according to the laws of nature and in keeping with the idea of pure justice, for someone to receive at the end of 2½ years a whole which he will not have created until the end of five years? This is so little "in accord with the laws of nature" that it is, quite on the contrary, just naturally impracticable. It is not feasible even if we free the worker from all the bonds of his much maligned wage contract, and put him into the most favorable conceivable position of an entrepreneur entirely "on his own." As a worker and entrepreneur he will of course get the whole $5,500, but not before they are produced, that is to say, not before the end of five years. And how is a thing to be brought to pass, in the name of the idea of pure justice, through the instrumentality of the wage contract, which the nature of things denies to the entrepreneur himself?

What the socialists want is, in plain English, for the workers to get under the wage contract, *more* than their work produces, more than they could get if they were entrepreneurs in business for themselves, and more than they bring in to the entrepreneur with whom they have made the wage contract. What they have created, and what they are justly entitled to is $5,500 at the end of five years. But the $5,500 at the end of 2½ years, which is what is being claimed for them, is more than that; in fact if the interest rate is 5%, it is equivalent to about $6,200 at the end of five years. And this state of relative valuations is not, mind you, the result of social institutions of debatable merit which have created interest and established a rate of 5%. It is a direct result of the fact that we humans live out our lives in a temporal world, that our Today with its needs and cares comes before our Tomorrow, and that our Day-After-Tomorrow may perhaps not be assured us at all. Not only the "profit grasping capitalist," but every worker as well, indeed every human being makes this difference between present value and future value. How the worker would complain of being cheated, if in place of $10 out of his week's wages which are due today he were offered $10 to be paid a year from today! And is something that is not a matter of indifference to the worker supposed to be such to the entrepreneur? Is he to pay $5,500 at the end of 2½ years for $5,500 which he is to receive, in the shape of a finished steam engine, at the end of five? That is neither just nor natural! The thing that is just and natural—I am glad to concede it again—is that the worker should receive the whole $5,500 at the end of five years. If he cannot or will not wait five years, he shall still receive the entire value of what he produces. But of course it must be the *present* value of his *present* product. This value however will necessarily be smaller than the future value of the product which his labor produces, because in the economic world the law obtains that the present value of future goods is less than that of present goods. It is a law which owes its existence to no social or governmental institution, but directly to human nature and to the nature of things.

If there is any excuse for discursiveness anywhere, it might be at this point where it is a question of the confutation of a doctrine as pregnant with possibilities as is the socialist exploitation theory. And so, at the risk of seeming tedious to my readers, I shall submit a second concrete case which will, I hope, afford me an opportunity of proving the socialists' error even more convincingly.

In our first example I ignored the fact that division of labor is an economic actuality. Now I shall change the conditions of the problem in this respect so as to approach the realities of economic life more closely. Let us assume that five different workers participate in the labor of producing a machine, and that each of them contributes one year's work. One worker, perhaps, is a miner who procures the necessary ore, the second prepares the iron from it, the third transforms the iron into steel, the fourth constructs the necessary steel parts, the fifth finally assembles these and, in general, does the finishing. Since each of these successive workers, by the nature of his work, cannot begin his work until the one before him has completed his preparatory stage of the work, the five years' work of our laborers cannot be carried on simultaneously, but only in succession. The completion of the machine, just as in our first example, will likewise take five years. The value of the machine we shall again assume to be $5,500. Now, in conformity with the principle that the worker is to receive the full price of what he produces, what can each of the five who share the labor claim for what he accomplishes?

Let us first solve the problem for a case in which there is no introduction of an outside entrepreneur, and in which therefore the claims to compensation, or the method of dividing the article produced need to be adjusted only among the five workmen. In such a case two things are certain.

The *first* of these is that a distribution of the product itself cannot take place *until the expiration of five years,* because before that time there is nothing there to divide. For if there were any desire, at the end of the second year let us say, to distribute to the individuals as compensation the ore and the iron that had been produced in the first two years, then the raw materials would be lacking for the succeeding stages. On the contrary, it is clear that the intermediary product that is achieved each year must be excluded from any early distribution and retained for the production process until its conclusion.

The *second* thing that is certain is that there will be a total of $5,500 to be distributed among the five workers. But in what proportions?

Certainly not, as one might easily suppose at a first—and superficial —glance, in equal fifths! For that would mean a distribution favoring the worker whose labor is performed in later stages, over those whose work was done early. The worker who puts the finishing touches on the machine would receive $1,100 for his year's work immediately after its conclusion. The one who prepared the individual parts for assembling into the complete machine would receive the same amount, but would have to wait a whole year after he had completed his work to collect his compensation for it. And then there is the extreme case of the worker who mined the ore, and who would not receive his wage until four years after he had completed his work. Since a delay of that sort could not possibly be a matter of indifference to the persons concerned, everyone would want to perform the final labor, which does not suffer any postponment of compensation, and no one would want to assume the work of the preparatory stages. In order to find anyone to assume those jobs, the workers in the late stages would be compelled to consent to an arrangement by which a larger portion of the ultimate exchange value of the product would be accorded to their co-workers in the preparatory stages, to compensate them for the delay. The amount of the difference would depend partly on the length of the postponement, and partly on the degree of difference in the valuation of present and future goods which prevails within our small society, as determined by the economic and cultural conditions which exist there. If the degree of that difference is, for instance, 5% per year, then the shares of the five workers would be graduated as shown below.

The first worker, whose wage is not paid to him until
    four years after the completion of his year's labor,
    receives $1,200
The second, who waits three years   1,150
The third, who waits two years   1,100
The fourth, who waits one year   1,050
The last, who receives his wage immediately upon com-
    pletion of his labor   1,000
                                                 Total $5,500

It would be inconceivable that each of the workers should receive
an equal share of $1,100, except under the hypothesis that the difference
in time is a matter of indifference to them. It would be conceivable only
if they all considered themselves equally well paid at $1,100, no matter
whether they received that sum three or four years later, or immediately
after finishing their labors. I hardly need to observe that such a hypothesis never holds, and never can hold. But in the absence of the introduction of a third party it is in any case *completely impossible for each
of them to receive $1,100 immediately after completion of his labors.*

It is probably worth while in passing to call special attention to
one circumstance. I do not think that anyone could find the distribution
plan that I have recorded above an unjust one. And I am especially
convinced that, since the workers share their own product only with
each other, there can be no contention that there has been an injustice
done by a capitalist entrepreneur. And yet the worker who completed
the next-to-last fifth does not receive a full fifth of the ultimate price of
the product. He gets only $1,050, and the last worker caps the climax
by receiving only $1,000!

Now let us make the further assumption, with which reality is ordinarily in agreement, that the workers cannot or will not wait for their
wages until the process of producing the machine has been completed.
That leads to their entering into an agreement with an entrepreneur
whereby they will receive their wage immediately upon completion of
their labor, in return for which he is to become the owner of the final
product. Now let us make the still further assumption that this entrepreneur is an entirely just and unselfish man, who would be thoroughly
incapable of making use of any possible distress to which the workers
might be a prey, in order to depress by extortionate measures their
claims to wages. Let us ask what the conditions would be of a wage
contract drawn up and signed under such circumstances.

The answer is fairly easy to find. Obviously the workers are being
treated with complete justice if the entrepreneur offers them as a wage
the same as they would have received as their distributive shares, had
they been engaged in independent production. This principle gives us
a reliable standard for one worker, to begin with, namely, the last of
the five. The latter would have received $1,000 immediately after per-
forming his work. So the entrepreneur, to be completely fair, must offer
him the same $1,000. But the rest of our table of shares does not give
us any direct standard. For since the point of time at which compensation is made is now different from the one that would have applied in
the case of their own distribution of shares, the amounts set up for the
latter would no longer be directly applicable. However, we have another
firm criterion. For since all five workers have contributed the same
amount of service toward the genesis of the product, they are in justice
entitled to equal wages. And since each one is paid immediately after
he has completed his labors, the wages will be equal sums. Justice is
served if each worker receives $1,000 at the end of his year's labor.

If anyone should think that that is too little, I refer him to the following easy example in arithmetic. It will prove that the workers now receive exactly the same amount as they would have received through a distribution among themselves—and that amount was shown to be indubitably just. Worker No. 5 receives $1,000 from the distribution, immediately after the end of the year's work, and in the case of the wage contract he receives the same amount at the same time. Worker No. 4 receives $1,050 through the distribution, one year after his work is completed; in the case of the wage contract he receives $1,000 immediately after his work is completed. Now if he puts that out at interest for a year, he achieves exactly the same position that he would have in the case of the distribution, for he then has $1,050 one year after completing his work. Worker No. 3 receives by the distribution $1,100 two years after his work ends, by the wage contract $1,000 immediately which, put out at interest, amounts to the same $1,100 at the same time. In the same way the $1,000 which the first and second workers receive under the wage contract, with the addition of interest are exactly equal to the $1,200 and the $1,150 which, under the distribution, would have been received after four and three years respectively. And if each of the individual wage sums is the equivalent of the corresponding distributional share, then the aggregate of the wage sums must be the equivalent of the aggregate of all the distributional shares. Hence the total of $5,000 which the entrepreneur pays immediately upon performance of the labor to the workers is the exact equivalent of the $5,500 which, in the other case, could have been distributed among the workers at the end of the fifth year.

Any higher wage, such as a yearly wage of $1,100, would be conceivable only under one of two alternatives. Either something to which the workers are not indifferent, namely the difference in time, would have to be a matter of complete indifference to the entrepreneur, or the entrepreneur would have to have the desire to make a gift to the workers of the difference between $1,100 in present funds and $1,100 in future funds. Neither the one alternative nor the other is to be expected of the private entrepreneur, at least not as a rule. Nor could one make it a matter of the slightest reproach, and least of all would it justify a charge of injustice, exploitation, or predacity. There is only one person of whom the workers could expect such behavior as a regular thing, and that is the *state*. For the state is, on the one hand, an entity that exists in perpetuity, and is not therefore compelled to take such strict account of the temporal difference in the giving and receiving of goods. And the state, whose ultimate purpose is the welfare of all its members, can, on the other hand, afford to give instead of to bargain. And so it would concededly be thinkable for the state—but *only* the state in its capacity of giant entrepreneur in the production field—to offer the workers a wage representing the entire future product of their future production and to give it to them *now*, that is to say, immediately after the performance of their labor. Whether the state shall or shall not do so, and thereby afford a practical solution of the social problem in terms of socialist doctrine, is a question of expediency, which it cannot be my purpose to discuss here. But one thing I should like to repeat here and with all possible emphasis, and that is this. If the socialist state pays out now to the workers, as wages, the entire future exchange value of their product, then that is not a *fulfillment but a violation* of the fundamental principle that the worker is entitled to receive as his wage the value of what he produces. And it is a deviation dictated by social and political considerations, rather than the restoration, as the socialists allege, of a situation which of itself is natural or which accords with the idea of pure justice, but has been upset through the avidity of the capitalists for exploitation. On the contrary, it is an artificial interference intended to render possible what in the natural course of things is an impossibility, and to make it possible by means of a veiled and perpetual gift by a generous communal entity known as the state, a gift granted to its more penurious members.

And now a short practical application. It is easily perceived that the stage of distribution which I last described in our example, is the one at which we have actually arrived in our market economy. In this system too, the full value of the product of labor is not distributed as wages, but only a lesser sum, though at an earlier point in time. But the worker suffers no unjust curtailment in his claim to the full amount of what he produces, provided one condition is fulfilled, and that condition provides as follows. The total sum of wages distributed in installments must not fall short of the ultimate price of the final product by a greater amount than is necessary to bridge the gap representing the prevailing difference in the valuation of present and future goods. In other words, the total wages must not be exceeded by the price of the final product to a greater degree than is represented by the prevailing interest rate. The workers in that case receive the full value of their product at a valuation which duly reflects the point in time at which they receive their wage. Only to the extent that·the total wage lags behind the ultimate exchange value of the product by a margin in excess of the prevailing interest can that lag, under some circumstances, indicate genuine exploitation of the workers.

Let us return to Rodbertus. The second decisive error with which I charged him in the immediately preceding pages was his interpretation of the statement that the worker is entitled to receive the entire value of his product. I conceded the correctness of the statement but not of his unjustified and illogical interpretation, to the effect that the worker is entitled to receive *now* the entire exchange value which his completed product *will some day have.*

A careful reader will realize that in the foregoing the reasoning of Böhm-Bawerk is "as tight as a drum," and is indeed irrefragable.

Therefore, in a **just** socialist society the exact equivalent of origin**ary** interest will exist openly or disguisedly, because **time** will have the same meaning in a socialist society that it has in a capitalist society.

Karl Marx's Fallacious Argument
On The Origin Of "Value"

Karl Marx declared that the value of goods and services should depend on the amount of labor in them. If there was much labor in a product, the price should be high; if little labor, the price should be low. He averred: nothing should be paid for except labor. This is, obviously, another way

of saying two things: (1) any natural resources,
as for example iron, should not be paid for because
iron should be a community resource; and (2) nothing should be paid for originary interest --
interest, rent and profit in the narrow sense.
These ideas sound plausible and reasonable, but
they are unsound.

Marx's idea can be compared to that of the five-
year-old child of a man whose wife was experiencing
the pains of childbirth for the second baby. Not
knowing what to do in the early hours of the morn-
ing with the five-year-old, the parents decided
that they and the child would all go to the hospital.
Father and child waited in the waiting room on the
obstetrical floor.

The hospital was inadequately insulated for sound
and the little girl heard ear-piercing screams of
her mother come echoing down the hall.

As the day began to dawn the nurse came to tell
the father that a baby son was born and that mother
and baby were fine. Later when the little girl saw
her brother she said to her mother: "When I grow
up then I shall scream too in order to get a baby."
In short, the cause or origin of babies, according
to the child, was the mother's screams.

Similarly, it was Marx's idea that labor creates
value. But Marx was as wrong as was the little girl.
The disturbing thing is that many people believe
the same thing that Marx believed (or said he believed; it is hard to understand that Marx could
have considered his view to be correct or believable).
Screams do not produce babies, and labor does not
create value. Both are equally fallacious. Indeed,
getting babies <u>can</u> be associated with screams, and
value <u>can</u> be associated with labor; but the association is not one with labor as cause of value, or
screams as cause of babies.

Marx was painstakingly refuted by Böhm-Bawerk
in his essay, "The Unresolved Contradiction in the
Marxian System," in <u>Shorter Classics of Böhm-Bawerk</u>
(Libertarian Press, South Holland, Illinois, USA,
1962).

But it is not necessary to follow Böhm-Bawerk's
complex argument, in his pursuit of the subtleties
that Marx had fabricated. Simple common sense will
make clear that the Marxian proposition is false.
Our argument can revert to the mother's screams and
the ideas of the five-year-old.

Something else had occurred (<u>before</u> the screams) which really produced the baby. Both father and mother knew that the screams were an effect, not a cause.

Exactly similarly something other than labor creates value, and that something other is also antecedent to any labor whatever. The two antecedent causes of value are (1) a <u>need</u> and a <u>demand</u> for the product, and (2) a <u>scarcity</u> of the product.

1. Suppose a man slaves to make what is neither useful nor beautiful nor wanted by anybody. Suppose the maker cannot give it away. Has his labor produced "value"? Indeed not.

2. Suppose, however, that what he produces has utility, namely, a pump for a water well. A person might be expected to want a pump and well in order to <u>get</u> water. But suppose at a particular location that there is a wonderful mountain stream right along side the house, and a whole lake below. Of all the things this person needs, the last is any more water; that is, there is no <u>scarcity</u> of water. The pump is then valueless, in this case. (A similar surplus of water may not exist elsewhere, and then the pump may have high value.)

What a man and woman are to babies, demand and scarcity are to value.

In the ultimate analysis, all value rests on demand <u>only</u>. It is competing demands which control the "distribution" of labor to various products. On-what-products-labor-is-spent is therefore an effect and not a cause; Marx made the error of declaring that labor was the cause of value, whereas he should have said that labor (1) is put forth, and (2) is allocated where it is allocated because we (1) need something (2) not in adequate supply unless labor is applied.

For the complete and lengthy and intricate problems involved, see the works of Carl Menger, Böhm-Bawerk and Mises (in the order mentioned).

There is such a thing as grossly overvaluing labor, in the Marxian sense; Scripture does not make that mistake anywhere. If a person has appreciation for logic, he cannot be a socialist. As the French expression goes: "There is something wrong with the heart of a young man who is not a socialist, and something wrong with the head of an old man who is a socialist."

Originary Interest Is Not Subtracted
From Anybody; A Believed-To-Exist
Value Was Never There!

The explanation previously given for the way originary interest will come into being, even in a socialist society, points to the answer to the question: who pays for originary interest?

The answer is, NOBODY. The fallacy involved is hidden in the gross but natural self-deception that value is unaffected by time differences. The man who seems to be adversely affected, but is not, is the man who wishes to be paid _before_ his product is ready. That proposition is worthy of some elaboration.

Production takes time; distribution through wholesale and retail channels takes time; and slowly "consumed" capital goods must be priced to allow for their wearing out only gradually. (See Böhm-Bawerk's CAPITAL AND INTEREST, Volume II entitled _Positive Theory of Capital_, especially pages 259-341.)

Karl Marx, and others, are right that there are, in the final analysis, presently two participants in the proceeds of production and distribution, namely,

1.   The laborer (who has been getting about
     89%, as mentioned in Chapter 29 in this
     section); and

2.   Whoever helps to PREPAY the laborer in
     the long time of production which exists
     in a complex and economically advanced
     society. (The folk who make this "advance"
     in the United States get about 11% of the
     total. However, this fraction is greater
     than the pure originary interest, as it
     also consists, in part, of profits from
     greater foresight and operating skill
     than competition possesses, insurance
     for risks, etc.)

Marx did not wish anything to go to the person who "prepaid." Again, see the works of Böhm-Bawerk and Mises.

Savers And Investors Constitute The
Group Who Enable Prepayment To The
Laborer, Whose Product Is Not
Immediately Available For Consumption

It will be helpful to consider who are the "pre-
payers." The answer is: the savers, but an elaboration of that should be helpful.

Basically, the five socialists building the steam
engine mentioned earlier in this chapter had to be
"supported" by the necessaries of life -- food,
clothing, shelter, etc.

A saver who buries his savings (money) in the
ground would not be contributing toward creating
the "stock" of goods on which this five-man, five-
year project to build a steam engine would have to
draw.

It is well to supplement the word savers with
the word investors. A man who buries his savings
is a saver but not an investor. (It may be wise
at times to bury your savings, but there is no
"income" from that, nor does it basically help
society.) Practically all saving is investing.

A rich society is one that is "organized" by
everybody participating in a grand production plan,
preferably of their own free will. The net result
is that there is approximately the right amount of
reserves of food, clothing, fuel, etc. These stocks
are in all stages of preparation -- raw materials,
goods-in-process and finished goods. No single
mind could plan it comprehensively, but every man
plans as well as he can for himself, and the over-
all result is that there is in a rich capitalist
society a mighty stream of goods becoming available
to "carry" our five steam engine builders until
their engine is ready, can be sold, and they can
use the proceeds to pay their bills, and then go to
work on additional production. It is fantastic how
well this seemingly unplanned, but in fact painstakingly planned, system works.

But is there never miscalculation? Are such miscalculations major or minor? What causes miscalculations?

Of course there are miscalculations, for example
on foodstuffs, if there is a crop failure. There
are miscalculations if there are earthquakes, storms,
pestilences. Except locally, these are minor miscalculations now, since good transportation has

opened up all areas to help to assist to make
necessary adjustments.

There may today be a major miscalculation because of world-wide war.

That Calamitous Cause Of Miscalcu-
lations, Which Cause Lies At The
Root Of Booms And Depressions

But the most important major miscalculation
results from an inappropriate rate of interest,
and its resultant effect on miscalculation by
planners who rely on the basic rate on loans to inform them of the real originary interest rate. A
brief statement may prove to be unforceful, but it
can serve at least as an affirmation.

A low rate of interest will naturally stimulate
expansion of business and fixed assets; a high rate
will do the reverse. In a complex society as in the
United States, a difference of one percent in the
interest rate has a big effect on plans regarding
the "stream of goods," by which stream of goods is
meant society's inventory on which to live while
production takes time -- moving along like a giant
river or glacier.

A low interest rate will indicate a large stream;
a high interest rate, a much smaller stream.

To force an unnaturally low interest rate will
make plans go awry; similarly, to force an unnaturally high interest rate. Society's stream of goods
is deceivingly indicated then by any unrealistic
interest rate.

Today, governments all over the world are meddling and tinkering with interest rates. They "sense"
that thereby they can influence plans. They want
booms, not mere prosperity. Therefore they tinker
with interest rates through their central banks and
their own fiscal policies, in order to have the rate
of interest lower than the real market rate, which
is based on the specific plans of individual savers
and dis-savers. An interest rate lower than the
populace's "discount of the future" results in an
unsound boom, based on the illusion that the plans
are "in gear" at that rate.

There is, therefore, in the present-day so-called
capitalist world a systematically disorganizing
factor in the form of interferring with the "natural"
rate of interest.

Society's progress largely depends on production becoming more and more long-term in order to become more efficient (productive). Of course, short-term plans can hardly be of major consequence; but long-term plans can (and should) develop massive proportions. Therefore, in a modern capitalist society there is a disorganizing factor in proportion as there is major "forcing" of interest rates. Then huge and long-term plans go awry; first there is a boom; then a depression. Both are undesirable and unnecessary. In a society as complex as that in the Western world in the latter half of the twentieth century booms and depressions are calamitous.

The interest rate is the most important "price" in the world. That is why rogues and fools devote more effort to influencing interest rates artificially than to all other business iniquities put together.

(This subject will be discussed in greater detail in Chapters 34 to 38.)

**The Two Different Ways That
Interest Is Computed Is Logical
But Confusing To Many**

The way that originary interest shows up often appears "inverted" and confusing to the average person. Originary interest has been explained to be a compensation to allow for the human good sense to "discount the future." One way that this is done is to take the price in the present time as a base; in order to make the price in the future equal in "value" to the present price something must be added to the future price in order to make it equivalent to the present price. If $100 worth of merchandise becomes available only after a year, then $5 must be added to the present value of $100 so that we end up with $105 after the lapse of a year being worth the equivalent of $100 now; (this assumes a 5% rate). The equation reads: $100 now = $105 one year in the future.

Naturally, it is possible to reverse the calculation by asking what is the present value of $100 a year from now. The answer to that is obtained by dividing $100 by 1.05 (assuming a prevailing discount rate of 5%); $100 ÷ 1.05 = $95.24, which is the _present_ value of $100 available a year hence. Then the equation reads: $95.24 now = $100 one year in the future.

Longer-term Production Is Generally
More Productive Than Short-Term

But someone may ask, if capitalistic production
which increases the time required to produce adds
to the cost, then it would be profitable to revert
back to short-time production methods. This is not
correct, because capitalistic (longer-term) production greatly increases productivity. This originally amply offsets the originary interest "addition"
or "discount" as just explained.

However, capitalistic (longer-term) production
is sure to expand to the point where the productivity
of the last unit of capital supplied just covers
the 5% originary interest rate (or whatever at a
given time and place the originary interest rate
may be). In other words, the greater productivity
of longer-term production enables the payment of
originary interest, but the origin -- the real
cause -- of originary interest is founded on dis-
count for delay in time.

Errors Of Capitalist Thinkers
On The Origin Of Interest

There are various logical errors made by capitalist thinkers (as distinguished from socialist thinkers) some of which it will be desirable to signalize,
although it will not be feasible to elaborate.

Traditional capitalist thinkers affirm that it
is the productivity of capital which explains and
justifies interest. See the analysis of the paralo-
gisms of traditional apologists for originary interest in Böhm-Bawerk's Volume I, Chapters IV through
XI. Justifications long employed by capitalist
thinkers are lamentably weak.

Böhm-Bawerk makes the important point that the
market evaluation of any greater productivity capability results in a higher price being placed on
the productive capability in question. A wonderfully designed machine that costs little to make
but which increases productivity 100% will not (long)
yield the owner 100%. This is true for a variety
of reasons. The fundamental one is that a machine
of such increased productivity will immediately be
priced higher, by many multiples, compared with
what it cost to make.

Then the yield is back to the basic originary

interest rate (here assumed to be 5%). This explanation is too brief to be readily understood and
therefore to be effective in destroying the customary capitalist justification for unearned income,
but further elaboration is not appropriate here.
See the works of Böhm-Bawerk and Mises.

The Price/Earnings Ratio And Its Significance

In the stock market and in other markets where
productive equipment or natural resources are
evaluated, veteran operators are accustomed to say,
"the most important factor in pricing stocks (or
other facilities) is the price/earnings ratio."
What something is worth as capital depends, basically, on what it will earn annually.

Something that will indefinitely yield $5 net a
year is priced as worth $100 as capital. This is
similar to the previous statement that a farm that
yields $4,000 net a year to the owner will be priced,
by discounting the future, at $80,000. (See page
205.)

The real explanation of the price of $80,000 for
a farm yielding $4,000 net a year is given in First
Principles In Morality And Economics, Volume VI,
pages 267-275. This is what is involved: An
originary interest rate shows in how many years
savers and investors in general want their full
capital back, after allowing for their discount of
the future.

The fact is that the distinction between capital
and income is basically confusing. Capital is
really a "flow of income in the future." It is the
term capital which is almost an unlucky abstraction.
One definition of capital, put forth here to elucidate the ideas involved, is that capital is the
present lower value in a lump sum of a larger future
stream of income. Penetrating thinkers in the field
of economics realize that it is the future income
discounted, which establishes today's capital value.

Capitalists Do Not Get A Return Equal To The Productivity Of The Tools They Provide

Capitalistic, longer-time production enormously
enhances production -- say, on the average today,
200%. (Compare production in the United States

with production in noncapitalistic countries.)
"Power" -- steam, electrical, mechanical -- and
"tooling," etc., accomplish that.

Do then the owners of the tools get a return of
200%? They certainly do not. They on the average
get a comparatively paltry 5%. Why do not the
owners of capital, which has increased production
so enormously (200%), get only 5%?

This is considered in the second chapter following.

Summary

The phenomena of originary interest do   not
rob the laborer; he still gets ALL that he has produced. What the man who provides advance payments
gets is merely an offset for differences in valuations. That which is available only after a lapse
of time is worth less than the same thing now.

The mechanism for equating between present and
future prices consists in adding the originary
interest rate, which we have here used at 5% per
annum; in other words, $100 now = $105 a year from
now.

That is exactly the same thing as saying that the
hundred individual dollar bills available a year
from now are worth only 95.24 cents each now. The
discount for time for the future bills was 4.76
cents on each single bill.

This discount (at varying rates) exists under
free capitalism.

A similar discount (at varying rates) must exist,
equally for justice   sake, under socialism.

This discount exists also under isolated, individual production. An isolated farmer can produce
something for immediate consumption worth $100; but
he will not divert himself from producing that product quickly, by using instead a longer production
method, yielding the same amount a year from now.
He will want 105 units a year from now to justify
the slow way to produce. The mere time difference
explains this. The isolated producer will take the
longer time only if he can gain 105 units in the
future versus 100 units now. (This assumes a 5%
originary interest rate.)

The simple fact is: the time discount is
<u>universal</u>, <u>because</u> <u>men</u> <u>are</u> <u>mortal</u>.

1.   Finally, to interfere with the free-market
originary interest rate by <u>eliminating</u> the discount
for the future would mean that men would receive
more value for their labor than they produce.   To
get now what will be available only in the future
is to want more than is <u>currently</u> being produced.
Only coercion (as by communism) can establish and
hold upright such an order for society.

2.   To interfere with this interest rate, not
by eliminating it under tyranny, but only to the
extent of lowering the "discount for the future"
below its free-market level, results first in a
boom which lacks a sound base, and which thereafter
and therefore collapses in a depression.   Men become so disconcerted by the "business cycle" that
they turn more and more to tyranny to escape its
repetition.   One of the seed-beds of socialism-
communism is the bewilderment created by booms and
depressions.   (See later chapters, beginning with
Chapter 34.)

N O T E

Is all this vital to ethics?   The answer is an
unqualified <u>Yes</u>.   The questions here discussed are
fundamental to one of the most controversial moral
issues in the modern world.

Interest Versus Usury

Legislation by Moses in the Old Testament against interest is against loans to the poor <u>only</u>, which exposed those folk extraordinarily to exploitation by the lender. The assumption in Scripture never is that the loans in question would be business loans, on which a borrower could expect to make a greater return than the cost of the interest.

The unsuccessful attempt to suppress loan interest which agitated the church for centuries was a consequence of "extensionism" in the interpretation of Scripture, instead of "strict constructionism"; it was a mistake to extend prohibitions on loans to the destitute, to loans for business (profit-making) purposes.

The church, however, never really condemned originary interest, because it did not undertake to condemn rents or profits. It was the socialists who "extended" the objection about loan interest to all unearned income. The church made an error on the first extension, from loans to needy persons to loans for business also; the socialists compounded the error by the further extension from loan interest to originary interest. (There is no phase of socialist ethics that can be reconciled with Hebrew-Christian ethics.)

Nevertheless, as by force of habit, churches today concern themselves still (although not conspicuously) about interest rates. Nearly all legislate or agitate against <u>usury</u>, by which is meant <u>excessive</u> loan interest. (And they also protest against rent <u>gougers</u> and <u>excessive</u> profits.)

These are clumsy remnants of the old objection to loan interest; it should probably be added that they are tainted somewhat with socialist ideas.

Churches are in fact generally incompetent to have an opinion in regard to what is a usurious interest rate, an excessive rent, or a so-called "profiteering" gain.

What is an <u>excessive</u> interest <u>rate</u>?

1. What if prices are being inflated 5% a year? (The interest rate should properly include a charge for this.)

2. What if serious political hazards in making
a loan or investment require an "insurance premium,"
in order to compensate for the risk of revolution
jeopardizing repayment, at the rate of 5% a year?

3. Suppose, too, that in the country involved
capital is scarce and the ordinary rate for (a) a
safe loan, (b) without there being inflationism,
is 8%.

Add those percentages together, 5% + 5% + 8%, and
you have a logical total rate of 18%! Excessive?
Not under those circumstances.

In any event, churchmen are not generally competent to pass on what is excessive or not excessive.
And circumstances alter cases.

In regard to excessive profits, they will be
discussed in the next chapter, but suffice it to
say here that from their very nature profits must
inevitably be variable in a free market -- which
means that sometimes they will be very high and at
other times very low or be replaced by losses. In
other words, the church's shift to opposing excessive profits is not impressively effective.

The issue of usury is an altogether different
subject from originary interest.

Originary interest arises only from the discounting of the future. Originary interest is a
part of, or fragment of, total interest.

The total interest charged always takes into
account risks of nonrepayment. If the risks are
high, a high insurance premium must be included in
the total interest rate. Further, if the loans are
small, and for a short period, there are relatively
high expenses for making and collecting the loan.
These, too, must be included in the total interest
charge, or else no lender will lend.

All in all the problems are so variable that
general rules are hard to formulate. The instinct
to protect the weak, foolish, and down-and-out is
sound. It is that instinct which underlay Moses's
rule. It is when his limited rule is extended from
personal loans to the destitute to business loans
to the rich and powerful that the meddling of the
church appears and is foolish.

The church was therefore right to shift from
originary interest to usury, but even usury prohibition can be applied properly by the church only
in the case of loans to the destitute and incompetent. But what the _rate_ should be in those cases,
in modern society, appears to be beyond the compe-
tence of a church to determine. There is, in fact,
no single rate that can apply. Under certain circumstances a 20% rate or higher might not be usury
in the sense that it would be appropriate to forbid it.

Details of usury problems are beyond the scope
of this book.

Competition Erodes Extraordinary Profits, But Not Originary Interest; Or (In Other Words) The Ethics Of The Hebrew-Christian Economic System And Capitalism Are "Socialistic" In Their "Distribution" Of The Proceeds Of Production To Those Who Participate In The Process

One way to divide economic problems and then consider their ethical aspects is to classify them (1) as production problems and (2) as distribution problems. What is here considered is distribution problems. The first question is: What is meant, in this connection, by distribution?

Distribution problems often (and in such connection properly) refer to problems of selling, including transportation, stocking, wholesale and retail pricing, sales promotion, advertising, credit granting, and other related problems. But that is not what is meant by the word, distribution, in this chapter.

Here distribution refers to the way the proceeds of cooperative human economic effort are divided between individuals; how much of the price to consumers does the inventor of the product get? the manufacturer? the workmen? sales people? wholesalers, retailers? suppliers of raw materials? lawyers? accountants? the government (by the collection of taxes)? the capitalist who advances money to pay participants before the merchandise is ready and finally paid for by consumers? and all others who obtain something of the final price? In economic theory, that is what is usually meant by problems of distribution.

This subject of distribution can be subdivided into questions of: (1) what is the distribution in fact; and (2) what ought the distribution to be, if that is different from existing distribution?

Economic Motives Alone Do Not Determine Ultimate Distribution

Free-market economics (based on what has been explained previously in Chapter 18 in this section) has its own simple answer: Each participant in

the operation should receive what he contributes;
and what he contributes is what his associates (not
he himself) think he is entitled to receive. Unless
somebody is to stand with the wisdom of a god or
the power of a dictator, and say what each is to
get, there is no other practical way to "distribute"
the proceeds of making and supplying consumers with
goods. Unless this procedure prevails, there will
be little real liberty left in the world. Further,
it conforms to Hebrew-Christian ethics because it
relies on each person exercising his own freedom.
But the foregoing statement remains ambiguous unless elucidated further, as is here proposed to be
done.

Almost without exception, nobody is willing to
accept that system unless there are modifications
to it. Nor do the principles of the Hebrew-Christian
religion permit accepting ultimately free market determination of "distribution" without modification.
The exception demanded by Hebrew-Christian ethics
is that charity (that is, almsgiving) should supplement the distribution based on productivity. Some
people cannot produce goods or serve society. For
reasons under their control, or beyond their control, they do not contribute enough, in the opinion
of buyers or users, toward making goods and services
available, to be paid enough in order to keep body
and soul together. These people require some kind
of help. The Hebrew-Christian religion says that
they should be given alms, voluntarily by the giver.
This restriction to voluntary gifts is certain to
make the lot of the needy hard, because men are
reluctant to support others. But whether adequate
or inadequate, voluntary almsgiving is a "correction"
or supplement of the "distribution" of the free
market, wonderful as the latter is, and benchmark
as that market is for "corrections" that are made.

In addition to voluntary almsgiving, some of the
other "corrections" of free market distribution are
as follows:

    1. By government
        a. Taxes, on a progressive-income-tax
           rather than straight-income-tax basis.
        b. Price controls.
        c. Patents.
        d. Tariffs, licenses, bounties, etc.

2. By lack of effective government disciplinary force

   a. Theft   )
   b. Deception) by "anti-social" individuals
   c. Coercion)

3. By friendship, caprice, nepotism, prejudice,
   reciprocity, ulterior motives, etc.

These make large alterations in the assumed
strictly economically motivated system.

The special purpose of this chapter is to show
that beyond charity, beyond taxes and government
controls, and beyond all nonmonetary motives for
altering the free-market distribution -- (1) the
actual distribution is not in proportion to contribution, and (2) that it should not be.

There is in the free-market "distribution" system,
and also in the Hebrew-Christian ethical system (even
aside from voluntary almsgiving), a powerful, pervasive leveling factor, so that great contributors
do not receive distribution fully proportionate to
their contribution to production. Capitalism -- a
free-market system -- tends to be "socialistic,"
that is, tends to equalize incomes. (Socialistic
here has a limited meaning of tending to equalize
incomes, one of the alleged objectives of socialism.)

There Are Three Differing Principles
According To Which To Distribute
The Proceeds of Cooperation

There are three premises, distinct from each
other, and inconsistent with each other, which under-
lie different positions in regard to distribution.

1. One principle is that a man should be rewarded by the extent of his labor, his fatigue, and
his boredom. This is the idea that pay should equal
the disutility of the work done. This is the idea
underlying Marxian socialism. In this case, productivity of the employee gets little attention. The
principle is that people should be rewarded for
their "blood, sweat and tears," or as the expression
goes in economics: they should be rewarded for the
disutility (to themselves) of their labor.

2. Another principle which is entirely different is that a man should be rewarded for his productivity, rather than for the extent and hardness
and wearisomeness of his work. Just as painfulness
of work appears worthy of consideration, so the
amount and utility of production appears worthy of
being considered, and even more so. Nevertheless,
men should not expect to be rewarded directly in
proportion to their contribution to productivity.
To expect a reward according to productivity looks
at the problem too much from the viewpoint of the
producer, just as those who think in terms of effort
(described in the preceding paragraph) wish society
to reward on the basis of fatigue. If one must
choose between rewarding on the basis of productivity
versus fatigue, then productivity is the better
basis. Still, it is genuinely unsatisfactory as
the real basis. Society must finally be "organized"
on the basis of the consumer. When naive capitalists look on _productivity_ as the basis for organizing society, their view is myopic.

3. In fact, society is organized on a third and
better principle. In matters of distribution it
disregards as much as it can either weariness or
productivity, and operates always to _get the most_
for the least. Clearly this is far from open-mouthed
admiration for strength or productivity. This is
a principle that says that society is organized on
the principle of _maximum utility to others_.

The claims of socialism based on _disutility of_
labor, and the hungry expectations of capitalists
based on _productivity_, must both make way for a
better principle, _marginal utility_, which cannot
afford to (and will not) reward on the basis of
either fatigue or productivity.

A Specific Example How Proceeds Of
New High Productivity Are Distributed

One way to state the problem, and to attempt to
find a correct solution, is to consider a specific
case; for example, farm implement manufacturing or
meat packing. The latter can serve well.

The facts in the case are the following:

1. Because fresh meat is perishable, it required
(from early history) that slaughtering be near the
place of consumption. That resulted in there being

no large slaughtering establishments; and only
local fresh meat peddling. (If anything was shipped
a long distance, it was the live animal. The man
who became the world's largest livestock slaughterer,
Gustavus Swift, originally slaughtered a cow or steer
in the afternoon and peddled the meat the next morn-
ing. This was in the town in New England in which
he lived as a young man.)

2. But "mechanical refrigeration" was invented
(as distinguished from refrigeration based on ice
cut from lakes in the winter, and put in ice houses
with sawdust insulation). This was revolutionary
eventually for the perishable food business, including meats. Livestock could now be slaughtered in
the agricultural Midwest, the carcasses dressed, the
cuts put in mechanical cold storage, and could then
be shipped in refrigerator cars, and put in coolers
or freezers in retail stores; finally, meat still
wholesome could be sold to consumers.

3. Mechanical refrigeration permitted an enormous reduction in costs. The first men fully to
realize that and to apply it were sure to make large
profits, quite out of the ordinary.

    a. It was not necessary to ship a live
       animal long distances, which distressed
       it, and shrank its weight.

    b. Slaughtering operations were moved to
       the center of livestock production.

    c. Mass production methods could be used
       to slaughter, dress and cut up the
       carcass products.

    d. By-products became available in quanti-
       ties permitting further processing and
       greater sales realization.

    e. Only the highly valuable products were
       subjected to long shipments and high
       freight charges.

    f. Inspection of the carcasses of slaughtered
       animals became feasible, and reduced the
       danger of human beings contracting cer-
       tain diseases, or becoming ill from con-
       sumption of meat of diseased animals.

These savings were so large that the end result was
that many local meat slaughterers went out of

business; meat packing developed into a giant and (temporarily) very profitable business in the Mid- west of the United States; farmers obtained higher prices for their livestock; packing house laborers earned more than they could have earned elsewhere or than the hired help of small slaughterers were paid; consumers obtained cheaper meat; many medicin- al products were developed from animal organs; and by-products generally were developed at lower costs and sold at lower prices than previously.

Analysis How Each Party At Interest Gained

No one acquainted with facts, as distinguished from being a propagandist or a sentimentalist, will dispute that. Such were the general, and widely dispersed gains. Benefits ranged from farmers to consumers, and included everybody inbetween. All parties at interest gained at once except those who were left behind in the more expensive, less utili- tarian older system (which it was against consumers' interests to retain). Eventually even those dis- placed persons, local slaughterers, because they were in an outmoded and expensive system, benefited from their own displacement. They were only tem- porarily "frictionally unemployed" but soon shifted to other production.

But the early large gainers were the men with the ability, courage, and vision to be the entre- preneurs pioneering in this new field, that is, the meat packers who became big.

Society will not go back to local slaughtering. Big meat packing is here to stay. Meat packing is presently (1964) a relatively unprofitable business; there is no rush into meat packing now. Nevertheless, there has been considerable critique that the early meat packers made too great profits, that they robbed farmers, exploited their employees, over- charged consumers. No one would undertake to de- fend every detail that occurred, but the system itself is worthy of unqualified defense. Let us consider alleged victims or beneficiaries one-by-one.

1. Farmers who sold livestock to slaughterers. They were accustomed to sell in the established way, to small slaughterers. They would continue to sell that way, unless a new buyer entered the scene who paid them more. Otherwise why would they change?

The growing meat packers in Chicago, St. Louis,
Omaha and elsewhere offered farmers more for livestock. Therefore, farmers diverted their sales to
the new buyers. The farmer was "ahead."

   2. Consumers who bought the various meat cuts
and carcass products. They were accustomed to buy
from a retail store or a peddler, who were local
slaughterers. Consumers naturally suspected that
products coming from the Midwest might not be so
wholesome. There was only one way to interest
east-coast consumers in Midwest-slaughtered products,
and that way was to lower the price to consumers.
The meat packers could get customers only by selling cheaper than the local slaughterers. The consumer was "ahead."

   3. Employees who came to work for the meat
packers. Meat packing happened to develop when
immigration into the United States was at a phenomenal height (that could not be indefinitely continued). People in Ireland, Lithuania, Poland, The
Netherlands and elsewhere in Europe were fleeing
bad living conditions to obtain improved conditions
in the United States. The question is: did they
better themselves? The answer is self-evident:
practically none went back; further, they nearly
all kept writing to friends and relatives still in
Europe: "Come on over; it is better here than
there." If the small slaughterers had offered more
wages, would not the immigrants have distributed
themselves among those small slaughterers? It is
not in accord with the facts to declare that the
humble employees of the growing packers were not
"ahead." The situation for packinghouse employees
has been caricatured by motivated and clever authors.

   4. The meat packers themselves, the capitalists,
constitute the fourth party at interest, and here
is where sentimentalists are inclined to be censor-
ious. Profits, they say, were conscienceless. That
is an error. Assume that the packers had passed
on all of their (temporarily) extraordinary profits
to farmers, consumers and employees. They would
then have had no funds with which to expand the
business. Nor would they have been able to borrow
funds on the outside with which to finance expansion;
lenders do not lend to a nonprofitable business.
The whole meat packing improvement would have been
like a baby that did not cry at birth -- stillborn --
dead. In order to expand the new operations fast,
profits just had to be large. To have reduced the
profits beyond the rate established by the free

market would have delayed proportionately the social
benefits from this marvelous new and lower-cost
method of operating. The original meat packing
tycoons were not extravagant people; they worked
long hours and hard; they made their families work;
they paid out as little as they could in order to
conserve funds to expand their businesses. They
did not sleep in two beds at once; nor sit on two
chairs; nor eat six meals a day.

5. Finally, the local slaughterers who were dis-
placed. These were no longer able to make so good
a living as formerly. They no longer belonged properly in the business. If they had been, for sentimental or other reasons, kept in business by subsi-
dies or other legislation, that would have been
against the interests of all others, and class
legislation.

How Self-Regarding Interests Of Others Crimp Extraordinary Earnings Of Great Innovators

Now it is possible to affirm that "productivity"
was rewarded after all, in an acquisitive, capitalist manner. The pioneering meat packers became
rich, did they not?

It is admitted that there can be no question that
the successful packers became rich. It was a reward
for their resourcefulness, courage and vision. Men
must be prepared to see entrepreneurs who take a
pioneering course receive large rewards (as well as
suffer disastrous losses which collectively may exceed gains). This is an incentive system without
which men have not found it possible to improve
their standard of living.

The fundamental question is: how long did the
extraordinary profits, which were (and still are)
so great an offense to many, continue?

Extraordinary profits continued only as long as
the new, lower-cost meat packing capability was
inadequate to supply the demand for lower-priced
meat.

Because expansion of meat packing capability

continued beyond the expansion of the market (a very
typical phenomenon), the packers eventually overshot
their market. Then profits dropped below normal.
It took some time to correct that.

Eventually, profits returned to normal. But normal
is modest, and few fortunes have been made, if any,
in the latest fifty years in the packing industry.

What might the terms "extraordinary profits" and
"normal" mean?

Normal here refers to originary interest, that
is, the prevailing "discount for the future," as
explained in Chapter 30. This is a return, as previously mentioned, of 3% to 5% on the investment,
presently in the United States.

The originary interest return is not basically
a return on productivity, but a discounting of what
is not consumed presently, but becomes available
only in the future.

We come then, finally, to consideration of how
an initial, unusually large profit because of increased productivity shrinks until it becomes a
stale "discount of the future."

Universal self-regarding interest, a laudable
motivation and a form of the instinct for self-
preservation, is the fundamental factor eventually
robbing the great producers in human history of
the fruits of their labors, so that finally they
get only originary interest.

1. That has already been foreshadowed in earlier
parts of this chapter. The innovator and great
producer must share, from the very beginning, with
suppliers, employees and customers. To gain volume,
the entrepreneur must offer inducements to all the
others, who are free agents properly looking out
for themselves. And so, a high-profit entrepreneur
himself, on his own initiative, passes on some of
his savings, and usually more and more, in order to
interest more and more collaborators. He must do
that to enlarge his business.

2. But there is an even more powerful additional
stimulus to the decline from extraordinary profits
to mere originary interest. This factor is direct
competition between the several entrepreneurs already
existing or who newly enter the market. If something is lush, and if entrance is free, as it ought

generally to be, the quicker others begin to compete, the better for suppliers, employees and customers.

The greatest leveller of extraordinary profits is competition. New competitors must offer to everybody involved even more than the first man in the field. And so profits come down rapidly and occasionally precipitously.

*   *   *

It should now be clear that unusual productivity contributes <u>temporarily</u> to higher returns than the basic originary interest rate. But universal self-interest chips away at those profits until they are gone.

The practical men of the world -- who greatly contribute to productivity -- are <u>never</u> fully rewarded nor long rewarded according to their productivity, and are progressively rewarded less and less until profits settle on their natural "floor," known as originary interest.

In other words, Hebrew-Christian ethics, and capitalism insofar as it conforms to Hebrew-Christian ethics, establishes what is really a mighty leveling system; it does not operate by envy and covetousness, but by legitimate self-interest and freedom to compete.

In short, Hebrew-Christian ethics and conformable Capitalism are naturally "levellers" or equalizers in their "distribution" of the proceeds of production.

N O T E

On goods, of which the quantity is augmentable or decreasable, the operation of the <u>free</u> market (free because it exists without government interference, or private combination, or monopoly) systematically brings selling prices down roughly to the level of cost of production and distribution. The result therefore is that the members of the community get (1) what they want most (2) at the lowest prices. Free markets are not only one form of freedom, but they create maximum prosperity for all.

Capitalism Is Christian Only In Theory

A standard definition of capitalism is that it is a system based (1) on the right of private ownership of property, and (2) on a free market for goods and services. (This is a good definition, but not an entirely comprehensive one.)

How relate that definition to Christian ethics? To do that is no problem.

1. The first part of the definition is based on the eighth commandment in the Decalogue, Thou shalt not steal. The premise underlying that commandment is that private ownership is normal, and that it should not be disorganized by theft.

2. The second part of the definition is based on the sixth commandment in the Decalogue, Thou shalt not kill, which of course is a generic expression forbidding also wounding, violence, threatening, and any coercion by an individual, or by a group, or by a state. A _free_ market for goods and services is merely another way of saying that human inter-relationships must not be disorganized by violence or coercion.

3. In a sense, too, the idea of a "free market" implies that the parties to exchange do not deceive each other. They would not freely exchange, if they realized they were being deceived. In that sense, the standard definition of capitalism really indicates that the system is based on three Hebrew-Christian ethical principles formulated in the sixth, eighth and ninth commandments in the Decalogue.

* * *

In fact, however -- as distinguished from theory -- capitalism presently in the Occidental world is substantially non-Christian; it flagrantly authorizes systematic theft and systematic violence. These cases will be discussed in the following chapters.

The real situation can be summarized in this manner: (1) Capitalism is based on Christian ethics in theory, but not in fact; and (2) Socialism is not based on Christian ethics either in theory or in fact.

That Counterfeiting Is Unethical, And Why

The mischief that is involved in counterfeiting needs careful explanation, in order that other undesirable actions identical <u>in</u> <u>principle</u>, but which (astonishingly!) are highly <u>approved</u>, may be revealed to be what they are, namely, theft also, and therefore immoral.

*   *   *

Christian ethical teachers sometimes have easy recourse for declaring something to be sin by saying that the particular action in question dishonors God. The sin then is supposed to consist in that <u>dishonoring</u>. A frequent (but not necessary) corollary to the emphasis on dishonoring God is that the sin in question is not supposed to have a <u>practical</u> consequence which is evil <u>per se</u>. The problem is viewed from a theological level, rather than from a practical, mundane cause-and-effect level. It is probably as correct to say that whatever dishonors God does that because its practical effects are bad, as to say it the opposite way, that the offense is bad because it "dishonors" God.

In a similar dubious way, it might be argued that counterfeiting is bad because it dishonors the State. The argument would be about as follows: the state has reserved to itself the regulation of money and the printing of paper bills. For anyone else to have the impudence to print paper bills is, therefore, an insult to the state, because the deed manifests disrespect to the state. But if that were all that could be said against counterfeiting, then the case against it would be weak.

Counterfeiting is wrong not because the state says that it is wrong, but the state says it is wrong because there is turpitude involved.

*   *   *

The objection against counterfeiting must rest on the fact that it is an effective way to be a thief, without revealing the customary aspects of theft, namely, taking property away from someone else, under cover of darkness or (hopefully) without being seen. A specific person is, by a theft, a gainer at the expense of another specific person or organization.

A mind-mannered printer operating a printing press seems to lack the hallmarks of a dangerous thief. Nevertheless, a counterfeiter is extraordinarily dangerous because of the <u>quantity</u> of counterfeit bills that he can print. If counterfeiting is theft, a counterfeiter can engage in enormous theft merely by printing faster, or in larger denominations.

As counterfeit bills are not permitted to continue to circulate in commerce after they are recognized to be counterfeit, no honest person wishes to have such bills in his possession at any time, regardless how innocently he may have acquired them.

The situation may appear to be different if the counterfeit bills are not discovered; then no individual who happens to get such a bill appears to be injured <u>directly</u>. It might then almost be argued that counterfeiting is not theft, <u>if</u> <u>not</u> <u>discovered</u>, because no man can singly be pointed out as having suffered (apparently) from the counterfeit bills which, together with government bills, are changing hands. Nevertheless, a theft has occurred. It is worth the time to explain this theft thoroughly -- the theft that exists even when the existence of the counterfeit bills remains undiscovered.

Successful counterfeiting robs society generally rather than individuals singly. It is, in fact, the hope of counterfeiters to be limited to robbing generally, rather than to have attention directed to them, by individuals having a loss from being obliged to turn in counterfeit bills of which they come into possession innocently by selling goods or services.

                    *   *   *

Let us consider a society of five men -- producers of (1) food, (2) clothing, (3) shelter, (4) personal services (repairs, delivery, printing, etc.), and (5) capital equipment.

By <u>specializing</u> in their respective industries these men increase their productivity, as has been explained previously (pages 87 to 99). These five men exchange their production, beyond their own needs, with the others. To facilitate these exchanges they use money. Let us assume that there are dollars in circulation with a face value of $10,000. In reality the men exchange goods, the money being merely a media to facilitate exchange. The $10,000 would mean nothing if there were nothing

for which to exchange it (except it would have the
heat value from burning the paper constituting the
$10,000).

Exchanges of products between the five men will
be "adjusted" by them to the known existence of the
$10,000 of money. Prices will be negotiated accord-
ingly. The exchanges will be "rational" because
each man will get in exchange for his own production
what others think his production is worth, considering that there is $10,000 of money in circulation
between the five. And, of course, a man having sold
for dollars (valued on the basis that there are
10,000 of them) will expect to buy other merchandise
on the basis of the same amount of money being in
existence.

The foregoing is a rational and honest world of
production, pricing, and exchange. (For illustrative purposes, the situation has been over-
simplified.)

                *   *   *

Suppose the fourth man in our society, the producer of personal services including printing,
decides he will print secretly an <u>additional</u> $1,000
worth of money. All he needs is the paper, the
dies for $10 bills, the ink and the press, and then
he can run off one hundred quickly and without much
trouble. There will then be $11,000 of money in
our little society instead of $10,000.

No house will have been broken into, no money
will have been taken from anybody. Therefore, so
one might reason, there has been and will be no
theft.

Surely, the printer has become a counterfeiter.
The state (the five men acting together) had decreed
only $10,000 of money; the printer (it must be ad-
mitted) has violated the state's rule against counterfeiting, and has "assaulted" the sovereignty of
the state; but has he perpetrated any violation of
the Decalogue? The answer is, Yes; the counterfeiter is a thief; he has violated the eighth
commandment, Thou shalt not steal.

The <u>process</u> by which the theft will be accomplished is worth tracing.

For simplicity sake, let us assume each of the
five men in the community has one-fifth of the
existing money, that is, one-fifth of $10,000; or
each has $2,000.

But after the printer has made the secret run
on his printing press, the amounts in each man's
possession are as follows:

Food producer	$ 2,000
Clothing producer	2,000
Shelter producer	2,000
Personal Services producer	3,000
Capital Equipment producer	2,000
T o t a l	$11,000

What will now happen?

The printer of course did not print the $1,000
of new bills for fun. He intended to use them to
make purchases of goods and services, and he puts
the new bills into circulation; unobtrusively, of
course, and without any notice to his four associates.

Let us assume that the printer spreads the $1,000
equally among the other four by buying goods from
them. We shall also assume that the turnover of
money is simply one turn for the time interval
involved.

In Table 12 we can see what will now happen to
each man's getting his one-fifth share of real production.

(The reader should have no difficulty understanding the data in this table, if he first reads the
column heads carefully. Some supplementary remarks
will be made in the text following the table.)

Table 12

What Happens When The Printer Counterfeits $1,000 Of Money

Goods	Each Man's Quantity of Real Goods & Services Available	Share of Each Good & Service Exchanged	Printer's Counterfeited $1,000 Spread Four Ways	Printer's Total Purchases Or Use	Aggregate Total Left For The Other Four	Each Man's Share Under The New Set-Up (Except The Printer)
	1	2	3	4	5	6
		(1 ÷ 4)	(1000 ÷ 4)	(2 + 3)	(1 - 4)	(5 ÷ 4)
Food	$ 2,000	$ 500	$ 250	$ 750	$ 1,250	$ 312.5
Clothing	2,000	500	250	750	1,250	312.5
Shelter	2,000	500	250	750	1,250	312.5
Services	2,000	0	0	0	2,000	500
Capital	2,000	500	250	750	1,250	312.5
Total	$10,000	$ 2,000	$ 1,000	$ 3,000	$ 7,000	$ 1,750

Naturally, the printer would not spend part of
his counterfeit money on his own production; but
only on the production of others. That is why there
is a zero in line 4 in columns 2 and 3, and other
appropriate differences.

It is important to keep in mind that this calculation assumes that prices have remained unchanged
for the time being.

The two most significant figures are the totals
of columns 4 and 6. The $3,000 total is what the
counterfeiting printer can buy. The $1,750 is the
total that each of his four associates can buy. The
figures "tie out." Suddenly there are no goods left,
and the four other than the printer have unspent and
unspendable money left.

The printer buys, or keeps of his own production	$3,000 worth
Each of the other four can keep or buy $1,750 worth, or	7,000 worth
T o t a l	$10,000

It has been assumed in the foregoing that the
printer has worked so adroitly that he buys up, for
example, $750 worth of food, whereas he ordinarily
would buy only $500, and that the food producer in
the community is not alarmed about whether there
will be enough left for himself and the other three.
But the fact is that if the printer buys $750 worth
of food, the others will be able to buy only $312.5
each, rather than the previous $500. This is a re-
duction of $187.5, or 37-1/2%. The bellies of some
people in the community will become flatter, and
they will have to tighten their belts.

However, the injection of the printer's $1,000
of counterfeit money will soon begin to affect the
price situation. In the foregoing it has been assumed that there would be no discovery of the extra
$1,000, and that prices would be unchanged. But
when the printer buys more than usually, his associates will think business is "booming" and will
eventually raise prices. This will reduce the
"effectiveness" of the printer's use of his extra
$1,000, but does not change the principle involved,
to wit, he will still be able to get more than his
"share" of production. He will still be a thief,
but not so big a one.

There will be consternation among the printer's
associates when they discover they have money left

($250 each) for which there is no merchandise or
services for them to buy (because the printer acted
ahead of them). Once they realize they are "stuck"
with some money, they will go out and bid more for
anything left, or soon to come on the market. In
time, _prices_ will all be adjusted upward to the
existence of $11,000 worth of money (rather than
$10,000), and the printer's advantage will prove
noncontinuing. (Unless, of course, he acquires the
habit of putting out another $1,000 of new money
regularly. But his neighbors will sooner or later
discover that, and put an end to it somehow.)

In the meantime, however, it is plain that the
printer has been a _subtle_ _thief_ by using counterfeit money.

*   *   *

Let us assume the printer is "successful" with
his counterfeit money for some time. Later, on
checking the amount of money existing, this little
society discovers that there are 11,000 dollars in
circulation rather than 10,000 dollars.

How, they ask, did that happen? The printer, if
he is a facile liar as well as a subtle thief, may
indicate shocked surprise and say, "The counting
mechanism on my printing press must have gone wrong."

Suppose it is decided to eliminate the extra
$1,000, each man being required to relinquish $200
for burning.

At the newly prevailing prices this reduction
from $11,000 of money to $10,000 will result in
unsold production.

As producers do not wish to retain unsold inventories, sooner or later prices will be reduced
(roughly 9%) in order to move the goods.

The situation can be summarized as follows:

1. Counterfeiting unduly enriches the man who
first uses additional counterfeit money. He can
buy more than the equivalent of what he produces.
He _is_ _a_ _thief_.

2. If the counterfeiting is not discovered and
corrected, prices will rise, and eventually dissi-
pate further benefit for him from his method of
theft, unless he counterfeits some more.

3. The community is generally deceived when

counterfeit money is injected into it. Demand appears greater than it really is. Prices are raised
by sellers, and they increase production if they
can. There·is a boom with nothing causing it other
than a printing press. (No person with capability
to think will <u>finally</u> conclude that prosperity can
<u>in the</u> least be created by operating a printing
press to produce counterfeit money. To think that
a little counterfeiting is good (because it stimu-
lates a fictitious demand) is still to lack the
capability of thinking soundly. A little counterfeiting is no better, nor more defensible, than a
great deal.)

4. When counterfeit money is withdrawn, the
activities of society, in a sense, go into reverse
gear: (a) products cannot be sold at the increased
prices; (b) inventories accumulate; (c) production
is then necessarily reduced; (d) unemployment increases; (e) then prices are finally lowered. These
are the hallmarks of what is known as a "depression."

Of course, if a person is so fond of booms that
he is willing to incur depressions, then counterfeiting, and next in sequence its elimination, will
appear desirable to him.

However, counterfeiting <u>never</u> promotes the real
welfare of any community; it does the reverse.

Seen under the clear light of morality and ethics,
counterfeiting is plain theft; and immoral; unethical; not reconcilable with Christian ethics.

*   *   *

(It is outside the scope of this book to pursue
all the effects of counterfeiting on prices, production, different individuals; etc.)

Capitalism, As It Manifests Itself, Is
Not Reconcilable With Biblical Ethics

Although capitalism, as a system for organizing
social cooperation (and in that sense as a system
of ethics), is generally founded on Christian principles, it neither has nor has had an entirely
Christian ethical foundation.

Insofar as capitalism lacks a <u>thoroughgoing</u>
Christian ethical foundation, its prosperity has
been, is, and will remain in jeopardy.

Throughout the western world, to which the appellation "capitalistic" is supplied, there has been
and continues to be a violation of Hebrew-Christian
ethical law which threatens to bring capitalism to
disaster. This violation involves the same principle of evil that was outlined in the preceding
chapter in regard to counterfeiting. The western
capitalist world has incorporated into its monetary
system <u>legalized</u> theft, in the form of permitting
and promoting the issuance of "money," which has
the same character and effect as putting out counterfeit bills.

This evil has arisen, in a sense, <u>naturally</u>.
The problem has been made complex. Honest men have
differed and disputed the question. The public,
generally uninformed and confused by the intricacies
of the system, and covetous of (hallucinary) benefits, has supported laws which create the evil and
which paralyze the efforts of the few who understand
the evil and foresee its eventual disastrous consequences.

Only an informed and aroused public opinion --
and a <u>reversed</u> public opinion -- can correct the
situation and put an end to the trouble. Financial
men who understand the situation, whether bankers,
economists or others, are powerless to develop a
corrective course on their own. Competitive conditions, established by law, will prevent individuals,
by their own action or their example as <u>individuals</u>,
from being able to remedy the situation.

The intricacies of the western monetary structure
are beyond the scope of this book. But it would be
a notable omission in this section on <u>Ethics</u> to
neglect to submit for consideration, in simplified
and schematic form, the <u>colossal</u> <u>alternation</u> <u>in</u>

<u>theft</u> <u>and</u> <u>in</u> <u>inequitable</u> <u>restoration</u> which bedevils
the so-called capitalist society, and which consti-
tutes the greatest public <u>sin</u> corrupting and threatening the capitalist world.

One proposition subscribed to in this book is
the well-known statement in Scripture: "Your sins
will find you out" (Numbers 32:23). Of course, a
publicly authorized and approved <u>theft</u> will not be
punished by a criminal sentence and jail term.
Either it will have to be punished differently, or
it will not be punished at all. If sins are inescapably punished sooner or later, despite public
opinion and permissive laws, then the punishment
must come <u>elsewhere</u>, in a <u>different</u> <u>form</u> (as what
may be called a "side-effect" of an antibiotic).

The "punishment" shows up in two ways, both of
which are harmful, (1) booms and (2) depressions.
The two can be combined under the one term, <u>business</u>
<u>instability</u>.

Socialism and communism hang on the outskirts of
capitalist society as wolves. These hostile systems
admit that capitalism is <u>now</u> more rewarding than
any socialist-communist system. But (1) they attack capitalism by saying it is <u>unstable</u> <u>because</u>
<u>of</u> <u>depressions</u>, and (2) they undermine capitalism
by promising a fabulous <u>future</u> utopia (which however is a siren song and wholly delusory).

Booms and depressions, because of the increasing
complexity of economic cooperation (which complexity,
however, makes it more productive) probably will become more severe rather than less severe. The
"mechanism," now being more complex, can grind to
a worse halt than ever before.

It is, therefore, probably only a question of
time before a worse-than-any-earlier depression
will afflict the world. That staggering probability
may be the <u>occasion</u> for the socialists-communists
to get a ready ear for their appeal to abandon
capitalism entirely, and for the world to become
socialist-communist. Such may be the <u>occasion</u>; but
the <u>cause</u> will be elsewhere; the cause will be the
<u>public</u> and <u>universally</u> perpetrated <u>sin</u> <u>of</u> <u>theft</u>,
officially and systematically incorporated within
the monetary structure of capitalism, presently and
for centuries.

The essential subject matter in order to understand the <u>idea</u> will be explained in Chapters 36 to

3. The actual monetary structure of the world is
   complex that only those can hope to understand
   who devote much of their life to understanding
  ts complexities.

   Any satisfactory monetary system should be kept
   simple that the average citizen can understand
  t; this is presently quite impossible. Material
  a the following chapters is merely schematic.

Can An Individual Cause A Boom And A Depression?

One nightmarish fear of the western world centers around depressions and consequent cyclical unemployment. Depressions are definite in fact; can be explicitly described by all; are denounced as great evils; but they are given varied and almost universally incorrect explanations of why and how they occur. On the question of <u>cause</u> or <u>causes</u> of a depression there are disagreements, confusions, and some hallucinations.

In order to put the problem simply to a layman, the question is asked, as in the title of this chapter: Can an individual <u>cause</u> a boom and a depression?

An illustration can be cited which none should have difficulty understanding.

Suppose a man earns $10,000 a year, and further that he spends or invests all that is not taken from him in income taxes. Say that his income taxes are $2,000; that he receives $8,000 in cash, and that he regularly spends or invests the $8,000. That, we assume, is his pattern of life. He annually buys $8,000 worth of goods, services and securities. The economists would say: He is contributing to an <u>evenly</u> <u>rotating</u> <u>economy</u>. No boom; no depression.

Suppose, now, that this householder develops an appetite or need to buy something that will suddenly cost him an additional $5,000 -- maybe a foreign car, or a complete refurnishing of his house, or a foreign trip, or that he unexpectedly must spend $5,000 for surgery and associated services in order to save the life of one of his children; and so instead of spending only $8,000 he spends in the given year $5,000 more than that, or $13,000.

He himself cannot pay, according to our assumption. His creditors in this situation must give him time to pay, or (maybe) he can go to a bank and borrow; or maybe he can counterfeit $5,000 of bills (if he has facilities for doing that, which however is not probable).

But this man is now spending thirteen-eighths of what he formerly spent, or an increase of 62-1/2 percent. That much <u>more</u> services or goods must be produced by others to meet this man's surge in purchasing. The rest of the community works harder

to respond to this demand, and has more employment
than before, possibly in the form of overtime.

Clearly our friend has <u>caused</u> a boom.

*   *   *

However, his creditors will expect to be paid
back. In the following year our boom creator cannot (we shall assume) pay back the $5,000 because
that would not leave him enough on which to live.
He aims to pay off the debt in two years, or $2,500
each year; instead of spending $8,000 each year, he
will spend only $5,500; the family tightens its
belt and begins to pay off.

But clearly our householder is now contributing
to a depression, because he is consuming less,
buying less, and taking away the opportunity of
others to work; he is causing unemployment. In the
language of ordinary conversation, and of the newspapers, this man is now acting so that a depression
will be caused. He caused a boom by buying what
he could not pay for; he is now causing a depression
by paying off the debt for which he splurged.

The variations in his buying are as follows:

Regular year $ 8,000

Buying-splurge year   13,000) Average for
First paying-off year   5,500) the three years
Second paying-off year   5,500) is $8,000

Future years   8,000

It should not be difficult for anyone to understand
the foregoing simple facts and the conclusion to
be reached from them, to wit, booms and depressions
are <u>caused</u> by variations in purchasing power stemming from variations in credit, first the expansion
and then the contraction of credit (the latter in
the form of paying off the debt).

The real <u>origin</u> of booms and depressions is then
<u>credit</u> <u>expansion</u> and <u>credit</u> <u>contraction</u>.

*   *   *

But there will be protests against
this reasoning, and under certain circumstances
validly so.

It may be argued that the $5,000 credit which
was granted was accompanied by somebody else decreas-

ing his expenditures $5,000. The surge of $5,000
in buying by our man is compensated by a balancing
shrinkage in the buying of another man or men who
saved the amount he borrowed.

Therefore, so it will be argued savings offset
spending; what one man saves, the other spends;
and vice versa, what one spends, another saves.
Then there would be neither booms nor depressions.

That is granted; the reasoning is correct.

But that is not the way the western world is
organized. Some of what one man spends more than
he has earned may indeed be offset by savings of
others who spend less than they earn. That does
not cause booms and depressions.

But if excess spending by one is not always
balanced by savings by others, then from where does
the extra money come?

The extra money comes from a feature systematically organized into the monetary and banking structure of the western world, and involves putting
out "fictitious money" in the form of "uncovered
bank notes" and "deposit credits," which are authorized and promoted by law. Another way of saying
this is that the monetary structure of the western
world is based on "fractional reserves."

The process by which banks create the equivalent
of counterfeit money is so smoothly organized that
practically no one questions it. You may wish to
borrow $5,000, and so you visit your banker. He
will appraise your means and character, and decide
whether or not to make the loan. If he decides
favorably for you, you sign a note and he credits
your deposit account book with $5,000. You can
then spend the $5,000. But -- and this is the
crucial feature in the situation -- the banker
really did not have the $5,000 to lend; he "created"
the $5,000; he did the equivalent of counterfeiting
it.

Under the system that exists, banks are authorized by law, and "coerced" by competition, to loan
out more than the savings or other funds deposited
with them. The system, in other words, is a species
of counterfeiting, but it is lawful and even obliga-
tory in the United States today.

                    *   *   *

It is unreasonable to blame the bankers, or the

rich, or businessmen, or politicians, or presidents, or Congress, for this situation. Such folk merely respond to the wishes of the public. It is "every man" himself in the United States who is responsible for this equivalent of counterfeiting, done on a colossal scale, compared to which private counterfeiting is a bagatelle.

Suppose there is a great depression and frightening unemployment. "People" may go to church to pray God for relief. But the cause of their trouble is themselves -- their own authorization (by their control over the laws) to have "legalized counterfeiting" in our monetary system.

Prayers in such a situation are an insult to the God who proclaimed the Decalogue; to pray for relief in such a situation is either blasphemous or ridiculous. What is needed are prayers for reform, and actual reform; not relief.

Who causes such a depression that afflicts these parishoners? They themselves and their preacher (possibly denouncing somebody else) have caused it. In all probability some of the houses they have bought, and some of their automobiles and some of their furniture (and possibly also the church building and the preacher's parsonage) have been partly bought (or built) with money not available as the result of the savings of others, but money available only by the equivalent of counterfeiting.

Naturally, they will be reluctant to have this source of funds for advance buying dry-up on them. Never yet in the history of this country have the "people" been prepared thoroughly to forswear this sin, and the present generation may not reform itself either.

But if there is no reform? What happens if the present practice continues? The answer is: the disorganization and maybe eventual destruction of the western world as we have it and know it.

The punishment -- and the wrath of God -- against theft will not be escaped because any people as voters have decreed by law that theft is not theft.

It should be granted that the "people" do not understand the situation. The monetary and banking structure of the western world, in the search for efficiency and to escape the affects of legalized theft by the equivalent of counterfeiting, has

become intolerably complex; it ought to be simplified. But it requires no great intellect to understand the foregoing illustration of a boom created
by a $5,000 credit (available but not through an-
other's prior saving); and a depression created by
paying off such a debt.

The answer to the question, Can an individual
cause a boom and depression, is: Yes. The individual citizens of the United States have been doing
that for 150 years; whenever their system gets them
into trouble they blame the wrong cause, and adopt
measures which will make future booms ever bigger
and depressions ever worse; or else they adopt a
program which will be even worse than booms and depressions (namely, continuing inflationism).

Booms and depressions are like malaria, the
patient's comfort goes up and down; but inflationism is like the bubonic plague, more surely deadly.

If this system requires reform, which it does,
how did it ever come into existence, and why is it
tolerated?

The Origin Of Legalized Counterfeiting

Money is that good which can be most easily exchanged for something else. People wish to have as their purchasing-power-"reserve" something that they can surrender easily to others in order to get something that they wish to have at once. The money of a society is then the "most liquid" transferable asset in it.

There are several reasons why precious metals, particularly silver and gold, and finally (in most of the world) gold only turned out to be "money." But the overwhelmingly determinative reason was: men cannot <u>cheat easily</u> on silver and gold, the quantity of which is steady and <u>not-quickly augmented</u> by <u>some will of a man or men</u>.

Silver and/or gold have, for thousands of years, been the "monetary media" of advanced societies, and will probably continue to be that permanently, because inanimate metal is not "corruptible" or "seducible" as men are (who can adopt a media that can be increased or adulterated by men) to which temptation it is in the nature of fallible mortal men sooner or later surely to succumb.

The precious metals are then, by their character and the convention of men, the <u>natural</u> money for the world. This was true in Abraham's time, almost 2,000 years before Christ. When he bought a grave lot (cave) for the burial of his wife Sarah, he paid in money "current with the merchants," which means that the weights and fineness were (in this case) not disputed. (Abraham had been smart enough not to accumulate "bad" money.)

As long as gold and silver functioned as money there was danger of cheating on the pureness of the metal, and the weight of the coins. Ancient merchants had to test such money all the time, and naturally were obliged to go to silversmiths and goldsmiths to have coins tested.

Several things were sure to happen:

1. The goldsmiths would have to have good safety vaults;

2. Merchants would be inclined to leave

their gold or silver there and take a
"receipt" for it from the silversmith;

3. If the silversmith guaranteed a certain
    fineness, then a merchant would be satisfied
    with a receipt for unminted silver or gold;

4. Merchants would hit on the idea of having
    many small receipts rather than one big
    receipt created by the silversmith;

5. Then in order to make a payment, instead of
    going to the silversmith and asking for so
    many ounces of silver or gold of specified
    fineness, the merchant would merely endorse
    a receipt or receipts for the required quan-
    tity to another man who could do either of
    two things:

    a. Go to the silversmith and claim the
        amount specified in the receipt; or

    b. He could simply leave the metal there
        and keep the receipt;

6. Then, that second man might endorse the
    receipt himself to a third man, who might
    in turn cash it, or keep it, or pass it on;

7. The silversmiths soon discovered that mer-
    chants seemed never all to want their silver
    or gold at one time, and the clever silver-
    smiths soon hit on the idea of putting out
    receipts greater in amount than they
    had precious metals on hand;

8. Of course, they "got something" for their
    fictitious receipts; they could buy a better
    living with their "phony" receipts; they
    were secret "counterfeiters";

9. Danger to them from doing this was not great
    as long as there was confidence in the "sound-
    ness" of the receipts; lack of confidence
    could only come when a particular silversmith
    who had put out too many receipts, suddenly
    upon presentation of too many at one time,
    was found not to have enough silver on hand;

10. Clearly, it was easy to be a thief, and
    almost safe to be a crook;

11. What one did, the others soon learned;

12. The "system" of <u>fractional</u> <u>reserves</u> was
    thereby naturally established; silver-
    smiths -- the forerunners of bankers --
    had learned that you could do a lot of
    "counterfeiting" of receipts (our modern
    paper bills) and not get caught -- unless
    you <u>over-did</u> it; or unless you were caught
    by an unlikely, unfortunate, unpredictable
    combination of circumstances;

13. In the meanwhile, as all the rest were
    doing this and competing hard, each silver-
    smith had to do the same thing, or else he
    could not compete <u>successfully</u>.

There is no mystery about the foregoing. It was
natural enough. The requirement was (and is):
just so you do not over-do it -- or, in other words,
just so you do not steal so much that you get caught!

The subject has many complications, and various
schools of thought have enlivened economic history
with arguments on the <u>pro</u> and <u>con</u> of putting out
"uncovered" receipts, that is, receipts without the
metal on hand behind them. The history of the dispute between the ideas of the so-called Banking
School and the Currency School is outside the scope
of this book.

It was inescapable that the controversy would
come to include the assertion that <u>merchandise</u> could
"cover" or "back up" a credit as well as silver or
gold. A manufacturer could "extend credit" secured
by the article manufactured; the wholesaler could
do the same; the retailer could in turn grant credit
to the consumer, if the "good" was durable and could
be repossessed.

After many years of argument the ideas of the
Banking School, which favored the issuance by banks
of receipts not covered with silver or gold has
triumphed <u>de facto</u>. This was a calamitous victory,
because since then the western world has a banking
system which explicitly is based on the assumption
made by silversmiths: we shall not be called on
to cash in <u>all</u> of our receipts (in the present day,
bank receipts are in the form of currency or depos-
its), and therefore we deliberately shall have more
receipts afloat than we have real money with which
to back them.

Eschewing the complexities of the situation, in
a general way a bank can create "money" at least

six times greater than the real reserves it has
behind it. With the passing of time this "multiplier" has been increasing. We have then, in the
western world, a "fractional reserve" banking
system. What is behind our money is not commodity
money that cannot be bastardized, but money largely
based on the faith that the consequences of theft
will not catch up with us; this is parallel to the
cynical calculation of silversmiths that they would
never at <u>one</u> time be called on to redeem <u>all</u> their
receipts (which they knew they could not redeem
under those circumstances).

Individual Bankers Cannot Correct
The Money Situation

An individual banker cannot correct the monetary structure in the United States. If he tries it, he will discover that he cannot earn profits and survive as a banker. Other bankers, as permitted by law, have utilized the profits on the equivalent of "counterfeiting" to lower their charges for appropriate monetary and banking services so that on such services the charges are not enough to permit a bank to continue to exist.

Furthermore, an individual banker is only a small cog today in the monetary machinery of the country, which is centralized in Federal Reserve Banks and under the Federal Reserve Board.

The Federal Reserve Board itself is not a free agent in following sound monetary policies. The Board is required by law to follow monetary and credit policies which insure "full employment." Unions, in turn, have special privileges (privileges are "private laws for themselves as favorites") which result in wage rates for some activities rising above the real market. This would inevitably cause unemployment, unless the Federal Reserve Board faithfully follows the law under which it must now operate -- to increase the money supply so that prices will go up enough to result in employment of those who would otherwise be unemployable (because they are too poor workmen to be employable at the artificially increased rates).

Inflationism is, therefore, the settled, legalized policy of the people of the United States. They, and they only, are to be held responsible for (1) labor union laws and (2) banking, credit and monetary laws of the country.

*   *   *

Banking is the <u>most-regulated</u> business in the United States. Bankers must conform to laws and regulations telling what they may, must and may not do.

Bankers are among the most law-abiding citizens of the country insofar as they are so extremely subject to laws and regulations from the government,

which government merely reflects what the public
wants, or thinks it wants, or does in blissful
ignorance, or does in defiance of the Decalogue (on
the assumption that they "can get away with it").

Surely, if the laws governing one man's business
were more detailed and more controlling than the
laws governing another man's business, it would not
be incorrect to say (assuming they both obey the
laws pertaining to them respectively) that the first
man is more law-abiding than the second (because
more laws control the former than the latter). In
that sense bankers are paragons of obedience to
law.

*   *   *

Law-abiding bankers are not permanently safe,
however, even though they conform to the law. Some
of them take on a responsibility which they should
reject. A historical case will illustrate the
point.

There was a financial panic in 1907. In 1908
and 1909 financial magazines contained lamentations
and self-incriminations by bankers that they had
made the mistake of extending too much credit prior
to the panic. They said: "If only we had been more
restrictive of credit, and more conservative, this
would not have happened."

Even today, one of the famous bank monthlies
regularly admonishes banks to be prudent and to
"exercise restraint" and not to do all that the
laws permit. They hold that only by "restraint"
can the financial structure be disciplined so that
it is sound.

Behind this worthy but feckless idea lies a fallacy, namely, that restraint is necessary where
something is not intrinsically unsound. A sounder
view is that the law permits something that is not
really sound -- is, in fact, bad; and so the urging
to exercise restraint really means "do not do too
much of what a bad law permits." If the law were
good -- effectually prohibited a real evil -- then
everybody could proceed with confidence, because by
doing the good that a good law would permit, no
further restraint would be necessary.

Admonitions to be careful on banking credits
and not overdo them is not properly to be understood
as courage on a good thing but caution on a bad
thing.

Bankers, although they operate under a bad law, should give testimony that the principles underlying the law are bad; are, in fact, theft. (The theft, by the way, does not accrue to bankers, but is diffused in various hard-to-trace ways -- to the public.)

*   *   *

Interlocked with all these problems are questions of domestic and foreign prices, foreign trade, and innumerable matters outside the scope of an elementary book on cosmology, ethics and religion, such as this sketchy text on <u>Minimal Religion</u>.

Bankers are necessarily technicians often largely engrossed in the details of banking. On the question here discussed maybe more should be expected from professional economists. In this case, the hope that the general opinion among them at the present time is in favor of stopping further credit expansion under the present system is probably not realistic.

*   *   *

It is impossible to correct the present situation without a severe economic and business adjustment. Anyone attempting to correct the situation, who fails to warn the public beforehand about the <u>immediate consequences</u> which will be frightening and will take time, is courting public disillusionment with his program and fickle withdrawal of support.

Inescapably there will be radical adjustments which must be made, which will temporarily <u>seriously</u> disturb business. But <u>thereafter</u> the trend could be expected to be the more favorable and sounder.

It is like a man who needs corrective surgery. The surgery is bad; immediately following it, it will look as if he is worse off. But after he recovers from the anesthesia, and the wound heals, then he is much better off.

There is no correction for the present situation without, according to our analogy, some major surgery, which will <u>temporarily</u> put the economy in difficulty.

*   *   *

Well-intentioned attempts to correct the situation may turn out to be ineffective.

Too-much and not-wisely-granted credits were

the explanations given by conscientious and responsible bankers after the 1907 panic. That event
stimulated substantial revision in the monetary and
banking laws of the country.

But did the new system reduce the amount of uncovered credit that could be extended? It did
quite the contrary. It permitted additional expan-
sion of credit <u>when</u> <u>the</u> <u>consequences</u> <u>of</u> <u>sin</u> <u>were</u>
<u>already</u> <u>heavy</u> <u>upon</u> <u>the</u> <u>economy</u>. In a metaphor,
the statute creating the Federal Reserve System
permitted a man to get more drunk than previously,
but then gave him more aspirin tablets and a longer
time to sleep off the effects of intoxication. The
statute aggravated the situation, by concentrating
on alleviating the effects, rather than doing the
reverse, concentrating on correcting the situation
and possibly even aggravating the discomfort from
getting inebriated, which would be a deterrent.

Famous economists foresaw,* as a result of the
initiation of the Federal Reserve System, a long-
drawn-out prosperity (taking up the new credit
slack granted), followed by a far-worse-than-usual
depression. They had superior prescience. That
boom lasted long in the 1920s and the depression
occurred in 1930-1934!

What the situation needed was something different from what the Federal Reserve System was organized to do.

*   *   / *

The price level of the United States and of the
world is based on and affected by credits which in
large part are the same kind of money as counterfeit
money. The amount of those credits is so great
that the effect of removing them all at once would
be devastating. <u>That</u> is not a practical solution.
The only feasible solution consists in "freezing"
the present amount of "counterfeit" money. Maybe
the freezing should be gradual. But once accomplished, it should be like the "laws of the Medes
and Persians, which changeth not."

*   *   *

Readers are referred to the great books on money
and credit by Ludwig von Mises and his associates.

---

* For example, the late Charles J. Bullock of
  Harvard University

Two of Von Mises's major books on the subject are
The Theory Of Money And Credit and Human Action.
To understand the problem comprehensively requires
accomplishing in the technical field of economics
what is a well-known requirement in the associated
field of ethics -- one needs to be "re-born" in
economics, too. Collateral reading will be helpful
adequately to understand Mises and his writings on
the business cycle. His ideas are often referred
to as the Austrian theory. This theory is the only
rigorously rational one, and the only one reconcilable with Hebrew-Christian ethics.

Unemployment And Its Causes

Depressions constitute one nightmare of the present-day American; unemployment is another.

The causes of these two evils, depressions and unemployment, are not inescapable <u>structural</u> defects of modern society as such, but are instead ethical deviations, violations of elementary rules of morality, which can and should be remedied. That is why these evils are being considered in a book on religion as is this one.

Whereas depressions occur as the delayed recoil of business from the boom caused by <u>theft</u> in the form of creation of money (equivalent to counterfeit money but legalized by law), and whereas this theft is a violation of the eighth commandment of the Decalogue, Thou shalt not steal -- the cause of unemployment is <u>coercion</u> by employees, operating through unions, who are given special protection under the laws of the land. This is a violation of the sixth commandment of the Decalogue, Thou shalt not coerce, which is clearly implied in the customary phrase, Thou shalt not kill.

Ordinarily coercion exposes a person to arrest, conviction and fines. One might think that, if coercion is legalized, its consequences are then escaped. This is a hallucination. In this case, the coercion brings no fine or imprisonment but unemployment. That is the "side effect" in this case.

Bankers unethically create money and enable others to <u>steal</u> with it. But it is not really the responsibility of bankers, but of society. The public has set the rules under which bankers must operate competitively. It is the public who is responsible for the equivalent of counterfeiting money through bankers.

Unions coerce in various ways, and violate the moral rule against violence and coercion. But it is not the moral responsibility of union members, but of society. Again, the public has set rules under which unions operate competitively. It is the public who is responsible for coercion which is exercisable by unions, and which the competition between them impels them to employ.

*   *   *

In order to have understanding of the unemploy-
ent problem, the term unemployment requires defin-
tion. It is well to distinguish several kinds of
1employment.

1. There is <u>seasonal</u> unemployment. There is
eed for harvest workers only at certain times of
1e year. Fortunately, each season brings its own
eeds, and a man can work at harvesting in the autumn,
itting trees and shovelling snow in winter, etc.
1en people worry about unemployment in a big way,
: is seldom about the inescapable seasonal change
f work. It is something to which men adjust
olerably.

2. Secondly, there is <u>frictional</u> unemployment.
r this is meant the unemployment associated with
1anging from one job to another. If a man does
ot like one job, he may quit it. Maybe he already
1s other employment, but maybe not. He may there-
ore be temporarily unemployed. The word <u>frictional</u>
1employment is a descriptive one; it refers to the
:riction" of matching work with workers. Sometimes
1e initiative comes from the employer's side; he
1y no longer have work, and he releases an employee.
·ictional unemployment can therefore be either
oluntary or involuntary. There will always be
ome frictional unemployment. There should be, too.
: there were no frictional unemployment, society
ould become static; further gains in the standard
: living would be almost impossible. It is by
·ople moving out of waning industries into growing
1dustries that society is benefited. Frictional
1employment should not be looked upon as evil, but
; good. That is why there is wide recognition
1at there is some unemployment that is "normal."

3. Thirdly, there is <u>cyclical</u> unemployment,
ssociated with the depression aspect of booms and
·pressions. Patently, this is different from
·asonal or frictional unemployment. People are
·t buying; inventories are excessive, plants can-
·t operate fully, and jobs are lost and few are to
· found. This situation can be devastating, as
: was in the great depression of 1930-34. Season-
. unemployment may be only for a season; frictional
1employment is not something associated with em-
oyment opportunities <u>generally</u> being bad; but
·clical unemployment shatters people's nerves and
·rale; and it often causes them to lose all their
·eserves" in cash and current purchasing power so
1at they "go broke," or must liquidate remaining
·sets under disadvantageous conditions. Cyclical

unemployment is a great evil. The cure for it is
to remove the cause of booms and depressions, as
explained in immediately preceding chapters. It is
really futile to work on alleviation instead of
cure; or to cover up symptoms; the cure for cyclical
unemployment is to end all granting of further credit which is not "covered" by real money (gold), or
some other <u>suitable</u> <u>metal</u> <u>the</u> <u>supply</u> <u>of</u> <u>which</u> <u>is</u>
<u>not</u> <u>augmentable</u> <u>easily</u>.

    4. Fourthly, there is <u>chronic</u> unemployment.
This refers to some persons being permanently unemployed, presumably people willing to work, but
who cannot find it. They are <u>chronically</u> out of
work. This is the class whom it is proposed to
consider in this chapter; none of those mentioned
in Nos. 1 to 3.

          *   *   *

    But what, someone may ask, about two other
classes: (1) those who really do not wish to work;
and (2) those who are not employable, in the sense
that they are not willing to work for wages as low
as their low potential production?

    There are always people who do not wish to work.
They may pretend that they do, but they conduct
themselves so that they are not able to get work,
or if they get it, they are soon discharged. But
this category does not include a large number of
people, and their associates eventually appraise
them realistically, and they do not get more sympa-
thy than they deserve. It is feasible to give these
individuals no further attention, in this book.

    The class of the unemployables is something quite
different.

    Some folk are not employable at prevailing rates
because of physical or mental handicaps. If employed
at specially slow speeds, and if paid accordingly,
some of these might find work, good both for them
and society. But presently there are minimum wage
laws which effectually prevent employment of such
handicapped folk. But these as a class are not of
primary concern in connection with unemployment.

    The great problem centers around those who have
no special handicaps, but are unemployable because
they demand more money, for either of three reasons,
than they are worth -- folk who want more than they
will produce.

These people, of three kinds, are:

1. Persons who claim a better job and ask more
    money than an employer, in his own appraisal,
    considers them to be worth;

2. Persons who are not worth to any employer
    the minimum wage set by legislation; and

3. Persons who are not worth to any employer
    the wage demanded by the union of which a
    man is a member.

All these reasons for unemployment are removable.
Therefore they are properly to be looked upon as
voluntary, rather than unavoidable.

A is unemployed chronically, maybe because he has
a fantastic idea of what he is worth. Maybe someone would be happy to employ him at $10,000 a year.
But A demands $15,000. A may consider an offer of
$10,000 an insult to him. But that A is unemployed
is really his voluntary act.

B may not exactly be handicapped, but everything
considered he is not worth the minimum wage set by
law. Of course, unless some employer does not know
what he is doing, B will remain unemployed. He,
too, swells the ranks of the chronically unemployed.
That B is unemployed is the public's responsibility;
the public had the minimum wage laws passed. The
remedy is easy and sensible -- rescind the minimum
wage laws. Laws cannot really legislate work for
men, unless employment terms become compulsory,
that is, that society reverts to slavery.

C may be employable far above the minimum rates,
but not employable at the still higher rates set
by a union wage contract. The rate may be $4 an
hour, but C may be worth only $3.25 an hour. Assum-
ing employers do not want an employee who produces
at a rate of $3.25 an hour but must be paid $4 an
hour, C remains unemployed. C is also, in a real
sense, voluntarily unemployed, assuming he agrees
with the policy of the union to which he belongs.

In a general way, this proposition is sound:
all chronic unemployment is really voluntary.

*   *   *

This truth, that chronic unemployment is really
voluntary (could be changed -- removed -- if

individuals and society were of a mind to do so)
can be approached and validated by a different
approach.

There is in economics a law known as Say's Law.
This law has a corollary that there never needs to
be chronic unemployment. The law says that in a
rather peculiar way; it is usually formulated
thus: production creates its own demand. The
statement however is too cryptic to be easily grasp-
ed and to be dynamic to most folk.

This is the idea: in the final analysis people
exchange their labor in the form of goods. What X
produces in excess of his own needs is what he offers
to Y who in turn offers what he has himself produced
in excess of his own needs. Units of labor are exchanged in the form of goods. The more goods that
are produced, the more that can be offered. The
greater the production, the better can be the induce-
ment offered to others to produce their goods, and
then make an exchange. Demand is then as plentiful
as production. Basically, it is always.

But a question is sure to be asked. What about
general overproduction?

There never has been and never will be general
overproduction. There is always a universal welfareshortage in the world. People always need
something. For example, no woman is ever satisfied
that she has all that she wants.

The only thing that exists in the field of overproduction is specific cases of overproduction.
There is, then, too much of one or more items; but
there remains a shortage of many other things still
wanted. It is not that too much in toto was produced, but too much of some things and not enough
of other things. It was wrong production rather
than too great general production.

The corrections for that are simple and obvious,
but may be painful. Cut the price of what was over-
produced; get rid of excess inventories; reduce
production of that item; and produce more of something else.

In markets where prices can fluctuate freely
goods can always be exchanged, supply and demand
are readily adjusted, and then chronic unemployment
disappears.

But the conditions are relentless: prices must

be prices determined in <u>free</u>, <u>uncoerced</u> markets;
production and exchange must be left flexible so
that they can "adjust."

There will <u>never</u> be any danger of <u>general</u> overproduction. All those who fear unemployment ought
to remove that fear from their imaginations.

There is nothing abstruse about Say's Law. It
is simple common sense. Nor will any economist by
fancy ratiocination of his own ever invalidate it.
He will only make himself ridiculous, and end with
embracing as a substitute a multitude of fallacies.

                    *   *   *

Were not another iniquity operating, factors 2
and 3 on page 269 would by this time have caused
<u>massive</u> chronic unemployment in the United States.

What may that "iniquitous correction" have been?
The answer, which will be clear when the situation
is seen in perspective, is as follows:

1.   The law of the United States permits unions
to do freely what a private citizen may not do,
and for which he would be put in jail.

2.   The result is that unions can bargain, with
the aid of strikes, threats, and other forms of
coercion, so that some wage rates exceed the natural
market for such labor. Goods made with labor
priced-over-the-market cannot be marketed profitably any more at prevailing prices. Therefore,
the back-lash of such coercive labor costs is
higher-priced merchandise that cannot be sold; and
so production will have to be reduced.

3.   Such potential reduced production entails
potential chronic unemployment. This chronic unemployment situation in this country would be
terrible, except that a clever (but eventually
futile) antidote has been believed to have been
discovered.

4.   The antidote is to inflate the money supply
more and more, by the equivalent of legalized
counterfeiting through the banking system (as was
explained in immediately preceding chapters), and
thereby increase purchasing power enough so that
consumers can and will pay the over-the-market
prices for goods caused by the union situation
(and also by the minimum wage laws). This dishonest

policy was explicitly formulated by the Britisher,
John Maynard Keynes. He said that employees would
be happier forcing their wages above the market,
and then have prices raised on them, in lieu of
contrary policies. This is an unduly low evaluation of the intelligence of employees.

5. Congress has passed a law _requiring_ the
Federal Reserve Board to adopt monetary policies
which will prevent chronic unemployment. The policies of the Federal Reserve Board are now to make
a slow and reluctant retreat from intrinsic honesty
to the equivalent of counterfeiting. The Federal
Reserve Board continues to inflate just enough to
prevent mass chronic unemployment. That is what
the law specifies that it is supposed to do. And
so it operates.

Summary: There is then in the unemployment
situation a teaming together of two serious sins,
which _temporarily_ neutralize each other: (1) the
sin of coercion by labor unions (a sin authorized
by law), and (2) the sin of theft by the banking
system (a sin also authorized by law).

But if they neutralize each other is it possible
that sins can become successful, by cancelling each
other out? That possibility may sound plausible,
but is not realistic; the combination will produce
inflationism, which is a degenerative and fatal
disease.

Universal Condonation Of Worst Public Sins

Coercion through unionism as it operates, and
heft via banking laws as they operate, which (as
utlined in the previous chapter) temporarily can
e so managed that they <u>neutralize</u> each other, is
ot a manifestation of the acuteness of the human
ind successfully to negate the Law of God. The
trick" will not "work" permanently. The longer
hat correction is delayed, the greater the bill
hat must be "footed," or the greater the "punish-
ent" that must be borne.

No, union members will not be put in jail for
heir <u>legalized</u> coercion. No, bankers will not be
ut in jail for their doing the <u>legalized</u> equiva-
ent of counterfeiting. But there will certainly
e a "day of reckoning." And it will be a <u>public</u>
ay of reckoning. The sin is national -- in fact,
orld-wide -- and the penalty should be expected
o be equally national; again, in fact, world-wide.

It becomes an interesting and practical endeavor
o attempt to anticipate the potential course of
vents. One might reason as follows:

1.   The coercion of unions will not soon be
iscontinued. There is, however, a sequence of
vents that can halt or "cure" the evil. That con-
ists of domestic United States wages rising fur-
ier and further under union pressure, followed
aturally by a corresponding rise in prices. But
ien, the United States will find it difficult to
xport any more, because it is no longer competitive
a price; contrarily, imports will increase. Then,
e would lose more of the gold we have left.
ventually, we would have a "runaway inflation."
it that will not necessarily happen. It depends
a) on whether the rest of the world inflates too;
id (b) on whether their rate is faster or slower.
ic first question is not hard to answer; the
econd is not so easy. The rest of the world <u>will</u>
aflate too; many smaller countries, faster; some
iropean countries, possibly slower. However, the
ost famous British financial weekly openly espouses
ie proposition that no country in its right mind
ill avoid <u>all</u> inflation; instead that weekly re-
ommends that country <u>A</u> help country <u>B</u> which is
aflating sharply, by country <u>A</u> inflating too!
ever is the whole correction to come from country

<u>B</u>. With such advice in such highly respected
quarters, unions can proceed with no great fear
that they will suddenly find themselves at the end
of their tether. They can long coerce, because
the world will long inflate.

2. "Theft" by proliferating "uncovered money"
(or as Mises calls it, <u>fiduciary media</u>) is also
likely to continue. Here again there is a "problem,
a hindrance in the path of continuing to doing more
of the same, namely, that the quantity of "paper
money" will become so large compared to the basic
gold stock (which <u>is</u> the only reliable money) that
the gold base becomes too small, and will be like
an inverted pyramid -- standing on its peak. Then
there will be more talk of "lack of liquidity."
The "corrective" movement for this problem is easy,
namely, to let the price of gold find its real market level, which real value is currently higher than
$35 an ounce. In other words, "legalized theft"
can go a long, long way yet, and probably will do
so. But to "release" the price of gold so that the
market for it reveals its true level will occasion
some powerful shocks.

The control valve that will give way first, con-
tinuously and finally disastrously, is <u>inflationism</u>.
People will eventually lose confidence in the ever-
increasing supply of money. They will then <u>immedi-
ately</u> spend money which they receive for tangible
goods; they will say to themselves: we can buy
cheaper now than later; therefore, let us buy <u>now</u>.
Savings will decrease; bonds will not be saleable;
insurance will become discredited; investments will
systematically "flee" from money (the dollar).
When that operation hits a "flash" point, events
are likely to move very fast. In a few months the
whole price and monetary structure of the world
may be destroyed by "runaway inflationism." Then
people will have their faith destroyed in the "system" they now think wonderful, but which is unethical and contrary to the commands of God. The
communists will say: "Did we not foretell to you
that it would be bad? Turn to our system." In the
meanwhile no acknowledged spokesman of Christian
ethics may have raised his "voice in the wilderness'
in solemn warning; and so Christian ethics not having been correctly prophetic may at that time properly get little hearing. The financial and commercial debacle may be followed by a moral and
political debacle in the form of a turning to social
ism-communism. Certainly none will be trusted <u>then</u>
who does not raise his voice in warning <u>now</u>. Of

course, to turn to socialism-communism is to jump
from the frying pan into the fire. It is exactly
the fact that the ideas of socialism-communism have
been borrowed by the western system, and accepted
under nonsocialist labels, which will ruin the present defective western system.

The ultimate consequences of inflationism can
effectively be registered on the mind of any modern
man who will carefully read the history of the
socialist German Weimar Republic after World War I.
That government spawned inflationism, which in turn
spawned Hitler, who precipitated World War II. What
is now being copied here in principle is the same
program that ruined Germany beginning with the 1920s,
and is now discredited there.

But it is not necessary to turn to the past. To
know what socialism stands for ultimately, look at
countries behind the Iron Curtain now. They cannot
even feed themselves.

                *   *   *

On these great issues there appears to be little
to be expected from "great captains" of industry.

These men are not generally in favor of inflationism, nor of union coercion. They will reject both
with some clarity and firmness in theory. But they
do not reject the unsound principles of theft and
coercion which underly the public sins under discussion.

What "captains of industry" are against, in
addition to their semi-vigorous objection to inflationism, is generally falling prices. They believe
in just enough "inflationism" of the money supply
to keep prices from falling.

Whereas John Maynard Keynes said that prices
should be raised artificially to compensate for wage
increases obtained by coercion or the threat of
coercion, captains of industry take the position
that the money supply should be increased enough to
prevent a general fall in prices. The principle,
therefore, that many businessmen and bankers of the
world have espoused is to offer little resistance
to a "managed money" system, which inescapably involves theft. Who is to call the halt between increasing the money supply to prevent a general decline in prices, versus to accomplish an increase
of prices? To authorize tinkering with the money

supply for <u>any</u> purpose is to open the door, be it
ever so little, for taking money from <u>A</u> to transfer
it to <u>B</u> (through the effect on prices). It is
<u>theft</u>.

Tinkering with the money supply should be condemned in comprehensive terms, but that is just
what few people are willing to do, including some
representative captains of industry and finance.

                *   *   *

No money system is satisfactory except one based
on a metal which is scarce and of which the supply
is <u>not-easily-augmented</u>. Gold is, therefore, presently the ideal money.

The present colossal paper money superstructure,
already built on the gold base, cannot be liquidated
without industrial, commercial and banking chaos.
It can, however, be frozen. It should be decided
that no more is to be created. Nothing already
existing would be extinguished. Doing even that --
i.e., stopping <u>further</u> inflationism -- will cause
temporary severe adjustment. The gain to come from
such honesty is worth that price. But men would
have to steel themselves for the temporary ordeal
anticipatorily.

The price of gold should become <u>free</u>. That can
simply be accomplished by permitting anyone to own
gold who wishes to do so.

Inert gold is much more reliable than are mortal
economists, bankers or politicians who might be
permitted to manipulate the quantity of nongold
money. Those who want a "managed" currency are
essentially naive about human character and strength;
they overestimate it grossly. Those who want gold
only as money (or more accurately under present
circumstances with all paper money frozen in quantity) are folk who are realists and have a correct
appraisal of the weakness of human judgment and
will.

The wise men and the nonwise men of the world
can be evaluated by noting (1) whether they believe
in gold only for money, or (2) whether they trust
a so-called managed currency.

                *   *   *

Nobody can predict how much gold will be mined
when the gold market is made <u>free.</u> Maybe much more;
possibly not.

Suppose that the gold supply just does not increase so fast as commerce increases with rising world production and trade. What will happen to prices?

The world will then experience the phenomenon of <u>generally</u> <u>falling</u> prices. Nothing could help the "common man" more than that. The pay check he gives his wife to meet household bills would then slowly but steadily buy more goods and services than previously. The family's standard of living would go up!

It is imaginable that a young man might earn $150 a week at the time he marries. Forty years later he might still be earning $150 a week; not a dollar increase in pay! BUT those $150 a week, when he is 63 years old might buy THREE times as much as they did when he was 23 years old. (The world will do well to eschew the cynical comment of John Maynard Keynes to let the "common man" beguile himself with wage increases, and <u>then</u> take <u>it</u> <u>away</u> <u>from</u> <u>him</u> <u>in</u> <u>price</u> <u>increases</u>.)

It is even possible a man might earn only $100 at 63 compared to $150 at 23. His gains would nevertheless come from an even greater reduction of prices.

*   *   *

No system of "cooperation" in society will work well, unless <u>all</u> prices of goods and services are <u>free</u>. Exceptions maim and may even destroy the system.

In any event, the ethics of the Christian religion are incompatible with either coercion or theft, or any partnership between them as there presently is in western capitalistic countries under labor unionism and the issuance of fiduciary media (money not covered by a metal, under present circumstances gold). A partnership in a dual evil may be able to survive a long time, but it cannot survive permanently; eventually it is doomed.

Chapters 34 to 40 have been devoted to two public sins, operating maybe in obscure partnership together but operating nevertheless, which are wholly incompatible with Christian ethics rightly understood.

If There Were No Shortage Of Things, Moral Problems Would Not Even Exist

David Hume in his <u>Autobiography</u> states that it was his personal opinion that his best work was <u>An Enquiry Concerning The Principles Of Morals</u>. It is not to be gainsaid that as a <u>moral</u> philosopher, Hume far exceeded Socrates or Plato or most others. In large outline, Hume's principles of morality are Christian.

Hume was an economist of some note. He had informed himself in regard to the writings of an English-French writer, Richard Cantillon, who may be looked upon as the founder of economics as a science.

That <u>morality</u> is a vital subject rests on the fact that there is a shortage of things; if there were no shortage of things, morality problems would be practically nonexistent. Hume saw this truism clearly. In the aforementioned work, he wrote:

> Let us suppose that nature has bestowed on the human race such profuse <u>abundance</u> of all <u>external</u> conveniences, that, without any uncertainty in the outcome, without any care or industry on our part, every individual finds himself fully provided with whatever his most voracious appetites can want, or luxurious imagination wish or desire.

> His natural beauty, we shall suppose, surpasses all acquired ornaments: the perpetual clemency of the seasons renders useless all clothes or covering: the raw herbage affords him the most delicious fare; the clear fountain, the richest beverage.

> No laborious occupation required: no tillage: no navigation. Music, poetry, and contemplation form his sole business: conversation, mirth, and friendship his sole amusement.

> It seems evident that, in such a happy state, every other social virtue would flourish, and receive tenfold increase; but the cautious, jealous virtue of justice*

---

* (Note of present writer: <u>Morality</u> can be substituted for <u>justice</u> here, if mates are also regarded as property.)

would never once have been dreamed of. For
what purpose make a partition of goods, where
every one has already more than enough? Why
give rise to property, where there cannot
possibly be any injury? Why call this object
mine, when upon the seizing of it by another,
I need but stretch out my hand to possess myself to what is equally valuable? Justice, in
that case, being totally useless, would be an
idle ceremonial, and could never possibly have
place in the catalogue of virtues.

We see, even in the present necessitous
condition of mankind, that, wherever any benefit
is bestowed by nature in an unlimited abundance,
we leave it always in common among the whole
human race, and make no subdivisions of right
and property. Water and air, though the most
necessary of all objects, are not challenged as
the property of individuals; nor can any man
commit injustice by the most lavish use and
enjoyment of these blessings.
                (Section III, Part I, paragraph 2ff.)

Böhm-Bawerk expressed a similar idea with an
important addition, previously noted in this book,
namely, that the relationships of men to things is
far more complex than naive thinkers realize. Neoclassical economics can be described as that school
in the science which analyzes especially the psychology and actions of men relative to things.

Declarations in regard to principles of morality
can be rather childish in those religious circles
where men are doctrinaire about the relationship
of men to men (ethics), but obviously without knowing the antecedent problems stemming from the relationship of men to things (economics).

Ignorance of economics plus doctrinaire morality
does not yield much. Erroneous economics such as
that of socialism-communism plus a sanctimonious
morality associated therewith gives a product still
worse.

It is prudence to beware of moral teachers who
remain ignorant of or are wrong on the relationship
of men to things.

Hume On Sex Morality

Blaise Pascal had a favorite author, Montaigne.
Pascal who was a devout believer once described
Montaigne's skepticism as a doubt that rolled over
and over itself and finally even "doubted whether
it doubted."

An interesting and stimulating English philosopher who similarly represents an excess of skepticism is David Hume (1711-1776). Hume, being an
extreme skeptic, gave no weight to revelation. He,
therefore, felt constrained to set up a system of
morality based on reason and ratiocination (logic).
He published his findings under the title, An
Enquiry Concerning The Principles Of Morals, already
referred to in the previous chapter.

The interesting thing, however, is that by his
cogent ratiocination Hume finally comes up with a
system of morals in most ways similar to that of
the Christian religion, but by no means so simply
and effectively expressed.

It will be interesting to compare what Hume has
to say about sex problems -- the relation between
the sexes, covered in the Decalogue, by the five
words, Thou shalt not commit adultery.

To the writer's knowledge, no system of ethics
associated with any other religion makes so simple
and unqualified a demand for sexual restraint and
discipline as does the Christian religion.

The Catholic church holds that a marriage is
indissoluble except by death. The historic position
of the Protestant churches has been similar, except
that an innocent party in a case of adultery has
been considered by Protestants properly to be re-
marriageable.

The ancient Hebrew religion left some freedom
for divorce and remarriage of a man, but Christ in
the New Testament tightened the rules. Christianity,
in short, if it is idealistic and adamant on any
subject, is so on the sex problem.

Hume took a semi-contradictory position. In
effect, he legislated against adultery for women,
but developed no cogent logic against fornication
or adultery by men. He is a "double standard"
writer.

Hume was a gentle person and a sedate and parsimonious bachelor. He says himself that he liked the company of "modest" women.

However, his opinion regarding the virtue of women was not high. He considered them all to be unreliable, saying that the logic for avoiding off-color stories (in mixed company) was that women were so seducible that their weakness should not be exploited by telling them about improper events; a woman's too eager laughter or too great interest in the tale of some scandal would betray her own vulnerability, according to Hume. It is interesting to note that in a large crowd a smutty story told publicly often elicits more noisy laughter from the women present than from the men.

But Hume was very sure of one thing, and it is a subject on which he is repetitious, namely, men will not tolerate adultery, or the suspicion of adultery, on the part of their wives.

Hume's argument is that a man refuses to pay the expense and trouble of bringing up any child that he is not confident is his own. In Hume's thinking, a woman must conform to the rule, Thou shalt not commit adultery, or she loses her meal ticket and financial support for her children.

Common observation supports Hume's logic. Men will at great burden to themselves support wives and children; seldom will they support a mistress and her children as well as they do for a wife and hers, except when they have ample riches; almost never will they support a prostitute and her children. The life of a mistress or a prostitute therefore is seldom as good as the life of a wife. Women know this well.

In short, Hume's view was that wives are by nature unreliable, and they should beware lest straying they get caught. If that happens, their financial support is endangered.

Solomon said something similar, when he wrote that a man will forgive another about anything except the second man's tampering with his (the first man's) wife. It is unforgiveable and will be avenged sooner or later when possible.

But Hume does not bind the man so tightly. He comes up with a logic that results in the conclusion that faithfulness on the part of the man is not equally enforceable; women simply do not have the

disciplinary power over their husbands that husbands
have over the wives, and the consequence is that
women cannot effectively demand so much as men can.

Even the most sophisticated of men have been as
"primitive" as Hume describes them. Julius Caesar,
according to Plutarch, selected a local woman as
companion wherever he went. But he divorced his wife,
and when asked whether he considered her guilty of
adultery (she at least having been indiscreet), he
answered, no, but that he "wished his wife to be
above suspicion." William the Silent, Prince of
Orange, had four wives, two of whom predeceased him,
one he divorced, and one of whom survived him; but
he also had concubine(s) and illegitimate children.
The wife whom he divorced, Anne of Saxony, had
involved herself with the portrait painter, Rubens.
In the effort to defend her position, Anne's relatives argued against the Prince that his own conduct
was tarnished by his open maintenance of mistresses.
Nevertheless, the Prince was adamant about divorcing
his wife, admittedly semi-demented and maybe half-
irresponsible; he was not willing to give her the
latitude he was exercising himself.

Scripture has no double standard of morality --
one for women, another for men -- but binds both
equally, the man as much as the woman. Scripture
is simpler and more consistent than Hume; or, if
you will, it substitutes revelation for logic.

As a celibate bachelor Hume may not have noted
a characteristic of women -- to be vengeful if they
cannot be disciplinary. Hume had noted the "sus-
ceptibility" of women to seduction. There is nothing
that a woman will use more as an excuse for her own
conscience when tempted to be irregular than to have
knowledge of -- or even flimsy suspicion of -- a
prior irregularity on the part of her husband. The
best way to keep a woman contented probably consists
in never letting a circumstance occur which will
permit her lively imagination to infer that her
husband has been unfaithful. But once she has been
through the trauma of concluding her husband has
been unfaithful, whether she chides him or not, he
may be sure she is at least an easier mark than
previously. This is a logic that Hume ignores in
his rationalistic system, but which Scripture fully
recognizes.

There are other logical reasons against adultery
by a man, which Hume fails to consider.

Monogamy -- _faithful_ monogamy -- is by far the
best system for a prosperous and good society.
Polygamy does not work. In the best of families,
polygamy ends in fratricide, or if not that bad, in
scheming and vicious competition between children
of different mothers and especially scheming by
those mothers themselves.

Promiscuity is even more disorganizing. Again,
following Hume, men will not "accumulate capital"
for a succeeding generation, specific and known
members of which they do not know to be their own
offspring.

A mate is "property." She may be homely, slovenly,
foolish, but if a man is confident she is "his own"
he will tolerate her, support her, etc. It is like
the statement about a man with a little ten-foot-
square garden versus a large and wonderful public
park. A man prefers his own little plot to the
grand public plot. Similarly, a man prefers _his_
own wife to any public woman no matter how beautiful and clever she may be. Security in marital
relationships is causally related to faithfulness.

The large advances in society are made by extraordinary people. First, they take care of themselves, and put themselves into a situation where
they are comfortable. Then, their motivation to
work and achieve might fail, unless they then continue to work hard and unsparing of themselves, _in_
order _to_ _help_ _their_ _offspring_. Monogamy and
certainly conviction in regard to who is and who
is not one's own child is essential to large property accumulation, which in turn is necessary for
a high standard of living for society generally,
because most of the benefit of property accumulation
goes to society generally rather than the accumulator
himself; see Chapter 32 in this section.

Property rights are considered necessary as a
foundation for a "good society." More fundamental
than property rights are rights in regard to a
monopolistically _possessed_ _mate_. The commandment,
Thou shalt not commit adultery, is even more a
foundation for society than the commandments against
violence, fraud, theft.

Christianity And Pacifism

Christianity is not pacifist in character.

It is true that Christ is reported to have said in the Sermon on the Mount, "Resist not evil," but that expression, in order to be reconciled with what else is taught in Scripture, must be elliptical, and must mean (as was previously indicated), "Resist not evil <u>with</u> <u>evil</u>." There is a further qualification necessary, which can be phrased in this manner: "Resist not evil with evil <u>for</u> <u>the</u> <u>sake</u> <u>of</u> <u>expressing</u> <u>personal</u> <u>hatred</u> <u>and</u> <u>exercising</u> <u>vengeance</u>"; it is, however, permissible in Christian ethics to punish evil, in order to motivate evildoers to desist and also to discourage others who may be contemplating doing the same or similar evil from perpetrating that. This is Christian utilitarianism. Society cannot exist if there is no resistance to evil, and to teach that evil should not be resisted in any way or circumstance is to teach a perverse doctrine.

Pacifism manifests itself in regard to international affairs; war is alleged to be wrong, and should never be permitted; it is alleged that it is better to submit than to fight. To fight is supposed to be contrary to Christian ethics and brotherly love, even when fighting is for a "righteous" cause.

It is a fact that Christ preferred not to resist arrest, and death by crucifixion. In fact, he courted death by going to Jerusalem. If he had fled he would not have died on the cross; but then neither would he have risen from the dead.

If he and his followers had put up a <u>successful</u> fight, he would not have died on the cross either; nor would there then have been a resurrection. Or, if he and his followers had put up an unsuccessful fight, the case would be unrecorded in history, and no grand drama of redemption could have taken place.

Nonresistance -- perfect meekness -- was the necessary corollary to his message and to his life. It was also the necessary requisite for grand drama -- for a history that could be told, and not forgot. Change the basic data, and it all is in the process of becoming meaningless.

The prevailing message of Scripture is that as a man sows, so shall he reap. If he sows well (in the figurative sense employed by Scripture), then he will reap pleasantly. If, however, he sows badly, his harvest for himself will be unpleasant. Evil, in the providence of God, is resisted by the experiencing of unsatisfactory results; in other words, evil is restrained.

The good, in turn, is rewarded. The righteous is promised that he shall flourish as a palm tree in a garden.

Naturally, the cause and effect (between doing good and rewards, and doing evil and penalties) here referred to pertains to inter-relations between men and men -- in the field of human action -- and does not refer to natural events such as sunshine and rain. These latter, except in most extraordinary cases, are declared in Scripture to be invariable, that is, God "makes his sun to shine and his rain to fall on the just and the unjust alike."

The genuineness of the convictions of pacifists should be tested by experiment. If they are genuinely pacifist by conviction, they will not resist evil in personal affairs either, because it would be inconsistent to be pacifist in international matters but not in personal matters. To test the situation, the thing to do is to beat them up; rob them; abuse their wives; terrify their children. Discover whether their pacifism is confusion or hypocrisy.

You will be able to do all this with genuine impunity, if you are dealing with a true-blue pacifist. If he resists, and especially if he retaliates, he is not a consistent pacifist, but a fraud. His betrayal into resistance has revealed that he is inconsistent, or insincere, or that he does not have the stuff in him to be a genuine pacifist.

Such pacifism, insofar as it is professed by some Christians and is declared by them to constitute a true part of Christian ethics, is really an unjustified deviation from what Scripture teaches.

*   *   *

The situation is quite different if a pacifist affirms that he does not hold to the principle of nonresistance to evil, but that he is against unjust wars, and that he is against a nation taking its own disciplinary action even in a just case; but

that he wishes that a judicial and penal machinery
be organized in order to settle international disputes in a grand, impartial court of some kind, and
that such a court should have a pooled international
police power behind it, to enforce the decisions of
the court.

This entails acceptance of the principle of resistance to evil, and shifts the question to whether
such a court could operate and enforce its decisions.

In the first place, is there a "law of nations"
that would set the guide lines for the court? Where
is such a law recorded? Will the nations of the
world accept it?

Is such a law the so-called "Natural Law" of the
Romans and of the historians, Grotius and others?
Is this Natural Law finally nothing else than the
Law of Survival? And is this survival accomplish-
able only by the Decalogue being accepted as the
only legitimate Law of Survival -- resistance to
coercion, fraud, deception, adultery, etc.?

The fact is that the Natural Law to which reference is made as being higher than any national manmade law is, when shorn of unneeded language, nothing
more than various applications of the Decalogue.

But the Decalogue is not universally acceptable
to the peoples of the globe today. The rules by
which a world court would operate are, therefore,
not likely to be either accepted or right. Scripture
condignly demurs on arranging for cooperation between
those who do not accept the same basic moral premises. Scripture does not approve of universal
cooperation.

The present practical difficulties of enforcing
world court decisions in vital cases affecting
national survival are even greater than the problems
just mentioned, but considering enforcement problems
is outside the scope of this book.

Pacifism, in short, is not now an essential or
practical program in Christianity's agenda. As
formulated by many avowed pacifists their program
can never be evaluated as essentially Christian;
Christianity is realistic and not utopian.

Depravity, But More Besides

After long and hard negotiations on a big deal in New York and after the last matters were settled, the negotiators (for relaxation) went to a restaurant for refreshments.

One of the lawyers proposed a question: "How should we look upon the contract we have just signed?" There were various answers.

Finally, the man who had posed the question answered it his own way. He said, "This contract is called an agreement, but it is really a careful and completely-worked-out expression of the suspicions and fears of the two parties who signed it; that is why the contract has the terms which it has."

This attorney had a sophisticated view of reality. A fundamentally significant proposition according to which to live is that men are _depraved_ and will not voluntarily and steadfastly hold to a right or an agreed-upon course, unless they are bound thereto by a contract which can be enforced in courts of law. A civil contract is founded as much on the concept of depravity as is criminal law.

Depravity is a basic datum to take into account in dealing with all others; this holds true for the depravity of others and for _our own_.

Depravity will be defined variously and, of course, not all definitions will be equally valid; some definitions may be almost grotesque. But wise people know themselves, and will correctly infer that others are not better.

Scripture is realistic about depravity, and it does not teach naively that man is good and needs no law to control him, or no contracts to make him consistent.

But more should be added to the definition quoted (in substance, not verbally) from this New York lawyer.

Granted that that contract had been hammered out under the blows of conflicting interests, which would tempt the parties to be faithless to the agreement they were making _unless_ _it_ _were_ _binding_, there is something even more important about

"hammering out a contract," and that is that neither
party to it was intellectually capable of "evaluating" all the interests of the other party, but
which could be incorporated in such a contract as
might be worked out after careful negotiations.

A "contract" is not solely an expression of
suspicion and a means of enforcement; most fundamental of all, neither party was intellectually
able to know at the beginning of negotiations how
the other party looked upon its own interests.
Hard bargaining by A against B is not solely "ill
will" against B's potential faithlessness toward A,
but also a real lack of knowledge of how B looks
at his own concerns. What is true of A not being
able fully to anticipate B's problems, is equally
true of B not being able fully to anticipate A's
problems.

All transactions between men are subject to two
basic complications: (1) mutual depravity, and
(2) intellectual incapability to anticipate wholly
the interests of the other party.

Does Scripture Teach The Ethics Of Morons?

"The reward (1) of humility and
(2) of the fear of Jehovah is riches,
and honor, and life." (Proverbs 22:4)

The text from Proverbs may sound naive; why should (to take the first part) "humility" (of all things!) be rewarded by riches and honors? (The humility referred to does not pertain to the spurious humility of Uriah Heep in Dickens's David Copperfield, but to a sober awareness of the limitations of the human mind.)

Great men are generally appraised according to their intellectual capabilities, the strength of their will, their courage, their industry, or according to their cruelty. Such characteristics are generally neglected in Scripture or condemned.

What is designated as wisdom in Scripture? The "fear of Jehovah" or "respect and love for Jehovah." The practical consequence of that is that a person recognizes he is a mere creature -- born feeble and helpless, soon to die and return to the dust, weak, foolish and wicked. Humility is a by-product of fear of Jehovah.

Avoidance of arrogance, or an even worse hubris, is a powerful note in Scripture.

The really positive note in Scripture, with regard to what constitutes supreme earthly wisdom, is that such wisdom consists in cooperation with fellow beings which cooperation is manifested by obedience to the Law of God. Scripture teaches that if you obey the commandments of God, you are very wise, and that the natural result (except when hindered by the violation by others of the commandments of God) will be prosperity, welfare, peace, happiness, etc.

The great deficiency in the world, according to Scripture, is not the intellectual incapabilities of people, but their unwillingness to cooperate among themselves. It is here only that potential future great gains are promised by Scripture.

One might almost say: Scripture is anti-intellectual, so that it can put a super-emphasis on ethics. Scripture promises more from right

will and right conduct than from a most superior
mind.

*   *   *

This supreme wisdom of Scripture is often not
recognized. In order to grasp the idea intellectually and analytically, instead of merely on the
authority of Scripture, it is profitable and illuminating to read that most excellent analysis of
the unconscious premises of the system of the
"Western world," by Friedrich A. von Hayek, especially in the early chapters of one of his major works,
The Constitution Of Liberty (or more briefly in his
essay Individualism, True and False, in the book of
essays carrying that name).

Hayek, relying on secular sources, shows that a
most important overlooked prerequisite for establishing a free and prosperous society, such as the
society of Western Europe and North America in
contrast to the rest of the world, is an awareness
of the limitations of any human mind, an idea which
(it may be added) is what Scripture means by humility
in the text quoted, and which constitutes its basic
note wherever it concerns itself with ethics, welfare, prosperity, peace.

It is true that some men in Scripture are described as talented, for example, Moses, David and
Solomon. But there is no paean of praise to
laud their capabilities. The emphasis instead is
whether they operated according to, or taught, or
accepted the appropriate rules of ethics. That
constitutes men's highest achievement. Analyses as
in Hayek's The Constitution Of Liberty are invaluable aids in understanding scriptural ethics, quite
apart from the purpose of that author, or other
secular authors.

*   *   *

In stark contrast to this approach is that of
the "planners." There is no humility in their
ideas. Instead of being elevated by the ethics of
the Christian religion, or of allowing freedom as
Hayek envisages, they would "plan" the activities
of all the peoples of the world in (ultimately) one
man's mind, or some super-committee. This is a
colossal hubris.

As illustrative of an approach irreconcilable
with Scripture, an undoubtedly sincere and well-
intentioned but erroneous and disastrous statement
can be quoted which has been attributed to a well-
known labor leader:

> Only a moron would believe that the
> millions of private economic decisions
> being made independently of each other
> will somehow harmonize in the end, and
> bring us out where we want to be.

That affirmation is a positive negation of the
highest practical wisdom taught in Scripture, provided of course it is understood that these "private
economic decisions" although purely self-regarding
do not involve coercion, theft and fraud. See
Chapters 4 through 7 in this section on Ricardo's
Law of Cooperation.

Scripture, if the quotation just given were
correct, would be moronic in its ideas!

MISCELLANEOUS NOTE:

Scripture is practical in character and interested
in how people "get along" in the world.

It might be expected, then, that emphasis would be
placed on native intellectual endowments, that is, on
a particular person's intelligence quotient, his so-
called IQ. Although not neglectful of a person's IQ,
Scripture basically makes a different approach, that is,
an approach which is more optimistic and hopeful for
personal improvement. That reveals a fine vista ahead
for every man who will follow the road. Scriptural
ideas are as follows:

1. It admonishes to self-knowledge; warns a man of
   his weaknesses, his proneness to evil, his mortality; and declares that all men are alike in
   those regards. Therefore, do not be naive, or
   "too trusting."

2. It urges cooperation with other men. Do not
   "withdraw." Do not fail to cooperate with others,
   especially not because they might be benefited;
   benefits are mutual in a free society.

3. It outlines a marvelous method of cooperation, by
   obedience to the Decalogue: do not coerce, deceive, plunder, etc.

4. It promises rewards for a steady will to do the
   right, and perseverence therein.

5. It advises industriousness -- hard work.

This characteristically Christian approach will yield a
man more than will anxiety when he is graded in IQ tests.
The scriptural proposition is that a moral approach will
yield more than an intellectual approach. An IQ test
may be able to tell you what your status is, but not your
opportunity.

The Interpretation Of Christian Ethics
Has Not Always Avoided Being In-Bred

It is doubtful that the Christian church should ever affirm that Scripture is _entirely_ and _solely_ its own interpreter, without being able to benefit by assistance from the sciences. If the church should do that, its wisdom should be questioned.

It is interesting to note that the churches have sometimes been, and continue not-too-wisely to be, laggard in utilizing all the sciences for assistance in interpreting Scripture.

This phenomenon occurred unhappily in the case of Galileo. The mother church of all the West, from its own nonscientific and in-bred interpretation of cosmological subjects referred to in Scripture, asserted that Galileo's views were in error, that the sun moved around the earth, rather than that the earth both rotated daily and moved in an ellipse around the sun annually.

Temporarily, the church enforced its will in this controversy, but we cannot look back, with satisfaction, on its action. Galileo's ideas universally prevail today; in other words, the church finally came to accept the assistance it could obtain, from the _natural_ sciences, when interpreting Scripture in questions of _cosmology_.

Maybe the churches have an inclination today to perpetrate the same error but now in ethics as distinguished from cosmology centuries ago.

Economics can contribute as much to the clarification of Christian _ethics_ as Copernican or Galilean natural science was (is) able to contribute to Christian _cosmology_.

Evidence has certainly not yet accumulated that the churches rely adequately on economics to contribute to the clarification of Christian ethics. Economics does not seem to have a place in theological curricula. The preaching and teaching of clerics do not give evidence that they have a utilizable knowledge of economics. There is evidence, too, that leaders in the churches look at economic problems in a naive manner (just as most people do), and see and consider only surface phenomena and

immediate consequences, rather than the <u>ultimate</u>
consequences which may be deduced if one engages
in a careful chain of reasoning. If economics can
be defined negatively, then it is not the science
of reasoning only t o the first consequences of
actions by men, but reasoning through to <u>eventual</u>
consequences.

Christian ethics should have a natural affinity
to economics. A basic characteristic of Christian
ethics is that it does <u>not</u> stop with superficial
observations and with first consequences of conduct.
Christian ethics does not dispute that violence,
theft and fraud may <u>temporarily</u> succeed; but it
declares that such conduct will not <u>permanently</u>
succeed. Christianity should, therefore, be naturally responsive to ideas it can learn from economics,
a science which also is based on taking the long
view (not the short one) of actions in the economic
field, which (as has been explained earlier) pertains substantially to the relationship of men to
things. See Eccl. 8:11-13; also pages 329-330.

Now if the <u>relationship of men to things</u> were
independent of, or posterior to, the <u>relationship</u>
<u>of men to men</u>, then economics would have little to
offer for the benefit of ethics. The situation,
however, is that the relationship of men to things
is <u>logically precedent</u> to most of the "relationships of men to men (ethics)," and the thought of
isolating economics from ethics is as unrealistic
as the isolation of the cosmological work of
Galileo from Biblical cosmology.

For moralists to turn to economics for interesting light on ethics entails a new problem,
namely, which branch of economics should they
select? Some good discrimination is necessary.
Old classical economics is like the Ptolomaic
system in cosmology; socialist economics is worse
and like the relation of astrology to astronomy;
if genuine and helpful assistance is to be obtained
by ethics, it can get it best from <u>neoclassical</u>
economics.

Not everything that passes for economics is of
genuine merit, no more than that everything which
has passed or still passes for cosmology is trust-
worthy. But neither economics nor cosmology is
inferior in this respect; not everything that
passes for ethics is perfect either; there is such
a thing as pseudo-ethics.

N O T E   No. 1   This footnote is apropos of
ideas on pages 44-6, 278-9, and 372-7.

Interpretations of what the Apostle Paul wrote
in Romans 5:12 (and elsewhere) differ; the text
there reads: "Therefore, as through one man sin
entered into the world, and death through sin; and
so death passed unto all men, for that all sinned."

The maximal interpretation is that Adam's one
fall condemns all men to temporal and eternal punishment. But that will give some pause. (1) There
will be no difficulty about Adam's sin being the
first of such events. (2) That spiritual death was
introduced by Adam's sin is not a difficulty either;
but that, only because of Adam's fall, physical
death exists reads too much into what Scripture and
commonsense teach. (3) That eternal punishment for
all derives causally from Adam's first sin, although
a possible interpretation, does not appear to be a
necessary one.

Suppose a man goes fishing, and catches twenty
fish. Suppose, too, that it took him a long time
to catch the first. Later he tells his wife: "When
I got the first one, I knew I was going to get a
good catch" -- as if catching the first fish might
be the "cause" for catching the next nineteen. This
would be a fallacy, namely, taking the first effect,
or the first piece of evidence on effect, as being
the cause. The cause for catching twenty fish was
not that one had been caught; but that one was caught
was evidence of the existence of the real requisites
for catching fish. The requisites included the lake
or stream; having fishing gear; proper bait; casting
correctly; fish present where the fisherman was working; etc. The first evidence that those requisites
were being met came to hand when the first fish was
caught.

Similarly, the "cause" or "causes" of sin being
present in the world can be ascribed to the first
evidence coming to hand, that is, to Adam's fall.
This is a case of not being pedantically meticulous
regarding cause and effect; or more accurately in
this instance, this is a case of the first evidence
of sin being, in a sense, mentioned as the cause.
The cause of our sins is not Adam's fall per se,
but the cosmology of existence: (1) the welfareshortage; (2) our needs; (3) our efforts to satisfy
those needs; (4) our inclination to get results by
the quickest method; (5) our getting those results
by injuring others. If we had no needs; if supplies
were redundant; if we did not endeavor to provide
what we need in the wrong manner, then there would
be no sin.

Paul can be excessively interpreted. The point he was surely and minimally making is that we all have the same potential propensities, under similar circumstances, from Adam on, to sin; and so it was natural to say that we all went down "in Adam"!

N O T E   No. 2

Readers, having finished this section on ethics, may wonder at its nontraditional approach. The explanations are:

1. The "origin" of sin is taken to be the cosmological constitution of the world; not any abstraction about goodness or badness of men; therefore, cosmology and ethics are not separated.

2. Sins of governments -- publicly approved policies, incorporated in their laws -- are treated extensively, because they are matters of ethics as much as private sins are. To treat private sins only, when public sins are jeopardizing the world's orderly existence, would be inexcusable.

3. A less attractive feature of the ideas of some Christians is "piosity"-- their excessive idealism and sentimental prattle about "love." Historically, such piosity has been alien to Christianity. The definition of "love" given by some is the communist definition; communism is a far more pious and sanctimonious religion than Christianity. Those who have a compulsive propensity for sanctimony should espouse communism, and formally abandon Christianity. Consider Dostoevsky's dictum: "Everyone is really responsible to all men for all men and for everything." This is blatant sanctimony. Sanctimony is denigrated in this book.

4. There are other Christians who concentrate on "getting saved." They hardly progress further than "grace." Their being Christians consists in subjective pleasure from their own grace, plus promoting grace to others, but a thorough study of the fruits of grace -- better private and public ethics useful in this life -- does not engross much of their attention. In contrast, Minimal Religion emphasizes this-worldly as much as future-worldly matters.

I V

Christian

Theology

FAITH VERSUS REASON

Without revelation, the origin, nature and
destiny of things cannot be known but only inferred
from phenomena. They are not known.

"To be incapable of proof by reasoning is common
to all first principles; to the first premises of
our knowledge, as well as to those of our conduct,"
wrote John Stuart Mill in his essay, Utilitarianism
(Chapter IV, the section one).

All answers to the "riddles of existence" are
manifestations of faith in one form or another, or,
if one wishes to use an alternative expression,
they are all manifestations of reason in one form
or another. But any one answer, whatever it may
be, is not to be distinguished from other answers
as if one were pure reason, and the other answers
were pure reason. On the basis of interpretation of
phenomena no explanation of existence has basic
preeminence over others.

It is the thesis of this book that it is an
error to believe that "science", as a closed system
of observations and inferred inter-related cause
and effect, is the highest "reason". "Science" is
here taken in the sense of Positivism as previously
explained (pages 6-.. and elsewhere), namely that
there is nothing beyond inanimate material, that the
previous universe has been self-generating, has
no purpose, and that the material only is a
"reasoned" explanation of that which we see which
to serve of existence. This proposition amounts to:
Just is God, for the Positivist; just as a
Transcendental Being is God for a Transcendentalist,
including Christians.

When placed on the horns of the dilemma -- namely
of being a Positivist or a Transcendentalist and
specifically, a Christian in this context -- the
choice made in this book is a vigorous choice against
Positivism and in favor of Transcendentalism. This
choice is not made because "faith" is preferred to
"reason", but because the reasoning behind the
Christian interpretation of life appears more
reasonable than that behind Positivism.

Faith Versus Reason

Without revelation, the origin, nature and destiny of things cannot be known but only inferred from phenomena. They are not known.

"To be incapable of proof by reasoning is common to all first principles, to the first premises of our knowledge, as well as to those of our conduct," wrote John Stuart Mill in his essay, Utilitarianism (Chapter IV, paragraph one).

All answers to the riddles of existence are manifestations of faith in one form or another; or, if one wishes to use an alternative expression, they are all manifestations of reason in one form or another. But any one answer, whatever it may be, is not to be distinguished from other answers as if one were pure reason, and the other answers were pure faith. On the basis of interpretation of phenomena no explanation of existence has basic preeminence over others.

It is the thesis of this book that it is an error to believe that "science," as a closed system of observations and inferred inter-related cause and effect, is the highest "reason." "Science" is here taken in the sense of Positivism as previously explained (pages 51-55 and elsewhere), namely, that there is nothing beyond the material, that the marvelous universe has been self-generating, has no purpose, and that the material only is a "reasoned" explanation of that which we are able to sense of existence. This proposition essentially is: Dust is God, for the Positivist, just as a Transcendental Being is God for a Transcendentalist, including Christians.

When placed on the horns of the dilemma -- namely, of being a Positivist or a Transcendentalist and, specifically, a Christian in this context -- the choice made in this book is a vigorous choice against Positivism and in favor of Transcendentalism. This choice is not made because "faith" is preferred to "reason," but because the reasoning behind the Christian interpretation of life appears more reasonable than that behind Positivism.

*   *   *

The initial foundation undergirding Christianity is
really not the Scriptures, but rather observations
of the world around us and rational deductions from
those observations.

It is standard among Christians to say that God
can be known out of two "books" -- (1) creation
(the phenomenal world) and (2) the Christian Scriptures. In this context, some Christians may put
the Scriptures first and creation second in sequence
of thought and rank of importance.

But an alternative is to reverse the order: to
wit, the interpretation of the phenomenal world
(creation and nature through the natural sciences,
etc.) comes first. In Romans 1:20, 21 the Apostle
Paul set the pattern: When one begins to discuss
with others the meaning of life one does well to
note the character of the universe and from that
deduce a guiding intelligence and purpose.

For the invisible things of him since the
creation of the world are clearly seen, being
perceived through the things that are made,
even his everlasting power and divinity; that
they may be without excuse: because that,
knowing God, they glorified him not as God,
neither gave thanks; but became vain in their
reasonings, and their senseless heart was
darkened.

What is more reasonable: to believe that two
eyes with adjustable lenses were developed by
chance, without purpose, in millions of years of
existence; or, instead, to believe that animals
and men have two eyes by some factor other than
chance?

An intelligent Christian cannot hold to his
faith without soul-searching uncertainty and
skepticism, in order to reassure himself that his
Hobson's choice -- between Christianity and Positivism -- is properly to be made in favor of
Christianity.

It is sometimes the Christian's verdict in the
natural field, designated here by creation, which
is (rationally) the initial foundation for his
faith.

                    *   *   *

But having concluded that the dirt in the
soiled cuff of his shirt does not constitute "God"

after all, he is then forced to a series of concerns about, who is the Transcendental God. At this point the significance of <u>special</u> <u>revelation</u> is decisive. It is <u>this</u> part of Christianity which builds all of the remaining superstructure.

Nor is this superstructure irrational; on the contrary, it is quite marvelous:

1. It presents an unsurpassable system of ethics;

2. It looks upon the Creator and Governor of the universe as beneficent, merciful, wise;

3. The welfare of human beings is one of its unalterable objectives;

4. It rejects the idea that the "setting" in which we see that we live and die here and now is comprehensive enough to interpret this life wisely, and it frames our present existence in a greater and spectacular framework beyond the temporal;

5. Its goal is happiness -- by mutual coopera- tion, good will, forgiveness, freedom.

Christianity appears to this writer to be an excellent and the <u>only</u> reasonable system by which to live and die.

Manoah's Wife

The strong man of the Old Testament was Sampson, son of Manoah.

Before the birth of Sampson an angel appeared to Manoah's wife, and announced the prospective conception and birth of Sampson. Later the angel appeared to <u>both</u> Manoah and his wife.

At that time it was apparently a belief that if you saw an angel (in human form, of course) that you would die. Manoah held to that superstition. He said to his wife (Judges 13:22):

> We shall surely die, because we have seen God.

This involved an inconsistency, to which the wife called attention: if they were to have a son, how could they, if they were to die? She was a rationalist in this matter. She said (Judges 13:23):

> If Jehovah were pleased to kill us, he would not have received a burnt-offering and a meal-offering at our hand, <u>neither</u> <u>would</u> <u>he</u> <u>have</u> <u>showed</u> <u>us</u> <u>all</u> <u>these</u> <u>things</u>, <u>nor</u> <u>would</u> <u>at</u> <u>this</u> <u>time</u> <u>have</u> <u>told</u> <u>such</u> <u>things</u> <u>as</u> <u>these</u>. (Emphasis supplied.)

In this book, the revelation of God has been approached in the same manner as that of Manoah's wife; our effort has been in the direction of her consistency rather than his inconsistency.

In every age there are people who approach revelation by God as did the wife of Manoah (on the one hand), and as did Manoah himself (on the other hand).

Two Ways To Learn Of God

The Christian religion is founded on special revelation, but it has really never been considered to be founded on special revelation <u>alone</u>.

Galileo wrote the following on that subject.

I am inclined to believe that the intention of the Sacred Scriptures is to give to mankind the information necessary for their salvation.

But I do not hold it necessary to believe that the same God who has endowed us with senses, with speech, with intellect, intended that we should neglect the use of these, and seek by other means for knowledge which these are sufficient to procure for us; especially in a science like astronomy, of which so little notice is taken by the Scriptures that none of the planets, except the sun and moon and once or twice only Venus, by the name of Lucifer, are so much as named at all.

This therefore being granted, me thinks that in the discussion of natural problems we ought not to begin at the authority of texts of Scriptures, but at sensible experiments and necessary demonstrations.

There is merit, in certain situations in certain fields of knowledge, in beginning as Galileo suggests, with "sensible experiments and necessary demonstrations," and then interpreting Scripture accordingly; rather than <u>in</u> <u>abstracto</u> really <u>imagining</u> something from Scripture and then rejecting sensible experiments and significant demonstrations. The proper "sequence" in different situations is a matter of importance.

It is not to be gainsaid that, as Galileo indicated, the data in Scripture on many natural phenomena are too meager to tell much and need to be supplemented greatly by either imagination (in the form of "exegesis"), or by facts.

The church father, Clement of Alexandria, wrote: "To know is more than to believe."

*   *   *

An ideal example of the employment of nature and
special revelation for the expression of Christian
thought is the Nineteenth Psalm. The first six
verses pertain to nature, and begin with the magnificent words:

> The heavens declare the glory of God;
> And the firmament showeth his handiwork,
> Day unto day uttereth speech,
> And night unto night showeth knowledge.

Then beginning with the seventh verse the theme
is shifted to special revelation, and the introduction has equally resounding words:

> The law of Jehovah is perfect, restoring
>   the soul:
> The testimony of Jehovah is sure, making
>   wise the simple.

The psalm ends with the prayer:

> Let the words of my mouth and the
>   meditation of my heart
> Be acceptable in thy sight,
> O Jehovah, my rock, and my redeemer.

Fourteen verses run the gamut (1) of the knowledge of God through nature, (2) of the significance
of the Decalogue for welfare, and (3) of the need
of and thankfulness for the mercy of God.

Evidence Regarding God From "Nature"

A notable argument from "nature" which occurs in the New Testament in the Epistle to the Romans, quoted on page 300, involves an extrapolation, a moving to a conclusion, which may not be obvious on first reading. The "approach" is fundamental and worth analyzing.

The argument is that there is a genuine Creator (not a manmade god), who can be "seen" (deduced) from the "Book of Nature," the world around us.

According to the argument, the "explanation" of the universe requires the concepts of purpose and design. This is in contrast to chance, aimlessness and unpurposeful causes arising out of the "dust" of the earth. Purpose is ascribed to God, just as it is known, in a smaller way, in the lives of men. Life, for mortals; is "unthinkable" in terms which would eliminate human purpose.

That there is a "jump" in the argument (an extrapolation, a mere deduction) is readily to be seen and admitted. An illustration should help understanding this.

Suppose a grandfather and a fourteen-year-old grandson wander over the old man's farm, where one of the objects is a gigantic tree. The grandson asks, "Grandfather, how high is the tree?" To which the grandfather replies, "I do not 'know' and never shall be able to verify it by climbing to the tipmost branch, but you can find out for yourself if you wish to do so. It will not be difficult. Do you wish to find out?" Let us assume that the grandson assents.

The grandfather sends him to the barn for a stick, a hammer, and a long tape measure. He has the grandson pound the stick in the ground, and then do three things: (1) measure the length of the stick above ground, (2) the length of the shadow of the stick, and (3) the length of the shadow of the tree. They are: the stick, 4 feet; the shadow, 6 feet; the shadow of the tree, 120 feet.

The grandfather next assigns the grandson the task of computing from the three measurements available the <u>unknown</u>, that is, the height of the tree. There must be an extrapolation, a "jump," a deduction from the <u>three</u> <u>knowns</u> to the <u>one</u> <u>unknown</u>.

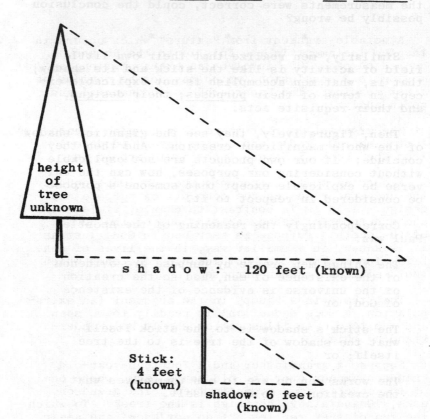

height
of
tree
unknown

s h a d o w :   120 feet (known)

Stick:
4 feet
(known)

shadow: 6 feet
(known)

(In order to avoid the necessity of a very
large drawing, the scales for the two
parts of the diagram are different, but
the idea will be readily understood.)

The grandson has his difficulties with the computation, but the grandfather finally makes it clear
that the stick's shadow and the stick itself had to
have a ratio, in this case, 6 feet to 4 feet; or a
<u>ratio</u> as 3 to 2; in other words, the stick is
2/3rds the length of the shadow. This the grandson
finally clearly understood. Then the grandfather
asked the question: Does it make sense to say then
that the height of the tree is 2/3rds as long as
the length of its shadow? The grandson agrees to

that, and then computes what 2/3rds of 120 feet of
shadow is, and finds the figure to be 80 feet,
which (necessarily) is the height of the tree. If
the measurements were correct, could the conclusion
possibly be wrong?

*   *   *

Similarly, men realize that their own little
field of activity is like the stick and its shadow;
that is, what men accomplish is not explicable except in terms of their purposes; their designs,
and their requisite acts.

Then, figuratively, they see the gigantic "shadow"
of the whole magnificent creation. And then they
conclude: if our own products are not explicable
without considering our purposes, how can the universe be explicable except that someone's purpose
be considered in respect to it?

Correspondingly the reasoning of the Apostle
Paul was:

The things men create by purpose are evidence
of the existence of men, and so the creation
of the universe is evidence of the existence
of God; or

The stick's shadow is to the stick itself
what the shadow of the tree is to the tree
itself; or

The works men do are to men themselves what
the creation is to God himself.

It is as irrational, according to Paul, to declare
that a sewing machine pulled out of the ocean in
operating condition just "happened" to come into
existence, as it is illogical to declare that the
universe all "just happened." There is, in this
reasoning which Paul attacks, no origin to the
sewing machine; no man made it! Similarly, there
is no origin to the universe; no creative intelligence made it!

The writer of the Epistle to the Romans held
that questioning the existence of God was unreasonable, the phenomena in the universe (his shadow)
being what it is.

A Strict Constructionist Approach To
Christian Dogma

If the method in this book in the earlier three sections has been strict-constructionist, it will be even more so in this fourth section on Christian dogma.

The broader a statement, the more difficult is its defense. It should be easier to prove that a man stole something in a specific case, than that he steals regularly.

If a man gets into an argument, the less restraint his opponent shows in what he affirms, the easier it will be to refute him. Schopenhauer recommended, in his cynical essay entitled The Art Of Controversy, as a strategem in order to win an argument in a dispute, purposely "to extend" the propositions of an opponent. He wrote:

The Extension. This consists in carrying your opponent's proposition beyond its natural limits; in giving it as general a signification and as wide a sense as possible, so as to exaggerate it; and, on the other hand, in giving your own proposition as restricted a sense and as narrow limits as you can, because the more general a statement becomes, the more numerous are the objections to which it is open. The defense consists in an accurate statement of the point or essential question at issue.

What Schopenhauer wrote about an argument is worth remembering when reading Scripture. There are various ways of interpreting its teachings, from extreme extensionism to extreme strict-constructionism.

The tendency of people who are enthusiastically convinced about their ideas is to extend them, that is, make them too broad. The more prudent a man is, the less inclined he is to make his statements broad or categorical.

Some devout church members have a propensity for an extensionist interpretation of Scripture. The consequence is that some things which Christians teach do not sound plausible to non-Christians unless these latter folk were in early youth taught those

same ideas. Because of such intellectual barriers
created by extensionism, some people are skeptical
of Christian dogmas and reject them, or are indifferent to them. There is some tendency for those
who are ignorant and naive to be Christians, but
for those who are rational and sophisticated to be
only nominal Christians, or to remain outside the
church.

As this book makes a strict constructionist
approach, it (instead of incautiously generalizing
and making a specific event in Scripture carry the
load of universal application) endeavors to avoid
generalizations which are not explicitly insisted
upon in Scripture.

To illustrate the method here employed and to
emphasize its importance, attention will first be
given to resurrection from the dead and to the
character of a future life.

These two doctrines are inseparable from Christian doctrine, but in order to put these doctrines
in a strict constructionist light, the fact will be
considered, in the next chapter, that <u>no</u> <u>one</u>,
Christian or non-Christian, wishes a <u>general</u> resurrection <u>in</u> <u>this</u> <u>life</u>.

After having established that, it should be
possible to make the point, effectively emphasized
by Christ himself, that a future life cannot be
imagined in terms of this life.

A Resurrection From The Dead Which Is
Not Wanted

Although resurrection is an essential doctrine
of Christianity, it cannot possibly mean what some
people imagine it to be.

In the first place, there are some problems connected with resurrection which necessarily constrict
the concept.

People think that they would like a resurrection
here and now, and in the present world and its environment (cosmology). But that they do not really
wish a resurrection of that sort is illustrated by
the following tale:

RESURRECTION IN _____ IN 1285

In the thirteenth century on a spring day a coach
came rolling down the road into _____, then as now
a thriving city in western Europe.

The coach was occupied by one man, in the prime of
life, alert in appearance, and obviously self-confident.
He gazed long and intently on the city before him.

At the back of the coach was a large, strongly built
oak chest, reinforced by wrought iron, and doubly pad-
locked.

Two vigorous armed guards on horseback followed the
coach.

Clearly, the traveller was a man of importance and
means.

In the city the company put up at the best hostelry,
and took the best rooms.

The visitor devoted several days to exploring the
town. He noted that it had outgrown its old walls. The
place was too crowded. The situation was aggravated because there was within the walls an old cemetery, which
occupied considerable space.

*   *   *

The Town Council of _____ met almost daily,
at least for a short session. At one of these there was
a rap on the door. The visitor was the man who had
ridden into the city in the coach.

In response to inquiry regarding what he wanted, he
came to business quickly. His somewhat halting speech
revealed him a foreigner. He said that he had arrived

three days earlier; that he had surveyed the town, and
that he had noted it was overcrowded within the ancient
walls; further, that there was considerable valuable
space occupied by the cemetery; and finally, that the
situation would be greatly relieved if the cemetery were
removed.

To solve that problem, he blandly proposed to the
town fathers that he would resurrect all the dead in
the cemetery -- for a fee of 10,000 florins.

The proposition was so astonishing that there was
a long silence. But the town councilmen were not the
most ignorant and credulous in the city. Mentally they
concluded that they were dealing with a bold impostor of
some sort, and that set the tone of the following discussion. They did not believe he <u>could</u> resurrect the
dead -- some were buried there already for 250 years;
nor would they pay the fee -- which the visitor wanted
in advance in gold pieces. However, he was aggressive
and argumentative. Finally, he was more or less hustled
out of the door by bailiffs.

No councilman would keep interesting news of that
kind to himself. The story was told later that day in
every house and public place in the city. The proposition was, however, so exciting and glamorous that a great
crowd gathered that evening outside the hotel of the
visitor; but he did not appear.

                    *   *   *

When the Town Council was meeting the next day,
there was again a rap on the door. It was the same
visitor who wished to resurrect the dead and earn a fee.
Behind him stood his two guards, carrying between them
the oak chest.

Without so much as, "By your leave, gentlemen," he
pushed his way in and motioned to his men to carry in
the chest. He produced keys and opened the chest, which
was full of documents.

One of these he handed to the mayor and asked him
to read it. Upon being unrolled and read, it turned out
to be an affidavit from a town council, properly signed
and sealed, in _____ in southeastern France. This
affidavit declared that Dr. Guglielmo Verranti had resurrected the dead in the cemetery of that city, in accordance to a contract signed by him and the Town Council
for an agreed upon number of gold pieces of such and
such a kind. The affidavit declared that the Town Council
of _____ was well pleased with the services performed.

Careful examination revealed the affidavit to appear
quite reliable. Paper, letterhead, signature and seal
appeared genuine.

One after another, Dr. Verranti showed letters,
affidavits and news reports of his marvelous achievements
at resurrecting the dead.

This evidence shook the councilmen. Conversation

revealed that several believed the evidence; others
wavered. But finally the skeptics prevailed, as is usual
and was proper, and again the visitor was rebuffed and
put out-of-doors with his papers, chest and guards.

That night the populace was excited. Exaggerated
rumors began to go around. The people, more credulous
than the councilmen, believed that a great miracle-worker
had come to their city, and that he could and would --
oh wonderful news! -- resurrect their dead, if the
councilmen would only pay him the 10,000 florins.

But following close behind this belief came an
uncomfortable awareness -- to many -- that they wanted
no resurrection from the dead. It would be a catastrophe
to have a resurrection!

There was a woman who had just remarried. At the
urgings of her lover, she had poisoned her first husband.
Dying, he had realized that he had been poisoned, and in
his last agony his wife had mocked him. Soon thereafter
she had married the lover. They wanted no resurrection,
because for them a resurrection would mean the gallows.

There was also the young man whose rich father had
just died. The family had been wealthy and aristocrats
for six generations, and all those generations were
buried in the cemetery. The young man was at first over-
joyed that he would get his father back, whom he had
loved dearly. Then he realized that he would have to
return the inheritance he had received; vacate the house
of his father which he had occupied; retire from the
management of family affairs; etc. All this, although
a shock, was worth getting his father back.

Then he thought of his grandfather, whom he remembered, a crotchety old man, with haughty air and almost
military discipline. He would get all the old property
back.

No, it would go to the great grandfather; no, no,
it would go back another three generations! The an-
cestor, sixth-removed would get nearly all, and the rest
would be property-less! He himself and his father --
the two for whom he had genuine affection -- would be
poor men!

In short, shamefacedly this young man realized --
with consternation -- that he did not want a resurrection
from the dead.

And similarly it was throughout the city.

Even many honorable people were confused and be-
wildered. Widowers and widows who had remarried asked
themselves: "With whom will I be married if the dead
are resurrected?"

*   *   *

The next day there was for a third time a rap on
the door of the council chamber. It was Verranti again.
He came in confidently, although respectfully. He asked
whether the Council had reconsidered. Upon receiving a

negative reply, he smiled and made a new proposition.
He said, "Your highnesses, I have decided to make you a
proposal so reasonable that you cannot reject it. It is
this: I will resurrect the dead, and will not ask for
payment until <u>after</u> the event. All that you will commit
yourself for is that you will pay me the 10,000 florins
upon my fulfilling my part of the agreement. No resurrection, no pay; resurrection, 10,000 florins."

       This proposition was something different. There
could be no trick to this, and no risk. Even the most
hard-headed councilmen were sobered. None argued back.
But Verranti could get no affirmative answer. Finally,
he left with the words, "I shall be back tomorrow at
this time."

       The latest news at the Town Council spread at once
through the city.

                    *   *   *

       The next day at the appointed time the city square
was packed by a muttering mob. Verranti and his men had
to elbow their way through. There were shouts, cat calls,
tremendous excitement.

       The council admitted Verranti.

       The clamor outside increased. Steadily the demand
became more uniform: "We want no resurrection of the
dead. No resurrection! NO RESURRECTION!"

       Upon Verranti's question, whether the council would
pay him 10,000 florins <u>after</u> he had resurrected the dead,
the answer given him was a sullen, "No."

                    *   *   *

       Then Verranti's air changed. Once he had been a
petitioner; then a bargainer; but now he became threatening. He radically reversed his position. He said, rais-
ing his voice so that those outside the windows could
clearly hear him, and report to the people:

       "I will resurrect the dead for nothing, then."

       Certainly, that proposition was reasonable enough.
It electrified the citizenry in the square and the streets
leading to it. The excitement became terrific. The
shouts became louder, "We want no resurrection of the
dead."

       The voice of the mayor betrayed his suppressed
anger: "Get out of here, and leave town at once."

       Verranti sauntered to the window, and then half
turned back to the council. He spoke slowly and clearly
so that those inside and outside could distinctly hear
him above all the clamor:

       "All right then, pay me 10,000 florins for <u>not</u>
resurrecting the dead."

It took only a short time for that proposition
to filter through the mob. Then the crowd began to shout:

"Pay him the 10,000 florins not to resurrect the
dead."

The councilmen deliberated. Delay only made matters
worse. Members of the mob attempted to force the door.
Some tried to climb through the windows.

The cries continued, "Pay him! Pay him!"

Finally, the councilmen proposed to Verranti that
they would pay him the 10,000 florins, if he would leave
town that afternoon yet without any resurrection.

Verranti rejected the proposition with disdain.
He had spent time and money. He had qualified himself
to resurrect locally. He could and would do it. The
10,000 florins, however, would no longer suffice. His
livelihood depended on his reputation; his reputation
depended on his performance. If they did not wish him
to perform, he could not forgo an affidavit that he had
resurrected the dead in _____. He would therefore
settle, only on two conditions, (1) payment of the 10,000
florins plus, (2) a statement signed and sealed by the
city clerk that he had raised the dead in _____.
The affidavit, under the circumstances, must accompany
the money.

That was the rogue's game. No wonder he had no
affidavits from other cities nearby. The shrewd men in
the council began to realize how they and the townsfolk
were being bilked.

It was too late, however, to do anything about it.
The mob was hysterical. Women were screaming. Men began
beating each other. The police were powerless.

The will of the council collapsed. They paid the
10,000 florins and gave Verranti the affidavit he wanted.

Announcement was made from the balcony to the crowd
that there would be no resurrection of the dead, and
that Dr. Verranti had promised to leave within an hour
if he were not in any way molested.

A great shout of joy went up.

That afternoon the same cavalcade which a week
earlier had come into the town left at a brisk pace,
until the horses slowed on the steeper climbs.

Dr. Verranti smiled. He had another affidavit in
his chest; and there were also 10,000 pleasant florins.

*   *   *

The purpose of the story is obvious. People do
not really wish a _general_ resurrection of the dead
in this life. Any resurrection generally wanted
must be in a radically different cosmology than
this present cosmology, that is, only in a future
and different world.

Indeed, people in _individual_ cases do wish a
resurrection from the dead; a lonely and hapless
widow wants her husband back; orphans weep for the
return of their parents; parents consider their life
blasted by the loss of a child. _Temporarily_, just
after a loss, survivors usually wish to restore the
old _status quo_.

It is a feature of life to "adjust" soon and
completely. (1) A widow who has remarried is hardly
in a position to wish to have her first husband back.
(2) Orphans grow up and become independent of the
need of parents; they may say: "It would be interesting to see what our parents looked like, but if
they would come back they would be younger than we
are now." (3) Parents, devastated by the loss of
an infant, when they are 25 years old, hardly wish
for the child back fifty years later when they are
75 years old! What would two old people do with a
two-months' old baby?

Because people and circumstances change, a _gen-
eral_ resurrection in _this_ life, and a restoration
of some past things into the present situation, is
not wanted nor feasible.

A _general_ resurrection in this life is simply
incompatible with the conditions of this life. A
general resurrection can be wanted only in a
future life.

Christ's Realistic View Of A Future Life

In the more than one thousand pages in the Old
and New Testaments, there are significant variations
in the attention given to <u>individual</u> <u>future</u> existence
after this life. Answers to the following questions
may be helpful.

1. What is the first reference in the Old
    Testament to a future life of some sort
    for all?

2. How much of a role does hope of resurrec-
    tion and a future life play in the Old
    Testament?

3. What is said about resurrection and future
    life in the New Testament?

*   *   *

1. The alleged first reference to a future life,
admittedly of a vague sort, comes as late as the
time of Jacob, about 1700 B.C.

When the sons of Jacob brought back the coat of
many colors which had belonged to Joseph (which
they had smeared with goat's blood), and when they
asked their father if that might be the special
garment that he had given to his favorite son,
Jacob looked at it, and answered (Genesis 37:33, 35):

> It is my son's coat; an evil beast hath
> devoured him; Joseph is without doubt
> torn to pieces. ... And all his sons
> and all his daughters rose up to comfort
> him; but he refused to be comforted; and
> he said, For I will go down to Sheol to
> my son mourning. And his father wept
> for him.

This statement by Jacob that he would "go down
to Sheol <u>to</u> <u>my</u> <u>son</u> mourning" is taken (by some) as
indication that Jacob expected to see his son again
after his own death. Jacob apparently did not
expect a good life because he would go down "mourning." But in any event, the words do not convey
much definite information.

*   *   *

2.   Centuries pass, and David makes a similar
remark on the death of his son (his first from his
adulterous union with Bathsheba) in II Samuel 12:23:

> But now he (the son) is dead, wherefore
> should I (David) fast? Can I bring him
> back again? I shall go to him, but he
> will not return to me. (Emphasis supplied.)

This is also considered by some as a proof-text that
there was belief in Old Testament times in a life
hereafter. But again, the evidence is not convincing. Might David have meant merely that he would,
sooner or later, follow his son to the grave?

The Old Testament is generally uninformative in
regard to a future life.

There are, of course, the two special cases of
unusual translation out of this life, of Enoch and
Elijah, but these cases are nontypical. And there
is the special case of Moses who died and whose
body was not found (was buried by God). But a
doctrine of resurrection and of a future life,
either good for all, indifferent for all, or bad
for all; or else, good for some and bad for some,
does not come to systematic or unequivocal expression.

Poetry probably best expresses fundamental emotions. Poetry in the Old Testament appears principally in the Psalms and in Job. The Psalms deal with
the problems of this life and of death, but not at
all (or so vaguely as not to register on the mind)
with a future life. That is a reason why some
extremely devout modern Christians (but who are in
a sense really this-worldly minded) are fond of the
Psalms; those Psalms give such folk comfort for
this life; that is why they like them. (These
Psalm-lovers generally act unworldly and are often
separatists; but they are practical folk, as well.)

There is also the expression in the dramatic and
poetical book of Job, where Job exclaims (Job 19:25):

> I know that my Redeemer liveth;

and then the additional words appear (Job 19:26-7):

> And after my skin, even this body, is
> destroyed, then without my flesh shall I
> see God; whom I, even I, shall see, on
> my side, and mine eyes shall behold, and
> not as a stranger.

It is not clear what is here meant by "without my
flesh"; possibly it means "without resurrection."

In Chapter 7, verses 9 and 10 Job sounds a different note:

> As the cloud is consumed and vanisheth away,
> So he that goeth down to Sheol shall come
> up no more.
> He shall return no more to his house,
> Neither shall his place know him anymore.

In a broad way it may be affirmed that the Old
Testament teaches a religion primarily oriented to
this life rather than to a future life.

*   *   *

3. In the New Testament the situation is
radically different.

Already, when Christ comes to the house of Martha
and Mary, after the death of their brother Lazarus,
there is the revealing dialogue between Martha and
Christ (John 11:21-25):

> Martha therefore said unto Jesus: Lord, if
> thou hadst been here, my brother had not
> died. And even now I know that, whatsoever
> thou shalt ask of God, God will give Thee.
> Jesus saith unto her: Thy brother shall
> rise again. Martha saith unto him: I know
> that he shall rise again in the resurrection
> of the last day. (Emphasis supplied.)

Obviously, Martha believed in a general resurrection
in the "last day." She here sounded a specific and
definite note not heard in the Old Testament.

The Apostle Paul's thinking on this subject
differed from that of Martha. Paul affirmed that
if Christ had not risen from the dead, nobody would.
But when Martha testified, as in the foregoing quotation, Christ had neither died nor risen yet;
therefore, the origin of her hope of resurrection
differed from Paul's, which was anchored in Christ's
resurrection.

Paul's argument is elaborated in I Corinthians
15:3-8, where he musters the testimony of those who
saw Christ after his resurrection, and he (Paul)
submits his own evidence on that subject. Then in
verses 12-19 he associates any future resurrection

from the dead with Christ's resurrection. He argues
brusquely: if Christ did not rise from the dead,
neither will anybody else in the future. For Paul
the resurrection of Christ was not a fanciful event,
but a "cause and effect" relationship; or, if it
was not that, then there was at least a common cause
behind Christ's resurrection and that of others in
the future. This is what Paul categorically asserts:

> Now if Christ be preached that he hath
> been raised from the dead, how say some
> among you that there is no resurrection
> of the dead? But if there is no resurrec-
> tion of the dead, neither hath Christ been
> raised; and if Christ hath not been raised,
> then is our preaching vain, your faith
> also is vain. Yea, and we are found false
> witnesses of God, because we witnessed of
> God that he raised up Christ; whom he
> raised not up, if so be that the dead are
> not raised. For if the dead are not raised,
> neither hath Christ been raised; and if
> Christ hath not been raised your faith is
> vain; ye are yet in your sins. Then they
> also that are fallen asleep in Christ have
> perished. If we have only hoped in Christ
> in this life, we are of all men most
> pitiable. (Emphasis supplied.)

                *   *   *

   In the first century of the Christian era the
two leading schools of thought among the Jews were
those of the Pharisees and the Sadducees. One of
the fundamental differences between the Pharisees
and the Sadducees was regarding a resurrection and
a future life. The Pharisees affirmed that there
would be a general resurrection. Paul had been
reared a Pharisee. It is not known (to this writer)
on what grounds the Pharisees believed in a resurrection. Nor does he know to what extent Paul as
a Pharisee, unconverted to Christianity, accepted
the Pharisean doctrine of a resurrection. But
this much appears certain: after his conversion
Paul founded a general resurrection on Christ's
resurrection, or on a cause which was common both
to Christ's resurrection and to the future resurrection of others.

   It has been said that the Sadducees, as skeptical
folk, affirmed that a man should do good because
it was good in itself, and not for the hope of a
future reward. Having disparaged the hope of a

future reward (entailing of course a future life),
they then (so it is reported) came to argue that
there was no future life at all. Whether the <u>early</u>
Sadducees believed in a future life as did the
Pharisees is unknown to this writer.

In short, in New Testament times, ideas about
resurrection were not uniform.

*   *   *

The well-known encounter between Christ and the
Sadducees in regard to a resurrection is described
in Matthew 22:23-33.

> On that day there came to him Sadducees,
> <u>they that say there is no resurrection</u>:
> and they asked him, saying, Teacher, Moses
> said, If a man die having no children,
> his brother shall marry his wife (widow)
> and raise up seed unto his brother. Now
> there were with us seven brethren: and
> the first married and deceased, and having
> no seed left his wife unto his brother;
> in like manner the second also, and the
> third, unto the seventh. And after them
> all, the woman died. In the resurrection
> therefore whose wife shall she be of the
> seven? for they all had her.

> But Jesus answered and said unto them,
> Ye do err, not knowing the Scriptures, nor
> the power of God. For in the resurrection
> they neither marry, nor are given in
> marriage, but are as angels in heaven.

> But as touching the resurrection of the
> dead, have ye not read that which was
> spoken unto you by God, saying, I <u>am</u> the
> God of Abraham, and the God of Isaac, and
> the God of Jacob? God is not the God of
> the dead, but of the living.

> And when the multitudes heard it, they were
> astonished at his teaching.

From the foregoing the following may be concluded:

1. That Christ accepted the doctrine of the
resurrection held by Martha, by the Pharisees, and
undoubtedly by many others. The corollary is that
he rejected the view of the Sadducees.

2. That Christ used the <u>tense</u> of a verb in a quotation from the Old Testament (Exodus 3:6) in order to affirm that the dead are still living. God in the book, Exodus, declares himself to Moses by the words, "I <u>am</u> the God of Abraham, Isaac and Jacob." But these three ancestors of Moses were long dead; if dead, the statement should read: "I <u>was</u> the God of Abraham, Isaac and Jacob." Christ affirmed that God is not a god of the dead but of the living. Therefore, when he said, (a) "I <u>am</u> the God of Abraham, Isaac and Jacob" (and (b) <u>if</u> he is a god of the living only), then these three men (although departed from this life) must nevertheless currently then have been having another existence. This argument was unusual enough to have astonished the people who heard Christ. So much for Christ's positive argument. But previously he had rebutted the argument of the Sadducees about the woman who had had seven husbands, and concerning whom they asked, "In the resurrection whose wife shall she be of the seven?"

3. That Christ declared that the character of life after the resurrection will be <u>radically different</u> from the character of this present life. It is as if the Sadducees had heard the story of the mountebank related in the preceding chapter who was going around offering, and finally threatening, to resurrect the dead <u>back into this kind of a life</u>. As told in the preceding chapter, that creates problems. Probably the Sadducees honestly felt that there could not be a general resurrection from the dead without there being chaos. The <u>assumption</u> underlying their argument was that there would be a perfect transfer of the conditions in this life to a future life, e.g., in regard to marriage and sex relations. <u>Christ categorically rejected that idea</u>. Conditions after the resurrection will be so different that they cannot be related to this life. He really affirmed two monumental propositions: (1) you cannot <u>reason</u> from this life to the next; to that proposition there is a corollary: (2) you cannot <u>reason</u> back from the next life to this one.

*   *   *

In fact, Scripture is generally vague about the character of life in the next world. It talks of gates of pearl, and streets of gold, and of fire never quenched (as in a smoking dump), but these are not necessarily to be taken literally; they may be more poetry and metaphor than description.

Folk who are very positive about the detailed
character of life in the future should probably be
suspected of affirming more than they know. Under
the rule of strict constructionism in this book,
there is preference for giving dominant weight to
Christ's intimation that the whole economy of life
in the resurrection will necessarily be so radically
different that <u>it</u> <u>cannot</u> <u>now</u> <u>even</u> <u>be</u> <u>imagined</u>!

                    *   *   *

The grand imagery of the last book in the Canon
of Scripture, <u>Revelation</u>, is written in such an
imaginative framework that it can only with difficulty be taken <u>literally</u>. It is vision and poetry;
not everything in it must needs be read as a literal description. Its style is obviously adapted to
create an overwhelming impression of difference from
what we know now.

The fact is that the long-established churches
have no <u>detailed</u> doctrine about the character of
life after the resurrection; (they <u>could</u> not have
on the basis of the limited data in Scripture);
anyone who would attempt the task would immediately
be daunted by its difficulties.

We now live in a finite world, with specific
needs, a welfareshortage of goods, the necessity
of work, a time factor, and death. The more one
thinks of extending these factors into a future life,
the more unreal the vision becomes. It may be
doubted that extensive time and effort should ever
go into trying to imagine the specific character of
a future life.

The combination, a resurrection and a future
life, is an undoubted datum of the Christian religion,
but its detailed character is unknown and unknowable
to men in this life. Nobody really <u>can</u> imagine it.
And that is what Scripture itself really teaches.
The controlling text probably is I Corinthians 2:9:
"Eye hath not seen and ear hath not heard, neither
has it entered into the heart of man what God hath
prepared for them that love him."

And so the scriptural doctrine of a resurrection
and a future life conforms to the fact (1) that men
do not wish a general resurrection in <u>this</u> life, and
(2) that they do not <u>know</u> in detail the character
of the radically new life after the resurrection.

                    *   *   *

There is a continuing dispute among Christians
about a millenium of a thousand years, during which
Christ will reign (essentially, some suppose) under
conditions prevailing in the present dispensation.
But such a situation will raise the kind of problems
the Sadducees found confusing, and which Christ
solved for them by saying there will not be a resurrection involving a present-day economy or order of
events. If it were otherwise, it would be proper
anew to ask concerning such a millenium: "Whose
wife shall she be then who has had several husbands
in this dispensation?" However, the fact that the
Sadducees picked the most obvious and puzzling
situation, marriage and sex relations, should not
stultify awareness that all the conditions of life
in the hereafter will be different and radically
so. It is dangerous to reason from now to then;
or from then to now.

Judgment And Punishment

In the early nineteenth century there was an important school of thought, customarily designated as Utilitarianism. The name of the man most prominently associated with this movement is Jeremy Bentham (1748-1832).

Utilitarianism made valuable contributions to ideas in regard to justice and punishment. In a certain sense Utilitarianism appears nobler in its ideas of justice and punishment than does Christianity.

*   *   *

There was in Old Testament thinking the idea of just reward, that is, "justice." There was that statement of "an eye for an eye, and a tooth for a tooth"; that is, as you hurt me, I may hurt you, in order to balance the account, in order that "justice" may prevail.

Striving for such "justice" may degenerate into vengeance -- the yearning just to "get even" for whatever ill another has done me.

However, vengeance is not countenanced in Scripture. There is the well-known text, "Vengeance is mine, saith the Lord, I will repay," with the clear implication that mere men must not engage in vengeance. But they may strive for justice, which appears in the Old Testament to include the idea of getting even for the sake of justice, although not for the sake of vengeance.

In Section III, Chapter 14 there was extensive discussion how Christ rejected "an eye for an eye and a tooth for a tooth" as a formula for justice. He called instead for forbearance. If I break the law against you, that is no ground, Christ averred, for you to break the law against me.

However, the essential idea of justice, that is, punishment according to sins, lives on in New Testament thought, especially in the form of a Final Judgment in the hereafter, at which time whoever did not get his deserved punishment or reward in this life would get it in the hereafter. In other words, God has reserved to himself not only vengeance but also ultimate "justice."

*   *   *

Utilitarianism rejected, in principle, the idea
of justice, and punishment for the sake of justice.

In Utilitarianism the idea of <u>utility</u> was substituted in place of <u>justice</u>. By <u>utility</u> was meant:
there is no utility, as far as Jones is concerned,
if he has committed a murder and now genuinely regrets
it and <u>will not repeat the act</u>, in hanging, electro-
cuting, or gassing him. If Jones has indeed reformed, he does not require punishment to deter him
from murdering again. There is no utility in the
old concept of justice; therefore, that idea of
justice should be rejected, and the only question
that should be asked for Jones's welfare is: what
has utility <u>for Jones</u>; and do indeed forget about
aboriginal concepts of vengeance and justice. In
short, utilitarianism was an advance over primitive
ideas of retaliation as justice.

This new approach to punishment has a high rationality; it says, punish murderer Jones <u>only</u> when he
needs that punishment to deter him from doing murder
again, but do not punish him if he will not murder
again anyway. Why hurt him when it has no utility
for him?

From a rationalist and humane viewpoint we may
all do well by giving thought to shifting from
Hebrew-Christian justice to utilitarianism's utility.
<u>Utility</u> as an ultimate principle for punishment is
something better than justice as an ultimate principle.

As strict constructionists of Scripture, and as,
at the moment, outlining only a <u>minimal</u> religion,
the utilitarian view just outlined is accepted.
The writer, too, is a utilitarian; at least in a
significant sense. Vengeance and justice, he believes, should yield to utility.

*   *   *

Does such an approach violate the teachings of
the Christian religion, or for that matter, of the
Hebrew religion?

To that question, the answer is an unequivocal
<u>no</u>.

The <u>Hebrew</u> religion was essentially utilitarian,
and the <u>Christian</u> religion is ostentatiously utilitarian.

The idea of the Utilitarians, that utility as a

substitute for justice was a new and revolutionarily
more rationalistic and humane idea than the idea
taught in the Old Testament and the New Testament,
was egotistic hallucination. There is nothing new
in Utilitarianism. It is only an old idea with a
new name. It is a sad case of violation of Occam's
Razor (that is, the rule that new names should not
be given to old ideas and be assumed, because of
the new name, to represent a genuinely new idea
merely because the name itself is new).

But on what grounds can it be alleged that Scripture is utilitarian in the sense of a Bentham or a
John Stuart Mill?

To that question the answer is that Scripture
keeps two ideas distinct, which are merged into
one idea in Utilitarianism; those two distinct ideas
are (1) punishment for sins, and (2) the instantaneous, effectual mercy of God immediately upon
any repentance. When the instantaneous mercy of
God, in response to penitence and reform, is proclaimed on practically every page of Scripture,
that is the same as saying that God is utilitarian
in his thinking. God is endlessly described in
Scripture as being a loving and forgiving God. The
refrain is: "Turn ye, turn ye, for why should ye
perish"; and "Good is the Lord and full of kind
compassion."

The idea of utilitarianism is, in other words,
merely the idea of punishment plus the idea of
mercy which is taught in Scripture. It is the
prompt mercy of God which makes Christian ethics
utilitarian.

The Utilitarians were unwittingly plagiarizers
of Hebrew-Christian ethics. They did not have a
nobler ethic; they merely did not as secular thinkers
feel any need of God in this situation, and they
called the same thing (when they as men did it)
utility or utilitarianism, what in Scripture is
called the combination of the wrath of God plus
the mercy of God.

But all this in no way lessens the claims of
the Utilitarians to some noble thinking. They
followed Scripture in one step, by utility, which
earlier Scripture covered in two steps, by wrath and
mercy.

*   *   *

The foregoing is simple and convincing, as long
as we think only of the individual sinner; and his
past and future acts; and what ought to be done
about them. The problem, however, is more complex
than the foregoing would indicate, and the complexities complicate the problem as much for Utilitarianism as they do for Christianity.

The complexity to which reference is made is:
what is the effect of "Utilitarianism" or of "Christian grace or mercy" on the folk in society other
than the actor himself whom, in the foregoing, we
have designated as Jones, a murderer who repents.

If Jones by his repentance (conversion in Christian terms) no longer needs punishment, because it
will have no utilitarian benefits for him, what about
Brown, a potential, deliberative, would-be murderer?
Brown sees that Jones gets off scot-free. Brown then
reasons: Jones murdered and was not punished, because he repented; then Brown says to himself: I
will murder, too, and I will then simulate repentance,
as Jones felt or pretended he felt, and then "they"
will let me off, too.

And so Brown destroys somebody whom he wishes
to destroy. This situation, it is obvious, is a
real problem for the theory of Utilitarianism; but
it is as much a problem for Christian ethics as it
is for Utilitarianism. God's grace can operate so
"broadly" that sinners are no longer deterred from
sinning!

What solutions did Utilitarianism adopt for that
problem?

*   *   *

Utilitarianism could adopt only one solution that
is rational, namely, that our original murderer Jones
will nevertheless have to be punished, not because
he subjectively needs it any more but because "society" needs his "symbolic" punishment as a deterrent to other future would-be murderers. There is,
in other words, utility in punishing Jones for the
sake of deterring others.

Incidentally, there may also be a "utility" for
Jones, all allegations to the contrary, because he
might sin the more facilely in the future if by
repentance he had wholly escaped earlier but "deserved" penalties.

Utilitarianism, therefore, inescapably uncovered

an internal conflict in its own system. And so also
does any Christian system based on the mercy of God.
Sin must still be punished for general deterrent
purposes, if not for individual deterrent purposes.
We are, in fact, back to where we started before we
took on utilitarianism. It turns out this way:
what is known as justice is really social utilitarianism. Society might have been better off if it
had always espoused utilitarianism in theory, and
consciously abandoned it in practice.

But as utilitarianism has problems, so Christian
mercy, judgment, condemnation and punishment have
corresponding problems. The wrath of God ought not
to be looked on as a capricious abstraction on his
part. Wrath against evil would seem to be an inescapable "problem" for God, too.

Curiously, just as utilitarianism is a super-
rationalistic and abstract principle for secular
rationalists, the combined (1) wrath and (2) mercy
of God is a corresponding rationalist principle for
rationalistic Christians. It is interesting to
note that it is primarily a differing nomenclature
which keeps them apart, and nonunderstanding of
each other.

*   *   *

If in this dispensation individualistic utilitarianism will not operate properly without adjustment for an in-essence conflicting principle, namely,
social utilitarianism, so neither, in this dispensation, will (can) the mercy of God operate properly
without adjustment for the wrath of God.

Now, even if "justice" prevails in this dispensation almost ideally, common observation nevertheless notes that some people given to wickedness
get along rather well at least for a time, and sometimes for a long time, and in some cases to their
dying day. On the other hand, some people, gentle
or noble, go through life with much trial and tribu-
lation. Rewards and penalties, simply, are not
exactly meted out in this life in accordance with
deserts. If there is a future life, it ought to be
an opportunity for adjusting the accounts! So at
least one might think, and not irrationally so.
One "reason" for expecting a future life, and one
justification for a final settling of the accounts
at that time, is that people think it would be
"just," that is, it will have a social utilitarian
purpose in the here and now.

*   *   *

Rationalism concerning the idea of the Final Judgment in the Christian religion is as follows:

1. Individual utilitarianism in dealing with a murderer (that is, mercy upon repentance and reform, just as God forgives) is marvelous. Between God and one man, between God and the individual, it is noble and wonderful.

2. But present-day society cannot operate on the basis of individual utilitarianism. In order to deter others, even repentant and reformed sinners must be punished. We must have social utilitarianism in this life. Christians and Utilitarians, as equally sharp rationalists, both know that social utilitarianism must supplement individual utilitarianism, and even supersede it.

3. But, in this life, the operation of social utilitarianism is not perfect. The accounts are not balanced. There is a great slippage between acts on the one hand, and punishments and rewards on the other. This slippage, a good part of which is really delay, can constitute a weak part of the battle-line of society against evil.

4. It was and is logical therefore for a profound ethic, such as the Christian ethic, to teach a future final judgment, as a deterrent to present evil. (This, it is conceded, is contrary to the idea of the Roman naturalist, Lucretius, who affirmed that one of the great evils in the world was the hope of future rewards and the fear of future punishment. Lucretius was irrational on this subject: the Christian concept of a day of Final Judgment and a day when exact justice will be dispensed is a powerful deterrent against present evil.)

5. The Christian religion would, therefore, be irrational if it did not teach a final judgment, and it would be failing to use a powerful deterrent to evil if it did not mention a final accounting. Scripture is not in the least equivocal on this subject. It teaches an overwhelming judgment day.

*   *   *

There is a basic difference between natural law and moral law.

Natural law works fast. If you walk off the edge of the roof of a forty-story building, you will be dead in a few minutes. Natural law is prompt and "automatic" and inexorable.

But the punishment of sin is often long delayed, and sometimes does not occur in this life. Ethical law is, then, neither prompt, nor "automatic," nor inexorable in this life.

The foregoing is no new truth, but an old one. Solomon long ago explained why men sin, namely, because the punishment is not instantaneous but is delayed, and is sometimes delayed very long. If the punishment were never delayed, so Solomon observes, men would do no evil; sin would disappear. Prompt punishment for evil is highly desirable, and the longer delayed the less effective. But better late, and sure and complete, than never.

Solomon wrote in Ecclesiastes 8:11-13:

> Because sentence against an evil work is not executed speedily, therefore the heart of the sons of men is fully set in them to do evil. Though a sinner do evil a hundred times, and prolong his days, yet surely I know that it shall be well with them that fear God, that fear before him: but it shall not be well with the wicked, neither shall he prolong his days, which are as a shadow, because he feareth not before God. (Emphasis supplied.)

*   *   *

How could it be meritorious of Christian ethics to teach that if the penalty for evil acts did not catch up with us in this life, that then we had "beat the game," and we had nothing more to fear. To have taught that would have been equivalent to winking at evil. So much for the logic of a final judgment.

But regardless of reason or nonreason, the fact remains that Scripture teaches a Final Judgment.

*   *   *

By making the rationalist approach which has been outlined in the foregoing, a new problem has been created. Utilitarian logic will carry us easily and well to the Judgment Day itself, but then it appears to fail.

Utility has been our lodestar, as it appears also to be the lodestar of Christianity. Now what utility is to be served by the Last Judgment for its own

purposes? Granted that the concept of a Judgment
Day serves well in this dispensation, will it
suddenly be converted into an arrangement for justice, with justice meaning vengeance. Is this the
time that the ominous words are carried into effect,
"Vengeance is mine, saith the Lord. I will repay."?

As was outlined in the preceding chapter, we do
not know the future economy, and in fact cannot
correctly imagine it. Further, the "this-worldly"
terms in which the New Dispensation is described
cannot (following Christ's principle in his conversation with the Sadducees) be taken literally. We do
not know and cannot know the "economy" of the New
Dispensation.

If we cannot now know the economy of the New Dispensation, we cannot anticipate its "purposes" either.
The nature of the punishments and rewards meted out
in the Great Day of Days are (for us in this dispensation) unimaginable. (We would, however, be inclined to believe that it would continue to be
utilitarian in some sense.)

*   *   *

Everyone can interpret as he sees fit statements
regarding Gehenna, or Hell. Jerusalem had a dump
as all cities have. Its dump was designated as Gehenna. To dispose of as much refuse as possible,
products dumped into a dump are burned if they are
combustible. But between moisture in what is dumped,
and rains as they come, and lack of air in close-
packed objects, the fire is seldom a roaring flame,
but smoulders perpetually and sends off odors and
smoke. A dump is indeed an area where the "fire is
never quenched, and the worm never dies."

The use of the name of a dump, and reference to
the fire in a dump, may have been useful to convey
an idea rather than have been submitted as an exact
description. As presented, the idea was understandable and graphic and horrible -- all of which fitted
into the purpose of mentioning Gehenna.

Dante had his own idea of purgatory and hell,
as he presented it in his Inferno.

*   *   *

That there is a day of reckoning for all men is
an inseparable part of the Christian religion. The
details are not known or are obscure. Nobody
k-n-o-w-s. A person will probably do well to
follow his church on this subject, but if he differs
he should probably hold his tongue. How could he
himself have special knowledge on this future
event, which could justify him being doctrinaire?

N O T E

This note pertains to the text on pages 122-3,
and on pages 327-8: (1) If utility is an essential
feature of proper correction for error; (2) if mercy
is a relevant feature of individual utilitarianism;
(3) if social utilitarianism in principle conflicts
with individual utilitarian mercy; then (4) if one
asks whether injured individuals qua individuals
should engage in social utilitarianism -- that is,
inflicting "an eye for an eye, and a tooth for a
tooth" -- then the answer should be obvious: at
most, individuals may engage in self-defense in
emergencies; but if there is no emergency and if an
evil has been perpetrated, social utilitarianism
should take over investigation, judgment and application of sanctions. Social utilitarianism should not
transfer its functions to an individual under stress
of spontaneous reactions and exposed to vengeful
motives, but obviously should be deliberative, calculating actions established by impartial agencies
of law and order. On all these subjects, Christian
ethics is most extraordinarily practical, and has
never been surpassed even in the latest ages.

Salvation By God, In Christ, As Grace
Through Faith

Salvation by grace, through faith, is the great theme of the Christian religion.

We are not saved by our good works, because they are neither uniform enough nor good enough.

We have sinned too often ("missed our mark" or "employed means not universally appropriate to the attainment of our ends") to justify our expecting salvation on the basis of our merits.

A politician or statesman may be appraised on the basis of the <u>net</u> total of his good acts and his bad acts; the pluses and the minuses are added algebraically, and if the total is a positive (plus), he is appraised as good; if the total is a negative (minus), he is appraised as bad.

Such a calculation may have a practical utility in a milieu admitted to be not perfect. But before a "just" and "righteous" God, operating "perfectly," a good cannot be used to neutralize an evil; an <u>evil</u> act is not obliterated by a <u>good</u> act. Men, therefore, must be saved by the "grace" of God to relieve them of the consequences (penalties) of their evil acts.

This phenomenon, as has previously been intimated, is related to the idea involved in Utilitarianism -- if after doing evil a man regrets it <u>per se</u> and currently has the resolve not to do it again, then punishment is no longer useful, nor desirable. Mercy is <u>then</u> greater than justice.

The Christian religion teaches that there is a "cut off" point after which repentance and good resolutions, "rewarded" by "grace" are no longer operative. If a man "dies in his sins," like a mosquito destroyed in the act, there is no hope for him.

That also is a utilitarian idea. Repentance, to be "useful," should come in this life, now -- before death. As previously outlined, the economy of a future life, must by definition be so different from this life that it would be rash to reason that repentance in a future existence will be applicable. Whatever the situation will turn out

to be, the Christian religion does not "extend"
ideas on "justice" suitable in this dispensation
into a later and (necessarily wholly different)
dispensation. "This (so Scripture teaches) is the
day of salvation." Now is the time to repent and
to reform.

The liturgy in connection with communion services,
employed in a particular denomination, reads: "We
...look to Jesus Christ for our salvation." Salvation is inextricably tied to an event associated
with Jesus Christ. The exact relationship of Jesus
Christ in the Trinity of God (of which more later)
and of Jesus Christ as man, must be complex enough
to be beyond human understanding. Certainly, the
Christian religion does not teach that we are saved
by a mere man. We have a relationship to Christ as
human beings, but salvation in Christ must rest on
his transcendental characteristics, that is, on his
divinity. As a "person" indissoluble from the Trinity,
Christ's achievements must be looked upon as phases
of the acts of God, and then the proposition quoted
above can be rephrased to read: "We...look to God
for our salvation."

That is the essence of both Old Testament and
New Testament teaching. We need the mercy of God,
the Creator and Administrator of the universe. God
extends his mercy (like a utilitarian idealist) --
he being interested especially in improvement following repentance -- to those who turn to him for grace,
help, and salvation.

The merits of Christ are often formulated as
being twofold: (1) He really "fulfilled" the law,
that is, kept it perfectly; and (2) he bore the
punishment for our sins. This is described in
Scripture as "fulfilling all righteousness."

The foregoing may be interpreted as meaning that
punishment was not utilitarian, but instead was
"legal," "forensic," "vindictive," and "just." This
may be correct, but mortal human beings are not
wise enough to be doctrinaire about the subject,
and within the Christian churches there are a variety
of opinions. These are outside the scope of a book
entitled Minimal Religion.

On a mathematically legalistic basis the burden
borne by Jesus Christ exactly balanced the grievous-
ness of the sins forgiven. Just what this might
amount to exactly nobody can know.

But one proposition is indisputable, if one wishes to claim being a Christian. In some way or other, Christ's life and death are inseparable from the scheme of "salvation by grace."

If the maximal view is that Christ's life and death were matters of finely balanced "justice" -- rewards for the <u>net</u> balance of good and evil that Christians perform -- then the minimal view must at least be that Christ's passive and terrible death, at the hands of a mob which utilized a Roman governor and troops, was a perfect manifestation of the forbearance which Christians are called upon to show, and the boundless extent of the mercy of God. As a minimum then, the death of Christ on the cross teaches the <u>ethics</u> of the Christian religion and the mercy of God, if not the <u>justice</u> of God in terms of a calculation of punishments and rewards. That makes death on the cross as significant for ethics as for justice.

Earlier in this chapter part of a sentence in a liturgy was quoted, namely, "We...look to Jesus Christ for our salvation." That was later rephrased as, "We...look to God for our salvation." The most exact way, probably, of conveying the idea is to say: "We...look to God for our salvation, in Jesus Christ." In the Christian Scripture, salvation is associated with understanding and accepting the concepts of righteousness, justice, repentance, mercy, salvation -- in Biblical terms, involving the grace of God as related to and manifested in the person of Jesus Christ. Whatever clearness the same basic ideas may have had in the theology of the Old Testament, it comes to an even better expression in the New Testament.

The Old Testament makes God the author of salvation (blessings of all kinds). The temple ritual symbolized need of repentance and reform, and made a fervent appeal to God's mercy and lovingkindness. But what was a blurred pencil drawing in the Old Testament but easy enough to read, has become in the New Testament an etching, cut deep and indelibly by acid, which makes obsolete the earlier symbolism. There was, probably, no better way to outline the scheme of salvation than the one outlined in the New Testament. When it is properly understood, the events themselves and the ideas associated therewith, tell better the mercy of God and the character of his government than anything else imaginable could have done. Indeed for a Christian, he must "look to God, in Jesus Christ, for mercy and salvation." This is <u>minimal</u> Christianity.

The Godhead Of Christ

The historical position of the church in regard
to Jesus Christ is unequivocal, namely, that he is
a member of the Trinity, coequal and coeval with
the Father and the Holy Ghost.

On this subject the name of Athanasius is inseparably connected with the formulation of the
creeds, and the controversy with Arius whose ideas
were rejected as heretical.

The anti-Trinitarians are classifiable into three
categories: (1) Arians; (2) Socinians; and
(3) Unitarians.

Arius assigned a unique position to Christ, but
disputed that he was coeval and therefore really
coequal with the Father, although begot before time
began and although creation was through him.

The Socinians deny that Christ existed before
his appearance on earth, but they consider he is a
proper person to whom to direct prayer.

The Unitarians consider Christ merely a man,
albeit an extraordinary one, and naturally he is
for them not an object of prayer.

John Milton was an Arian. Sir Isaac Newton,
who spent the last years of his life endeavoring
to interpret the prophesies in the latter part of
the Old Testament book of Daniel, was also an Arian.

There are statements by Christ, quoted in the
New Testament, which indicate that in his human
nature he did not know when certain events, controlled by God the Father, would occur; for example,
the end of the present world. This is the basis
for the creedal doctrine that Christ when on earth
took on the <u>humiliated</u> nature of fallen man, and
also the limitations of men generally, sin excepted.

As the nature of the Trinity is by definition
unfathomable by a finite man, the same can be said
in regard to the doctrine of the Incarnation and
the God-man characteristics which Christ possessed.

Certainly, according to Scripture, Christ is
the supreme revelation of God to man, both in

teaching and in life. The main branches of Christendom have steadfastly refused to diminish their
evaluation of the Second Person, Jesus Christ, in
the Trinity.

If the question is posed as one of reason or
logic, then there are as many objections to the
Arian position as the Athanasian; and also the
Socinian position. The Unitarian position so radically rejects the scriptural presentation of who
Christ was that it is not considered here. This
book on Minimal Religion is Athanasian.

N O T E

The appellation, Christian, probably necessarily
covers a wide range of ideas. This will be confusing to anyone not already definitely oriented to
the different denominations and sects which claim
that they are Christian.

Further, in some denominations priests or
preachers are not required, by the existence of
effective church discipline, to preach and teach
what the creeds of that particular denomination
affirm.

On the crucial question of the nature and person
of Jesus Christ, those claiming to be Christian will
vary from Athanasian to Socinian! This is a very,
very broad range.

In a general way, the largest classification is
into Greek Orthodox, Roman Catholic and Protestant.
The latter in turn are fragmented into many denominations, which can be sub-classified as Evangelical,
Lutheran and Calvinist.

Some churches have historical or place names;
others are named after their doctrine, as Baptists.
Others are named after their organization, as for
example Presbyterians, who have a democratic system
of church government. In doctrine Presbyterians
are Calvinists.

A person will do well to investigate broadly and
thoroughly which church appears to him to teach and
operate most conformably to revelation in Scripture.
The question, "What think ye of the Christ," is absolutely crucial.

Atonement And Crucifixion

The Christian plan of salvation may appear to have unreasonable and irrational features in it, but these should be explicable.

It is repeated again and again in Scripture that God is merciful (which is one way of saying that he is utilitarian), and that he does not always punish when doing that would have no purpose with the (individual) sinner; instead, he <u>forgives</u>. This is the grandest note in the Christian religion.

In contrast to that, Scripture also teaches that Christ came on earth as a very special person; with no earthly father; that he was perfectly exemplary in his life; without sin; that in his prime at about 33 years of age he was crucified near Jerusalem at the instigation of a malignant mob; not for evil doing, but for his self-claims that he was a wholly, unique being in his relation to God.

His death was a very bloody business, gruesome in details, and a permanent stain on the reputation of those who had anything to do with it.

But the question may well be asked: In the plan of God could not this <u>atonement</u> by crucifixion with its horrid and shocking features have been avoided? How much more dignified and less humiliating it would have been to have accomplished atonement without such a requirement!

The "problem" of "revelation" in this connection can be outlined as follows: Granted that God was working according to a plan of redemption that would contribute to welfare in this world under existing conditions, and also in the world to come, he could hardly be accomplishing that purpose if he did not indicate his objection to and his wrath toward what is known as sin. If he should ever-blithely wipe the slates of sin clean, without so much as a frown, there would be inadequate deterrent against sin.

The fact that society has no sure way to resolve uncertainty about the genuineness of repentance on the part of a <u>repentant</u> murderer is one reason that it adopts in self-defense a policy that murder must be restrained by punishment even though there may be repentance that is genuine.

If the state in this dispensation has this problem, and reacts to it as <u>logically</u> as it does -- and must do -- then there is no good reason to believe that God either would adopt some esoteric solution when endeavoring to restrain sin in this world.   There was one obvious way to establish the idea that sin must be restrained, and that way consisted in a <u>spectacular</u> infliction of punishment. The event employed, according to Scripture, was death of Christ on the cross.

As a matter of fact, probably no other influence toward conversion and toward obedience to God could have had the effect that Christ's death on the cross has had.   The church, wherever it has been effective, has founded its program on the message of atonement, by the merits and sacrifice by Christ, as being applied by God, in mercy, to repentant and true believers.

But patently, the disciplinary effect of God's scheme in the world would have collapsed -- would not even have obtained a start -- if mercy and forgiveness were so cheaply purchasable, that God did not exact as a minimum representative punishment, and even go so far as "an eye for an eye and a tooth for a tooth."   In limited, mortal human logic, it was necessary that there be a "scapegoat" for sins committed, or else the idea that sins were wrong and worthy of punishment as a deterrent would have lost its force.

The program of atonement through Christ is in Scripture put together logically, and should be rational to those who have an objective mind.   The steps in the situation are as follows:

1.   People sin; it is blindness to deny that
     we do evil.

2.   The good that we do should not be considered
     as neutralizing the evil that we do.   If we
help <u>C</u> but hurt <u>B</u>, can anyone reasonably say in court: surely I hurt <u>B</u> grievously, but do not punish me for that, because a week earlier I did <u>C</u> a good turn.   No court would accept that defense as relevant; nor should we believe that God will accept it.

3.   But God has an offer outstanding of forgive-
     ness, merely upon contrition and reform.
This is his overwhelming utilitarianism, or in scriptural language, his unending mercy and loving-

kindness. In this gracious offer, however, everything becomes cheap and unreal unless someone becomes
the punishment-bearer, or at least the representative
punishment-bearer.

    4.   In Scripture, Jesus Christ is the punishment-
        bearer.

    5.   Patently, for any _single_ and _ordinary_ person
        to take on the load of punishment for the
sins of the world would entail ridiculous exaggera-
tion, and therefore the "person" selected would have
to be truly extraordinary. Scripture claims that
Jesus Christ was a member of the Trinity; that he
took on mortal existence; was exemplary in life and
doctrine; was unjustly crucified; that he arose from
the dead; and ascended into heaven. He took on,
according to Scripture, his human nature from his
mother, but was in essence a member of the Godhead.
True God and man.

    6.   By the grace of God, men can, through Christ,
        be saved, under a utilitarian system. But
the "sense" of that would be lost, if Christ had
not undertaken to "bear" the sins of the world.

    7.   A sense of unreality about this _can_ stem from
        the way the vicarious sin-bearing is
interpreted. There are several interpretations.

        a.   One interpretation is that God is
            vengeful and finally exacts "an eye for
an eye and a tooth for a tooth" (despite Christ's
specific rejection of that policy for men). God
then finally proves to be a hard rather than a
merciful judge. This is a widely accepted interpretation. The infinite _number_ of sins in the
world, insofar as atoned for by Christ, is
"compensated for" by his infinite _suffering_. Under
this system there is then, finally, no real mercy
from God; he punishes men directly, or the appointed
substitute, Jesus Christ.

        b.   Another way is not to be so doctrinaire
            about the justice of God. One can in-
stead look upon Christ as truly the mediator, and
the atoner, but not as bearing to the last ounce
all the sins of the world, in all lands and in all
times. Christ then becomes the great embodiment of
mercy rather than of _justice_. His unique character
is not attacked by this. His agonizing sacrifice
is not repudiated. The wrath of God against sin

continues to be indicated, and deterrence of sin
is effectuated by memory of what Christ did. This
view does not arrogantly weigh the scales of justice, as saying Christ bore more than the sins of
the world, or exactly the sins of the world, or
less than the sins of the world. What _exact_ justice may have been cannot be known humanly anyway.

      c. In a utilitarian frame of ideas, the
          necessity of Christ's being a punishment
bearer can be expressed as follows: When God, by
his mercy, facilely desists from punishing the
individual sinner who repents genuinely, then personal utilitarianism is in operation; but just as
society cannot operate under _personal_ utilitarianism only, but must proceed to employ _social_ utilitarianism in order to establish general deterrents,
so the bearing of punishment by Christ was an
essential part of the structure to resist and reduce sin. Christ's atonement is in the social
utilitarianism of God, what social utilitarianism
is in present-day society; see pages 327 and 328.

*   *   *

In a book as this one, on _minimal_ religion, the
matter on how to measure the exact amount of atonement is left to the various churches. But there
is an absolute minimum: salvation is by grace; good
works are important as effects of redemption but
not as cause; Christ is the God-man who takes away
the sin of the world.

Whoever expects to be saved by works alone, cannot aver that he accepts the essence of the revelation of Scripture on atonement, redemption and
salvation.

Grace And Works

To someone looking at the Christian church from
the outside, the <u>differing</u> emphases on <u>grace</u> versus
<u>conduct</u>, or <u>faith</u> versus <u>law</u> should not be surpris-
ing nor disconcerting. The emphasis is in various
ratios.

Grace and works are not really separable. In the
Christian religion, an atonement had to be and was
made for sins. If the sins had been unimportant,
then the measure of atonement would not need to have
been significant. Therefore, sins are the counter-
poise for atonement.

Sins can be looked upon as the absence of good
works, and so atonement became necessary because
of the lack of good works. In other words, a church
which teaches grace only can hardly be called Christian. And contrarily, a church which teaches works
only is not Christian either. Christianity is a
religion of grace <u>and</u> works.

What does Christianity really demand as works
from men? The answer is: submission to God and
genuine cooperation between men. And what might
genuine cooperation be? Unbounded freedom of one
and all <u>except</u> without injury to others. In short,
you may do what you please except you must acknowledge God and you may not damage your neighbor.

*   *   *

The Apostle Paul seems to disparage the "law"
and "works" and "cooperation," and instead to exalt
grace. But he can easily be misinterpreted.

What good could atonement and grace have <u>per se</u>?
If there were no sin, then neither incarnation,
humiliation, suffering and death would have been
necessary. It is because "works" failed, it is
because sin came, it is because men injure each
other that grace is required. But, therefore, it
follows, as Socrates also affirmed, that ethics is
the science of sciences, the good of all good, and
the most critical phase of practical life.

Prosperity, among men, beyond the animal level
results from <u>cooperation</u> -- that cooperation derived
solely from the benefits of the moral law.

The whole system of salvation is a necessary
"consequence" of failure of men to "cooperate"
under the rules of the Decalogue.

It is when people fail to "cooperate," but
instead injure each other and despise the idea of
the existence of God, that the whole scheme of
costly salvation comes into play.

Some might think that it is correct to say that
the importance of grace is determined by the greatness of sin. Reduce the sins, and grace can then
abound less. The Apostle Paul formulated his objection to placing a high abstract value on "grace"
by posing the curious question about sinning more
so that grace would abound more. His own answer
was a startled one -- at such folly: "God forbid."
The Apostle Paul, therefore, warned against overvaluing grace in the form of: sinning more so
that grace might abound the more! Grace is indeed
wonderful, but it is lamentable that it is necessary.

The corollary of that is that grace needs to be
crowned by good works, or else, as the Apostle
James averred, faith is dead.

N O T E   Dogmas, sacraments, church organization, discipline and other internal church matters are not considered in this introductory book, although they are of
great importance.
For example, consider the "mystical union" of members
of a denomination or congregation. Such a union can be
significant or insignificant, real or farcical. The
"union" can consist in concentration on the thought of
sharing grace together, especially in the hereafter.
From another viewpoint, that "union" can be looked upon
as sharing "works" together, in the here and now. In
the first instance, the unity consists in saying, "Lord,
Lord" together; in the second, the unity consists in working together because the same interpretation of Scripture
is given for a practical program in the church and in the
world at large.
In a system in which grace, ethics and cosmology are
combined as in this book, the "mystical union" is not
great unless there is substantial concurrence on the active program of works as well as the passive program of
grace.
Sophisticated folk should therefore fortify themselves
for the shock of noting unity in matters of grace accompanied by disagreement, conflicting programs, and dislike
in matters of practical action -- within denominations
as well as across denominational lines. In other words,
some slogans of unity (sometimes fictions) in the churches,
need to be interpreted with sophistication rather than
naiveté.

Supplementary Meaning To Crucifixion Of
Christ

Some folk may have difficulty with a mathematical calculus between the sufferings of Christ and the sins for which he atoned. They may doubtingly ask: Is then the note of mercy and forgiveness, sounded all through the Scriptures, not really controlling? Is there after all no mercy -- forgiveness in the complete sense -- with God?

Granting such reasoners the satisfaction of their own thoughts, is there supplementarily any overwhelming other and _additional_ significance to Christ's death by crucifixion? The answer is that there is.

It was one thing to proclaim a superb and unsurpassable system of ethics and to recommend long-suffering, meekness, doing well to enemies, and such like. But how much attention would have been given to such teaching, and what character would be assigned to Christ, if his own application of his ethics were never tested and remained mere fine talk which in an evil hour he himself abandoned; and what if he had reverted to protest, resistance, anger, hatred, vengeance against his persecutors?

Talk would then have been negated by _conduct_.

It, therefore, in a sense became "necessary" for the test to be applied, in any heavenly controlled economy; and in a most appalling and frightening manner, sufficient to disintegrate any insincerity in himself, or lack of perseverance in his own principles, or faltering in fortitude in holding to what he taught. It can logically be argued that in some shattering way a trial would have to be presented to find whether the gold was pure gold, or an alloy, or brass, or really pretense.

The events associated with capture, trial, torture, crucifixion and death are such that the imprimatur -- the seal of authenticity -- had to be stamped on Christ's teachings. It was necessary that he validate his personal claims by his conformity to those teachings in as evil an hour as the mind of man can imagine.

On this ground also or alone, the crucifixion

is the most epoch-making event in human history,
in ethics and in general conduct.

Although the analogy may properly be considered
inappropriate, the observation naturally comes to
mind: how much smaller a place would Socrates have
come to occupy in human thought if he had not been
required by the citizens of Athens to commit
suicide by drinking hemlock? Did not that fate
and his fortitude in meeting it add greatly to
Socrates's stature?

But, of course, neither the ethics of Socrates --
or, if you wish, Plato speaking through words
ascribed to Socrates -- nor the circumstances attending his death are to be compared to those of
Christ; if for no other reason than that the ethics
are grossly defective; nor was his manner of death
comparable. There is nothing else like Christ's
teaching, life and death in recorded history. The
event was wholly unique!

"The Kingdom Of God Is At Hand"

There have been, in the history of man, some strange and unrealistic hallucinations. At the present time, for example, the head of a country which is a member of a world organization declares that he is God!

But on the eastern edge of the Mediterranean world 2,000 years ago a person was born who made an equal or greater claim for himself. Scripture declares that at the beginning of the public career of Jesus Christ, a "forerunner," known as John the Baptist, called the people in Palestine to repentance with (besides other statements) the pretentious declaration, "The Kingdom of God is at hand." This statement was taken over by Jesus Christ himself, and became an expression for impressing the public generally, for mustering followers, and for firing them with proselyting and testifying zeal.

What might be some aspects of the statement, "The Kingdom of God is at hand"?

*   *   *

Anatole France wrote imaginatively about Pontius Pilate in his book, The Procurator of Judea. France imagines Pontius Pilate as living in retirement in his old age in Baiae, which in those times was a fashionable and corrupt seaside resort near Naples.

Pilate meets there another old Roman, named Aelius Lamia, who for misconduct when young had been banished from Rome, and lived in Palestine during Pilate's administration as procurator. The two recall in their conversation their earlier lives among the Hebrews.

Pilate complains about the obstreperousness of the Jews, and their complaints to Rome about his administration, which made his life as procurator unpleasant and difficult.

Lamia had been banished from Rome for adultery with the wife of a Roman of senatorial rank, but he had not thereby lost his interest in women, and he turns the talk to his pursuit of Palestinian women. The old roué's memory shifts from Pilate's

politics to his own amorous episodes, and he relates
his pursuit of Mary Magdalene, whose name in Scripture is not untarnished. He says:

> I knew a Jewess at Jerusalem who used to
> dance in a little room, on a threadbare
> carpet, by the light of a smoky lamp,
> waving her arms as she clanged her cymbals.
> Her loins arched, her head thrown back, as
> if it were dragged down by her red hair;
> her eyes voluptuous; eager, languishing,
> compliant. I was in love with her barbaric
> dances, her voice, the perfume she used,
> ...and I followed her everywhere.

Then he complains that she suddenly disappeared.
He says he sought her in all the honky-tonks of
Jerusalem, until he learned she had reformed and
attached herself to a company of men and women who
were followers of a young Galilean miracle worker.
Lamia remembers the man's name as Jesus, and recalls
that he came from Nazareth, and that later he was
crucified for some crime. He asks: "Pontius, do
you remember anything about that man?"

Pilate struggles to recall the name but fails.
"Jesus?" he mutters, "Jesus of Nazareth?   I cannot
call him to mind."

Whether Anatole France's imagination is trust-
worthy is not of great importance; anyone can let
his imagination wander over the later career of
Pontius Pilate. But imagine him, if you will, as
France does, living a life of indolence at a corrupt
Roman seaside resort near Naples. Imagine him taking his ease in a litter carried by slaves. Further,
imagine Pilate in conversation with a worn-out
voluptuary, an Aelius Lamia, seducer of the wife of
a Roman of consular rank and pursuer of Mary Magdalene, a man who remembers that he lost Mary Magdalene because she joined a small group of people
associated with a "miracle-worker." The old roué,
regretting that he had lost Mary Magdalene, can
remember the name of Jesus of Nazareth. But Pontius
Pilate, without the aid of a passion-heated memory,
shakes his head and says: "Jesus of Nazareth?   I
cannot call him to mind."

Maybe for later generations the most familiar
of all Roman names has been Pontius Pilate, who is
mentioned (dishonorably) in the Apostles' Creed, in
the clause, "suffered under Pontius Pilate." If he
might return to the living and visit Rome, and hear

his name repeated in the liturgy in the churches
there, he might discover that he is the best known
of all Romans merely because he relinquished Jesus
Christ, innocent (as Pilate himself testified) of
crime, to a mob for crucifixion.

Again, whether Pontius Pilate could recall Jesus
Christ or not, the confident words of Christ come
down the centuries: "The kingdom of God is at
hand... The gates of hell shall not prevail against
it... My kingdom is not of this world" -- and
similar expressions.

*   *   *

If you read the products of Roman oratory in the
centuries near Christ's birth, then the language,
ideas and descriptions sound modern; for example,
consider the speeches by Cicero.

If, further, one reads the philosophers of that
period, as Seneca, one is astounded at the high
and noble morality of the ideas advanced.

If one also reads histories of those times, as
the one by Tacitus, one is astonished at the corrup-
tion of the age. Nothing new in evil has apparently
since been developed by men, as compared to what
was done under the government of Rome, before,
during and after Christ's time. That government
was sophisticated, calculating, ambitious, worldly,
realistic, "western."

In contrast, consider the simple narratives in
the four Gospels: the ideas are primitive, peculiarly Hebraic, idealistic, apparently not this-worldly,
seemingly almost hallucinary.

Here, at the center of the Christian religion
stands the figure of a man born in poverty, of
grandiose claims even as to earthly lineage, trained
as a carpenter in a small village in Galilee, not
even remembered (maybe) by the Roman governor who
surrendered him (Christ) to be crucified. This
crucified man nevertheless categorically declared
that everything shall pass away except his kingdom;
that kingdom, he affirms, will triumph over everything else in time and eternity.

*   *   *

The best-known family in Roman history is the
Julio-Claudian family. This "family" includes

Caius Julius Caesar (102-44 B.C.), then his grandnephew, the Emperor Augustus Caesar (27 B.C. -
14 A.D.); Tiberius (14-37 A.D.); Caligula (37-41);
Claudius (41-54); Nero (54-68).* The period covered,
beginning with Augustus, is 95 years. The Roman
emperors were proclaimed by the senate to be "divine."
Let us look at the powerful and talented and "divine"
Caesars. (* The latest five dates show time as emperor.)

What this family's history records may be taken
as an index to what the Roman world was like at
that time. (It is worth remembering that Cicero,
contemporary to Julius Caesar, admonished the leading families of Rome to be exemplary in their conduct, because what the leaders did the commoner
folk imitated.)

Tacitus, greatest of Roman historians, begins
his The Annals by briefly referring to Augustus, and
then devoting major time to the reign of Tiberius,
and later to the other emperors of the Julio-Claudian
family. (Some sections of The Annals are lost.)

Tacitus explicitly avers that what he would write
would have certain characteristics. He wrote on
the first page of The Annals:

> The histories of Tiberius, Gaius Caligula,
> Claudius and Nero, while they were in power,
> were falsified through terror, and after
> their death were written under the irri-
> tation of a recent hatred. Hence my pur-
> pose is to relate a few facts about
> Augustus -- more particularly his last
> acts, then the reign of Tiberius (Augus-
> tus's stepson), and all which follows,
> without either bitterness or partiality,
> from any motives to which I am far re-
> moved.

In general, Suetonius in The Twelve Caesars confirms
what Tacitus writes. Tacitus will be relied on
principally, when available.

It is outside the scope of this book to do more
than contrast the emperors of the Romans with Christ,
and their respective empires.

              *   *   *

The main characteristics of the Julio-Claudian
family may be summarized as follows:

Caius Julius Caesar (102-44 B.C.) himself,
endowed with great abilities, was a demagogue;
licentious; à homosexual; a man who was interested
in the acquisition of power and the satisfaction
of his ambitions and pleasures. If Scipio Africanus
150 years earlier had ushered in the greatness of
Rome, Caesar was the initiator of its great decline.
It is not to be disputed that he was not so vicious,
cruel and vindictive as practically all of those
who came after him in the Julio-Claudian family.
But "principles of morals" per se to control himself
he did not have conspicuously. "Principles," or
"rules" of conduct were subordinated to his self-
aggrandizement and pleasure. His program was not
even to develop a "set of rules," which would establish a "kingdom" which would be unimpeachable, in-
destructible, or everlasting; the thought was foreign
to and far beyond him.

Caius Julius Caesar's grandnephew (through his
sister Julia) later became the emperor Octavius
Augustus. Augustus's paternal grandfather had been
a rich money lender with no distinction in ancestry.
Augustus's father bought himself a seat in the Roman
senate. That Augustus's qualities were exceptional
is not disputed. That he, in general, aimed at
good government and a wise "constitution" for Rome
is conceded. Augustus may be taken to be the man
who "set in concrete" the Julio-Claudian family
characteristics. What were these?

1.   First, family aggrandizement. To accomplish
that he instituted the practice of close inter-
marriage. The Julio-Claudian family tree after
Augustus is an intolerably complex mess of descendants of the Caesars, Claudii, Agrippae and Antonii.
The family came to be bedevilled by officially
tolerated and approved incest. In addition to the
legalized incest, the unauthorized incest and licen-
tiousness is almost unbelievable. (See a Julio-
Claudian family tree.)

2.   Secondly, in the maneuvering for power by
parents for children, siblings against siblings,
cousins against cousins, etc., the in-fighting became merciless and suicidal for the family. Members
of the family had recourse to banishment, compulsory
suicide, poison, daggers, purposeful shipwreck, and
what have you. No man of respectable character
survived after Augustus himself. Tiberius, Gaius
Caligula, Claudius and Nero must all be described
as monsters of infamy and wickedness (and consequently of folly).

3. Thirdly, maniacal <u>cruelty</u> became an outstanding characteristic of this most-famous of Roman families. The people groaned under the burden. Informers enriched themselves by falsely accusing people they wished to destroy or see impoverished. Wives and favorites, freedmen, slaves, women without morality, and the like, became important in determining policy and caprice. Death of an emperor became occasions for popular rejoicing and new hope.

4. Fourthly, the women of the Caesars appeared to become more vicious and depraved than the men.

*   *   *

Let us consider the several generations of the Julio-Claudian emperors.

1. <u>Augustus</u> (emperor, 27 B.C. - 14 A.D.), having had other wives, developed a passion for a Roman matron named Livia, young wife of an elderly husband of the patrician branch of the Claudian family, with the name of Tiberius Claudius Nero. Livia had already borne one son to Tiberius Claudius Nero; this son is known to later history as emperor under the name Tiberius. She was again six-months pregnant, but Augustus impatiently claimed Livia. After the baby, named Claudius Drusus, was born in Augustus's house, he sent the child back to the natural father, old Tiberius Claudius Nero, but he (Augustus) kept Livia. (Augustus had no children by her, but he already had a daughter Julia by an earlier marriage with Scribonia.)

This Julia, by her first marriage, had five children; one, Gaius, died in 4 A.D.; another, Lucius, in 2 A.D., possibly both by the treachery of their step-grandmother, Livia. Julia's youngest son, Agrippa Posthumous, was executed in 14 A.D., by Tiberius (who succeeded Augustus). This leaves two other natural granddaughters, one who had no children, and the other Agrippina the Elder who married Germanicus. This couple, one a Julian and the other a Claudian, had six children (great-grandchildren of Augustus).

But returning to Augustus's daughter Julia for a moment: he was disappointed in her. He eventually required his step-son Tiberius to marry her, but Augustus then discovered to his consternation that

politics to his own amorous episodes, and he relates
his pursuit of Mary Magdalene, whose name in Scripture is not untarnished. He says:

> I knew a Jewess at Jerusalem who used to
> dance in a little room, on a threadbare
> carpet, by the light of a smoky lamp,
> waving her arms as she clanged her cymbals.
> Her loins arched, her head thrown back, as
> if it were dragged down by her red hair;
> her eyes voluptuous; eager, languishing,
> compliant. I was in love with her barbaric
> dances, her voice, the perfume she used,
> ...and I followed her everywhere.

Then he complains that she suddenly disappeared.
He says he sought her in all the honky-tonks of
Jerusalem, until he learned she had reformed and
attached herself to a company of men and women who
were followers of a young Galilean miracle worker.
Lamia remembers the man's name as Jesus, and recalls
that he came from Nazareth, and that later he was
crucified for some crime. He asks: "Pontius, do
you remember anything about that man?"

   Pilate struggles to recall the name but fails.
"Jesus?" he mutters, "Jesus of Nazareth? I cannot
call him to mind."

   Whether Anatole France's imagination is trust-
worthy is not of great importance; anyone can let
his imagination wander over the later career of
Pontius Pilate. But imagine him, if you will, as
France does, living a life of indolence at a corrupt
Roman seaside resort near Naples. Imagine him taking his ease in a litter carried by slaves. Further,
imagine Pilate in conversation with a worn-out
voluptuary, an Aelius Lamia, seducer of the wife of
a Roman of consular rank and pursuer of Mary Magdalene, a man who remembers that he lost Mary Magdalene because she joined a small group of people
associated with a "miracle-worker." The old roué,
regretting that he had lost Mary Magdalene, can
remember the name of Jesus of Nazareth. But Pontius
Pilate, without the aid of a passion-heated memory,
shakes his head and says: "Jesus of Nazareth? I
cannot call him to mind."

   Maybe for later generations the most familiar
of all Roman names has been Pontius Pilate, who is
mentioned (dishonorably) in the Apostles' Creed, in
the clause, "suffered under Pontius Pilate." If he
might return to the living and visit Rome, and hear

his name repeated in the liturgy in the churches
there, he might discover that he is the best known
of all Romans merely because he relinquished Jesus
Christ, innocent (as Pilate himself testified) of
crime, to a mob for crucifixion.

Again, whether Pontius Pilate could recall Jesus
Christ or not, the confident words of Christ come
down the centuries: "The kingdom of God is at
hand... The gates of hell shall not prevail against
it... My kingdom is not of this world" -- and
similar expressions.

*   *   *

If you read the products of Roman oratory in the
centuries near Christ's birth, then the language,
ideas and descriptions sound modern; for example,
consider the speeches by Cicero.

If, further, one reads the philosophers of that
period, as Seneca, one is astounded at the high
and noble morality of the ideas advanced.

If one also reads histories of those times, as
the one by Tacitus, one is astonished at the corrup-
tion of the age. Nothing new in evil has apparently
since been developed by men, as compared to what
was done under the government of Rome, before,
during and after Christ's time. That government
was sophisticated, calculating, ambitious, worldly,
realistic, "western."

In contrast, consider the simple narratives in
the four Gospels: the ideas are primitive, peculiarly Hebraic, idealistic, apparently not this-worldly,
seemingly almost hallucinary.

Here, at the center of the Christian religion
stands the figure of a man born in poverty, of
grandiose claims even as to earthly lineage, trained
as a carpenter in a small village in Galilee, not
even remembered (maybe) by the Roman governor who
surrendered him (Christ) to be crucified. This
crucified man nevertheless categorically declared
that everything shall pass away except his kingdom;
that kingdom, he affirms, will triumph over everything else in time and eternity.

*   *   *

The best-known family in Roman history is the
Julio-Claudian family. This "family" includes

Tiberius developed an appetite to see people suffer. Toward the end of his life he retired to the island of Capri, apparently with the particular purpose of being unhindered in licentious habits.

Suetonius writes (The Twelve Caesars, pages 139-141):

Soon Tiberius broke out in every sort of cruelty and never lacked for victims: these were, first, his mother's friends and less intimate acquaintances; then those of Agrippina, Nero and Drusus; finally, those of Sejanus. With Sejanus out of the way his savageries increased; which proved that Sejanus had not, as some thought, been inciting him to commit them, but merely providing the opportunities that he demanded. Nevertheless, in Tiberius's dry, brief autobiography we find him daring to assert that Sejanus had been killed for persecuting Nero and Drusus; the fact being that he had himself put Nero to death when Sejanus was already an object of suspicion, and Drusus after he had fallen from power. A detailed list of Tiberius's barbarities would take a long time to compile; I shall content myself with a few samples. Not a day, however holy, passed without an execution; he even desecrated New Year's Day. Many of his men victims were accused and punished with their children -- some actually by their children -- and the relatives were forbidden to go into mourning. Special awards were voted to the informers who had denounced them and, in certain circumstances, to the witnesses too. An informer's word was always believed. Every crime became a capital one, even the utterance of a few careless words. . . . Some of the accused, on being warned to appear in court, felt sure that the verdict would be "guilty" and, to avoid the humiliation of a trial, stayed at home and severed an artery; yet Tiberius's men bandaged their wounds and hurried them, half-dead, to prison. Others obeyed their summons and then drank poison in full view of the Senate. The bodies of all executed persons were flung on the Stairs of Mourning, and dragged to the Tiber with hooks -- as many as twenty a day, including women and children. Tradition forbade the strangling of virgins; so, when little girls had been condemned to die in this way, the

executioner began by violating them. Tiberius used to punish with life those who wished
to die. He regarded death as a comparatively
light affliction, and on hearing that a man
named Carnalus had forestalled his execution
by suicide, exclaimed: "Carnalus has got
away!"

*   *   *

In Capri they still show the place at the
cliff top where Tiberius used to watch his
victims being thrown into the sea after pro-
longed and exquisite tortures. A party of
marines were stationed below, and when the
bodies came hurtling down they whacked at them
with oars and boat hooks, to make sure that
they were completely dead. An ingenious
torture of Tiberius's devising was to trick
men into drinking huge draughts of wine, and
then suddenly to knot a cord tightly around
their genitals, which not only cut into the
flesh but prevented them from urinating. Even
more people would have died, it is thought,
had Thrasyllus the astrologer not cleverly
persuaded him to postpone his designs by an
assurance that he still had many years of life
in hand. These victims would have included
Germanicus's sole surviving son, Gaius Caligula,
and his own grandson Tiberius, whom he hated
as having been born from adultery.

Suetonius also wrote (page 131):

On retiring to Capri he (Tiberius) made
himself a private sporting-house, where
sexual extravagances were practised for his
secret pleasure. Bevies of girls and young
men, whom he had collected from all over the
Empire as adepts in unnatural practices, and
known as spintriae, would perform before him
in groups of three, to excite his waning
passions. A number of small rooms were fur-
nished with the most indecent pictures and
statuary obtainable, also certain erotic
manuals from Elephantis in Egypt; the inmates
of the establishment would know from these
exactly what was expected of them.

Tacitus refers to the same events as follows
(page 195):

Tiberius (living on Capri) often landed at
points in the neighborhood (on the mainland),
visited the gardens by the Tiber, but went back
again to the cliffs and to the solitude of the
sea shores, in shame at the vices and proflig-
acies into which he had plunged so unrestrain-
edly that in the fashion of a despot he de-
bauched the children of free-born citizens. It
was not merely beauty and a handsome person
which he felt as an incentive to his lust, but
the modesty of childhood in some, and noble
ancestry in others. Hitherto unknown terms were
then for the first time invented, derived from
the abominations of the place and the endless
phases of sensuality.

The last lines that Tacitus wrote of Tiberius are
as follows (page 226-7):

His character too had its distinct periods.
It was a bright time in his life and reputation, while under Augustus he was a private
citizen or held high offices; a time of reserve and crafty assumption of virtue, as
long as Germanicus and Drusus were alive.
Again, while his mother lived, he was a compound of good and evil; he was infamous for
his cruelty, though he veiled his debaucher-
ies, while he loved or feared Sejanus. Finally,
he plunged into every wickedness and disgrace,
when fear and shame being cast off, he simply
indulged his own inclinations.

This is the Roman emperor who ruled the world
when Christ was a humble and gentle teacher in
Palestine, lived blamelessly, and was crucified by
the Jews with the permission of Pontius Pilate,
Tiberius's appointee.

3. Gaius Caligula (emperor, 37-41 A.D.). This
man was a descendant of Augustus and also of Mark
Antony.

Caligula forced his father-in-law to cut his own
throat.

It was his habit to commit incest with each
of his three sisters in turn and, at large
banquets, when his wife reclined above him,

placed them all in turn below him. . . . He
took his sister Drusilla from her husband...quite
unashamedly treating her as his wife;... . . .
He showed no such extreme love or respect for
the (other) two sisters, and often, indeed, let
his favorites sleep with them; (but he also denounced) them as adulteresses who were party
to plots against him...　　(Suetonius, page 161.)

*　　　　　*　　　　　*

Caesonia (his wife) was neither young nor beautiful, and had three daughters by a former husband, besides being recklessly extravagant and
utterly promiscuous...　For his friends he even
paraded her naked...　He named her child (daughter)
Julia Drusilla...　What finally convinced him
of his own paternity was her violent temper...
(Suetonius, page 162.)

According to Ferrero, Caligula thought in Egyp-
tian terms; the Pharoahs had a policy of systematic
incest, marrying sisters and other　near kin.

Many men...were branded at his (Caligula's)
command...or thrown to the wild beasts.
Others were confined in narrow cages where
they had to crouch on all fours like animals;
or were sawn in half...merely for criticizing
his shows, failing to swear by his genius...
(Suetonius, page 163.)

*　　　　　*　　　　　*

The method of execution (Caligula) preferred
was to inflict numerous small wounds, avoiding
the prisoner's vital organs; and his...proverb-
ial order (was): "Make him feel that he is
dying!"　(Suetonius, page 164.)

*　　　　　*　　　　　*

He never missed a chance of making profits;
setting aside a suite of palace rooms, he
decorated them worthily, opened a brothel,
stocked it with married women and boys, and
then sent his pages around the squares and
public places, inviting all men of whatever
age, to enjoy themselves...
When Caligula played at dice, he would
always cheat and lie...
(Suetonius, page 170.)

*　　　　　*　　　　　*

After less than four years of reign, he was
destroyed by two military men who had special reasons
to fear he would destroy them. He was 29 years old.
Most of what Suetonius wrote about Caligula is under
the caption, "Caligula the Monster."

4. _Claudius_ (emperor, 41-54 A.D.). Claudius,
a nit-wit, succeeded Caligula. He was dominated
by his wife Messalina (his third), and also by
other worthless folk, which resulted in his decisions
being arbitrary, variable and nonsensical. Claudius
was married four times; to Plautia, whom he divorced
for scandalous behavior and the suspicion of murder;
then to Aelia Paetina; then to Messalina, his
cousin's daughter; and finally to Agrippina the
Younger.

> Suffice it to record that (Claudius) executed
> his father-in-law, Appius Silanus; Julia, grand-
> daughter of Tiberius; and Julia his niece,
> daughter of his brother Germanicus -- all on
> unsupported charges and without the right to
> plead in self-defense. Gnaeus Pompey, who had
> married Claudius's daughter Antonia was stabbed
> to death while in bed with his favorite cata-
> mite; and Lucius Silanus whom Claudius had be-
> trothed to his daughter Octavia...had orders to
> commit suicide... He executed 35 senators and
> 300 Roman knights with...little apparent
> concern... (Suetonius, page 200.)

Messalina had a lover named Silius. Finally,
she decided to marry him, without so much as a "by
your leave" from Claudius. She waited until
Claudius was out of the city; then the marriage
farce was performed, and they lived together.

> Nor did this insulting behaviour of
> Messalina destroy the extravagant love he
> bore her, so much as terror that she planned
> to seat her lover Silius on the throne; and
> when the news of their marriage reached
> Claudius he fled ignominiously to the Guard's
> Camp, asking again and again as he went, "Am
> I still Emperor?" (Suetonius, page 202.)

Messalina and Silius were executed. Claudius
then went to dinner, and was (according to Suetonius) so absentminded as to ask, "Why is her ladyship
not here?"

Finally, he remarried again, to Agrippina the
Younger, his niece, and mother of the infamous Nero.
He adopted Nero as his son. He repented both actions
later.

Most people think that Claudius was poisoned;
but when and by whom is disputed. Some say that
(it was) the eunuch Halotus; ...others that
Agrippina did so herself... Claudius's death
was not revealed until all arrangements had
been completed to secure Nero's succession...
(Suetonius, pages 206-7.)

5. Nero (emperor, 54-68 A.D.) was a great-great
grandson of Augustus. In him five generations of
in-breeding in the first imperial family of Rome
comes to its zenith of folly and wickedness -- and
to its end as a line of emperors.

Nero first married his (adoptive) sister Octavia,
daughter of Claudius.

Nero's mother, Agrippina the Younger, soon made
away with a member of Augustus's family, Junius
Silanus, by poison. (She had previously contrived
the murder of Junius's brother, Lucius Silanus.)

Two men, Burrus, a soldier, and Seneca, the
famous philosopher, did what they could to frustrate
the fatal course of Agrippina and Nero.

Nero "fell in love" with a freedwoman, Acte.
This at first incited the rage of Agrippina, his
mother; later she reversed her attitude and tactics.

Next, Nero destroyed his step-brother, Brittanicus, son of Claudius, by poison. Brittanicus was
in his middle teens.

Nero would roam the streets of Rome at night in
a slave's disguise, with companions, in order to
assault and rob.

Eventually Nero took as paramour Poppaea, a woman
of beauty, and without character. First she had been
the wife of a Roman knight, Crispinus; then of Otho,
a friend of Nero; and then she was transferred to
Nero. Otho willingly released her. (Eventually,
Otho was the second emperor after Nero.)

In order to retain her power over her son, it

is alleged that Agrippina offered her person to
him. Suetonius indicates that there was incest
between them.

Eventually, Nero decided to destroy his mother,
Agrippina. Various plans were devised; the one
finally adopted was to get her to take a boat ride,
and contrive an accident (collapse part of the
boat) by which she would be destroyed, or, if that
failed, drowned. But she escaped, fully realizing,
however, her son's frustrated attempt. He was
desperate. Finally, he sent to her the commander
of the fleet, a boat captain and a centurion. The
captain hit her on the head with a club, and the
centurion stabbed her to death with his sword.
Her body was burned that night on a dining couch.
Nor was she decently buried.

Nero disposed of his wife Octavia by banishment;
then ordered her to die. She was tightly bound
with cords, her veins opened, and then killed "outright by the steam of an intensely hot bath. To
this was added the yet more appalling horror of
Poppaea beholding the severed head which was con-
veyed to Rome." (Tacitus, page 356.)   Octavia,
descendant of the emperor Augustus, daughter of
the emperor Claudius, and wife of Nero was 20 years
old at her death.

Then there was the great fire in Rome when Nero
fiddled.

Nero blamed the Christians. He had some of them
dipped in pitch, and lighted to be torches in his
gardens. Tacitus writes (page 380f.):

But all human efforts, all the lavish gifts of
the emperor, and the propitiations of the
gods, did not banish the sinister belief that
the conflagration was the result of an order
(from Nero). Consequently, to get rid of the
report, Nero fastened the guilt and inflicted
the most exquisite tortures on a class hated
for their abominations, called Christians by
the populace. Christus, from whom the name
had its origin, suffered the extreme penalty
during the reign of Tiberius at the hands of
one of our procurators, Pontius Pilatus, and a
most mischievous superstition, thus checked
for the moment, again broke out not only in
Judaea, the first source of the evil, but even
in Rome, where all things hideous and shameful
from every part of the world find their centre

and become popular. Accordingly, an arrest
was first made of all who pleaded guilty; then,
upon their information, an immense multitude
was convicted, not so much of the crime of
firing the city, as of hatred against mankind.
Mockery of every sort was added to their deaths.
Covered with the skins of beasts, they were
torn by dogs and perished, or were nailed to
crosses, or were doomed to the flames and
burnt, to serve as a nightly illumination,
when daylight had expired.

Nero offered his gardens for the spectacle,
and was exhibiting a show in the circus, while
he mingled with the people in the dress of a
charioteer or stood aloft on a car. Hence,
even for criminals who deserved extreme and
exemplary punishment, there arose a feeling
of compassion; for it was not, as it seemed,
for the public good, but to glut one man's
cruelty, that they were being destroyed.

A conspiracy was organized against Nero, but
was betrayed. Nero reacted by ordering frightful
tortures and executions.

In the persecutions following the conspiracy,
Nero secured the death of Seneca by ordering suicide. Seneca cut his veins, and when the bleeding
threatened to stop, was rushed to the baths to
keep the wounds open, and to be suffocated.

Nero next disposed of his wife, Poppaea, by
kicking her in the abdomen when she was pregnant,
as a consequence of which she died.

Tacitus's _Annals_ are incomplete and do not
report the end of Nero. Suetonius writes: "At
last, after nearly fourteen years of Nero's
misrule, the earth rid herself of him."

First, there was a revolt in Gaul. But Nero
neglected this and was instead interested more
in "demonstrating a new type of water-organ."
Then Galba revolted in Spain. That frightened him.
He proposed ridiculous and fantastic courses of
action.

News came to Rome of further revolts in the
provinces.

Suetonius tells of Nero's end as follows (pages
237-239):

Nero suspended his deliberations until the
following day, but woke at midnight to find
that his bodyguard had deserted him. He
leaped out of bed and summoned his friends who
were staying in the Palace. When they did not
appear he went with a few members of his staff
to knock at their doors. But nobody either
opened or answered. He returned to his room.
By now even the valets had absconded with the
bed linen and the box of poison. He shouted
for Spiculus the gladiator or any other trained
executioner, to end his misery at one blow.
No one came. "What? Have I then neither
friends nor enemies left?" he cried, and dashed
out of the Palace. Apparently he intended to
hurl himself into the Tiber.

Changing his mind once more, however, he
said that all he wanted was some secluded spot
where he could collect his thoughts at leisure.
Phaon, an Imperial freedman, suggested his own
suburban villa, four miles away, between the
Nomentanan and the Salarian Ways. Nero jumped
at the offer. He was in undershirt and slippers;
but simply pulled on a faded cloak and hat,
took horse and trotted off, holding a handker-
chief over his face. Four servants went with
him, including Sporus. Suddenly a slight
earth-tremor was felt and lightning flashed
in their eyes, which terrified Nero. Then,
from the near-by camp soldiers began shouting
about the defeat which Galba would inflict on
him. He heard one man exclaim as they passed:
"Those fellows are in pursuit of the Emperor,"
and another: "What's the latest news of him
in town?" Then Nero's horse took fright at
the smell of a dead body lying by the roadside;
which made him expose his face. He was immediately recognized and saluted by a Guards'
veteran. They reached a lane leading to
Phaon's villa and, abandoning their horses,
followed a path which ran through a briar patch
and a plantation of reeds to the rear wall of
the house. Because the going was difficult
Nero made them spread a cloak for him to walk
on. When begged by Phaon to lie low for
awhile in a gravel pit, he answered: "No, I
refuse to go underground before I die." While
the servants tunneled through the wall he
scooped up some water in his hands from a
neighbouring pool and drank it, saying: "This
is Nero's own special brew." Then he pulled
out all the thorns from his ragged cloak and

crawled into the villa by way of the tunnel.
Finding himself in a slave's bedroom, beside
a couch with a poor mattress over which an
old cape had been thrown, he sank down on it
and, although hungry, refused some coarse bread;
but confessed himself still thirsty and sipped
a little warm water.

Finally, when his companions unanimously
insisted on his trying to escape from the
miserable fate threatening him, he ordered
them to dig a grave at once, of the right size,
and then collect any pieces of marble that
they could find and fetch wood and water for
the disposal of the corpse. As they bustled
about obediently he muttered through his tears:
"Dead! And so great an artist!"

A runner brought him a letter from Phaon.
Nero tore it from the man's hands and read
that, having been declared a public enemy by
the Senate, he would be punished "in ancient
style" when arrested. He asked what "ancient
style" meant, and learned that the executioners
stripped their victim naked, thrust his head
into a wooden fork, and then flogged him to
death with sticks. In terror he snatched up
the two daggers which he had brought along and
tried their points; but threw them down again,
protesting that the fatal hour had not yet come.
Then he begged Sporus to weep and mourn for him,
but also begged one of the other three to set
him an example by committing suicide first. He
kept moaning about his cowardice, and muttering:
"How ugly and vulgar my life has become!" And
then in Greek: "This certainly is no credit to
Nero, no credit at all," and: "Come, pull yourself together, man!" By this time the troop
of cavalry who had orders to take him alive were
coming up the road. Nero gasped:

"Hark to the sound I hear! It is
hooves of galloping horses."

Then, with the help of his scribe, Epaphroditus,
he stabbed himself in the throat and was already
half dead when a cavalry officer entered, pretending to have rushed to his rescue, and staunched
the wound with his cloak. Nero muttered: "Too
late! But, ah, what fidelity!" He died, with
eyes glazed and bulging from their sockets, a
sight which horrified everybody present. He had
made his companions promise, whatever happened,

not to let his head be cut off, but to have
him buried all in one piece.* Galba's freedman
Icelus, who had been imprisoned when the first
news came of the revolt and was now at liberty
again, granted this indulgence.

They laid Nero on his pyre, dressed in the
gold-embroidered white robes which he had worn
on 1 January. The funeral cost 2,000 gold
pieces. Ecloge and Alexandria, his old nurses,
helped Acte, his mistress, to carry the remains
to the Pincian Hill, which can be seen from the
Campus Martius. His coffin, of white porphyry,
stands there in the Domitian family tomb behind
a rail of Thasian stone and overshadowed by an
altar of Luna marble.

*   *   *

So _lived_, so _ruled_ and so _died_ the imperial
Caesars of the Julio-Claudian family.

Anyone wishing to evaluate the person of the
founder of the Christian religion may well compare
how _he_ lived (whether virtuously?); and how he
legislated (whether to protect the weak and restrict
the strong?); and how he died (justly or unjustly?);
or whimpering like the last of the Julio-Claudian
Caesars, scion of famous Claudii, Agrippae, Antonii
and Caesars.

*   *   *

Rome today would be a tenth-rate city if it had
nothing to live on except the memories of the days
of republican and imperial Rome.

What makes Rome today one of the greatest cities
in the world is the fact that it is the headquarters
of the largest church in Christendom, the Roman
Catholic. Remove the Catholic church from Rome and
it will almost be what in the United States is known
as a "ghost town."

What is true in regard to the city of Rome is
equally true about the whole western world, which
constitutes the so-called Christian part of the earth.

---

* (As previously related, Nero had had (in contrast)
  the head cut off of his first wife, Octavia, and
  brought for examination to his last wife, Poppaea.)

The "west" is not what it is today because of the
Romans, but because of Jesus Christ, who declared
that the "gates of hell" could not prevail against
his own kingdom. The term "gates of hell" can
possibly be admitted to be metaphorical, but it is
not farfetched to consider it to be any government
on different principles, as that of Rome, under
Tiberius, and his procurator Pontius Pilate, under
whose rule Christ himself was crucified.

This is not to say that everything Roman was
vicious, cruel and depraved. The Romans were great
lawgivers, wise in many of their policies, orderly
in much of their administration. But they did not,
and could not, bequeath to future generations a
kingdom of which it could be said, "The gates of
hell shall not prevail against it."

                *   *   *

One meaning of the expression, "The kingdom of
God is at hand"; and, "My kingdom is not of this
world"; and, "The gates of hell shall not prevail
against it," is undoubtedly eschatological, and pertains to the dispensation to come after this one.
Nevertheless, those expressions have proved also
to be true in the latest 1900 years, and may be
counted on to remain true in the remaining time in
this dispensation, whatever that may be.

If such is the case, if the kingdom of Christ is
everlasting, imperishable, pertinacious in survival,
and triumphant at the end, then why? There must
be a logic or a rationale that will explain such
phenomena.

It is sufficient, of course, to accept the sure
promises of Christ about his kingdom on "faith";
that is, merely because he said it, therefore it
is to be believed.

It is even possible (probable?) that successful
searching for a logical explanation of the validity
of Christ's bold assertions about his kingdom will
undermine simple and naive faith. If there is a
grand rationality to what Christ declared, then (so
some may reason) faith is not a requisite; reason
can be sufficient.

Nevertheless, at the risk of someone thinking
in that way, what follows is an outline of the
reason why Christ's statements about the triumph
of his "kingdom" appear indubitable.

                *   *   *

The propositions underlying Christ's apodictical statements about "his kingdom" are as follows:

1.   Any kingdom that is imperishable must agree with the nature of things; must agree with the way existence was created.

2.   Men were created in the "image of God," with the ability to reason and to have purposes.

3.   The objectives of men for their lives are to act so that they will <u>survive</u>; associated and included in that idea is that they seek not only barely to survive, but to be able to live as well as possible, that is, with maximum personal welfare.

4.   The universal formula for this is that men will act so that they can "obtain what they prefer more to what they prefer less." Call this selfishness, if you will, but the reasoning will then be confused, because of the connotation of the word, selfishness. It is important to keep in mind that nowhere in Scripture is there condemnation of that general idea which consists in seeking what you prefer more to what you prefer less.

5.   The <u>natural needs</u> of human beings are not sin. If a week-old baby cries because she is hungry, her annoying cry cannot properly be considered <u>sin</u>.

6.   The seeking of means in order to satisfy the natural needs of a person is not sin <u>per se</u> either. There is nothing wrong <u>per se</u> in trying to satisfy needs <u>at the lowest cost or with the least effort and greatest ease</u>. It cannot be described as sin for a baby to prefer to be nursed rather than to be fed a formula.

7.   Trouble comes, and sin comes into a situation, when and only when a legitimate need and an efficient method of satisfying it also <u>injures other people in inappropriate (and forbidden) ways</u>; by violence, theft, falsehood, particularly when these evils are aggravated by indifference toward others or (even worse) by ill-will.

8.   What happens when imperial Caesars commit violence, adultery, theft and falsehood? The victims do not like it. They resist, individually; collectively; and via public opinion, or by violence, or by rebellion. Sooner or later, in one way or another, despite earlier failures and despite immediate dangers, people <u>resist</u>. They do no more

than engage in "self-preservation" and in "acting
to obtain what they prefer more to what they prefer
less," and further "acting to obtain that which they
prefer more by the lowest-cost method that is legitimate." This is human nature; and this is common
sense. This is a pervasive phenomena; eventually
it is overwhelming and decisive.

9. The "Kingdom of God" to which Christ repeatedly made reference as a <u>minimum</u> (as the method
is in this book on <u>Minimal Religion</u>) certainly is
based (a) on the law of nature (or creation), and
(b) on the law of revelation (or reason as revealed
in the moral law of Scripture, namely, that self-
defense and self-welfare are legitimate motivations
in this life).

10. The character of the rule of the Julio-
Claudian Caesars was, therefore, eventually doomed.
It was not a question whether their rule would survive, but only when it would collapse. That sure
collapse did not require mysterious or arbitrary
intervention by God. The cumulative resistance of
the victims of Julio-Claudian rule would sooner or
later destroy it. That is what happened when Nero
put an end to his life, a moment before he would
have been killed by others anyway.

11. By reasoning from the same principles one
comes to the opposite conclusion regarding the
"kingdom of heaven" to which Christ referred. This,
he alleged, was an "everlasting kingdom" against
which the "gates of hell" would not prevail. The
explanation is this: the rules underlying the
kingdom of heaven are the everlasting rules underlying human relationships. Human nature, the closer
it is to desperation, will the more certainly endeavor to restore the rules of personal relations
which Christ laid down. Those rules are the opposite of violence, adultery, theft, deception.

There is then no error and no arrogance in
Christ's statements: "The kingdom of heaven is at
hand"; "the gates of hell shall not prevail against
it"; "my kingdom is an everlasting kingdom." The
<u>character</u> of that kingdom, its definition, is in-
trinsically rational; it agrees with the nature of
things and the laws of profitable cooperation.

*   *   *

Scripture reading is highly praised and strongly

recommended in Christian circles. If you wish to
benefit more from reading Scripture, and if you
wish to strengthen your faith, then alternate your
reading; read first, a chapter or so in one of the
gospels; then a chapter from Suetonius; then another
chapter from the gospels; then a chapter from
Tacitus.

The contrasts will reduce your doubts about the
transcendental claims of the Christian religion;
and also which is the more probable: whether Christ
is divine, or the so-called "divine" Caesars were
divine.

                    *   *   *

The empire of the Caesars was based on the
principle of force. The empire of Christ is based
on the principle of cooperation, which is the exact
opposite, because cooperation without the use of
force is really service.

                    *   *   *

"And being asked by the Pharisees when the
kingdom of God cometh, he (Christ) answered them
and said, The Kingdom of God cometh not with observation; neither shall they say, Lo, here! or Lo,
there! for lo, the Kingdom of God is within you."
(Luke 17:20-21.)

                    *   *   *

Reflective men who know human nature and its
weakness, and who have pondered the events in the
life and death of Christ, have come to a conclusion
to which all men may well give thought.

Sometimes ideas are more forcefully expressed
in poetry or in novels than in history itself.
Conrad Ferdinand Meyer tells in his novel, Der
Heilige, about the wonderfully sagacious Thomas à
Becket, chancellor of England in the twelfth century,
for Henry II. Becket, waiting one day in the anti-
rooms of the king, had soliliquized with great
introspective psychological discernment with a
powerful crucifix on the wall, as if the latter
could hear him. Later espying Hans the Crossbowman as one who had overheard him, Becket says to
Hans (according to Meyer), "Son of Japhet (a gentile),
you know that the children of Shem (Mohammedans)
among whom you have lived, do not believe that the
Eternal permitted his Only Begotten Son to be

nailed to the cross -- how would you instruct them
better?"

To that Meyer has Hans answer: "My saviour
kissed the traitorous Judas and forgave those who
tormented him; an ordinary man is not capable of
that, because it goes against nature and blood."

Thomas à Becket gently nodded his head, and
expressed himself, "You have said it correctly; it
is difficult and impossible."

N O T E

As to the importance of the "Kingdom of God,"
versus any earthly kingdom, note the prominence
given in the Lord's Prayer, in the clause: "Thy
kingdom come, thy will be done, on earth as it is
in heaven."

Limitations Of The Human Mind

Although human intelligence is amazing --
consider the discoveries of this atomic and space
age (1964) -- it nevertheless has limitations
which will keep it from ever <u>solving</u> all the
mysteries in the universe.

People ought not to let what has already been
discovered by human intelligence lead them to the
conclusion that mortal men will <u>eventually</u> discover
<u>all</u> the answers to existence. What has been dis-
covered thus far does not warrant a jump to such
a conclusion.

Slowly for many centuries, and more rapidly
later, men have learned what they call the "Laws
of Nature." We can formulate in mathematical terms
some of the laws of motion, of electricity, of
chemistry, and other natural sciences in the inanimate world. We have learned much in the fields
of living things -- botany, zoology, bacteriology,
anatomy, hygiene, psychology, etc. -- and we have
the prospect of learning much more.

Advances have been made, or are thought to have
been made, in the sciences of human action --
economics, government, jurisprudence, ethics.

Grant all that; grant that we can describe
present phenomena and can reconstruct the history
of some things that have happened in the past, we
still lack definitive evidence about the <u>origin</u> or
the <u>destiny</u> of everything. Find a man, if you
can, who really believes that the minds of mortal
men will finally understand those ultimate unknowns.

Massive and terrifying phenomena long monopolized
the subject matter of science. Generally people
thought that that which was <u>big</u> revealed God. But
then science turned from the great to the small.
Science, in order to understand a physical man, no
longer concentrates on a whole man who weighs
175 pounds, but on the infinitely small cells
smaller than an eye can see which make up the body
of that man. If there is a creator, what reveals
him most: the big things and the aggregates, or
the little things and the protons and neutrons?

But each new discovery -- explanation -- pushes
the mysteries of the universe another step "backward." But in the place of what was "discovered"
there is an antecedent and often even greater
mystery.

The character of our knowledge has changed, and
in a sense it has enormously increased. But simultaneously we have enlarged our awareness of that
which we do not yet know. The boundaries of our
lack of knowledge have expanded as fast as the
boundaries of our knowledge.

N O T E

    If there is anything in the nature of
things which the mind and reason of man and
human might and power cannot produce, the
being that has produced it is certainly
better than man. All the heavenly things,
and all that has an everlasting order, cannot
be made by man. Therefore, that which has
made all this is better than man. Yet how
should you call it, if not God?

                              -- Cicero

The Poorest Hypothesis To Explain Existence

Nobody lives without "faith," not even the greatest skeptic.

The origin of things is not known now and probably never will be. Any hypothesis regarding that origin is expression of a faith. Man cannot "live by bread alone"; neither can a man "live by knowledge alone."

The two basic faiths are: (1) Dust is God, and (2) a Being-super-the-dust is God. The second proposition sounds more plausible (to this writer) than the former.

There is a third position to which men are inclined to retreat, to wit: "We do not know." This is, in effect, a denial of the necessity of any faith. And to be such an agnostic sounds prudent, wise and humble. But agnosticism is beguiling salesmanship and never reality.

The proposition which is subtly inchoate in the modest expression, "We do not know," is really: There is no explanation.

That proposition is not the "foolishness" of a faith, but a pure denial of the possibility of an attempt at rationalism. Agnosticism is not the highest form of reason, but the denial of reason. It is the least acceptable formulation of the most basic question of life.

In this book (1) agnosticism is scorned; (2) atheism (materialism, that Dust is God) is rejected; and (3) transcendentalism (that there is a Super-the-dust Being) is accepted.

The Approach Made In This Book

What is spoken or written is ever subject to
various interpretations by those who hear or read.
That is true of what is written in the Hebrew-
Christian Scriptures, about the many and various
complex problems of life and death, of the origin
of things and the destiny of things.

Varying interpretations of Scripture can be
classified as one of three: (1) maximal; (2) average (or median); or (3) minimal.

Scripture is generally particularistic and sees
problems (1) in a particular setting; (2) with
individual actors; and (3) under given circumstances.
Consequently, it seems to judge very diversely;
some would say that that is confusing; others may
even allege that there are contradictions, making
part or all of the record invalid. (Scripture had
to be that way in principle, in order to see the
various sides of a problem.)

1. Take, for example, a given subject or problem and compile out of Scripture all statements that
bear on that problem. Then analyze and rank them.
Then take the strongest, most comprehensive statement, and accept that as the scriptural position.
If you do that, you aim at maximal religion.

(If you go further and extend the strongest
statement in any manner -- over-emphasize it --
and thereby conclude a super-powerful dogma, you
have over-maximized the ideas of the Christian
religion. Such a policy is unjustified.)

2. Or, approach Scripture differently -- say
in an average or median manner -- you then concentrate on the inbetween statements. (The word median
means mid-most; to find the median strike out, first,
the two extreme statements at the two ends; next,
strike out the second group of two most extreme
statements, and so on. Then you are finally left
with the median or mid-most statement.) Maybe
this principle of interpretation has more to commend it than maximization or minimization.

3. Finally, there is that third approach --
the least-strong propositions are accepted; or, at

least are begun with. That is the approach made
in this book, whence it derives the title, Minimal
Religion.

These minimal propositions will be found to be
honorable, and promoting the good of the individual
and of mankind generally.

They will also be found to be rational on mundane
subjects -- the practical matters of this world;
and additionally, to offer some of the less objec-
tionable answers to that which is not to be mastered
by finite human minds, but for which the human mind
needs a hypothesis according to which to think and
act.

Of course, what is here presented is only one
man's formulation of the ideas of minimal Christianity. Someone else might formulate the propositions
of minimal Christianity differently. There is no
claim made that what appears in this book is the
only proper formulation of the minimum for which
Christianity stands.

Maybe readers will wish (1) to read Scripture
by themselves and formulate their own beliefs; and
(2) to consult official representatives of the
several denominations to obtain help and guidance.

Interest in religious problems is timeless, and
exists among the most cultured and the most primitive peoples. It is animals, birds, insects and
vegetation -- which have no interest in religion.
Why vegetate?

*   *   *

A was talking one day to B about a mutual friend,
whose interest in religion was inconsequential, but
who (because the Bible is a most significant book)
had decided to read it from cover to cover. This
Bible reader, call him C, had had little religious
training.

Alone, C was setting out solitarily to read a
book written over a period of fifteen centuries
by very diverse authors, and from all kinds of
differing viewpoints, and consequently (potentially)
confusing in its real teaching.

The churches have been working for centuries to
help readers of Scripture. They have matched texts.
They have accumulated data on historical circumstances.

Therefore, the churches can be genuinely helpful
to anyone setting out to inform himself on what
the Christian religion teaches and proclaims.

B was, in a sense, aghast at the idea that C
(without a background, and half-skeptically and
cursorily) was undertaking to read the Bible, just
because many people considered it a great book.
How great or small was the prospect that C would
read with profit!

Therefore, consult priests or clergymen for
assistance in exploring what the Christian religion
teaches. This suggestion is rational. Most people
study physics, mathematics, history and other
subjects usually only with the assistance of someone already informed on the subject.

Although denominations differ in their interpretations and formal propositions about Christianity, solicit help (if you wish from several), and
decide whether you wish to be a Christian and
rational, or a Positivist and (in a special sense)
irrational.

N O T E   There are intellectuals and nonintellec-
            tuals in every denomination. Nonintellec-
tuals will be taught didactively and authoritatively
a program which fits the circumstances. Intellectuals will need to explore for and seek out the intellectual cadre in a particular denomination; then
they can by discussion and exchange of ideas progressively come to clarity on what Scripture teaches;
this is a learning process by intellectual activity
rather than by memory.

Naturally, denominational representatives will
react against dissent from their respective creeds.
But it is hardly wise for them to take offense.
Doctrines wholly accepted and never in dispute anymore become "dead" in a practical sense. To remain
alive, the great subjects of religion must continue
to be actively discussed and even disputed. Such
discussions conducted in a wisdom-seeking and non-
contentious spirit are invaluable.

That other problem, that denominations have representatives who do not vigorously hold to their respective creeds, may cause confusion and difficulty.
But no church has infallible representatives.

Participate actively intellectually yourself in
coming to the preferred answers. It is written in
Scripture: "Search the Scriptures." Do it yourself.

Supplement

It is not to be disputed that <u>grace</u> is a central
idea in the Christian religion, that is, redemption
from punishment by the grace of God, granted freely
to individuals who are really unworthy of such
grace.

But it would be a grievous error to affirm that
grace is the objective or purpose of the Christian
religion. It is, instead, a lamentable need, an
attempt to make good what has been done amiss, and
to balance accounts.

The need for grace is because of prior sin. If
there were no prior sin, grace would be superfluous.
Sin must therefore be an item which balances with
grace.

*　　　*　　　*

And why is there sin? <u>Because</u> the supply of
natural things is not equal to, nor immediately
responsive to, variable human needs. If the things
of this world were not finite -- limited in quantity --
there would be no occasion for violence, fraud, theft,
coveting. Why should any man engage in violence,
deception, envy if there was enough available to
satisfy his every need in immediate response to his
wishes? Clearly, the "cause" for sin rests in the
character of creation, in the relationship of men
to things. See pages 278-9.

Were there no welfareshortage there would be no
motivation to sin; if there were no sin, grace would
be redundant.

If then a man has a religion which begins and ends
with salvation -- but never comes to results, never
produces -- he has a fractional religion. In any
event, he is a superficial thinker.

If a man has a religion which begins with grace
and then proceeds to consideration and correction
of sin, he has done better. He is dealing with at
least two related facts -- <u>grace</u> and <u>sin</u>.

But if a man has a religion which begins with the
problem of the relationship of men to things (a relationship which, in a sense, is the "cause" of sin,
and which in this book has been dealt with under the
question of cosmology); and if that man then proceeds

to the problem of the relationship of men to men
(here treated as ethics); and if that man then
finally proceeds to grace, the relationship of men
to God, then the thought would appear to be
"logically" organized.

A redemptive approach consists of beginning with
grace (and maybe working back to men and to things).

An analytical approach consists of beginning with
cosmology and economics; proceeding to ethics; and
ending with grace.

Scripture is essentially redemptive in method,
and not analytical. Or maybe it is better said as
follows: the interpretors of Scripture and their
interpretations have followed the short-cut method,
of beginning with grace (as an urgent need) and sometimes ending there; or, in other cases, advancing
from grace to consideration of sin; but seldom going beyond sin to cosmology and economics.

The atypical method in this book has been to
emphasize complexities about the relationship of men
to things; then proceeding to ethics; and finally
to theology and grace.

Böhm-Bawerk, the economist, has emphatically made
the point that the relationship of men to things is
far more complex than men generally realize.

The present _purpose_ of the Christian religion
should be the reduction and removal of sin. Certainly, we are not called on to sin energetically
so that grace may abound more. The purpose of
revelation must therefore be that sin will be reduced rather than that the need for grace be magni-
fied.

                *   *   *

There are several approaches to the problem of
the solution of the "cause" or "origin" of sin.

One is the approach of the ascetic, the type
which withdraws from life. He says, solve your sin
problem caused by "things" by devaluing things;
reduce your evaluation of the utility of things to
satisfy needs; and discipline yourself to want less
so that you will have less incitement to sin by
violence, etc.

Another approach is that of the socialist-
communist. Sensing that men's relationships to

things lie at the root of sin -- and really blaming
the shortage of things rather than man's improper
adjustment to things -- socialism-communism says,
let us make everything public property, and let us
ban private ownership.

Over-pious Christianity can designate the wish
to have things, which really rests in the need for
things, as sin. But if one wishes to approach life
with gusto, then a pious approach does not appeal.
Christians with gusto will see no sin in loving the
good things of life, and therefore they restrict
their definition of sin to improper means to get
things. Such Christians will see nothing wrong with
fine houses and fine clothes honestly obtained for
"value received." Of course, such folk are appropriately vitally interested in increasing the
quantity of goods which are needed, which entails
high productivity per capita, by which poverty is
universally reduced.

The psychology of the writer of this book is that
of a Christian with a natural gusto for life. Work,
obey the commandments of God, and enjoy the appropriate and good things of life!

Unfortunately, because sins are ubiquitous among
men, every man still needs grace.

Without in any way subtracting from grace what
is due to it in Christian theology, it may be
correct to say that the Protestant Reformation
fixated attention on grace in a manner which can
result in undervaluing good works. The Mother
Church had developed an extensive doctrine on good
works. The Reformers took exception to that "calculus" which weighed good works in one balance of
a scale and sins in the other; they alleged in
effect that the good works were intrinsically an
obligation of a kind that could not be used as a
credit against sins.

Eschewing this Roman Catholic and Protestant
difference entirely, the position here taken is
that the performance of good works (The Decalogue)
should be the rule of life, and that that reduces
the amount of grace needed.

                    *   *   *

But to begin with the relationship of men to
things introduces problems of education in that
field. Certainly, the most valuable "science" to

employ in this connection is economics. But there
are all kinds of economics.

There is hardly a philosopher of note who has
not dabbled with various subjects in economics.
But much of their work was amateurish -- from
Socrates, Plato and Aristotle on.

The works of the "classical" economists are not
really "classical." The name was applied to men
who were too early in the science.

What is known as Neoclassical should really be
considered as classical. The Neoclassical writers
reconstructed the very foundation of economics.

The outstanding writers among the Neoclassical
are (1) Carl Menger, whose Principles of Economics
(The Free Press, Glencoe, Illinois, $6) is the
really primary work in Neoclassical economics. It
concerns itself in an elementary manner with the
relationship of men to things. He was closely
followed by (2) Eugen von Böhm-Bawerk, whose
greatest work available in English is Capital and
Interest (Libertarian Press, South Holland, Illinois;
three-volume set, $25; three volumes in one, $15),
which consists of three separate books:

1. History and Critique Of Interest Theories

2. Positive Theory Of Capital

3. Further Essays on Capital and Interest

In addition there is available in English a separate
volume of essays under the general title, Shorter
Classics of Böhm-Bawerk (Libertarian Press, South
Holland, Illinois, $7.50).

Then there is (3) Ludwig von Mises, whose more
famous works include:

1. Human Action (Yale University Press,
        New Haven, Connecticut, $15)

2. Theory Of Money and Credit (Yale, $7)

3. Socialism (Yale, $6)

4. Theory and History (Yale, $6)

5. The Ultimate Foundation of Economic
        Science (D. Van Nostrand, Princeton,
        New Jersey, $4.50)

6. Epistemological Problems Of Economics
        (D. Van Nostrand, $5.50)

But to read these books is a serious discipline
in itself. Once understood, they appear easy.
Read for the first time, or without care, they
appear abstruse and difficult. They are difficult
because they open up a new "world," complex but
finally more rational than any other.

*   *   *

The author of <u>Minimal Religion</u>, in 1955-1960,
published for six years a monthly, with the eventual
title, <u>First Principles In Morality And Economics</u>.
It is because these six volumes are an easy introduction to Menger, Böhm-Bawerk and Mises that their
contents will be briefly described. For those
interested in the social sciences and in religion,
these volumes have the feature of being hybrids,
half ethics and half economics. There is a treatment of the subject matter in a manner to show
regularly the relation between ethics and economics.

A <u>monthly</u> cannot be expected to be so systematically organized as a book, and there are diverse
materials in <u>First Principles In Morality And
Economics</u>. In fact, instead of beginning with cosmology and economics, the first volume (1955) is
primarily devoted to ethics. The main problem
there considered is: what is meant by being required to <u>love your neighbor as yourself</u>. See pages
21-23; 28-42; 54-77; 83-112; 113-144.

1.   The purpose of material in Volume I was to
"debunk" exaggerated ethical claims made in the
name of the Christian religion. Volume I and in
steadily lessening degrees later volumes make in
part a sectarian and controversial approach. Comment of a reader that the positive material was
not restricted really to a particular sect was
eventually conceded, and the original sectarian
title dropped. Later volumes are nonsectarian.

2.   Volume II in 1956 in the June issue, pages
162-190, has informative material on money problems.
The September 1956 issue considers a thesis of the
sociologist Max Weber about being "worldly minded"
and acquisitive. The October 1956 issue questions
the validity of claims of devout people of receiving a charisma from God.

3.   Volume III for 1957 considers among other
subjects the question of "unearned income," that
great offense to socialists and the insoluble
moral problem of philosophers who were not economists.

See pages 43-92. This volume especially questions
sanctimony -- pious prattle and exaggerated demands
made in the name of religion. The August issue is
devoted to exposing the biased, untruthful and
unsound principles underlying programs as are dram-
atized in Upton Sinclair's book, The Jungle. The
issues for September, October, November and December contain helpful introductory economic material.

4. Volume IV for 1958 contains critical material
on socialism and Keynesianism. See on another vital
subject the material beginning on page 147 and ending on 159, and continued on 174 to 199. But the
volume is valuable to have just for the material
alone on Ricardo and his famous but little-known
Law of Association. See issues for July, pages
200-224; also August, pages 229-255; also September,
pages 259-288; the treatment is much more detailed
than in Minimal Religion. See also the material on
John C. Calhoun's A Disquisition On Government in
the November and December issues.

5. Volume V for 1959 is mostly economics. The
approach is Neoclassical.

6. Volume VI for 1960 is devoted even more to
economics. There is an extensive analysis (beginning
with the March issue) to discover who gets the benefit from inventions; the analysis shows that the
benefits are widely diffused and accrue mostly to
consumers (pages 89-96; 123-128; 184-192; 200-212).
Even more important are extracts from Böhm-Bawerk's
Volume I, portraying the fallacies of the socialists; see pages 235-256. The last four issues are
devoted to pricing problems. Again there are quotations, this time from Böhm-Bawerk's Volume II.
These quotations are from some of the most famous
parts of Böhm-Bawerk's works.

All told, there are in these six volumes 2,344
pages. The set of six paperbound volumes is priced
at $9. If funds are sent with the order, the price
is postpaid; otherwise postage is extra.

*   *   *

There are many other famous men in the Neoclassical school of thought whose works should eventually
be examined -- Frank H. Knight, Friedrich von Hayek,
Friedrich von Wieser, Henry Hazlitt, Wilhelm Röpke,
Verrijn-Stuart, Sr., Edwin Cannan, Philip H. Wick-
steed, William Stanley Jevons, Hans F. Sennholz,
Murray N. Rothbard, and many others of similar
distinction.

The economic rebuilders in the countries of Europe which have recovered most rapidly since World War II are distinguished members of the Neoclassical school of thought. Neoclassical thought is not merely theoretically sound, but is practically successful.

References

Acte 358,363
Adams, John vii
Aelia Paetina 357
Agrippa Posthumous 351-2
Agrippina (Elder) 351-3
Agrippina (Younger) 357-9
Alexandria 363
Anne of Saxony 282
Antonia 357
Aristotle 378
Arius 336
Augustine 17
Augustus, Octavius 349-52,
355,358-9

Baumgardt, Carola 55
Becket, Thomas à 367-8
Böhm-Bawerk, Eugen von
vii,156,169,192,201-2,
209-10,217-220,224-5,
279,376-80
Bridges, Dr. 54
Brittanicus 358
Bullock, Charles J. 264
Burke vii
Burrus 358

Caesar, Caius Julius 282,
349-50
Caesonia 356
Calhoun, John C.vii,40-2,
380
Caligula, Gaius 349-50,
354-7
Cannan, Edwin 49-50,86,380
Cantillon, Richard 278
Carnalus 354
Charnwood 13
Cicero 348-9, 370
Claudius 349-50,357-9
Claudius Tib. Nero 351-2

Clement of Alexandria 303
Comte, Auguste v-vii,6,
24-6,51-4,56-7,60
Crispinus 358

Dante 331
Darwin 22
De Tocqueville 104
Dewey, John 23
Dickens 289
Dostoevsky 295
Drusilla 356
Drusus 351-3,355

Ecloge 363
Einstein, Albert 55
Elephantis 354
Epaphroditus 362
Erasmus 188

Ferrero 356
France, Anatole 346-7

Gaius 351
Galba 360-1,363
Galileo 292-3,303
Germanicus 351-2,354-5,357
Gracchus, Tiberius 174
Grotius 286

Halotus 358
Hannibal 174
Hans the Crossbowman 367-8
Hayek, Friedrich von 104,
290,380
Hazlitt, Henry 380
Henry II 367
Hobbes 177
Hume, David 47,166,174-7,
278,280-3